David Tremayne is a freelance m  the FIA Formula 1 World Cha leading expert in the history of breaking, he has himself raced hydroplanes and driven a rocket dragster from zero to 247mph in 1.8 seconds.

DONALD CAMPBELL

THE MAN BEHIND THE MASK

DAVID TREMAYNE

BANTAM BOOKS

LONDON • TORONTO • SYDNEY • AUCKLAND • JOHANNESBURG

DONALD CAMPBELL
A BANTAM BOOK : 9780553815115

Originally published in Great Britain by Bantam Press,
a division of Transworld Publishers

PRINTING HISTORY
Bantam Press edition published 2004
Bantam edition published 2005

3 5 7 9 10 8 6 4

Inside cover photograph: Captured by a fell-walker on Christmas Day 1966,
Donald Campbell streaks down Coniston Water after launching the boat
with the help of just a few close friends. (Ken Norris)

Set in 11.5/14pt Minion by
Falcon Oast Graphic Art Ltd.

Bantam Books are published by Transworld Publishers,
61–63 Uxbridge Road, London W5 5SA,
a division of The Random House Group Ltd.

Addresses for Random House Group Ltd companies outside the UK
can be found at: www.randomhouse.co.uk
The Random House Group Ltd Reg. No. 954009.

Printed and bound in Great Britain by
Cox & Wyman Ltd, Reading, Berkshire.

The Random House Group Limited supports The Forest Stewardship
Council (FSC), the leading international forest certification organisation.
All our titles that are printed on Greenpeace approved FSC certified paper
carry the FSC logo. Our paper procurement policy can be found at:
www.rbooks.co.uk/environment.

CONTENTS

ELEGY TO CAMPBELL

by Andrew Wintersgill

A man sits alone in the grey light of morning,
The heart and the brain of a powerful machine.
The eyes of a hawk glare bright with a purpose;
A helmet he dons, the battle begins.

Months of preparing, bitter despairing,
The funds have run out, so it's on the attack.
A cold winter's morning, like an ice age is dawning,
The engine screams out, and the gods answer back.

OVER THE MOUNTAINS, FOLLOW THE RIVER
DOWN THROUGH THE VALLEY AND TO THE LAKE
  SHORE
WHERE BLUEBIRD LIES BURIED 'NEATH CONISTON
  WATER
AS GREY AS A GHOST AND AS STILL AS THE DAWN.

See how she runs as she climbs on the water,
See how she flies as the spray falls like rain.
Plus forty-seven and the waiting is over,
Wait for the calm and try once again.

Frozen in time now the black and white newsreel,
As Bluebird leapt forward in a circle of death.
Shot in mid-flight she plunges face downwards,
Ballast bags bobbing was all that was left . . .

OVER THE MOUNTAINS, FOLLOW THE RIVER
DOWN THROUGH THE VALLEY AND TO THE
LAKE SHORE
WHERE BLUEBIRD LIES BURIED 'NEATH
   CONISTON WATER
AS GREY AS A GHOST AND AS STILL AS THE DAWN.

The boathouse is empty, the jetty lies rotten.
New heroes are basking in the spray of champagne.
Speed is the king in the realm of ambition,
Great are the glories but short is the reign.

FOREWORD

When David Tremayne came to see me while he was writing this book, at some point I said, 'I've never read anything about my family.' David looked at me rather quizzically, so I went on to explain that it can be so annoying to hear people say that they are going to write the 'definitive true story' etc. and then when you read it it is full of errors and inaccuracies. In fact, it is probably nigh on impossible for someone to write a 'definitive' account of the lives, loves and fast machines of a family that has achieved so much, particularly when it has to be put together from hearsay, hefty research and word of mouth; so much boils down to how the author and the reader interpret the information put before them. Also, the main characters will have made sure that their own accounts of events are favourable to themselves, and where the Campbells come into the equation there are, I am sure, some minor embellishments of the facts!

Then I read David's highly researched and very accurate interpretation of all the information he has amassed, in the most part from people he has made a huge effort to track down and visit. In my view, he has written the best 'definitive' account that will ever be available for the many people who are still intrigued by and interested in the achievements of my forefathers.

This account – and I prefer to call it that – has imparted to me more information and facts about my family than I ever thought was possible. There were so many things I hadn't either appreciated or known that they had got up to. The more I read, the prouder I became, and the more I came to understand after so many years why my forefathers had, and still have, such a huge following, not only in their homeland but all over the world. It has taken me a lifetime to realize that I have the blood of truly amazing characters and achievers flowing through my veins. David gave me this insight. This in turn leaves one with a huge responsibility and a heavy burden to carry. I always wanted to feel and be 'worthy' of this precious blood, but however hard you try you can never quite match these astounding men.

I'm so delighted now that I complied with David's request, broke with tradition and read 'something' about my family. We are all fortunate to have this most fascinating, painstakingly accurate piece of literature, the research for which has taken more than twelve years. It will, I know, enthral people, irrespective of whether they are full-blown 'Campbell anoraks', folk with a keen interest in the history of water and land speed records, or those interested in historical achievements and heroes. We had men like Sir Henry Segrave, John Cobb, Sir Malcolm and Donald Campbell, true heroes who battled against adversity to realize their dreams and ambitions by the seat of their pants. There was not the technology available then as there is today; their exploits were truly life or death. Some paid the ultimate price, but none of them shirked his commitment to enhancing the greatness of Great Britain.

David, whom I am honoured to call a friend, God bless you, this is a marvellous piece of work. You have done my family and yourself proud. Thank you, too, for the privilege of contributing this foreword. And to all who have the good sense to include this book in their libraries, I know you will now get the best possible account of 'The Man Behind the Mask'.

Gina Campbell, QSO
Leeds, July 2003

INTRODUCTION

It is a beautiful tale, Maurice Maeterlinck's play *The Blue Bird*. The children Mytyl and Tyltyl wander through the Land of Memory, having been told by the Fairy Beryline that if they find the Blue Bird they will again meet their departed brothers and sisters. Tyltyl is a little god in the eyes of his faithful dog Tylo, and how like Donald Campbell and Leo Villa the two characters are: when the brave Tyltyl stands to fight his enemies, it is always Tylo who remains steadfast by his side. There is danger in pursuing the Blue Bird, for it is said that all who accompany the children will also die at journey's end. Yet still, just like Campbell, they keep pushing ahead, past the point of no return.

It is an emotional story, yet it radiates happiness too. When the children meet their late grandparents, they learn how the dead can always be made gloriously happy whenever the living remember them. They learn, too, that the Blue Bird is the great secret of happiness, that it cannot be caught and caged, but may only be shared with others. There was pathos, too, in the story of Donald Campbell's life. 'I have always burned to write a book,' he once told Peter Costigan of the *Sydney Morning Herald*. 'Not about speed, but about the human struggle and suffering behind the Campbell efforts to break speed records. Behind the glamour of the record runs was an incredible story of frustration and human effort.'

I had just turned fourteen when I saw the television news film of Campbell's accident on the evening of 4 January 1967. Weeks later, I happened upon a copy of Richard Hough's *BP Book of the Racing Campbells* in a local department store sale. It cost me at least a week's pocket money, so much that I didn't dare tell my parents. I read it in one go, and was hooked for ever, on the Campbell legend, on land and water speed records, on the whole speed thing. I had found a calling.

But who was Donald Campbell?

The writer Leslie Charteris once wrote of his most famous creation, 'I sought to create a situation whereby the man who has not heard of The Saint is like the boy who has never heard of Robin Hood.' One might substitute the name Donald Campbell for that of The Saint. Generations of adults watched the television footage as the *Boy's Own* speedking of the fifties and sixties somersaulted to his death. His achievements and the drama of his passing are thus forever remembered, but what of the man himself? Only two books ever got anywhere close to probing the fascinating riddle of Campbell, John Pearson's *Bluebird and the Dead Lake* and Arthur Knowles' *With Campbell at Coniston.* But each focused more on individual attempts than on the overall character and career of the actor on centre stage, because they were written when he was alive, and that was the way Campbell wanted it.

So who was he? The playboy adventurer, as Fleet Street so often portrayed him? A reckless daredevil with a death wish, as a radio producer tried to suggest on the twentieth anniversary of his passing? Or a man in his later years often frightened, continually trying to prove himself to himself and to his illustrious late father, in whose long, long shadow he forever felt trapped? Why were there so few written interviews with him? What really caused the crashes at Bonneville in 1960 and Coniston in 1967? Did Bonneville really change him? Why was he so obsessed with spiritualism? Was he really just trying all along to prove himself to the memory of his dead father?

These were some of the questions that kept spilling around my head until my friend, the motorsport writer Nigel Roebuck, finally cajoled me into concrete action. I wanted to tackle Campbell in a way he had never allowed anyone to in life. To shrug off the tired opinions based on superficial perceptions, established dogma which turned out to have little factual basis, even Campbell's own carefully orchestrated publicity. To cover a fifties and sixties story with a fresh perspective, but without the contemporary spite of icon-debunking. I wanted to look at the man himself, in the context of his well-chronicled achievements and his elegant machinery, by talking to those who were closest to him. I knew what he had done, and what he had done it in, but there was a still undiscovered prize: what made him do it the way he did? What factors pushed him in the direction he went, and how did they affect him and those around him? Could it ever have ended other than the way it did?

I have an open mind on spiritualism, a subject with which Campbell was obsessed, but during the course of researching this book I had some interesting experiences. While I was interviewing the medium Marjorie Staves, she spoke of my making trips abroad, across water. That mightn't have been too difficult to suggest, given what little she knew of my profession. She also mentioned that I had recently been in a bungalow. That could conceivably have been the one

Donald Campbell had stayed in during his final spell at Coniston. I was intrigued by that, because she couldn't possibly have known that I had been there the previous week. But it was hardly unconditional, and it could have been interpreted any number of different ways.

Then she mentioned the names Leonard and Peter, the month of March, and news that would please me. Leonard Peter is my doctor, and I wondered if it might have something to do with the medical I was about to undertake for my hydroplane racing licence. It wasn't. The Leonard part proved to be a red herring. But the Peter bit wasn't. I saw Marjorie on a Tuesday. She had been convinced that whatever relevance Leonard or Peter had, it was to do with something that was worrying me, something I wanted. At the end of that week, on the Friday, I received a phone call. It was Peter Collins, one of my closest friends and at that time the managing director of Team Lotus. Moreover, a man whose sister Chris claims to have had psychic conversations with his former boss and Team Lotus founder Colin Chapman. PC wanted to know if I was interested in writing daily press releases for Team Lotus at each Grand Prix. It was a timely offer that eased some financial worries, and an honour given my regard for the team's heritage and aspirations. The job would start in March . . .

The other odd experience came, fittingly enough, at Coniston. Each January the Speed Record Club meets in the village in commemoration of Campbell's death. It's a chance to see old faces, meet some new ones, and to share record-breaking stories and swap memorabilia in a glorious setting and a friendly atmosphere. In 1994, I stayed as usual with Tony and Elizabeth Robinson at the Coniston Lodge Hotel, and, as tends to be my habit, I retired late to bed after an evening of camaraderie at the Sun. I turned in around one in the morning but rose early. I love to drive around Coniston in the very early hours, although on this occasion my six o'clock start rather backfired as the sky steadfastly remained black until minutes before eight. More than once I ventured onto the jetty near the Bluebird Café on the western shore to marvel at the flatness of the water. It was a cold morning, born of the previous night's clear sky. Ice all over the jetty demanded care. A few lights peppered the darkness of the Grisedale Forest behind the eastern shore. Though I could see little by the moon's feeble light, I felt peacefully alone. Only the incessant yadder of the wild ducks broke the morning's stillness each time I walked out there. I found myself wondering how similar it was to another 4 January so many years ago. The third time I drove down there, the light was just beginning to reveal Coniston in its mirror-calm beauty. I sat in the car and played Andrew Wintersgill's wonderful 'Elegy to Campbell' tape as my own little tribute. Watched a robin so tame that it damn near hopped in through the open window.

Each of the three times that I walked from the car to the jetty and back I was struck by a smell of paint. It was strong enough for me to know that I hadn't imagined it, yet initially faint enough not to be all-pervading. The first time I thought little of it. The second, I subconsciously took care to avoid stepping in anything and treading it into the car. I even checked that I hadn't. The third time it finally struck me consciously as being downright odd. There was no sign whatsoever of any spillage. No discarded cans. The Bluebird Café had not been redecorated recently. The boatyard was surely too far away to matter. Yet the smell was now definite enough.

Later that day, I collared Carolynn Seggie, an ardent believer in the paranormal, who had brought along for me that weekend some photocopies of newspaper features about Campbell and his interest in psychic phenomena. She had absolutely no idea what had happened by the lake, nor of the context, when I asked her what, if anything, a smell of paint meant in the psychic world. 'It upsets me sometimes,' she said straight away, 'how strong the smell can be for me. In the psychic context it means that somebody is trying to pass on a message, trying to communicate.'

Well, who knows? I can't explain it.

Donald Campbell has been without question the greatest influence on my life, consciously and subconsciously. Some may simply view this book as an unconditional tribute to him, but I promised myself from the start that it would be warts and all. There are warts here, but there are no skeletons in the cupboard, simply because there were none to find. Much has been made of Campbell's infidelity, but he was always open about it, especially with his last wife Tonia, who admits that she herself was far from blameless. And of his fears . . . what man would not have been apprehensive about such a cold-blooded game, especially after the horrific accident in Bluebird CN7 at Bonneville in 1960? His record (and his records) speaks for itself.

He never did get beyond a brief draft of the book, *The Eternal Challenge*, about which he had spoken so passionately. I hope this may be the next best thing.

David Tremayne
Harrow and Stapleton,
October 2003

1

THE LAST THROW OF THE DICE

Winter 1966

'You look over there and you can see another mountain, the real
mountain, and you are going for it, boy. And what hurts, what
really hurts, is when you come to the last one and you go down
the other side.'

DONALD CAMPBELL TO JOURNALIST GEOFFREY MATHER, CONISTON WATER,
DECEMBER 1966

As Donald Campbell's life moved into its final full year in
1966, he was torn by doubt. Should he carry on with the
project to design a rocket car, not just to return the land
speed record to Britain but to go supersonic? Should he
make another attempt with the venerable Bluebird K7
hydroplane with which he had set his seven water speed
records? Have a crack at the 300mph mark? Or was it time
to quit a dangerous profession while he was still young
enough to enjoy a more peaceful existence? He had, after all,
planned precisely that six years earlier, voicing his intention
to quit should he reach the land speed barrier of 400mph at
Bonneville.

The 1960s were largely unkind to him. He had been the toast of the 1950s, a glamorous young knight on a blue charger doing dangerous and daring deeds for Queen and country at a time when the post-war world was still fascinated by such things. His exploits with his Bluebird K7 speedboat had made him a household name. He was a celebrity. But the 1960s had begun with a spectacular crash at more than 300mph in the Bluebird CN7 car on the Bonneville Salt Flats in America, where his father Sir Malcolm had broken that very barrier a quarter of a century before. Then his subsequent attempts in Australia with a rebuilt Bluebird had been washed out. Eventually he reached 403.1mph to break the official land speed record, but when success finally came, after an abnormally brave effort in nightmare conditions, it was qualified. Time, ill fortune and an American hot-rodder called Craig Breedlove had over-taken his project.

He had considered settling in Australia. After the land record, during a demonstration run down King William Street in Adelaide, Australia had given him the sort of ticker-tape welcome his own country had never even considered. Later, on the last day of 1964 on an Australian lake, he had broken his own water speed record too, becoming the only man in history to break both records in the same year. It was the apogee of his career.

Quitting was anathema to a charismatic man who had spent his childhood indulging in the sort of scrapes that induce wrath in parents and give them white hairs, his adult years chasing the elusive Blue Bird of happiness on the dark waters of a cold lake or across the mesmerizing white glare of a lonely salt flat. But suddenly Campbell had become less sure of himself and his place in things. Australia had given him his finest hour, but he was still desperate to lay to rest the ghosts of Bonneville, and to wipe away the accusations that his desperate triumph at Lake Eyre had somehow fallen short. He wanted, too, to redress the inescapable fact that his Bluebird car had become a white elephant. It was a 1950s project that had played by the rules but had overrun, for a variety of reasons, into the 1960s. There it had been overtaken by a bunch of American speed merchants who turned their noses up at regulations which demanded that a car should drive through its wheels. Even before Campbell had achieved his 403.1mph on the treacherous surface of Lake Eyre, Breedlove had done 407.45mph, literally blown along on his wheels by a pure jet engine. And he had done it at Bonneville. Even before its desperate moment of triumph, Bluebird, the car to end all cars, was obsolete. Now Campbell passionately wanted the chance to play the Americans at their own game, to build his own jet-powered projectile.

But times had changed. He could not shake off his own self-made mask. He remained the pin-striped Establishment figure with The Voice. The plummy, perfect vowels, the deliberate, clipped inflections. The carefully combed-back hair. He was almost a Churchillian caricature to a new generation interested only in escaping such things. New raiders who basked in the glory of speed, such as Breedlove, wore their hair like the hippies with whom the younger generation more readily identified. They preferred to speak the hip argot of the new breed of role models. In appearance, at any rate, the two cultures of record breaker were as different as champagne and chardonnay. The real Donald Campbell was in reality Craig Breedlove's kindred spirit, and had practised his own philosophy of free love long before it became the mantra of the sixties, but the new teens and twentysomethings freshly weaned on the Beatles and the Rolling Stones weren't about to waste time looking beneath a middle-aged man's apparently fuddy-duddy external appearance.

It might have been the right time to stop, for though Lake Eyre *was* a qualified victory, the subsequent water record at Lake Dumbleyung at the end of 1964 was a brilliant triumph against the odds. Proof that he really *was* a speed-king. But there was something else old-fashioned about a man who drove Bentleys, Jaguars and Aston Martins and who usually looked more like a merchant banker than the fastest man in the world on water. He was intensely patriotic. He believed, so intrinsically that he never even considered questioning the belief, that a country's virility could be measured by the willingness of its inhabitants to push frontiers. He admired the Scotts and the Shackletons that Britain had spawned, just as he admired the men whose explorations had been of a different nature, airmen such as John Boothman and Sidney Webster, or racing drivers and record breakers such as Sir Henry Segrave and John Cobb. And, of course, the most prolific of that genre, his own father, Sir Malcolm.

Record breaking was the family tradition. The wire in the blood. It was what he did. It was what he saw himself doing whenever he considered his self-image. Donald Campbell, speedking. 'Speed is my life,' he once said. No four words better summarized his *raison d'être*.

So he vacillated. He ought to have stopped, but he couldn't. Something inside kept prodding him forward.

There was talk of dragging CN7 out of mothballs and getting it to run again in the hope of achieving the 500mph for which it had been designed, but it didn't take the American jetcars long to shatter that milestone too. So he talked instead of a new boat to do the 300. But what he really wanted to do was the supersonic record car – until press reaction to it in 1965 proved so feeble that for perhaps the first time in his life he became genuinely demoralized. Still, speaking of the Bluebird legacy, he once wrote:

> The name passed from one car to another, from track racing to world speed records, from land to water, from father to son. In the passage of time, as world record succeeded world record, each became just one more milestone of human progress, a single word in the book of human endeavour. A book, perhaps, without an end. A book in which every man has something to write, of his struggles, successes and failures on his ascent of the mountain of progress. But each can only go so far since the mountain has no summit, for it leads to the stars. It has to be climbed, for man cannot regress; he may pause momentarily, but there is no going back on the path of life.

Early in 1966 he went on a trip to America, and returned to Britain refreshed. Exploration was still big news in the United States, where man was reaching for the moon. There was none of the apathy he had encountered in Britain. The idea of someone wanting to strap himself into a landbound rocket to become the first man at ground level to blast along faster than the speed of sound was still cool. Something magical and worthwhile. That naive enthusiasm kickstarted his own once again. It was so devoid of the youthful cynicism of Carnaby Street, or the boardrooms of a jaded British industry fatigued after the prolonged encounter with Bluebird CN7. It was precisely the antidote he needed.

So he was not going to stop. He now understood that he had just been pausing on his ascent of that mountain of progress. He was not going to give up, or let the apathy drag him down into the oblivion he so detested and feared. By his own code of classification, he was a runner. And runners ran. So he would carry on running, and to hell with those who did not want to come along for the ride.

A new boat was out of the question, not just because of the timescale but because he could no longer afford to have one designed and built, as he had with Bluebird K7 back in 1953. But with a more powerful engine he believed that the old warhorse had one last great run in it, so he set about making plans accordingly. Two American firms had indicated their interest in paying him worthwhile bonuses if he could deliver a 300mph water speed record by the end of the year. He never identified them, but the bonuses would help to generate support for the all-important supersonic car.

When Donald Campbell had set out on what he liked to call 'this rather stony path' back in 1949, using his father's old Bluebird K4 boat, it had been just him, his faithful companion Leo Villa, and a small but dedicated team. They had toiled on with their backs against the wall, and with the thousand-yard stares of men with distant horizons as their target. Now the wheel had come full circle and they would be a tight little team once again. There was none of the big-budget backing and support of the past from publicity-hungry fuel companies such as Mobil, BP or Ampol. He would have one last daring throw of the dice, one final push to break the 300mph barrier, with the old hydroplane that had served him so well. Together they would recapture the old glories at Coniston. 'Who says Campbell is old hat?' he demanded to know.

But not everyone shared his fresh enthusiasm. Some were worried about Bluebird's age, not the least among them Leo Villa. 'You can't put new wine in old bottles,' the old man grumbled. But Campbell and designer Ken Norris were satisfied that the twelve-year-old boat was still up to the task despite the rigours of its numerous record attacks and a long tour of Australia. 'The only way to beat the Americans, who are spending thousands of dollars trying to break our record,' Campbell said, 'is to bump it beyond their reach.'

There was much scepticism about the American challenge. To some it was merely a figment of Campbell's imagination, something convenient he had dreamed up in jingoistic self-justification. But the Americans *were* coming. There was no doubt about that. Even a modicum of basic research would have confirmed it. In 1958, the famed American hydroplane designer/builder Les Staudacher had created a jet-engined boat perhaps presciently called the Slug, which handled like its namesake. Equally revered rival Ted Jones envisaged a Bluebird-like jet craft shortly afterwards. But though neither project amounted to much, the Tempo Alcoa challenger created for bandleader and race boat driver Guy Lombardo by Staudacher in 1959 was much more serious. Lombardo had aspired to the record back in 1949, and his plans for Aluminum First had been the spark that ignited Donald Campbell's fire and determination to protect his father's mark set in 1939. Testing had shown Tempo Alcoa to have clear 300mph potential, even though Staudacher damaged it in an incident at Pyramid Lake in Nevada. But in 1960, the boat exploded when a sponson broke during further testing under remote control on the Salton Sea near Los Angeles. Still Staudacher would not relent. The Miss Stars & Stripes II that he built for industrialist Robert Beverley Evans in 1963 showed even greater potential, hitting 285mph, until a mishap on Lake Hubbard left the boat severely damaged and Staudacher hospitalized with extensive injuries.

Still Campbell could not rest on his laurels. American challengers just kept on coming. That same year, Californian Lee Taylor commissioned well-known boatbuilder Rich Hallett to create a record contender around a Westinghouse jet motor with far greater power than Bluebird's Metropolitan-Vickers Beryl engine. Taylor, like Staudacher, was lucky to survive an accident after crashing his Harvey Aluminum Hustler on Lake Havasu on the California/ Arizona border in April 1964. He spent eighteen months learning how to walk and talk again, then went back on the water to build up to a fresh attempt. Like Campbell, Taylor was not a man who gave up.

As if all that was not enough to have any record holder looking anxiously over his shoulder, two land speed record gunslingers were also considering aquatic attempts. In 1964 and 1965, Craig Breedlove and Art Arfons had played a high-speed game of Russian roulette on the Bonneville Salt Flats; the victim was the land speed record as they boosted it in stages from 413mph to 600mph. Both had survived terrifying high-speed accidents along the way that reminded Campbell of his own upset at Bonneville. Now Breedlove planned his twin-engined Aquamerica, Arfons another Green Monster based on his Cyclops jetcar mounted atop two aluminium pontoons. Neither was a man to dismiss lightly, however unorthodox or bizarre their concepts.

So if Donald Campbell had decided that he was not going gentle into that good night, he had only one realistic option: breaking 300mph on the water. Through his old friend Bill Coley, who had given him invaluable moral support and the seed capital to finance the initial design of K7 back in 1953, he was able to buy a complete Folland Gnat trainer aircraft. Stories of him paying £10,000 (£112,600 at today's values) were laughably wide of the mark, given the parlous state of his finances; he actually paid £200 (£2,250). The Gnat came complete with a Bristol-Siddeley Orpheus turbojet engine, capable of generating 4,800lb of thrust. This was comfortably more than the Beryl he had used for all of his previous runs, and the engine was lighter too. Campbell once again engaged Norris Brothers to design the installation, and to incorporate the tail fin from the Gnat to enhance Bluebird's directional stability.

He had no problem deflecting the comments of the doubters:

Life is to be lived, lived to the full. We all live close to death or failure, or some kind of disaster. It could be a disaster of life, or status, or just any small personal ambition. It is a question of sphere.

So what is the point? The point is this, chum. There are in this life the starters, the runners and the critics.

Everyone can do something splendid, or heroic, or even just worthwhile and exciting. The war showed that. Folk who thought they weren't cut out for heroes found that they were doing fantastic things.

Well, all folk are starters. Some get a better start than others. But most get stuck with the idea that they are ordinary folk – the nine-to-fivers. The runners are those who try. I am one of the runners.

Then there are the critics. I don't know if they are in the majority or not nowadays.[1]

In the middle of 1966 he moved from his home, Roundwood, to Prior's Ford, in Horley, and by November he was ready to go back to Coniston Water, scene of so many of the heartaches and triumphs that lay in his golden past. Typically, he had dismissed Villa's misgivings about the new project with his own brand of bonhomie and gung-ho enthusiasm, and pushed forward with his customary determination and courage. But as winter wrapped its cold embrace around the little Bluebird team, the omens multiplied and gripped them as surely as Sir Ernest Shackleton's Endurance had so famously become trapped in the ice half a century before. There were technical problems. Then, when they appeared to be solved, the weather gods scowled. Campbell found himself becalmed and at bay again, an animal caught haplessly in a trap of its own making. Perhaps the mantle had been preordained for him. He worried about his dwindling finances, and became more edgy in the face of continual press criticism. There was little tolerance for the ongoing failure, despite the mechanical woes and inclement weather that so obviously kept him from his goal.

Record breaking makes a poor spectator sport for those not directly involved, especially when they understand little or nothing of it. Ennui can be as destructive a visitor as rain and high wind. Coniston's chill exacerbated the problems. The pressure gradually became intolerable as the enforced inactive days drew out, until the scene was finally set for the disaster that would elevate Campbell to the pantheon. 'The game can be hell,' Campbell admitted:

One often wonders how Hillary might have felt. They have climbed the highest mountain there is, and that's it. In my life, the top at the moment is 300mph. Life is a succession of these mountains. All of us are struggling up and, oh God, isn't it a swine? You get there and you look around and it's great. And you just have time to breathe before you start getting everything in perspective. Then you realize it wasn't a mountain after all. It was a molehill. You look over there and you can see another mountain, the real mountain, and you are going for it, boy. And what hurts, what *really* hurts, is when you come to the last one and you go down the other side.[2]

But there would be no last peak on Donald Campbell's journey into legend. Not for him the lonely vigil he had described atop a final summit. Nor the horrible awareness that his greatest achievements lay in his past.

What drove him on in the face of such inhuman and intolerable odds? What train of cruel circumstances ultimately pushed a lonely, beleaguered, frightened yet determined man to take the final chance that cost him his life? To understand the complex and deep-rooted forces that took him to the brink of disaster at Coniston Water in that harsh winter of 1966/67, we have to go back. A long way back. For it is impossible to understand Donald Campbell without knowing also the character and achievements of the man who so profoundly influenced his life. One of the greatest record breakers of them all. His illustrious father, Sir Malcolm Campbell.

2

THE BIRTH OF THE SHADOW

1885 to 1921

'Fined ten shillings, and let that be a lesson to you not to go so fast in future, Malcolm Campbell.'

MAGISTRATE TO SPEEDING CYCLIST MALCOLM CAMPBELL, 1897

It was typical of Malcolm Donald Campbell that when he decided to change the colour of his racing cars in search of better luck, the thought occurred to him late at night when the shops were closed; he still went out, located one in Kingston, and knocked up the shopkeeper so he could obtain the paint he wanted immediately.

Photographic images capture the essence of the man: small and wiry, with the mien of a lightweight pugilist; thin brown hair neatly brushed flat, oiled and parted in the centre; eyes blue, their stare piercing and intimidating. He was charismatic, but those eyes were the signal that he was not one to let circumstance dictate to him. They could see right through you, as if he could look into your soul and see what lay there.

Campbell knew what he wanted in life. And he would not

be thwarted when he set his mind on something. That day in 1912, his decision to change the colour of his car could never have been seen as the momentous event it became. He sought only better luck, but he would be starting the most famous dynasty in motorsport.

A friend had advised him to see a new opera that had opened in London, written by the celebrated Maurice Maeterlinck. It was called *The Blue Bird*. Campbell enjoyed it, and was feeling benign as he drove home to Sundridge Park in Bromley. And then it suddenly occurred to him. *The Blue Bird* was a play about the pursuit of happiness, synonymous with hope and success. It was the perfect name at a time when the cars that raced at Brooklands were habitually given colourful sobriquets. Count Louis Zborowski had his Chitty Bang Bangs, Parry Thomas his Babs; even more exotic were Hoieh Wayarych Giontoo or Winnie Praps Praps. Campbell's cars were called Flapper, after a partner at Lloyd's who owned and bred racehorses advised him to place his bets on one of his stock bearing that name. It also appealed because he liked to pull the pigtails of his flapper cousins. But both horse and car failed to win with the name.

Campbell followed through his spur-of-the-moment idea with immediate action. He was due to race at Brooklands later that day, and once he had an idea in his head he would pursue it relentlessly. It was gone midnight, but he found an oil chandler and hammered on his door until the bewildered man opened up and sold him all the pale-blue paint, brushes and turpentine he had. In the small hours, Campbell's Flapper III was transformed, and the first Blue Bird was born. He finished the job at four o'clock and the paint was still wet in places when he lined up for his first race.

When Malcolm Campbell saw something he wanted, he

pursued it with a determination and speed that bordered on obsession.

Malcolm Donald Campbell was born in Chislehurst on 11 March 1885 to William and Ada Campbell. Sister Freda was five years old. The family came from Tain, Scotland, where clansmen had fought for Mary Queen of Scots, and for Bonnie Prince Charlie at Culloden. In 1745, one Campbell declared himself for the 'Young Pretender', and his son David, born in 1730, is the first of Malcolm Campbell's ancestors it is possible to trace with authority. David Campbell married Isabella MacGregor, and their son Andrew was the first to move down to London where he set up as a diamond merchant. He handed the business on to his son Joseph when he retired in 1838, and Joseph later passed it on to one of his four sons, another Andrew, who married Jane Mosley from Wolverhampton. Andrew and Jane Campbell had two sons, Andrew and William, the latter born in Chislehurst in 1845. He continued to work in the diamond business, and his success in expanding the enterprise into other spheres saw him leave an estate worth £250,000 (some £10 million today) when he died in 1920.

Donald Campbell liked to describe his grandfather William as 'an astute, industrious man with a broad sense of humour and a kindly disposition', and his grandmother Ada as 'a fabulously beautiful woman, insular, narrow-minded and not a little selfish'. They believed in discipline. Given his ancestry, it was perhaps not surprising that William's word was law in his house, and he was a firm believer in the adage that sparing the rod spoiled the child.

Malcolm grew up self-sufficient and confident. He was sent to a preparatory school in Guildford, where he taught himself to box as a defence against bullying. 'The gruesome

34

stories he used to recount about the floggings, burnings and brandings made the place sound more akin to *Oliver Twist*,' Donald wrote. Later, Malcolm went to Uppingham public school in Rutland, near Grantham, where he got by without ever distinguishing himself as a scholar. His reports always provoked paternal wrath. On the one occasion that he won an award, and returned home bristling with pride, he was intensely annoyed when his father dismissed it on the grounds that the other pupils must have been worse rather than him being better. History would repeat itself when Donald's only daughter Georgina was born; she never remembers her father offering her praise to her face for deeds she knew made him proud from his discussions with others. A reluctance, or inability, to show emotion, and that refusal to offer praise to offspring, was a family trait, and goes a long way towards explaining the restless need to outdo himself that was the cornerstone of Malcolm's life.

He didn't like team games, preferring the solace of cross-country running or the thrill of riding the local rams. He was an adventurous young man who never flinched from confrontation or challenge. Against the strictest head-masterly orders, he and a friend once walked the railway tunnel at Glaston on the Kettering–Manton line. A predecessor had received twenty-four strokes of the cane for a similar offence. Halfway through the tunnel the two boys heard the sound of an oncoming express but, unable to figure out which of the two tracks it was on, they had to wait until the last second for it to appear around the curve before leaping to safety.

Courage was always the dominant Campbell gene.

After his son had finished at Uppingham in 1901, William Campbell took his family to Egypt for four months to broaden their outlook, then sent Malcolm to an engineering works in Neu Brandenburg in Germany to learn its business methods. Bored, Campbell frequently chose not to attend and fell in with a young German, Freido Geertz, whom he called 'Fritz'. Freed from the inhibitions and frustrations of home, he was at liberty to indulge his rambunctious nature.

His German sojourn came at the time of the Boer War, when anti-British feelings were rampant. Campbell hoisted a Union Jack on the small sailing dinghy he kept on Lake Tollensee. Incensed to find one day that it had been torn down, he raised another the following night and lay in wait. As the perpetrator attempted to sabotage the second flag, Campbell shoved him into the freezing water. He might have enjoyed indulging a juvenile streak of irresponsibility, but his patriotism was deeply rooted even at that early stage.

He would satisfy his lust for adventure by riding out storms in his boat, enjoying the sense of control. He and Fritz liked poaching, and defying authority in whatever form they encountered it. They had a keg of gunpowder and made their own cartridges. One afternoon, each anxious to know how soldiers in the war must feel under fire, they took up positions and fired at each other. They stopped only when each had enjoyed the experience of bullets passing inches above his head. One night their hut caught fire. Despite the danger, Campbell rushed in to rescue the precious gunpowder. There were other near misses, such as the incident in which he came close to accidentally shooting himself in the head with his revolver. It would, he admitted, have seemed like the perfect suicide. Later, as winter drew on, he and Fritz decided to excavate a cave in a vertical hill face, to replace their hut. Fortunately neither was present when a post-thaw mudslide sent tons of earth and trees crashing down on their new hideout.

Fate had something much more esoteric in store for Malcolm Campbell.

Prior to his return to England he went to stay with a clergyman and his family in Caen, to assimilate French business methods. There was no scope for adventure there, but he could not resist spending the fare his father had sent him for his return home at Christmas on a gun that caught his eye. He was down to his last three-penny piece, which he subsequently lost, when his mother met his train.

Campbell could have settled for working in the family diamond business, in which he would naturally retain an interest. But right from the start the humdrum business-man's life was anathema to him. He built up many interests, but far preferred to be out fighting the odds in the manner of his more illustrious ancestors. When he intimated to his father that his interest lay in the newly emergent motor trade, William Campbell's reaction was so severe that Malcolm shelved his aspirations temporarily and in 1902 settled for an introduction to a firm of insurance brokers in the City, Tizer & Co., which was attached to Lloyd's. He earned fifteen shillings a week and initially lived at home, until another argument with his father finally prompted him to leave for good. Ada Campbell disapproved of a relationship her son had developed with the daughter of a local squire, and when a row ensued over it between parents and son, the outcome of a father/son tug-of-war over a light chain was that the light fitting pulled away from the ceiling and landed on William Campbell's balding pate. Malcolm left home the next day, and though reconciliation followed, he never went back there to live. From that moment on he was his own man.

At Tizer's, his individual instincts overrode everyday

practicalities. He stayed long enough to learn the rudiments, but as a twenty-first birthday present in 1906, William Campbell bought his son a partnership in the firm of Pitman & Dean. He was now a Lloyd's underwriter.

During the Russo-Japanese War the fortunes of Campbell's business fluctuated. At first he made money as ships ran the gauntlet of the blockade in Vladivostok. But when the Japanese captured Port Arthur and began confiscating ships and cargoes, serious losses arose. Campbell and his business partner went through a lean spell. He had temporarily gone to live in a hydro at the health resort Sundridge Park and learned all about penury during this unedifying spell, but soon a silver lining banished the cloud and helped to set him up for the future.

A newspaper journalist had written an account of a car rally in Dieppe, but to spice it up he had ascribed some disreputable behaviour to a fictitious English spectator. Through unfortunate coincidence the writer happened to choose the name of an Englishman who actually existed, and the latter brought a legal action against the newspaper. Both paper and writer pleaded ignorance of his existence, but he produced witnesses who swore that he had been the first one to come to their minds when they read the story. The court found in the claimant's favour and awarded him massive damages of £1,750 (£103,400 at today's values). One of Campbell's uncles in the printing ink business then suggested that Campbell should develop a new line of insurance to combat such cases. After weeks of trudging round trying to sell policies, Campbell was just in time to cash in on a flood of copycat legal actions. Before the test case no newspaper had insured against libel; within a year it was *de rigueur*. Odham, Southwood & Co. was Campbell's first client. He never looked back.

By the age of seventeen he had paid £15 (£950) of his pocket money for a Rex motorcycle. Now mobile, he learned all about the thrill of speed, and the danger. He crashed several times. By 1906 he was obsessed with motorcycles and was racing them, winning a gold medal in the London to Land's End Trial riding a Quadrant. He was pleased with himself, but his pride was piqued when friends suggested it had been a fluke and he was reminded of his father's put-downs. Perhaps that was where the seed of his future success was really sown. The scepticism hurt. He boasted that he would win a gold medal in three successive years, and went on to do precisely that.

The year 1908 brought a new passion, after he had watched a film of the Wright Brothers' famous first flight at Kitty Hawk, North Carolina, on a visit to the Egyptian Hall in Piccadilly. He would create his own aeroplane. Newspapers were offering fabulous sums to those who conquered the air: the man who first flew across the Atlantic stood to win £10,000 (£584,250) from newspaper baron Lord Northcliffe; flights around Britain, or from London to Manchester, stood to win £1,000 (£58,425) apiece; and there was £4,000 (£233,700) on offer for the longest non-stop flight from Britain to the Continent. These were heady figures for any man, let alone a determined twenty-one-year-old Scot anxious to make his mark.

In the early years of the twentieth century, the spirit of adventure counted for more than any designer's plans. Devoid of any flying experience when he embarked on his audacious project, Campbell was fascinated by the sheer challenge of it all. He had little money to go with his minimal knowledge of aeronautics, but his enthusiasm carried him up the steep learning curve as he experimented with models and boned up on the theory. In 1909, when

Hubert Latham's attempt to cross the English Channel ended in failure, pundits gave his rival Louis Blériot scant chance. But Campbell did not share their pessimism and took out an insurance on the Frenchman succeeding. When Blériot achieved his historic goal on 25 July, Campbell pocketed £750 (£43,220) from the underwriters. When the successful monoplane was briefly put on display at a London store, he was able to gain further valuable insights into its construction. Later he went out via packet steamer to the first European aviation meeting at Reims, down in the champagne vineyards of France. His ship ran aground in fog off Calais, but Campbell hitched a ride and, with typical opportunism, he and his companion arrived just in time to latch onto an official party led by President Emile Loubet that was due to inspect the assembled aeroplanes. Campbell was shrewd and bold as well as resolute.

Knowing his limitations, he employed a carpenter to construct the Campbell Flyer. Every day he rushed down from London to Kent the moment he had finished work. They would work through the night, and he would just have time to clean up before setting off again for the City the following morning. Eventually the craft, powered by a two-cylinder JAP motorcycle engine developing little more than 6hp, was ready for its maiden flight from a small aerodrome near Orpington. Locals staged a protest as Campbell tried to take off from a site that was too short, but he shrugged off his lack of experience and in a daring face-off got the plane airborne, though not for long enough. It lifted only feet off the ground before crashing back down. While he was surveying the wreckage, his barn was burgled and somebody stole a chunk of money.

Most would have been daunted by such an experience, but failure was a spur to Campbell. The more circumstances conspired to rob him of something he desired, the more he would dig his heels in to pursue it.

One by one the great aviation prizes were won by more successful pilots, but Campbell remained at work on the Flyer throughout 1910. Several times the craft would hop aloft for a few feet, but always the result was failure and expensive damage. Attempts to raise money also failed, and in desperation he offered his creation as the first aircraft ever to go up for public auction. Bidding rose steadily from £50 (£3,070) to £270 (£16,570), at which point Campbell made a fatal error and indulged in some surreptitious bidding to boost the price. Another bidder topped his £10 (£610) increment first time round, but not the second, so Malcolm Campbell, failed aviator, now found himself buying from himself for £300 (£18,400) the very craft he had been trying to offload. When it was put up for auction again a week later he was wise enough to quit while he was behind and accept the sole bid of £22 10s. (£1,380), which matched the commission he owed from the previous week's fiasco.

Campbell's depression in this brave new world didn't last. He threw himself into his business at Lloyd's and, in contrast to his aviation adventures, enjoyed significant success. By 1911 he was prospering, and gradually motor racing came to replace aviation in his affections, just as aviation had replaced motorcycles.

In Germany he had ridden a secondhand bicycle to third place against professionals in a closed-circuit race. He'd first raced at the great concrete saucer at Brooklands, which had been completed by Hugh Fortescue Locke-King the previous year, in 1908. He had made his debut on a motorcycle, and later driven a three-cylinder Renault car. But his career really took off when he got his restless hands on a big 4.9-litre French Darracq. This was a potent car. It had

41

finished third in the Tourist Trophy race on the Isle of Man in 1908 after leading until a carburettor fire delayed it on the final lap. In quick succession, Campbell replaced that monster with a Lion-Peugeot and then another Darracq, each faster than its predecessor. These were the first two cars to bear the name Flapper. When he acquired a third Darracq, this time developing 60hp from its 10.5-litre engine, he finally began to make his mark. He bought it from a dealer in Kennington and survived a hair-raising trip on his journey back to Bromley. This was the Flapper III that would metamorphose into the first Blue Bird and establish the Campbell legend.

The day he repainted Blue Bird, he won two races at Brooklands. But during the August Bank Holiday meeting in 1912 he duelled with death when a front tyre burst at 100mph and he slithered down the banking, perilously close to spectators, as the steering broke under the strain. A young girl was watching at the fork where the incident occurred. Dorothy Whitall had gone to Brooklands with her father, Major William Whitall, one of Britain's pioneer motorists, who had press accreditation that enabled them to get into the paddock. There she watched enthralled as Malcolm Campbell calmly described how he had come within a hair's breadth of oblivion.

I remember marvelling how any man who had just looked death squarely in the face could have remained so utterly calm and unconcerned as he appeared to be. He took the matter quite seriously, but only seemed to be concerned at what might have happened to the spectators had his car gone through the railings instead of providentially taking the course it did.

I had the impression forced upon me that here was a man

quite out of the ordinary. Although I was at a very impressionable age, I had never so far met anyone I felt I could idealize. But here was someone different – one that on the instant I thought worthy to be installed in the gallery of heroes. And there in my young mind I placed him.[3]

Campbell was a fatalist. He believed implacably that everything was preordained. 'It is all written in the book,' he would say. His son shared similar beliefs and copied the expression.

Campbell did not forget his meeting with Dorothy Whitall, but at the time his affections were occupied by another attractive woman called Marjorie Trott. They married in 1913. She was a charmer, wealthy enough to fund his passion for racing. When the outbreak of war in 1914 put a temporary stop to his activities, which had taken precedence in his life over everything else, he owned five cars. Marjorie had paid for most of them. She had also given him a motor yacht, the White Heather.

When war was declared, Campbell applied for a commission in the Royal West Kent Regiment, but before that came through his impatience drove him to enlist as a motorcycle despatch rider and to do his bit to help the War Office's drive to persuade private car owners to travel to France, where they could ferry around senior staff. He fought at Mons before his commission as a second lieutenant came through. He moved on to look after the horses in the transportation department and left a lasting memory by replacing his men's infantry equipment and ammunition pouches with cavalry uniforms and bandoliers. Just under a year later he was seconded to the Royal Flying Corps, and learned to fly properly during training at Gosport. But the RFC had an unpleasant truth in store for him. His instructors were impressed by his reactions and assessment of fighting situations, but turned him down as a fighter pilot because he was too hamfisted. It was an ignominious failure for a man who would go on to set nine land speed records and four on water, and he had to content himself ferrying damaged craft from France to England for repair.

That work was not without its dangers, however. On one memorable occasion he flew two new planes from Lyme in Kent to St Omer, flew two old ones back, and was then obliged after a second trip over the Channel to land at St Omer in fog, before being asked to take yet another old plane back to Kent. Shortly after take-off the engine cut out at 5,000ft and he was forced to glide back through fog to Calais aerodrome. By pure good chance his blind flying brought him out of the fog in time for him to recognize two of the aerodrome's hangars, just as he was contemplating the bleak possibility of having to ditch in the Channel. He was shaken by the ensuing crash-landing.

Once recovered, Campbell struck out as a flying instructor, passing on his hard-won experience to raw recruits. He recorded his observations in his first publication, *Hints to Beginners on Flying*. At his own expense he had five thousand copies printed, and he handed them out to the men who looked to him for the means of keeping themselves alive. Later, now promoted to captain, he was awarded the MBE for services to wartime aviation.

One casualty of the Great War was Campbell's marriage. Though he could be generous when the mood took him, Marjorie soon tired of Malcolm's egotistical pursuit of his racing aspirations, his inability to see her point of view, and the arguments that blighted their lives. She was no longer content to stand by as he flitted after publicity like a moth chasing a flame. They divorced in 1915. Dorothy Whitall, who five years later became the second Mrs Malcom Campbell, had this to say of Campbell's character:

> His make-up was very well defined by one who knew him best and who once told him that one of the greatest obstacles to his social success was that he had no absolutely normal personality. 'You know Malcolm,' he said, 'the trouble you are up against is that you have a unique personality. Most of us have a normal line; sometimes we are a bit above that line, and sometimes we are a little below, but there is nevertheless a normal line we follow generally. You have *no* normal line. You are either the most charming person one can meet in a day's march or you are the most perfect son of a —— it is possible to imagine.' That was indeed his trouble. You never knew which of the two characters you had to deal with almost from hour to hour. Without the slightest desire to reflect upon the memory of a man who in many ways deserved and achieved greatness in his chosen career, it must in truth be set down that it was the second aspect of his character which seems to have dominated him in this early marriage.[4]

It was typical of Campbell that he invested so much of himself in his wartime roles, but the moment hostilities ceased he prepared to return to racing. His libel insurance business had been outclassed by other operators who had flooded the market. But despite their differences, William Campbell had prior to the war lodged sufficient deposit so that his son could become a member of Lloyd's. His membership of syndicates covering maritime business had provided a very healthy income that more than compensated for the downturn in his libel insurance fortunes. The bonus now was that he had plenty of free time to indulge his racing aspirations.

From 1919, cars became the real focus of his life. Besides refettling his racers, he persuaded friends to invest in a motor trading operation that aimed to cash in on the inevitable shortage of new cars by offering a specialist service to locate them for clamouring buyers. Unfortunately, he chose the wrong marque; after he had taken deposits from a number of customers, the manufacturer failed to deliver. It did, however, return the deposits plus interest, so he was able to offset the damage to his reputation. In desperation, he revitalized a pre-war link and began importing a French car, the Grégoire, which he marketed as the Grégoire-Campbell. Later he added the famous Mors marque, well known for its prowess in pre-war land speed record breaking and racing. The business never recovered from its shaky start, however, not helped by his lack of foresight in turning down William Morris, later Viscount Nuffield, after suggesting that his Morris cars were not sufficiently well finished. Close friends suggested that he had fallen victim to what they called his 'Rolls-Royce mentality'.

In business, Campbell had a reputation as a prickly individual who refused to delegate, and staff turnover was high. He began to realize that his future lay not in selling cars but in racing them, and he moved from his expensive West End premises to something cheaper in South Kensington. The business would struggle on until 1927 before going into liquidation. A subsequent effort also ended unhappily with dissent among directors tired of his forthright speech and frequent absences on record-breaking forays. His backers were £25,000 (£1,020,000) out of pocket.

Campbell was rather more successful when racing, ham-fisted or not. He took part in hillclimbs, and then went back to racing at Brooklands. The first post-war race there took place over Easter in 1920, the year in which he would marry Dorothy Whitall, the young girl who had witnessed his heroic fight with the Darracq eight years earlier. Campbell slid around regulations that banned the import of foreign cars by describing his French Lorraine-Dietrich as a British army staff car. Trivial rules never bothered him. After winning one race, he promptly sold the car and acquired a Schneider, but was subsequently distinctly unamused when his old Lorraine beat him to win the prestigious 100mph Long Handicap race.

That race was portentous in another way, however, for it saw the debut of the car that would play a key role in Campbell's future. This was the 350hp Sunbeam, built by an irascible Frenchman called Louis Coatalen at the Sunbeam factory in Wolverhampton around a war-surplus 18.3-litre Sunbeam Manitou V12 aero engine. It was the first of a new wave of monsters that would be created in the immediate post-war years. The moment Campbell saw the great car, he realized its potential.

Even on the road he was competitive. If he encountered another fast driver on his daily commute from the City to his home, Canbury, on Kingston Hill, he might well over-shoot his own front door until the challenger had been overcome. He became a familiar figure to police officers in the days long before speed cameras had been thought of. His new wife found, as Marjorie had before her, that he would frequently be late for dinner and, having consumed it, would soon change into overalls and head for the workshop to fettle yet another racing car. Not for him the pipe and slippers of domesticity.

There was one thing on the home front that brought him to a temporary halt, however. On 23 March 1921 another event occurred in his life that was to have far-reaching effects in the world of record breaking. While her husband was reportedly building a dog kennel, Dorothy Campbell gave birth to a son at home.

Just before the Armistice had been signed, Campbell had been flying a Bristol Fighter alongside another flown by his closest friend, Donald Hay. While they were indulging in some aerobatics and pretend dog-fighting, the wings of Hay's plane had suddenly folded up and he plunged to his death. Now Campbell honoured the promise he made to himself that day to name his first son in his friend's memory.

3

SON OF SPEEDKING

1921 to 1935

'Donald could stand up for himself. He had plenty of guts in him, and he wouldn't be browbeaten.'

JEAN WALES, DONALD CAMPBELL'S SISTER

Malcolm Campbell continued to race cars, but from the moment he saw the 350hp Sunbeam he had become captivated with the idea of record breaking. On 17 May 1922, Kenelm Lee Guinness, founder of the KLG spark plug company, realized the potential of the great car at Brooklands by setting a new land speed record of 133.75mph. Campbell knew that he had to have the car, and found himself in the grip of a fresh obsession.

He wanted to be the fastest man on earth.

Had he succeeded at his first attempt, history might have been very different. Sated, Campbell might have moved on to other things. But as he found himself beset by setbacks and frustration, he became more determined than ever that he would not be beaten.

First he had to persuade Louis Coatalen, a man every bit

as capricious as himself, to lend him the car. He began by hiring it, and in June 1922 took it to Saltburn Sands near Redcar in the north-east of England. Despite poor conditions and the massive power that was an embarrassment on skinny Dunlop tyres, Campbell handled the car with a deftness that would have pleased his old RFC instructors and a courage that would not have surprised them. According to hand-held stopwatches, he exceeded 134mph in one direction, but runs were required in opposite directions so his effort could not be ratified. That didn't bother Campbell. He had found his new vocation.

Now he redoubled his efforts to persuade Coatalen to sell him the Sunbeam. They began a battle of wits, the Breton shrewdly upping the ante as Campbell's ambition burned. By April the following year Campbell was winning the struggle, but Coatalen drove a hard bargain. Campbell paid a significant sum for the Sunbeam, and though the amount remained a secret between him and the Frenchman it is interesting to note that a year later, after setting his first record at Pendine Sands, Campbell would offer it for sale at £1,500 (£52,500 at today's values).

Immediately, he entered the car for a speed trial on the holiday island of Fanoe, off Jutland, where an eight-mile section of beach had been prepared. What happened there set the scene for all Malcolm Campbell's subsequent record attempts. The sand was soft in places and frequent bumps also triggered wheelspin in a 3,500lb car whose 350hp was transmitted through tyres less than four inches wide. None of this bothered Campbell, whose sole aim was to extract the maximum from the potent machine. This time he achieved fast speeds in two directions, averaging 136.31mph through the measured kilometre and 137.72mph through the mile. It was a quite remarkable display of fearlessness.

Campbell was ecstatic to have attained his goal with such apparent ease, but his delight was shortlived. The Danes used electrical timing apparatus that was not acceptable to the Association Internationale des Automobiles Clubs Reconnus (the AIACR) which governed such attempts in Europe. The Danish Club was embarrassed and sent the apparatus to Paris for inspection, but though AIACR officials agreed it was accurate they still refused to recognize Campbell's speed.

Momentarily incensed, Campbell resolved to try again. He commissioned the Boulton and Paul aircraft company to manufacture a sleek extended tail with head fairing and a revised radiator cowling to improve the car's aerodynamics. By the middle of 1924 it had been repainted in the familiar pale blue that was now synonymous with the Blue Bird name. He entered the Fanoe trials once again, this time ensuring that the timing equipment met AIACR standards. But he was no longer alone in the record-seeking arena. In France, the racing driver and former Indianapolis 500 winner René Thomas was preparing a 10.5-litre V12 Delage for an attempt, and in England, Brooklands *habitué* Ernest Eldridge was readying his much-modified aero-engined Fiat, affectionately known as 'Mephistopheles'. Before Campbell could run, these two contenders waged an intrepid duel on a section of French public road at Arpajon in July. Thomas drew first blood, upping Guinness's record to 143.31mph. Eldridge fought back with 146.80mph before Thomas protested that the Fiat was not eligible since it lacked reverse gear. The resourceful Eldridge corrected the shortcoming and a week later gained his revenge on Thomas with a new record of 146.01mph.

Campbell had to wait until August to run at Fanoe, but this time his attempt was blighted by tragedy. The beach was in even worse condition than before, and during test runs the Sunbeam persistently threw off its rear tyres as it broke traction and skidded. Campbell fitted wired-edge tyres in place of the beaded-edge Dunlops, but when the car went into another skid at 150mph during the record attempt, the offside front tyre was torn off. Campbell had earlier expressed his concern that spectators were held back from the course only by rope barriers; now the errant tyre struck a boy, who later succumbed to his injuries. Campbell's feelings can be imagined. Driving the car had been nerve-racking, and now he had the boy's death on his conscience, even though he was exonerated at the subsequent inquest.

A month later he appeared at Pendine Sands in Carmarthenshire, North Wales. Again he was forced to run on wet sand, the damp patches snatching at the car intermittently, acting like giant brakes, but this time a new type of Dunlop tyre held up. And this time he was not to be denied. On 25 September he squeaked past Eldridge's record at 146.16mph, thankful that at that time there was no minimum mandatory percentage increment governing new speeds. And his reaction to his success was typical: he said he wanted to reach 150mph next. On 21 July 1925, again at Pendine, he achieved that aim with 150.76mph in the Sunbeam, commenting afterwards, 'My previous record was an odd sort of number that didn't mean much. But 150mph is two and a half miles a minute. A better landmark. I felt it would be an honour well worth having to become the first man in the world to travel at this speed on land.'

Suddenly he was a national celebrity, his achievement flashed from one end of the country to another. His new record was a significant milestone, and a bold achievement. Today one would hesitate to drive a sophisticated sportscar such as a Jaguar XKR at such speeds down Pendine Sands, let alone a crude chain-driven monster that weighed little short of two tons and on which the intrepid driver was perched with zero protection from the elements or an accident while trying to maintain control via narrow tyres. Whatever Malcolm Campbell's shortcomings from the point of view of patience or social grace, he did not lack cold courage. Right from the start of his new ventures he came to learn a key lesson about record breaking: it has nothing in common with the adrenalin rush of competing wheel to wheel with other drivers on a track; instead, it is as much a battle of man against himself as it is man against the capriciousness of Mother Nature and things mechanical. Both required courage, skill and judgement, but record breaking was a much more cold-blooded affair. And now Malcolm Campbell, failed aviator, failed fighter pilot and failed motor trader, had shown himself to be its consummate master.

Even in his moment of triumph, he knew something that no-one else could. Two and a half miles a minute certainly did have a ring to it, especially to the man in the street in search of a vicarious thrill. But already Campbell's restless spirit was thinking of bigger numbers. Something nice and simple. Something like three miles a minute – 180mph. He was convinced that it could be done, but he also knew that the Sunbeam had reached its limit. Now he had a new challenge. He would build a completely new car, designed from the outset to break records. Thus was the first pukka Blue Bird record breaker conceived.

Both Malcolm and Donald Campbell were the sort of men who would still have tasted success had some of their circumstances been different, but neither could have achieved what he did without the small, wiry mechanic who stood alongside them in so many of their duels with death. This was the inestimable Leopoldo Alphonso 'Leo' Villa. If the Campbells were Don Quixotes, then Villa was their Sancho Panza. He was the cornerstone upon whom they both came to rely totally as they tilted at the windmill of speed.

Villa was born in London on 30 November 1899, just under a year after Count Gaston de Chasseloup-Laubat had piloted his electric Jeantaud racer to the heady speed of 39.24mph to establish the world's first ever land speed record. Villa's father was Italian, his mother Scottish, and he inherited the former's emotional disdain for authority and the latter's calmness in the face of problems. At one stage in his youth, however, he was sacked from his job as a page boy at Romano's in the Strand when his temperament got the better of him and he threw a bottle of ink over the hall porter.

A gifted artist, Villa had drawn many sketches of the internal combustion engine and was increasingly attracted to the emergent motor car. It was with some relief that his vexed parents were able to move him along to his Uncle Ferdy, who was in the trade. Through him, Villa ended up working for the mercurial Italian racing driver Giulio Foresti, who held the British franchise for the Itala automobile. Between 1915 and 1922, Villa and Foresti escaped serious injury after a number of hair-raising exploits in motor racing, but during preparations for the French Grand Prix at Strasbourg, in which Foresti was to drive a works Ballot, Villa's luck ran out. He was badly burned when a generator exploded.

After a period of convalescence in England, he returned to Paris to work on engine development in the Ballot factory. Foresti had continued racing with another riding mechanic, so Villa was temporarily on the shelf. But then came the sort of chance encounter that shapes destinies. Malcolm Campbell held the Ballot agency in England and raced one of its models at Brooklands. Now he was considering buying a new Ballot for a Grand Prix campaign, so Foresti and Villa were despatched to London with the car that French star Jules Goux had driven in the Grand Prix Villa had missed. Campbell was taken with Villa's manner and ability, and offered him a job.

He was very much Malcolm Campbell's paid employee, but he would be much more than that to the easier-going Donald, whom he would know for most of the younger man's life. Donald would call him Unc. As both the Campbells chased their dreams, Villa would be the glue that held the fabric of their projects together.

Malcolm Campbell lived in an age that fêted achievers. Inter-war Britain was anxious to re-establish and redefine its place in world society, and a new generation wanted to forget the carnage of the Somme and to exploit the stimulus to technical development the 1914–1918 conflict had provided. The men who flew aeroplanes or drove fast cars and boats in this era were heroes. Their death-defying exploits and successes were an affirmation of life. Those with the courage and finances necessary to indulge in such things earned great popularity. On the race tracks there were the peerless Major Henry O'Neil de Hane Segrave, Campbell himself, Kaye Don, and quiet giants of speed such as John Rhodes Cobb and George Eyston; on the water, Segrave, the enigmatic Betty 'Joe' Carstairs and Hubert Scott-Paine flew the flag.

Campbell was as tough as they came, and would stop at nothing. Frustration merely drove him on. Taking on allcomers, he and Villa developed a succession of Blue Birds, employing the best technical brains Campbell's money could hire. In February 1927, the first true Blue Bird, a Napier-powered monster designed by Amherst Villiers and Josef Maina, finally pushed the record to 174.883mph on Pendine Sands after myriad teething problems. When Segrave beat him to 200mph that same season, Campbell hit back in 1928 at Daytona Beach with 206.956mph in a modified version of his new car. A year later, as Segrave prepared to ace everyone and retrieve British honours from the American Ray Keech with his singular Golden Arrow, Campbell's bid at Verneuk Pan in South Africa failed. He had sunk thousands of pounds into having the Blue Bird modified yet again, but still he would not give up. By the time he was ready to go back to Daytona in the late winter of 1931, rivals such as America's Frank Lockhart, Keech and Lee Bible, and England's Segrave, were dead, while Kaye Don was now involved in attempts on the water speed record after a 1930 fiasco with his Sunbeam Silver Bullet car. But Campbell wanted his record back. After Blue Bird had benefited from the design ministrations of Reid Railton, a gifted genius, he succeeded – at 246.09mph. Then he nudged that beyond the 250 mark a year later with 253.97mph. Still he would not rest. For 1933, the further-modified Blue Bird was powered by a Rolls-Royce R Schneider Trophy-winning engine, and with greater horsepower Campbell crept closer to his ultimate goal, the five-miles-a-minute 300mph on which he had now set his heart.

Again working with Railton, Campbell took the final model of the car to Daytona Beach in March 1935, but he was incensed to better his new record of just over 272mph by only 4mph. He needed a firmer course where wheelspin would not rob Blue Bird of its true potential, so, with fourteen-year-old Donald at his side, he went to the Bonneville Salt Flats in Utah. There, on 3 September that same year, he overcame a terrifying first run when a front tyre punctured and fumes filled the cockpit to complete his attack with an average of 301.13mph. His son loved every moment. At school he had his own business cards, stressing his middle name: Donald *Malcolm* Campbell. He aped his father's signature, and basked in the hero worship of his peers.

This, then, was the public hero whom King George VI had knighted in 1932. Record breaker, businessman, author, journalist, yachtsman, politician. An often testy man who nevertheless possessed great personal magnetism. But there were telling signs in his public life that Malcolm Campbell could be too self-centred. On one newsreel, a young Donald Campbell rushes up the gangplank to greet his father at Southampton after his successful 1933 campaign. In a poignant little vignette the boy moves to shake the man's hand but the gesture goes unnoticed. He stands there, hand outstretched. Ignored. If every picture tells a story, that film raises volumes of questions about the relationship between a father and son who between them pushed Britain to the very forefront of speed with eleven records on water and ten on land to their joint credit.

I once happened to mention this film to Donald Campbell's widow, Tonia Bern, who clapped her hands in recollection and shrieked, 'I know! I know the film you mean! You know, it was watching that film, when Donald showed it to me, that made me fall in love with him! There was this little boy, so proud of his father, and his father didn't even notice . . .' But you can interpret the footage in various ways. Maybe Tonia was right: maybe Malcolm simply wasn't the demonstrative type; maybe he just didn't see his son's hand. But few relationships between public figures can have been as complex. Malcolm reportedly once told Donald, 'You will never be like me, we're built different.'

Shortly after their son was born, Malcolm and Dorothy Campbell moved to a sprawling house on the old Reigate road near Horley, called Povey Cross. Within two years Donald had a playmate when sister Jean was born there in 1923. These were carefree days for children, especially those born to a wealthy adventurer. Gatwick was just a small town with a race course the Campbell children walked past every Sunday on their reluctant way to church. 'We were brought up with not a lot of contact with the family, because Father was away a lot,' Jean Wales recalled. 'I had a governess and a nanny, and we were brought down to tea on a Sunday afternoon with all these strange people who had come down from London, sitting in our best clothes, and then we were taken back upstairs to the nursery with our governess. My day school was only about a mile and a half away, so we used to have other children coming for tea on Saturday and Sunday. Mother was the most beautiful woman. She was always up in London, at banquets and things.'

When they were old enough, both children were sent to boarding schools. At eight, Donald headed for a prep school in Horsham, and then at Easter in 1932 to St Peter's Preparatory in Seaford. There are stories that he was bullied there, but Jean was quick to defend her brother. 'There might have been, but I don't recollect that. In any case, Donald could stand up for himself. He had plenty of guts in him, and he wouldn't be browbeaten.' In July 1934 he went to Uppingham in Rutland, his father's old school. But though the siblings were separated, they still spent plenty of holiday time together at Povey Cross. As a combination they had always been lethal. Whatever Donald did, Jean would copy. Malcolm Campbell did not believe in mercy when misbehaviour went beyond the limits he defined, but though Donald was often spanked it did nothing to diminish his feelings for his father. Jean recalled some of their mischievous exploits:

> We got punished for breaking all these tiles one day. Dad was having a summerhouse built and there was a stack of beautiful roof tiles. We decided that in our little cars – one was a Bugatti, the other the 1928 Blue Bird – we would play our favourite game of Earl Howe and Malcolm Campbell. And we smashed them all up.
>
> We'd ride our bikes round and round, and when we weren't having head-on collisions we'd sometimes fall off straight into the lavender bush. One time I was laughing: 'Ha, ha, wouldn't it be funny if Dad came home early from the office and found us!' And this voice came round the corner, 'Wouldn't it!' He caught us red-handed. Donald was taken upstairs and walloped, I was sent to bed. If Donald was punished, if he was in trouble, I would just go and sit and cry my heart out for him. But Dad never hit me.
>
> He sent us to bed for breaking those tiles, but I remember at four o'clock he said, 'Come on, kids, I'll take you to the cinema.' Up we got, and trotted into Reigate with him. Dad couldn't bear to see us punished for long.

Then there was the time they played Howe and Campbell on the brand-new tennis court, their skidding cars cutting great ruts in the flat turf.

There was no television, of course, so they had to make their own amusement. 'I had a dolls' house,' Jean continued, 'and I wanted some mats. So Donald said, "I know what we'll use!" And he proceeded to cut all my hair off! He thought my fringe would make a nice mat. He literally scalped me! We couldn't understand why all the hair wouldn't stay together. Stupid, isn't it? He got hell for that. So did I.'

Malcolm Campbell was fond of lighting bonfires, and his offspring caught the bug early. 'Dad had a big party one night, when we were eight and ten probably, and the cigarette boxes were full of the finest cigarettes,' Jean remembered. She and Donald played truant from their governess, Ivy Whiteman, whose husband Reg was the family chauffeur, and escaped to their tent in the garden with handfuls of cigarettes and a box of matches. 'We didn't know how to smoke and we couldn't figure out why the cigarettes wouldn't stay lit. I thought, "This is no use," so we'd stub them out and have another one. All this horrible smoke. In the end we burned the tent down, and I have never been so sick in my life. And I wouldn't come clean about what we'd done until they discovered that the cigarettes were all missing.' Then there was the haystack episode. 'Dad had just had these thatched haystacks done in the fields on the road to Charlewood. God knows what that had cost him. Donald and I decided we'd go down and see if we could do fire engines. So we got some matches and lit a fire. That was fun, and we put it out. Next time we let it go a bit further. All right, we put it out. The third time we couldn't put it out. We had to get the real fire brigade. Luckily for us the wind was in the wrong direction, otherwise the whole load would have gone up.'

Campbell had a reputation for being high-handed with staff and colleagues, and for being a difficult man to get along with if you had an opposing view. But his daughter was adamant that with his children his bark was usually worse than his bite. The stern disciplinarian was an adventurer who still had enough of the small boy in him to pursue the romantic notion of hunting buried treasure during an unsuccessful expedition with his friend Kenelm Lee Guinness to the Cocos Islands in 1926. Few children would not have looked up to such a swashbuckling figure.

He buried all this treasure during the war. All his cups from Headley Grove [where the family lived from 1936]. Had them all cemented in so that if the Germans came they'd never know they were there. And he had marvellous wine. Everything was blocked in, bolted down under concrete. He buried God knows what.

He had some lakes at Tilgate [another of Malcolm Campbell's properties], two beautiful lakes. Now they're a pleasure park. And he had a little island, with a drawbridge that Leo designed. Dad had a little place there, and later in his life he just loved being there. Though he had a beautiful house in Reigate when he died, he used to go out regularly to Tilgate on his own. He had a couple of boats and he'd go fishing, and if he caught a certain fish he'd chuck it back. He'd cut the undergrowth back, put on his old plus fours, and potter. That's what he loved doing. One day we went down at the weekend, and he was putting a stake in the ground and he missed, and he went flat on his face into muddy water. And Donald and I didn't know what to do. He was furious! But then he saw the funny side of it. And at Tilgate he had Huntley and Palmer's biscuit tins full of the old two bob pieces, half crowns, all green as green. One Sunday, he said, 'Now, kids, if you find a couple of tins, you can have them.' So he watched us, and we were poring around, and we found them. I don't know how much was in them – twenty, thirty quid – but they were so green you'd have needed caustic soda. I reckon there's still some other money buried at Headley Grove and at Tilgate, but it will never be found.

I think in another life he was a pirate. At home he was digging things up, looking for treasure, and he did that treasure hunting in the Cocos. And he hoarded towards the end. He never bought just one thing, he'd buy six or seven at a time.

Jean Wales also admitted that she became deeply upset whenever she heard negative stories about her father.

That's because Dad *wasn't* a bully. He used to have us in for our school reports at the end of term, and I didn't know how to keep a straight face. He'd sit at his desk, in his swivel chair, and look at us. Donald would be sitting there, and Dad would read our reports out. Could do better, could do better, everything but what we should have done, but he didn't give us stick over that. He hadn't really got a temper. When he got mad I suppose we drove him to it with the things that we did.

He was strict with us because he'd been brought up in the Victorian era. And I thank him for it. We weren't spoiled. Oh God no! We had to walk or bike, and we were never given everything we wanted. We had to earn pocket money, doing odd little things. We never really wanted for anything, but we certainly weren't spoiled. In fact, I was very strictly brought up. In my late teens, if I had a boyfriend back, when Dad and Mum went to bed *I* went to bed. None of this sitting downstairs snogging or anything, oh no!

He was a good father. He did frighten me a little bit,

because he could look at you, you know, if you'd been behaving badly, and you would freeze. But he never touched me, never laid a hand on me. And I don't think he enjoyed giving Donald the odd wallop on the backside. He didn't really hurt him.

Several stories, however, portray Campbell as a tough father. According to one, when Donald fluffed his good-nights to dinner guests before going to bed, Malcolm held him by the throat and forced the correct words from him. Another recalled his buying Donald a train set but taking it away after his son caused a crash when he set the points wrong. Some of that is dressed up in a trite Pathé news story which shows a benign little scene where the train derails. Father says to contrite son, 'I'm afraid you've broken this, old chap.' But things were rather less quaint beyond the camera. Malcolm later took over the train set for himself, allowing Donald access to it only on request. But again, Jean leapt plaintively to her father's defence.

I can't remember him being bullied by Dad. I don't know where this has come from. I never remember Dad ever bullying Donald. That story about the train in a *Sunday Times* article was appalling! I don't know where that came from, or the grabbing by the scruff of the throat. I never, ever – this is on my life – saw Dad ill-treat Donald, other than taking him up and giving him a quick wallop when he'd done something. But that was normal in those days. Dad never bullied Donald when I was around so I don't see why he would behave differently when I wasn't. He gave him a wallop when he deserved it, and in any case I can tell you that none of it had any lasting effect on Donald.

In family life, Malcolm Campbell had a soft side that he permitted few others to see. As little children, Donald and Jean would go into his bedroom some mornings and watch while he did his regular exercise on a pull-up bar, and would then have a sugar and cinnamon breakfast with him. 'Then we'd hide, under the bedclothes or in his clothes basket, and he'd go round looking for us, saying, "I can't see those kids anywhere!" And it would be so obvious where we were. But it was a ritual. I've got a china Alsatian that I gave Dad back in 1930. Every day we went to make sure this dog was there, and we'd create havoc.'

Real pets mattered, too. Though Jeyes Fluid once proved so attractive that Donald unwittingly used it to wash some of his father's ferrets, it was a child's mistake. Both he and his father were dyed-in-the-wool animal lovers. 'Dad used to breed pheasants. We used to have a big sweeping lawn, and his joy every morning was to feed them with raisins. Donald shot one once by mistake, and Dad was livid. He couldn't bear anything being shot.' Both father and son enjoyed clay-pigeon shooting, and Malcolm had a shotgun case in his study at Headley Grove that was twenty feet long. He didn't like shooting live things, but he enjoyed collecting guns. Later, while he was at Lake Eyre, Donald would go target shooting in the outback, but he never took shots at the plentiful kangaroos and dingoes that were popular targets for the locals. 'Dad once found this sick little baby rabbit on the golf course,' Jean remembered, 'and we managed to suckle it on a little feeding bottle. He was gorgeous. Mother had a Peke, and the rabbit played with this dog. It loved chocolate peppermints; it used to sit up and eat them. It would follow the Peke around, it was absolutely like a puppy. Well, Dad *would* kill rats, and one morning he thought he saw one in the shrubbery and shot it. But it was our rabbit.' That was the only time she ever saw her father cry. 'Donald was an animal idiot, too. In the fifties he had Maxie the Labrador, and Mocha. When Maxie died, Donald was in a terrible state.'

As brother and sister, Donald and Jean were always very close. They had their inevitable ups and downs, of course – once, their impromptu boxing lessons went awry when she bloodied his nose and he whacked her so hard that they had to be stopped – but when one was in trouble the other would be at his or her side. Still, they had more solitary pursuits, too: Jean had her 'fairy' dell in the woods, where Ivy Whiteman indulged her childhood fantasies, and Donald would spend his time in the workshop with Leo Villa. He was an inquisitive child and loved to take things to pieces. Jean had a cooking stove that he dismantled, then it was a bike. Mechanical things fascinated him, though Villa was often called upon to help when it came to reassembling them. Once he'd figured out what made them tick, he would lose interest.

Christmas was a time, according to Jean, when they were 'always out of control'.

Dad bought us lovely presents. One year they fooled us and we went to bed quite happy, not realizing it was Christmas Eve until Donald woke up about two o'clock in the morning and shrieked, 'Sis, quick, quick, there's a huge giraffe at the bottom of my bed!' It was Christmas morning. We got our own back. We went straight into their bedroom, at about three o'clock, and tipped our bags of toys all over the bed.

There was one Christmas when Donald had reached the age when he was starting to think that there wasn't a Father Christmas. Probably when we were ten and eight. He said to me, 'Right, this Christmas we're gonna fool them. We're

65

going to find out who Father Christmas is!' He got some string, tied it on one of his big toes, ran it along the floor and under the door, and then tied it to one of my big toes. And I don't know whether it was Mother or Father who came in, but they went smack on their face after they caught their foot in the string! And we just sat there laughing, shouting, 'Ha, ha, we don't believe in Father Christmas!'

But I was terrified of Father Christmas, terrified! I think it was the beard. I remember going into the spare room at Povey one morning and I saw Father Christmas's outfit lying on the chair and I went screaming to Dad, who thought I'd been killed. I couldn't work out what it was! We had a lift in our house that brought our food up from the kitchen, and I'd been naughty. Dad's voice from the bottom said, 'Father Christmas is here, he's coming up! You've been naughty!' God, I was lost for words.

He was always Father Christmas. We had a minstrels' gallery, and I can see him now standing there in his outfit and coming downstairs with all that was left of the toys for us for Christmas Day. But I wouldn't kiss him. I would scream and run a mile, wouldn't go near him. He was very good at Easter, too. I remember the little things, like the chocolate Easter bunny. He was very good with things like that.

He was a funny mixture, Dad. We used to have a summerhouse, with hammocks, camp beds and things in it. I remember he really got me believing that the lights that were flashing from aircraft were fairies. The light went out for me when he died. I just couldn't imagine it because he was just so full of life. He never sat still, he was always on the go. I never looked upon him as getting old.

Both Donald and Jean went out to Cape Town with their father in April 1929 for his abortive record attempt at

Verneuk Pan. Apart from an image of Malcolm Campbell's battered nose, a legacy of a nasty flying accident out there, Jean's principal memory of that trip is of Donald dealing with an old boy with a flowing beard who kept jumping out of his deckchair and annoying them during the outward boat trip. Donald crawled under the deckchair and tried to set the septuagenarian's bottom alight. Jean also went to Florida in 1935. Donald didn't go because he was at boarding school, whereas she was only a weekly boarder.

I used to hate Dad going away, and I went up to his room and put my arms round him to say goodbye, and just burst into tears. And he said, 'Right, you're coming!' So he rushed off to get my passport and off I went on the *Aquitania* with him. It was just ridiculous, when I look back now. They met us off the train, gave us a police escort to the hotel. I couldn't even dance, yet we were dancing in my honour. It was just crazy! But he was a god, and I didn't appreciate it.

When you're brought up with speed, it isn't very nice in a way. You just don't like to see your father going off, and not know whether he's coming back. It's hard when you're old enough, ten or eleven, to know what he's doing, that it's a risky thing.

Donald's consolation came when he went out to Bonneville with his father later that year.

During his youth, Donald Campbell had several bouts of illness. The Campbells had good friends, the Burts, down at Bracklesham Bay in Sussex, and they used to go there sand yachting during the holidays. But one year Donald contracted typhoid after drinking water at the Bracklesham Hotel. Then he contracted rheumatic fever after a bout of German measles at Uppingham, and developed a problem with two valves in his heart. He was brought home, very sick, and spent weeks on his back recovering. The problem would have long-term repercussions. On another occasion, in 1940, Jean answered a knock on the door at Headley Grove to find some Canadians who had brought her brother home with blood pouring from his mouth. 'We thought he'd punctured his lung. He'd come off his motorbike outside the cemetery. I thought it was curtains then.' It was the second time he had fractured his skull in an accident. Indeed, Donald Campbell seemed to attract trouble. 'We had these Alsatians. One was Nimrod, a most docile black and tan. [Donald remembered it as Carlos in his autobiography, *Into the Water Barrier*.] It was Donald's fault. He put his head on the dog's back and it tickled; the dog went to scratch it and took a bit of the lobe of Donald's ear off.'

But for all the setbacks he developed into a young man of good humour and coltish effervescence, and though he only scraped by academically, he was a keen sportsman who won his boxing colours at Uppingham before he contracted rheumatic fever. Malcolm was a horseman and golfer, and the moment he achieved a new record at Daytona he would head straight for the links. 'You couldn't keep up with him,' Jean remembered. 'You needed a motorbike. And God help you if you moved when he was about to swing.' Donald, too, was a good golfer, as Jean confirmed. 'He hit the ball a mile. I remember playing with him at Reigate Heath and he hit the ball so hard he broke his club in half. If he'd had time, he could have been a very good golfer. He was very powerful, thicker set than Dad. Not much taller, but stockier. Dad was a very small man. He had lovely legs; he should have been a woman, actually! He was very chiselled, with very fine features. He had lovely blue eyes, and that look that penetrated.'

Donald said of this man who cast such a long shadow over his entire life, 'He was a terrific example. Courageous, colourful, dour, unbending, uncompromising. He and I were very different characters. I'm the sort of idiot who, once he gets tucked into a job, just puts on the blinkers and sees nothing else. Spirit counts very much. It is infectious. All you know is that there is a fire burning inside.'[5] Freud might have had a field day analysing their relationship, but no matter what Malcolm might or might not have been as a father – and there is only one person alive today genuinely qualified to pass true judgement – his son continued to worship him. Everything he would do in record breaking would always be done with one thought in mind: would the Old Man have approved?

4

'KAISER'S NOT GOING TO GET THE OLD MAN'S RECORD'

1935 to 1949

'I'll have a crack at improving the record myself. To hell with Kaiser. We'll give him a run for his money.'
DONALD CAMPBELL, FEBRUARY 1949

If anyone expected Malcolm Campbell to rest on his laurels during a quiet retirement, it was not long before he was hatching plans to disappoint them.

Initially, however, he spent his time on his return from Utah in the autumn of 1935 looking for a bigger house. Eventually he settled on a Georgian mansion in eighty acres of parkland overlooking Surrey's North Downs, Headley Grove. It needed work, and typically the penny-conscious Campbell told Dorothy that he did not mind what was needed so long as it didn't cost much. As she was often moved to observe, when it came to buying new cars or equipment he never batted an eyelid, but on less esoteric matters he could be stingy. Dorothy Campbell was a woman of wiles, however, and eventually the interior was completely refurbished at a cost of several thousand pounds. By the time he received the bill, Campbell had long forgotten his initial objections.

Campbell worked happily away, restyling the out-buildings and gardens and creating new workshops and garages and a complicated road system, but character-istically he had such an explosive falling-out with his architect that the matter nearly went to court. Once his temper had cooled, he was obliged to make a financial settlement. Whatever the undertaking, his maxim was always the same: my way, or the highway. Some were prepared to tolerate such dictatorship, others kicked against the traces.

Headley Grove was habitable by early 1936, but before moving in Campbell headed off for an ocean cruise to North Africa, leaving Dorothy to cope. He was never a man to concern himself with domestic trivia. On his return, when she had the house functioning properly, Campbell threw several lavish parties, indulging the other side of his complex character. This was his way of returning the favours he enjoyed as a national celebrity. Normally he detested such events, but he felt more comfortable reciprocating as he was on home turf. Entertaining was nevertheless an ordeal, since he hated the inevitable upheaval and seeing his precious possessions being moved even slightly out of place. Several times, when he and Dorothy had been invited to stay with friends, they returned home early after Campbell had grown homesick. He was a recluse at heart, impelled by an inherent homing instinct. He loved the public limelight, but hated anything that interrupted his private peace.

Three hundred miles an hour on land had long been his goal, but even in its achievement there had been an upset.

He was incensed that the timekeepers had rendered his greatest triumph an anti-climax by initially giving him his speed as 299mph, and though a recheck had confirmed that he did indeed exceed his target, it still rankled. It had taken something from the victory.

While Campbell had been busy with the continual rebuilds of Blue Bird that would take it from 174mph to 301mph, he had monitored the progress of his race-track rivals, Henry Segrave and later Kaye Don. They had fought America not only for the prestigious Harmsworth Trophy, an international competition instigated by *Daily Mail* proprietor Lord Northcliffe to stimulate speedboat development, but also the water speed record. Segrave was long dead, killed in a tragedy on Windermere on 13 June 1930; Don had taken up his mantle in the same boat, Miss England II, and in its less technologically adventurous successor, Miss England III. Four times Don had broken the record, but the final honours remained with the man who had been Britain's great rival, Commodore Garfield Wood, known in American racing circles as the Old Grey Fox of Algonac. At the same time, Campbell's old Brooklands rivals, Captain George Eyston and John Cobb, were preparing dramatic new machines to attack his land record. Eyston created a seven-ton, eight-wheeled, Rolls-Royce-engined behemoth known as Thunderbolt; Cobb went to Reid Railton for a four-wheel-drive, twin Napier-powered teardrop called the Railton Special.

Campbell could have built a new Blue Bird car, but now he was more interested in Wood's record. Late in 1936 he commissioned Miss England II designer Fred Cooper, Britain's leading marine architect, to create the first in a line of Blue Bird hydroplanes. Railton was a consultant on the project. The craft was a conventional hydroplane hull, 24ft long and 9½ft wide, with a shallow V beneath the waterline and the usual step part of the way along which would help it to get 'on the plane' in order to run partly out of the water at high speed. The boat, built by Saunders-Roe, weighed just under 5,000lb and was officially registered as K3, K being the British insurance symbol to denote that this was an unlimited-class boat, and the 3 to indicate that it was the third such craft since the system had been instigated with the Miss Englands. Campbell took the trusty Rolls-Royce R37 engine from the Blue Bird car.

He was venturing away from his realm of expertise, and his anxieties in ceding control in some areas manifested themselves in his behaviour. He simply did not believe that anyone could do things as well as he could, and when he found himself in a position in which he had to let others make key decisions he was psychologically incapable of accepting it. Some saw this as arrogance, but Campbell had always lived his life on his own decision-making. Now he began to fidget and fret, and he became a nightmare to live with. Dorothy complained of his malignant penchant for fault finding. At times he would simply take himself off for a few days before returning in his normal humour, having worked out whatever problem was vexing him.

Early in June 1937, K3 was taken to Loch Lomond, and though Campbell steadfastly maintained that it was an experimental boat that would not necessarily be used for breaking records, nobody was fooled. Subsequently, Blue Bird went to Locarno, at the Swiss end of Lake Maggiore, since Leo Villa's Uncle Ferdy was friendly with the local mayor. On 21 August the first attempt on Gar Wood's record failed when the thermostat controlling the closed-circuit water cooling system malfunctioned and damaged the engine. Then there was a near miss with some fishing nets, but on Wednesday, 1 September Campbell got what he wanted. In ideal conditions he sped one way through the measured mile at 125mph and then came back at 127.66mph for an official average of 126.32mph. It seemed easy, but Campbell had found K3 a brute to handle and had struggled to keep it running straight. Typically, he was not satisfied with his new record, and went out again the following day. This time he touched 130mph on the outward run (130.43mph) and came back at 128.57mph for an average of 129.5mph and another new record. It would do for a while.

He was ready again a year later, with K3 now wearing a sleeker metal tail to improve its aerodynamics and directional stability. He did some trial runs on Lac Leman in Switzerland before deciding that the venue was unsuitable because of submerged springs that upset the surface; nevertheless, at the League of Nations international meeting there he won the Coupes des Nations after attaining the highest speed over the mile at 120mph. He was advised to switch to Lake Hallwil, close to the border. Blue Bird remained brutish, though. By this time Fred Cooper had been replaced by Peter Du Cane, and on one occasion Campbell sent Du Cane out in it and the marine architect reached 120mph before encountering the same unpleasant behaviour Campbell had complained of. K3 had reached its limit around 130mph, and Hallwil's 1,000ft elevation above sea level did not help, but he persevered. On Saturday, 17 September 1938, he achieved his third water speed record with a mean of 130.86mph. But for Campbell that was too close to Wood's old mark for comfort. His wake had barely died down before he announced his intention to try again in 1939 with a new boat already under construction.

In America, the spur of competition lent great impetus to speedboat development. In Atlantic City, Arno Apel and his brother Adolf had long been experimenting at their Ventnor Boat Corporation with a dramatic new type of hull. It was still a hydroplane, but effectively the boat had been halved longitudinally along its centreline, and a flat bottom was inserted between the two halves. On either side of the pilot an integral sponson now supported the front of the craft at speed, while the rear end rode on a planing shoe just ahead of the propeller. The effect of this new principle was to lift the hull almost entirely clear of the water so that the boat ran on just those three points. Top speed was dramatically improved, as hydrodynamic drag was reduced. When Apel declined to build him a new boat in 1938, Campbell ordered a brand-new design along similar lines from Peter Du Cane at Vosper. Thus was born Blue Bird K4, the 27ft-long craft that would become the mechanical link between the racing careers of the Campbells, father and son.

Due to the uncertainty in world politics at that time, K4 was taken to Coniston Water in the British Lake District in August 1939, where it was christened by Donald Campbell with the words, 'May God bless this craft and her pilot.' He was eighteen years old, and had no way of knowing that ten years down the road his young wife would similarly be seeking God's protection on his behalf. Father and son were getting on well as Campbell grew to manhood. Jean Wales recalled one incident when they larked around with their caps turned back to front and Malcolm drove them up to the forecourt of an expensive restaurant. 'The doorman took one look, sniffed, and said, "Round the back, if you please." He was mortified when he belatedly recognized Sir Malcolm Campbell.'

This was one of the smoothest record attempts in Malcolm Campbell's lengthy career, and it would be his last successful one. Some 485 residents of Coniston took him to their hearts and formed the Friends of Campbell to fight protest action from a self-styled group of early-day conservationists who called themselves the Friends of Brantwood after the house on the east shore of the lake in which the long-departed poet John Ruskin had lived. Campbell's supporters won the day amid promises from the Blue Bird team that they had no intention of doing anything to upset the ecological equilibrium, and were just trying to do something for British prestige. Blue Bird needed only test runs on the Thursday and the Friday after arriving at Coniston on Monday, 14 August. These revealed that the water scoop beneath the hull needed to be repositioned after an overheating problem, but Du Cane was shaken rigid by Campbell's first assessment of the boat. He told him it felt terrible and that he didn't think he could attain 80mph with it. Campbell was unable to describe the behaviour he so disliked with sufficient clarity for Du Cane to get a handle on it, so that Friday Campbell agreed to let Du Cane have a run on Saturday morning, the 19th, and Villa and his team worked through the night to reposition the scoop. In the event, Campbell took the controls right from the start and sped smoothly up and down the glassy lake. Blue Bird's trim was perfect. His first run was 142.86mph, the second 140.62mph for an average of 141.74mph. Troubled or not at eighty, Blue Bird ran well enough to secure for Malcolm Campbell his fourth water speed record, and the success could not have been better timed. Within days, Britain declared war on Germany.

Campbell went back into the services. He had believed that war was inevitable and had written books to that effect that later made Neville Chamberlain look as foolish as the piece of paper he had so naively flourished. In many ways it was a relief for Campbell to get back into harness again working at Combined Operations, where he was in charge of testing new weapons and mechanical systems.

His father's streak of patriotism ran right through Donald Campbell, who immediately made his own plans. In 1939, he took a preliminary medical and soon found himself at RAF Cardington in Bedfordshire as an AC2 rank trainee pilot, serial number ACH964147. It was the one branch of the services that appealed to him. But soon his world crashed around him when a simple electro-cardiogram at RAF Halton Hospital revealed the heart murmur that was the corollary of his rheumatic fever at Uppingham. It was a shattering blow that would leave its subconscious mark on him for ever. 'That was all such a shame,' commented Donald's sister, Jean, 'because he loved the outdoor life. With that rheumatic fever he was flat on his back for weeks at Headley. That was pure neglect, letting him up too soon. He was in his prime then, about sixteen.' Campbell switched to a job installing special equipment at airfields, and later went to work for Briggs Motor Bodies in Dagenham, where Malcolm had connections. It was hardly fulfilling work.

Though they saw less of each other as Malcolm worked in London, the tensions in family life became too much for the highly strung Dorothy. She went into a nursing home after suffering a nervous breakdown and stomach problems. While she was convalescing by the coast, Jean decided to move out of Headley Grove to be with her. After twenty years, Malcolm and Dorothy's marriage was in trouble. Life at Headley Grove became intolerable, and by 1940 they had divorced. Later in the war they were reconciled when Jean, living full-time now with her mother in Chelsea, fell ill with the skin infection erysipelas. Malcolm insisted that they should both go down to Headley Grove, where he and Dorothy talked through their problems. Both agreed that there was little point in starting over, but the rapprochement gave them a measure of peace. They remained friends until the end, in many ways closer than they had been during their marriage.

Before then, several times Dorothy and Jean prepared to go back to London; more than once Malcolm begged Dorothy to stay. On one occasion he faced charges of laying dangerous traps on his property at Tilbury, which had been plagued by trespassers. One of his staff had forgotten to switch off the traps – shotguns with blank cartridges – and another employee lost a leg after accidentally triggering one. Campbell needed moral support. At other times he pleaded with Dorothy to accompany him on the rare occasions when he could be persuaded to go to the dentist or the doctor. He was also worried that she and Jean would be targets for bombing raids in London, and urged them to remain at Headley Grove. Whenever bombs fell anywhere near Headley Grove, he was secretly pleased because it afforded him the opportunity to use the air-raid shelters he had built long before hostilities became inevitable, when his frequent penmanship on the likelihood of conflict had earned him a reputation as a warmonger.

After the war, Campbell decided that Headley Grove was far too big for him and he moved to Little Gatton, near Reigate, a smaller property that stood in fourteen acres and had once been owned by the well-known novelist Sax Rohmer, creator of the character Dr Fu Manchu. Shortly after his return from duty in Ceylon, Campbell stunned his family by marrying for a third time. For Dorothy, it was as if he was simply relating news that he had bought a new car. His marriage to divorcee Betty Humphrey lasted little more than three months before she departed for France, and he stayed on at Little Gatton living the reclusive life to which he felt far better suited. They divorced in 1948.

Dorothy and Malcolm once again resumed their friendship when Betty disappeared from the scene, but Dorothy was becoming increasingly concerned with the deterioration in her former husband's eyesight. That did not stop him getting back on the record-breaking trail. He commissioned Vosper to convert Blue Bird K4 to accept one of the legacies of the war, a loaned de Havilland Goblin turbojet engine capable of producing 3,000lb of thrust. This was a major refit, since the boat now no longer needed a propeller, and the upper bodywork was dramatically reworked. Vosper also carried out numerous experiments in the Admiralty Experimental Works' water tank at Haslar in Hampshire with a Jetex rocket-propelled scale model. On its arrival in the Lake District, the fullsize boat was quickly nicknamed the Coniston Slipper because of its distinctive new twin-nostrilled appearance.

Malcolm Campbell was sixty-two years old when in the summer of 1947 he attempted his last speed record, and he entertained very high hopes for Blue Bird in its new guise. But this time the attempt was dogged by problems. With jet propulsion he was moving into completely uncharted territory. Nobody knew how a hydroplane would behave with pure thrust pushing it along instead of a conventional propeller, because Blue Bird was the first of its type. Early indications suggested that the answer was 'badly'. The boat had been built in 1939 for piston power, and eight years later it was being asked to do something for which it had not been designed. At speed, it showed an unpleasant tendency to porpoise, or flutter up and down violently, and to slew off course. This would have been unnerving for any pilot, but for a man in his early sixties who was also suffering from glaucoma – even if he was Malcolm Campbell – the whole thing was a nightmare. Typically, Campbell gave no indication of his problems outside his immediate circle, nor did he show the slightest sign of giving up.

He first ran on 12 and 13 June, the latter the seventeenth anniversary of Segrave's death. After that, K4 was taken back to Vosper to have a central fin added to enhance directional stability, and Campbell briefly tried the boat on Poole Harbour before preparing to test it again at Coniston on Sunday, 1 July. Jean Wales went with her father on this last attempt, and remembers how trying K4's behaviour was.

For the first time in his waterborne career, Campbell now had to wait for the weather gods to smile. He ran briefly on the Tuesday, when directional stability seemed better, but then mist and rain moved in the following day. He still insisted on having a run, but it only proved that while Blue Bird now ran in a straight line, it still porpoised violently. Campbell also went perilously close to a support boat and the rocky shoreline at one stage. Peter Du Cane was summoned back specially from an overseas trip, made a run, and confirmed Campbell's findings. On another occasion when Leo Villa had trouble getting Campbell up one morning, he told him that Du Cane was ready and waiting to drive Blue Bird, which got Campbell out of bed at record speed.

It was the last hurrah. Blue Bird would be returned to Vosper for further modifications. According to Du Cane, the problem lay in the relative angles of the forward and aft planing shoes, but before work could begin on that de Havilland took its engine back.

Campbell had more pressing problems, of a personal nature. Within weeks of the Coniston débâcle his glaucoma became so bad that he finally needed medical help. He was also suffering from high blood pressure. 'Poor Dad was struck down,' Jean recalled.

I think his glaucoma came about through not wearing goggles, not looking after his eyes properly in the earlier days. He had too much fluid, and he had this operation where they bored holes to drain it. I remember going into his room afterwards and watching him night and morning. He had this liquid to massage into his eyes to keep these holes open so the fluid could disperse. I remember going up on the train to London to see him at one of the big hospitals, and him lying there with the eyes bandaged up. Eventually he could see all right, and then in September 1948 I went with him to this big Park Lane dinner for Riley Cars. He wouldn't let me drive him. Oh no. We got up there and were having drinks in the cocktail bar. I was standing very close to him. And I suddenly saw it happen. He just went whoomph! Blacked out. I just stood there, mesmerized. That was the first stroke.

Racing driver Goldie Gardner retrieved Campbell's car from Duke Street and put him into it, and Jean rushed him back to Little Gatton. It was the first time she had ever driven her father. Campbell refused to let her call a doctor.

Donald was abroad when his father fell ill. A couple of years earlier he had used a £1,200 (£30,950 at today's values) legacy from his grandfather to buy a half share as a director and partner in Kine (pronounced Kinney) Engineering in Horley, a company that among other things made wood-working machine tools. It would do very well in the immediate post-war years, and in the summer of 1948 he and his wife Daphne, whom he'd married just after the war, went on a trip to Portugal in a converted motor torpedo boat, the Leonus, intent on selling Kine Engineering goods abroad. They sailed with the DuCann brothers, Edward and Dick, and all of them endured a gruelling outward journey in heavy seas that took three weeks. Business was brisk, though the trip ended in disaster when an explosion, thought to be caused by a faulty gas cooker, destroyed the boat in Lisbon's port.

On his return, Campbell was shocked to see how his father had deteriorated, though he recovered for a while in the autumn and winter of 1948 and was content just to potter. Blue Bird and all its problems were forgotten. On Christmas Eve he insisted on making his usual trip to hand out Christmas boxes to the staff. He was at the property at Tilbury with Villa when he suffered another stroke, this one massive. Somehow, Villa managed to get him back to Little Gatton. Jean recalled her father's last days:

We knew he'd had that one stroke, but it didn't seem to affect him. But the one he had with Leo . . . I don't know how poor Leo got him back because the lakeside at Tilgate was out in the wilderness. Donald called me and said, 'For God's sake, come round quickly, Dad's had a monumental stroke.' And there he was, poor darling. He didn't know what day it was. He tried to tell us things, and sometimes you could vaguely work out what he was trying to say, but he got frustrated because he couldn't get it out. It was terrible to see somebody like that. He always wanted to go at the wheel of something, not to have a death like that. Dad was paralysed down one side. I prayed for him to go. I knew there was no hope. There was nothing worse than seeing that man like that. He would have shot himself. He wouldn't have lived in a wheelchair, paralysed and not able to speak. He was a cabbage. Absolutely poleaxed.

Doctor Benjafield told us that Dad *had* been to see him and that he had diagnosed his blood pressure trouble, but Dad had just said, 'Oh, he doesn't know what he's talking about. I'm not interested in what they say, these doctors.' We rang Benjy up, and he said, 'If I can do anything I will come down. But all you can hope is that he will go through the night.' We just prayed when Benjy said this for him to go as soon as possible. Poor man. And he went peacefully, thank God. But, nevertheless, it was such a shock.

It was a traumatic experience for both of Malcolm Campbell's children, seeing a man they thought immortal suffering such debilitating ill health. In his delirium and distress, Campbell even struck out at his daughter, though the feeble blow did not connect. 'He didn't know what he was doing,' Jean said, 'but it was terrible.' After he had driven hot-foot from Reigate upon receiving the initial news, Donald remembered how haggard his father looked. 'I kneeled at his bedside and broke down. Father, with an effort, pulled out the handkerchief from my jacket pocket. He dried my eyes. "It's all right, old chap," he said. "I'm quite finished."'[6]

On Christmas Day, Jean and Donald decided not to tell their father what day it was, but he found out from his nurse. With a flash of his old character he demanded to know why he had not been told. 'I do hate being taken for a bloody fool,' Donald recalled him saying. 'Why didn't you tell me? Go and get a bottle of champagne, boy.'[7]

Malcolm Campbell rallied enough to ask his family to drink to his health in the upstairs bedroom that overlooked his beloved garden. He seemed a little better as he summoned them to gather round as he lay there, strapped down for his own safety. A table had been set, with festive decorations and crackers. Despite his failing strength and paralysis, Campbell insisted on being lifted into a sitting position and he raised a glass of champagne to wish his children Merry Christmas. Jean and Donald took it in turns to be with him through the night. Not long after that final, courageous effort, he began to lapse in and out of unconsciousness.

On New Year's Eve, 1948, we both went in and he was gesturing to us, beckoning. It was quite eerie. He pulled us right down to his face as if he was blessing us. He did this to me, and then he got Donald and did the same. And there's no two ways about what happened as he did this. He saw something. I could understand more or less what he was trying to say, and he was looking all around him. He had a light on in his room at night, a dim light, and the whole thing was really weird. He was looking from corner to corner, and he said something about how he'd just seen Segrave.

He'd seen somebody he knew from the racing world who had passed on, no two ways about it. It was the way he was looking, staring at these corners as if he'd seen something or someone.

Some years after de Hane Segrave's death on Windermere in 1930, Doris Segrave claimed that her late husband had visited her during a séance she had reluctantly and sceptically attended. At another, a single red rose had dropped onto the table. She later discovered that it had come from a bunch of twelve in a vase in the room above the séance. Jean Wales didn't pretend to understand such matters, but added, 'It wouldn't surprise me if Dad had seen Segrave that night, given Doris's experiences.

'I don't know how much Dad suffered. You don't know how much of the brain is working. I mean, he knew us, but he couldn't talk to us. It was such an unfortunate time. And now, I don't know what comes over me at Christmas time, I cannot describe it, but I get the most odd feeling at the beginning of December until January is over. Something comes over me as if I have been taken over. It's horrible.'

After a while that night, Jean and Donald returned to their bedrooms. Before New Year, a nurse awoke them with the news that their father had passed away.

Sir Malcolm Campbell was buried in Chislehurst, in the same grave as his mother and father. On 17 January 1949 a memorial service was held at St Margaret's, Westminster. Hundreds attended, including many of the celebrities who had counted him as a friend.

Over in America, the famous Canadian band leader Guy Lombardo had already been casting covetous eyes at Campbell's water speed record, now nearly ten years old. The previous year he had begun working closer to Gar Wood's 124.915mph mark which, though beaten by Campbell back in 1937, was still an American record. Now Lombardo was working with automotive industrialist Henry Kaiser, who was investing $60,000 ($445,920/£279,000) to create a dramatic new challenger. The Ventnor Boat Corporation, which had developed the three-point suspension principle Campbell had so quickly embraced for Blue Bird K4, was building a 32ft-long, 8,500lb monster that would be powered by a 3,000hp Allison aero-engine. It was the design work of Arno Apel himself, the man who had refused to build Malcolm Campbell's new boat in 1939, and chief engineer Norm Lauterbach. It would be called Aluminum First.

While Malcolm Campbell was alive there was only ever room for one record breaker in the family, but one day in February 1949, while Donald Campbell was keeping out of a bitterly cold wind by pottering around his father's old workshop at Little Gatton, Malcolm's old friend Goldie Gardner came visiting. Selling the house and its contents, Donald admitted, was one of the hardest things he'd ever had to do. Under the terms of the will everything had to be sold at auction, which was to be held the following day. He was feeling melancholy when Gardner arrived, and in his father's study they shared the last bottle of whisky from the sideboard. They reminisced about his father's many achievements, then Gardner broke the news of Lombardo's imminent record attempt.

Campbell sat smoking in his father's favourite chair for some time after Gardner had left. First he imagined how his father would have reacted, how his nose would have twitched at the challenge. And then he found himself gripped by a deep anger. Everything his father had stood for was up for grabs, and now Lombardo wanted his record. He himself had never driven a speedboat before, nor any kind of racing car. His experiences on motorcycles had twice left him injured. His father had actually once said, 'I am lucky in that I was born with very fast reactions. But I hope to God that Donald never goes in for this business. He is accident prone, and if he does he will kill himself.' But there and then he made his decision: he would carry on his father's work. He and Leo Villa would get Blue Bird K4 going again. 'I'll have a crack at improving the record myself,' Donald announced. 'To hell with Kaiser. We'll give him a run for his money.'[8]

Was Donald Campbell merely stung to uphold family honour, or was the American challenge the catalyst he needed subconsciously, something that finally gave him the spur to achieve something his late father might really have been proud of? 'Dad never wanted Donald to do it, but then I don't think any father would,' Jean Wales confirmed. 'I never heard Dad say, "You're not going to do it," because kids will do it the more anyway, won't they? But it was too good an opportunity for Donald when Dad died. Blue Bird was in the garage, and there was Leo, who said he'd join forces with him. But I never really thought the whole thing would happen.'

Was there another reason? *Daily Express* journalist Geoffrey Mather, who would be there at Coniston all those years later, postulated two interesting questions. First, would Campbell have felt the need to emulate his father to the extent that he did had he been able to fly fighter planes in the war? Second, would the acquisition of a medal or two have preserved him from 'improvident' peacetime acts? 'As it was,' Mather wrote, 'he desperately needed an enemy, and if the enemy was a stretch of water, so be it. He could fight the water for England.'

Whatever the reason or reasons, it was a remarkable decision Campbell took that day. He had never raced a car or a boat himself, yet was prepared to step into a 2,350bhp monster to take on the world. Certainly there was no lack of courage in the family genes.

Villa, naturally, was the first person Campbell apprised of his intention, seeking him out in the workshop moments after he had made it. He almost casually mentioned to the older man the plans of Kaiser and Lombardo, and then stood back to watch the sparkle come back into his lifelong friend's eyes. Villa was approaching fifty, and post-war Britain was a hard place for a man that age to find alternative employment to the life he had known for so long.

Secretly he was excited, but his first thought was for Campbell's safety. But Campbell talked him round, and Villa pledged that he would work with him, 'to the bitter end'.

It was a promise that he would keep, literally.

5

'THIS JOB'S BLOODY DANGEROUS!'

1949 to 1950

*'I'm terribly sorry, Donald. There's been a mistake. We've checked up
. . . a simple error . . . quite an easy thing to happen . . . you were
about two miles an hour under the record.'*

TIMEKEEPER PHILIP MAYNE TO DONALD CAMPBELL, CONISTON WATER,

23 AUGUST 1949

Donald Campbell's plan to take over his father's mantle was
nowhere near as straightforward as it seemed on paper.
Malcolm Campbell had made his wishes pretty clear that his
son should live a quieter life than his own with his decision
not to leave him either the Blue Bird car or either of the
hydroplanes. His will left Dorothy a £500 payment and a
£400 annuity (£9,700 and £7,750 respectively at today's
values), and £1,000 (£19,400) to Leo Villa together with the
house known as Melbourne, in Josephine Avenue, Lower
Kingswood, near Reigate. There were other cash disburse-
ments to old faithfuls such as chauffeur Reg Whiteman, and
all his silver cups and trophies were to be shared equally
between Dorothy, his two children and his sister, Winifred

Mather. All his other properties, including Little Gatton and Tilgate, and remaining personal possessions, including the car and boats, were to be sold and the proceeds put into two equal sums in trust for his son and daughter. He left his third wife Betty nothing, 'in view of the fact that she has adequate means of her own and for other reasons which are referred to in a Memorandum signed by me'.

If Donald Campbell wanted to keep the Blue Birds, he had to buy them from the trustees of his father's will. Under its terms, he and Jean had no right to the possessions they had taken for granted during their childhood years, though there was a clause that enabled them to buy anything of sentimental value prior to the public auction. Campbell immediately bought the Blue Bird car, now long past its active years and of little value. He also bought Blue Bird K4.

Malcolm Campbell's legacy to his only son included more esoteric things than hard cash and possessions, however. Some of it would be of immediate short-term use, such as empirical data on the limitations of the piston-powered unlimited speedboat. Some, such as the only knowledge in the world on the subject of jet-propelled craft, would not be useful for many years. But perhaps the greatest gift was his towering example of steely courage and determination. As he took up his father's work, Donald Campbell would prove without question that such attributes had been passed down through the genes.

K4 lay in storage in Porchester, not far from Portsmouth. Campbell and Villa went down to Vosper to see Peter Du Cane, and discussed the route they should take. The obvious option was to continue with jet power and tame the wayward hull with the modifications that would have been made had Malcolm Campbell lived. De Havilland had taken back its engine and said it was too busy to spare the time for the project. Almost certainly the company had reservations about a rookie pilot. They fell back on the three Rolls-Royce piston engines: R19, which had set the current water record back in 1939; R37, which had set the land record at Bonneville and could be squeezed to produce another 200bhp, or 350bhp with different fuel; and R39 as the spare. Vosper agreed to refit the Blue Bird to accept the R-type engine, and Campbell signed away another chunk of his inheritance. Naturally, he intended to retain his father's name for the famous old craft, but where it had always been Blue Bird, it now evolved into Bluebird. He was buoyed by the fact that when his father had set the record, he had barely scratched the surface of K4's potential.

Then an unforeseen problem threatened to stop the project in its tracks. They planned to overhaul the engines and gearbox, and drove to the premises of Thompson and Taylor, a well-known motor racing engineering firm in Cobham, to inspect them, but Ken Taylor told them that Malcolm Campbell had already sold all the equipment as part of the sale of Blue Bird K3 in 1947 to a car dealer named John Simpson. It was a crushing blow. Campbell tracked Simpson down but was in the weaker position, and finally had to buy back Blue Bird K3 and its precious equipment in exchange for the 1935 Blue Bird car and a further £750 (£14,500). But it was the only way to secure the equipment that would make him a record challenger in his own right.

Kine Engineering was still very busy, so Campbell was able to spare only limited time as Villa completed Bluebird's refurbishment, but as England basked in a glorious summer it was finally ready for its journey north on 22 July 1949, and arrived two days later. A week after that, Campbell prepared for his first moment of truth. But almost as if the gods felt the young pretender needed a warning of what he had so blithely undertaken, the weather turned sour and Coniston was drenched by heavy rain. Every day he would rise at four, only to go back to bed again, disappointed. It was not until 10 August that conditions were good enough for him to make his long-awaited debut.

By first light the little team was gathered on the water. Campbell was the new boy, Villa had seen it all before. He counselled caution. Malcolm Campbell had been his employer, but his relationship with Donald Campbell was a friendship. He had known Malcolm's son for all but the first year of his life, and on many occasions had lied to the Old Man to protect him. The fact that the younger Campbell would affectionately call him Unc, a name bestowed upon him by Gina Campbell in 1956, said it all. Then there was Harry Leech, a veteran of Malcolm's previous attempts and one of only six who had survived the tragedy of the R101 airship by punching his way out of the burning craft when it crashed at Beauvais in October 1930. Mechanic Sid Randall also knew the score. Campbell felt an inner compulsion to perform quickly in order to win the respect of such men, and was more than a little nervous.

Bluebird's starting procedure was complex. The Rolls-Royce R engine would be fired first on 'soft' spark plugs and with a dog-clutch engaged so that the boat did not move. Then it would be switched off, and restarted with the dog-clutch out on 'hard' plugs better suited to high-speed running. With the dog-clutch out, Bluebird had direct drive and would begin to move forward the moment the engine fired, since it was now connected directly to the propeller shaft. On this occasion intermediate heat range plugs were used since Campbell would not need full power on his first run. In the cockpit he went over his procedure again and again in his head. He was ready for the challenge. With the intermediate plugs installed, Bluebird was towed out onto the lake. After months of preparation and planning, Campbell's moment had finally come.

With almost 2,400hp, Bluebird was not an easy craft to handle. Too much initial throttle would cause the stern to dip violently and the bows to rise alarmingly as if it was trying to go over backwards, until the boat gained forward speed and climbed onto its planing points. Even then, too much throttle would cause it to slide violently, like a car being driven fast on ice, and an indelicate touch could induce the engine's massive torque to try to rotate the craft around its own propeller. The moment Bluebird's bows dropped down after the initial acceleration, it shot down Coniston like an arrow from a powerful bow. Campbell found himself intoxicated with the sensation of speed, the slap of the water as it pounded the hull, and the bellow of the engine. 'I was exhilarated,' he wrote. 'The steady roar of the engine behind me was not too loud but rather comforting, the lake slipped by, and out of the corners of my eyes I could see the green-wooded shores gliding by. I had to learn to sense their distance, for, at high speed, they could be reached in three or four seconds if Bluebird began to slide about.'[9]

First, he passed the marker that signalled the start of the measured mile, a great triangle with a canvas top lovingly made for the occasion by Villa's wife, Joan. Then the black and white marker at the halfway point. Finally, the red marker that signalled the end of the mile. He had completed his first run, without mishap. And he had noticed that a water pressure gauge wasn't registering the expected figure. He was pleased that he had attention to spare to note such things. He would describe the run back as 'one of the biggest thrills of my life'. After pitching around at 70 to 75mph, Bluebird became a lady again as it picked up speed.

Villa greeted him as the launch drew alongside ready to tow him back to shore. 'Just like the Old Man,' he said, beaming. 'A chip off the old block.'

They were just the words Campbell had hoped to hear. He laughed boyishly, in relief and exhilaration, and replied, 'It's a piece of cake, Leo. What the hell are you worrying about?'

As they turned in for bed, Campbell said something that chilled Villa. 'Right,' he declared, 'tomorrow I'll give her the works.'

The older man knew everything there was to know about record breaking. He had watched Malcolm Campbell in victory and defeat, and men such as the American genius Frank Lockhart, killed when his Stutz Black Hawk streamliner crashed at over 200mph on Daytona Beach. He knew that impatience had lain at the root of Lockhart's demise, and that he had had a mountain of experience behind him that included victory on his first attempt at the Indianapolis 500. Donald Campbell might be keen, and he might be his father's progeny, but he was nowhere near as competent at this stage as Lockhart had been. Villa's face darkened.

'Now look, Don, take it easy, boy. Everything went all right today, but let's give her a little more time to settle down. You've still got a bit to learn, you know.'

But Campbell was worried about the threat of Lombardo and Aluminum First, and he was feeling cocky after his first run had gone so well. 'To hell with it, Leo,' he said. 'It's a piece of cake. We'll put in the hot plugs and see what she'll do.'

Villa thumped the table angrily. 'Don't be a bloody fool,' he snapped. 'Have another go on soft plugs.'

Campbell also banged the table. 'Let's get on with the job. Time's going by, we've been up here long enough. Put in the hot plugs.'

'Now listen. Take my advice and do as I tell you.'

'No. You do as I tell you.'

Such exchanges were rare between the two men, given the depth of their mutual affection. They turned in, Campbell with Villa's parting shot ringing in his ears: 'All right. You'll learn. It's on your own head . . .'

Campbell ran with the hot plugs the next day, and scared himself silly. At only 90mph he accelerated too hard and suddenly Bluebird snaked violently as the torque reaction forced the port sponson to dip. Feeling frightened and contrite, he continued the run after straightening out and pushed on to 120mph. But the lesson was not over yet. Just as he was regaining his confidence he spotted a water-logged fence post a hundred yards ahead. Again Bluebird snaked violently as he steered round it.

Back on shore, he felt less cocky. Villa caught his eye, and Campbell grinned at him. 'Leo! This job's bloody dangerous!' They laughed, and the small storm was over. But the team never let him forget that remark. 'Leo,' Campbell wrote, 'never even whispered "I told you so".'[10]

The following day, Campbell took Bluebird out again, now more circumspect and aware of the things he needed to avoid doing. At 120mph he pushed the throttle all the way down and was surprised as Bluebird's engine note deepened and she accelerated closer to the speed of his father's record. 'I kept my right foot hard down and the lake became a different place. No longer were the water and the buoys and the lakeside slipping by; now everything seemed to be rush-ing towards me. The horizon was no longer flat, but curved. I felt that Bluebird was tearing straight towards a gigantic waterfall, and in a moment would go slap over the edge. The air-speed indicator showed 135, the boat was running dead straight. I kept the pressure on my foot. Now the speed mounted – 140, 145 – and I thought, "That's good enough. You're over the top of the Old Man's speed. Ease her." [11]

That night they developed cine film of the run and watched it on the bedroom wall, the needle on the air-speed indicator running well over the current record speed. They were elated, and immediately settled on 19 August for a crack at the record. It would be ten years to the day since Campbell had christened Bluebird K4 at Coniston.

If Donald Campbell had known then what a Chrysler dealer called Stanley St Clair Sayres was doing in Seattle, his elation would have been tempered. Aluminum First had proved a complete flop during unhappy runs on the Potomac River, but Sayres had a new boat that had been designed by Ted Jones, who would become the father of unlimited hydroplane design as a result, and built at Anchor Jensen's boatworks in the Pacific NorthWest. Sayres called it Slo-mo-shun IV, but there was nothing tardy about it beyond the deliberately ironic name. First time out, Jones discovered that his new boat would accelerate from 160mph to 190mph faster than he could think. Sayres was planning to race for the Harmsworth Trophy and the Gold Cup, the Indianapolis 500 of unlimited boat racing, but the primary aim was always to break Malcolm Campbell's speed record.

Saturday the 19th dawned with high wind and rough water, and the shoreline of Coniston was a riot of colour as hundreds of spectators turned out. Hopes were to be frustrated. The weather kept Bluebird in her rudimentary boathouse through Sunday as well. Campbell was disappointed, but his innate good humour demanded that those around should be cheered up, and at late notice he threw a fancy dress party at the Bull Hotel.

Bluebird didn't take to the water again until Wednesday the 23rd. Initially the eerie calm out on the lake heightened

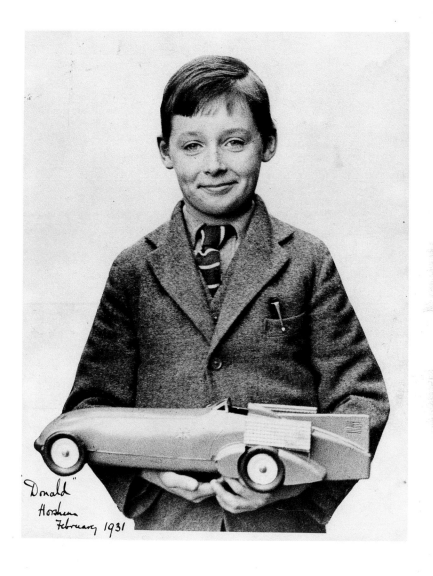

Donald "
Horsham
February 1931

At the age of ten, clutching a model of his father's 1928 Bluebird,
Donald Campbell's cheeky expression is hardly that of an abused child.

Photographs are from the David Tremayne Archive unless otherwise stated.

Left: A happy domestic scene at Headley Grove, with parents Malcolm and Dorothy, captures the idyllic childhood that Donald Campbell enjoyed.

Below: By the age of ten Donald already worshipped his father. What small boy would not have been held in thrall by a father whose monster aero-engined cars had made him the fastest man on earth?

Right: Animal lovers both, Donald and Malcolm could not resist taking in this scruffy little stray when the elder Campbell (looking less sartorially elegant than normal) aimed for 300 mph at Bonneville in 1935.

As Donald approached his seventeenth birthday and manhood, he continued to ape his illustrious father's mannerisms, even down to affecting a pipe.

Above: Donald loved motorbikes, but he had more than one accident on them. Aged seventeen, he poses outside Headley Grove. GINA CAMPBELL

Below: In August 1939 at Coniston Water in the Lake District, seventeen-year-old Donald christened his father's dramatic new Bluebird K4 hydroplane, before playing a pukka role in the record attempt itself.

Left: Young love 1: Donald and Daphne. GINA CAMPBELL

Below: Young love 2: Donald and Dottie outside Little Abbotts, *c.* 1953.

KEYSTONE PRESS AGENCY

Above: Bluebird K4 was not an easy boat to handle and habitually adopted this unusual pose until the transom came up and the boat began planing. Donald Campbell and Leo Villa make waves on Coniston in 1950. PRESS ASSOCIATION

Opposite page, top: Modified with two sleeker cockpits for 1951, Bluebird K4 won the Oltranza Cup but was disembowelled by gearbox failure when finally running at record speed on Coniston in 1951. PRESS ASSOCIATION

Opposite page, bottom: At great personal cost Campbell finally got his own hydroplane, the turbojet-powered Bluebird K7, running on Ullswater in February 1955, but only after temporary modifications helped it to plane.

Left: Campbell had plenty of emotional support at Ullswater. Here he walks off the jetty with sister Jean, mother Dolly and wife Dottie. SANDERSON & DIXON

Below: Campbell's activities always attracted huge crowds in the Lake District. As usual, here at Ullswater in July 1955, his back gave him trouble, but the lake yielded his first record at 202.32 mph. LAT

Campbell's tension, leaving him more alone in the cockpit than he had ever felt in his life. The feeling would become familiar over the years, but would never leave him altogether. Action suppressed the butterflies, and this time he exceeded 150mph as he sped down the lake on the first of his mandatory two runs. But just before he cleared the measured mile, a plume of white smoke preceded scalding oil squirting onto the vestigial windscreen, then his goggles and face. His reaction was momentarily to lift his foot quickly from the throttle, and once again Bluebird became an animal as he fought for control. Despite his inexperience he did the right things, correcting the slide by reopening the throttle and steering into the skid. He reached the end of the course shaken but intact. Once again he took Bluebird through the measured mile, but this time it slid and bucked as he hit his own wake from the previous run, wasting time he didn't have. He accelerated again, but the boat lacked a sharp edge. At the end of the run he was amused to discover that when he deliberately drove close to a launch full of photographers, one had jumped overboard in panic.

Campbell tried to convince himself that he had done enough to squeak past his father's 141.74mph record, but he was sceptical as the timekeepers, Frank Lydall, Philip Mayne and Les Lumby, made their deliberations. When they approached, their faces were wreathed in smiles. He had succeeded. Word spread quickly, and soon the spectators around the lake were celebrating too. The BBC broadcast the news on its eight o'clock bulletin. Campbell and Villa experienced the wonder of the moment, one for the first time, the other for the fourteenth. Campbell admitted later that his emotions embraced pride, relief from the fear and tension, and gladness that it was all over.

But it wasn't. The timekeepers had made a mistake. He

had seen it before, at Bonneville in 1935 when his father exceeded 300mph. He was walking towards Mayne when the latter, tears in his eyes, started heading his way. As they met, Campbell already knew what the other man was going to say.

'I'm terribly sorry, Donald. There's been a mistake. We've checked up ... a simple error ... quite an easy thing to happen ... you were about two miles an hour under the record.'

He accepted the news with good grace, for he was never a man to rail against misfortune, in public or in private. It did not surprise him that his average speed was only 135.34mph; he had gone down the lake at 138.46mph and come back at only 132.35mph. It was a bitter blow, but there was nothing to do but accept the hand Fate had dealt.

Deflated and dispirited, the little team set about examining Bluebird to find out why it had been sluggish on that second run. They found more bad news. The oil mist had been caused by bearing failure in the gearbox, and there was also serious damage to the propeller shaft bearings. Later they would discover water in the engine, too. The true import of these discoveries would not be understood for another year. As it was, they were through. Campbell had already spent far too much money and far too much time away from Kine Engineering. It was time to be thankful that Lombardo had not yet succeeded, to head back to Reigate, and to figure out why the propeller shaft bearings, hitherto bulletproof, were now running dry, as if they were clear of the water that normally cooled them.

When you leave Coniston, heading north on the road that leads to Tarn Hows, there is a spot where you can stop and look back and see the full length of Coniston Water in all its majesty. Donald Campbell stopped there the following evening on his way home. 'As I was on the point of turning to settle into my car again,' he wrote, 'the sun glittered on Coniston. It seemed almost as though the lake were alive, winking at me and mocking me for my failure. "You bitch," I thought. "But we'll be back."' [12]

An interlude of technological brainstorming followed. Campbell and his team could not understand the damage to Bluebird. They had talks with Professor R.W.L. Gawn, superintendent of the Admiralty Experimental Works at Haslar and an expert on propeller design who had overseen water-tank testing of Blue Bird K3 in 1937. He had designed a new propeller for K4 and conducted some tank tests up to 155mph. At the same time, a young engineer from Kine, Lew Norris, designed a new propeller shaft. In between work at Kine and work on Bluebird, Campbell embarked on a series of lectures and talks about the project, visiting clubs up and down the country.

The team was back at Coniston by the end of June 1950, but poor weather was not the only bad news to greet Campbell and his supporters. One day while they were there, the 27th, they learned that Stan Sayres and Ted Jones had the day before sped to a new mark of 160.323mph on Seattle's Lake Washington. The news was shattering, for tests had indicated that if it ever succeeded in reaching such a colossal speed – and that was doubtful – Bluebird's aerodynamics would turn it on its back. It was as if they had been beaten before they had really hit their stride. And had Campbell known that Slo-mo-shun IV had achieved its record while almost loafing along, he would have been even more depressed. Instead, he was sceptical initially, but soon there was no denying the achievement of a boat that would set American racing on its ear and determine unlimited hydroplane design for the next decade. Slo-mo-shun went on to win both the Gold Cup (becoming the first craft ever to win it at the first try) and the Harmsworth Trophy (becoming the first craft ever to win both big racing prizes in the same year). It would also become the first boat to win a full race at 100mph, and would repeat its Gold Cup wins in 1952 and 1953 (its sister, Slo-mo-shun V, won the races in 1951 and 1954). Not for nothing was this wonderful boat, which still makes exhibition runs today after a major rebuild by Seattle's Hydroplane and Raceboat Museum, known as the Grand Old Lady. The only consolation came later, when the Campbell team obtained a photograph which showed Slo-mo-shun to be similar in most respects to Bluebird, with three-point suspension and the engine placed ahead of the pilot. But what the photograph could not show was the revolution Sayres, Jones and Jensen had incorporated. It was only after a lot of painstaking, almost soul-destroying experimentation that the Campbell team discovered what the Americans already knew.

In the meantime, they could only carry on. They would stay at Coniston until Gawn's new propeller was ready, and learn what they could. When Villa decided that he wanted to travel with Campbell so that he could monitor the boat's behaviour, they spent time cutting out a rudimentary cockpit for him to the right of Campbell's.

Then an old face returned to help. Jack Hutchinson was a veteran of the famous Borwick's boatyard in Windermere. He had met, and disliked, Malcolm Campbell when Borwick's helped build a slipway for Blue Bird at Coniston in 1947. He had found the speedking not at all to his taste, and no comparison to Segrave, whom he had met as a young child during the racing knight's fateful attempt on the record at Windermere in June 1930. 'I met Malcolm as an adult, when I was working in the game, so to speak. He was a horrible man, though one must admire what he did with his racing. But it didn't matter who was there when he cussed, women or anybody. But Donald, now, he was a real gentleman – a showman. He liked the glory of it. And he rather exploited things to the full, which of course these chaps had to do.' Now, as Donald Campbell and Leo Villa worked away on the very same boat, Hutchinson came back into the family orbit once again.

They had some new bearings in the propshaft, and they were too tight. Arthur [Borwick] asked me to go over and help. They were simple Cutlass bearings, rubber-lined. And Donald and Leo had an ex-army three-tonner as their workshop. I went over there, and there was Leo in this truck. I was looking at this prop he was filing bits off. Now when we did that at Borwick's we'd scribe a line round it to give us something to work to, then we'd put it on a mandrill in the lathe and cut off what we wanted. Then we'd put it on two knife edges to balance it all up again. But here they were, with a record-breaking boat, and as far as I could tell they didn't have any of that stuff. Leo seemed to be doing it all by eye. That's not said to disparage anybody, it's just the way things looked to me.

Donald was a nice chap, but I felt to some extent that in many ways he was trying to live up to his father's good name. He felt a calling, that he had to do it. What kid wouldn't? There was always an element of risk with these things, of course. In most cases that seems to be the driving force. But Donald always seemed to me to want a mental picture of what might happen. He always wanted more instruments on the dashboard than were probably necessary or that he would have time to read at the speeds he was doing. It was as if he had to try to figure out every eventuality.

Early in July, Campbell and Villa were ready to run again, and Bluebird behaved perfectly at more than 130mph. By the beginning of August the new prop was ready, but again the weather intervened until the 17th, when once again Villa took over the role of riding mechanic that he had played with Giulio Foresti and Malcolm Campbell. Once again the engine note deepened as Bluebird exceeded 140mph. Both men watched for signs of the bows rising as the speed crept up, but then came the same sluggishness that had marred the last run in 1949. On the return run the same thing happened until they reached 145mph, when suddenly Bluebird accelerated alarmingly as the needle swept over 150 and closer to 160. Campbell just had time to feel elated before Villa thumped him in the ribs and pointed frantically to the water temperature gauge. The needle was off the clock.

Back on shore, they discovered that R37 was cooked. Bluebird had a scoop beneath the hull to pick up cooling water from the lake, but somehow it was no longer doing its job. And there was serious hull damage where the propshaft bearings had again overheated. The cine film footage revealed that the engine temperature had gone from 85°C to 110°C in three seconds. Even though Campbell had lifted off before he exited the measured mile, his average speed on that final disastrous run had been 142mph. He had equalled his father's record.

He and Villa were now convinced that, far from trying to rise at speeds approaching 160mph, Bluebird's bows were actually being pushed down as the stern persistently tried to climb out of the water. But that flew in the face of all perceived aerodynamic wisdom, and in some quarters they became a laughing stock. Others believed it was a moot point. Bluebird was past its shelf life, and they should quit before they hurt themselves. Such talk stung Campbell, who became more determined than ever to prove that he and Villa were right. But what was really happening to the boat?

Ted Jones could have told them. Together with a scientist called Dr Euan Corlett, it was Reid Railton, the man who had overseen some of the updates to Malcolm Campbell's Blue Bird cars and designed John Cobb's land speed record-holding Railton Special, who came to the rescue. Railton had spoken to people in America, had actually viewed Slo-mo-shun IV, and now understood what Jones knew. Railton went up to Coniston to watch Bluebird do a couple of runs once the damage had been patched up. Around 150mph the propeller of a big hydroplane ran immersed, but at higher speeds it tried to climb until its hub was on the surface. With the further decrease in hydrodynamic drag – as the propeller shafting was lifted clear of the water and only one of the propeller's blades remained immersed – the speed increased dramatically. Slo-mo-shun IV had been designed from the outset as a prop-rider, but Bluebird had not.

At Coniston, Campbell and Villa faced some harsh facts. In its current state, the old boat had nothing left to offer. Just to rub their noses in it, flash floods hit Coniston and nearly washed away much of their equipment. But they had the last laugh this time. After moving the water scoop, they worked Bluebird up to 150mph without further trouble, confirming the view that had been ridiculed. They went back again in October and coaxed Bluebird closer to 160mph despite more weather delays, but they just could not find those few extra miles an hour that would have taken them past Sayres' record.

That year's effort was not entirely without reward, however. Dorothy McKegg was a vivacious New Zealand girl living in Earls Court, on a scholarship to study at the Royal College of Music. 'I was twenty-one going on seventeen, very young and living on a government bursary of five pounds a week,' she recalled. She had arrived in England in 1949, and met Donald Campbell in that summer of 1950.

I'd been in the theatre all my life. I'd done every facet you could think of: backstage, sitting on the book; painting the sets; wardrobe; playing the leading role time and again; playing the walk-on part. Everything! Loved it to bits. But I could also sing. That's why I went to England. And the reason I went to Coniston is that in college one of the girls had a station wagon, so in the holidays we decided to do England and Ireland. There were five of us. We'd stop and ask a farmer if we could pop up our tent on their property. It was just after the war, and thanks to the behaviour of the New Zealand boys, our stock was pretty high.

When we got to the Lake District, we went to one little dairy in Coniston and said we were looking for somewhere to pitch up. They said that we had to go and see the Bluebird. We said, 'What's that?' 'Oh,' they said, 'Sir Malcolm Campbell's son!' And suddenly I remembered all those old cigarette cards. Well, Ava Wells was our leader. A great big Kiwi girl, lots of blonde hair which she used to wear in plaits. Scared of nothing. A real Amazon. 'Right,' she said, 'we're off to see Bluebird!'

We got to this field and there was a big notice on it: KEEP OUT. That didn't stop us. We were over the top. And then Leo Villa appeared. 'Excuse me! Excuse me, girls! This road's private . . .' 'Oh yes,' said Ava. 'We've come to see the man that matters. We've come thirteen thousand miles.' I can still hear her now. The man that matters! Well, Leo just turned round and yelled, 'Don, you're wanted!'

In later years, Don used to tell the story, how within ten minutes all these Kiwi girls were climbing all over his precious boat. And we were! Photographing each other, sitting in the cockpit. We took our shoes off, of course. He didn't mind at all. I think he was vastly amused by the whole thing. We were all pretty extrovert. And we were entranced. He and Leo were so nice. We pitched our tent not far away, and Don and Leo invited us all up to the Bull for dinner that night. Don showed us movies of his father. We stayed there several days, manned the support boats. We had a lovely time.

Campbell welcomed the distraction, little realizing the part Dorothy McKegg would come to play in his life.

When it became clear that he and Villa would have to go back to Reigate and regroup yet again, he was undeterred. They would carry out a fundamental redesign to enable K4 to run as a prop-rider, and they would be back. 'If I had succeeded then, I might have escaped,' he wrote in 1955. 'There was a good chance that by now I might have been firmly settled into the routine of a respectable, reasonably successful sort of business life. As far as I am concerned there is nothing challenging about success. If I had taken the record in 1949 I would probably have written the whole adventure off as a short, very agreeable episode in my life, and that would almost certainly have been that. But I failed. And failure has always been a very dangerous thing in my family.'[13]

Donald Campbell might not have broken anything yet but his precious equipment, but already he was evincing all the courage and resolve of his father.

6

TRIALS AND TRIBULATIONS

May to October 1951

'To hell with the laps, to hell with the Oltranza Cup, and to hell with you too!'

LEO VILLA TO DONALD CAMPBELL DURING THE OLTRANZA CUP ON
LAKE GARDA, JUNE 1951

The following year, 1951, was to be intensely frustrating for Donald Campbell. He was still living at the Reigate Hill Hotel and working for Kine Engineering, and redesign work on Bluebird K4 was not completed until the end of January. The engine and gearbox were moved six feet further forward, necessitating two new cockpits, one on either side. Both Campbell and Villa were convinced of the benefit of retaining the two-seat configuration. There was a new propeller and shaft, rudder and steering gear, and the angles of the forward planing points were altered. Campbell was hardly disadvantaged, but there was no question of Vosper doing the work. Instead, Villa toiled away in the hotel's old stable, Campbell helping him whenever work commitments permitted. Even with friends such as carpenter Len Coles,

Australian Doug Floyd and Leo's son Tim helping, the work still cost £1,000 (£16,675 at today's values).

Early in the year Campbell received an invitation from the Club Motonautico Gabriel d'Annunzio on Italy's Gardone Riviera to compete in the Oltranza Grand Prix meeting in May. D'Annunzio, one of Italy's foremost poets, had first presented the Oltranza Cup in 1931 as a memorial to Sir Henry Segrave. The implied compliment was the tonic Campbell and Villa needed. For Villa, with his fluent Italian, the trip recalled the old days at Maggiore and Lake Hallwil. But this trip to Garda would cost Campbell £2,000 (£33,350), and even with a massive effort the boat was only just ready in time.

Campbell and Villa were soon making test runs on the triangular five-mile course on Lake Garda, where Bluebird proved as adept at sliding round corners as it was in a straight line. Campbell could not resist the temptation to show one of his Italian competitors Bluebird's potential. He had never raced anything, and had only driven Bluebird on a handful of test runs, but Villa was pleased and impressed with the confidence with which the rookie 'Skipper' handled the big blue and silver craft. On one occasion Villa had to leap onto the deck to extinguish a brief engine fire, and he subsequently fell off when Campbell came into the pits a little too fast and had to manoeuvre in a hurry to keep Bluebird off the jetty wall. Still, the revised weight distribution made the boat unstable. It took giant corkscrew leaps across the water. Eventually it landed so hard that a blade on the 1939 record-setting propeller was bent completely back. 'It was incredible to realize that an impact with water could cause this,' Villa observed. The new propeller simply brought the period of instability lower down the speed range. Then the R19 engine was damaged.

Due to poor weather, the race was delayed a fortnight. It finally took place on 10 June. Campbell had settled on the finest-pitch propeller, which limited top speed to around 135mph but made the boat less of a handful. Two prizes were at stake: the Grand Prix, for the fastest overall time from the start, and the Oltranza Cup, for the two fastest consecutive laps. Among Campbell's rivals were Italian aces Mario Verga and Ezio Selva (both of whom would later entertain aspirations to water speed record challenges), as well as fellow Englishman Norman Buckley, a Manchester-based solicitor and close friend of Campbell's who was racing his Jaguar-powered Miss Windermere. Reid Railton was also there, spectating with John Cobb. The burly fur broker had already announced his intention of building a bespoke jetboat to challenge the water speed record. They were looking at the suitability of Italian lakes for their challenge.

Bluebird had been fitted with the R39 engine after the damage to R19, but as the five-minute gun sounded it failed to fire up and the boat lay stricken as rivals rallied for the flying start. Frantically, Campbell and Villa leapt from their cockpits and began changing the spark plugs before trying again. By the time the Rolls-Royce engine finally spluttered into life the race had begun and all chance of winning the Grand Prix itself was over. But they could still win the Oltranza Cup for the two fastest laps.

Villa would never forget that ride, for Donald Campbell handled Bluebird with a brilliance that easily achieved their revised goal. Far from being accident prone, as Malcolm Campbell had suggested, Campbell proved a quick and courageous pilot as the boat skipped down the straights and slithered through the corners. At one stage the fin under the right sponson was torn away; it whistled over their heads like a scythe. The race was over four laps, and it was Villa's job to punch out four scraps of paper to denote each lap covered. Campbell repeatedly yelled across at him, asking if they had covered the distance. Villa ignored him. 'I looked over to his cockpit,' Campbell wrote. 'He seemed pale and shaken. Suddenly I appreciated that our wild ride and Bluebird's antics at the turns must have been a considerable strain for him; he was just sitting there hanging on, wondering what might happen next, while I knew my purpose exactly.'[14] Eventually, once they had returned to the dock, Villa stirred.

I'm afraid I felt so disgusted that I let him ask the question several times before I replied: 'I don't know. I don't know anything. To hell with the laps, to hell with the Oltranza Cup, and to hell with you too!' To add to my discomfort I had worn no crash helmet or headgear, despite Donald's insistence that I should do so. After the race my forehead was one big sting owing to myriad small insects and flies that had collided with me during the race.

Later, thinking back over it, I suddenly realized what a splendid effort it had been. It was his first race, in a craft designed for straightforward record runs. My fears had been completely unfounded; the consistent lap times which Donald had recorded proved that he knew exactly what he was doing. It was far from being the neck-or-nothing gamble that it had seemed to me; he had driven the boat with cool and calculating skill and had beaten all existing records for the course by a very substantial margin. Donald hadn't got a record yet, but at least he had proved that he could drive the boat.[15]

All four of Campbell's laps were over 95mph, and he completed the 20-mile race in 12 minutes 18.25 seconds at an average speed of 96.94mph. Subsequently he received notification from Giuseppe Mayr, vice president of the Organizing Committee, and Nico Moederle, commissioner general, that the race had been declared void on a technicality, but he had proved his point, even if the Oltranza Cup did have to go back.

By September, Bluebird was back at Coniston, ready for another challenge to Slo-mo-shun's record, though before that Campbell had insisted that Villa take Joan back to Garda for a holiday. Campbell and Villa were accompanied by Lew Norris and Leo's son Tim. The primary aim was to work through Bluebird's period of instability and find the cause. Eventually they concluded that the problem lay in the angle of the front planing shoes. Sayres, over in Seattle, had access to top-level facilities, but they had to make do. They were on their own now, and in bitterly cold conditions they set about undoing the hundreds of screws in each shoe and making the necessary alterations. Their boathouse was open-sided, with just a rudimentary tarpaulin roof stretched over tubular steel poles. It offered no protection from Coniston's elements as autumn caught up with them. Connie Robinson – who ran the Black Bull Hotel, and later the Sun, and had known Malcolm Campbell in his days up at Coniston – brought them sandwiches and hot coffee laced with rum, and made them their evening meal whenever they could finally be persuaded to stop. It was the unseen side of record breaking, the grind behind the glamour.

At this time, the prolific Lakeland writer Harry Griffin of the *Lancashire Evening Post* became one of the few people apart from Villa to ride with Campbell.

It probably came about as a bit of a laugh, a joke. My great interest was rock-climbing and I was always trying to get Donald to come with me. I almost got him to go, but it never came off.

Leo and Donald were very anxious about the stability of the boat. Leo wanted to study what it looked like from the outside, so most likely Donald dared me to take over. I was shoved into the right-hand cockpit. The impression I got was of lying on the water, not sitting above it. It was fairly frightening. Donald fixed an aiming point at the southern end and was trying to keep the boat level. He had quite a job, because the surface of the water affected the boat quite considerably. There were two types of surface that day: there were the dark bits of water, and there were the bits where it was absolutely clear, like a mirror. When the boat was on dark water Donald was able to hold her perfectly, but as soon as he hit the completely calm water it felt exactly as if it was sliding on ice. That was frightening, and it was a relief when we got back onto the dark stuff.

We ran south, then came back. I asked him what speed we'd done and he said about 125mph. The record at that time was 160mph. He turned to me and said, 'You, Harry my boy, are now the eighth fastest man on water!' He'd just worked it out in his head, having included Leo in his calculations.

Nobody else saw the run. There were many times when I was the only press man up there, so I got to know Donald personally, all his problems.

The work on Bluebird was finally finished in time for a run on 24 October. It was a cold morning, but conditions were perfect. Running south, Campbell hit 150mph and at last Bluebird behaved perfectly. Suddenly the old vices were a thing of the past. They had turned a corner. At the end of the run, Campbell turned to Villa with a massive grin, determined to give Bluebird everything on the return. He was now completely familiar with the vagaries of the old boat, and confident that he could surpass Sayres' record. Villa felt that he was driving Bluebird at least as well as his father had, probably better since his mechanical sympathy was far superior. The boy was a chip off the old block all right, whatever the Old Man might have thought.

'We started the return run and were soon past the unstable period at 90mph,' Villa recalled. 'Rpm steady and speed increasing at an alarming rate. 160mph, and the rpm not yet on max. 3,200 rpm, really going now, 165 mph. Good old Skipper. 170.' They had been travelling at a speed well above the record, with complete stability. In their tight cockpits, they were elated. After all the months of struggle and heartache, they were finally on their way. This was what they had been living for. With a surge of adrenalin, Campbell had watched the air-speed needle flicker up to 170mph. At 140mph during previous runs Bluebird had been a bitch; now she was a lady. Suddenly, 170mph seemed easy. Campbell was learning what so many winners know: when everything finally runs right, success comes far more easily than you could possibly have believed when you were struggling to find your way.

But equally suddenly, success became a mirage out on the lake. Bluebird swept past the end of the measured mile on the last run it would ever make. Campbell felt a shudder run through it, likening it to a red-hot coal being dropped onto naked flesh. 'Then,' Villa remembered, 'the most almighty crash, and within split seconds Bluebird was bumping and sliding all over the place.' This was accompanied by a massive explosion so loud it was heard by workers in a slate quarry ten miles away. In Coniston, shopkeeper David Watt was later told that Campbell and Villa had been killed.

Something had gone terribly wrong. One moment they were travelling in excess of Sayres' record, the next, Bluebird was slewing to a halt in little more than fifty yards. Dumbfounded, Campbell and Villa looked at each other, their mouths open in sheer astonishment. Then, as they heard the unmistakable gurgle of water pouring into the hull, they began frantically to scramble out. On deck, the two men who had breathed so much of their own life into the boat threw off their lifejackets in dismay and lit cigarettes as they tried to figure out just how disaster had overtaken them in their moment of elation. As the launch approached, they yelled more urgently for a tow rope. Bluebird was filling up. 'My God, Donald,' Villa suddenly exclaimed, 'she's sinking!' They got close to the old boat-house that Malcolm Campbell had used back in 1947, but before they reached shore Bluebird slipped gracefully beneath the surface to rest on a bank. Campbell and Villa were left scrabbling in Coniston's icy waters. 'I stared down at Bluebird,' Campbell wrote. 'Under the clear, slightly greeny water of the lake, she lay on a shallow bank, her nose tilted slightly towards the surface, her bright sapphire dulled. She looked very lonely and deserted and, somehow, rather tired.'[16]

As he looked at his old friend, Campbell realized with a mixture of pain and guilt that Villa had aged. He was in his fifty-second year, well past the age when normal men climb aboard 170mph speedboats, let alone survive terrifying accidents. He placed a hand on the older man's shoulder and together they looked down at the craft which had carried their hopes. For long moments, neither could say a word.

The following day, they dragged the wreckage ashore, and

the extent of the damage became apparent. Bluebird had been disembowelled. There was nothing more to do but remove the engine and other mechanical equipment, patch the boat up enough to float it back to the boathouse, and then ship everything back to Reigate. The dream was over. Campbell wrote that they winced as they broke up all that beautiful machinery. Repairs were out of the question. The damage was heavy, and despite Bluebird's fabulous spurt at 170mph her chances of beating Slo-mo-shun IV by any significant margin were now slim. Campbell asked his old friend Bill Coley, of Coley Metals, to store it. It would lie for many years in a yard in Hounslow, forgotten and unloved, until it was eventually dragged out. 'We set fire to it,' Coley admitted. 'I don't remember just when, but I know it was there for a long time and it was rotting away. It was in an awful state; we couldn't do anything with it. I told Donald that, eventually, we had to get it out. So we had a ceremonial burn of it.'

It was an inglorious end for one of the most important boats in British marine history. But what had caused its accident? In his book *Into the Water Barrier*, Campbell wrote that he believed they had hit a submerged railway sleeper. He described it as a thousand to one chance. Villa agreed: 'There was no doubt that we had struck something hefty, possibly a submerged rail sleeper.' But many years later, in a television interview, Campbell was asked to describe his sensations of fear and alluded to the effort with Bluebird K4. 'That was just as darn difficult,' he told Border Television's John Pett. 'We had our worries and troubles. I got frightened over that one as I've never been before in my life – and never want to be again for that matter – when that gearbox cracked up at 150mph. And 150mph in that boat, you believe me, was really quite an experience, because you were sitting out in an open cockpit, you had this huge engine behind the back of your head, exhausting away, making the air feel like it was going to vibrate to the point where the earth was going to split asunder, and then this gearbox went.'[17] 'The sleeper was what we said at the time . . .' Lew Norris confided many years later, but the more likely reason is that the gearbox mountings failed, though Ken Reaks of Smiths Instruments believed that a blade had come off the propeller and gone through the bottom of the hull.

It was the end of the line for Bluebird K4 and for the aspirations of her intrepid pilot and engineer. They were out of the record-breaking business. Since 1912 there had been a Campbell and a Bluebird, but now it seemed the dynasty had come to an end. John Cobb was now well advanced with his plans to build his revolutionary jet-powered Crusader, which had the potential to obliterate all previous speed marks. Campbell's only hope had been to set a record before Crusader ran, and now there was no chance of that.

It was typical that, despite his desperate disappointment, Donald Campbell took consolation from the fact that another Briton was going to challenge the Americans for the record. As he was forced to take a bow and leave the world stage, with no likelihood of ever stepping onto it again, he genuinely wished Cobb success.

7

THE CALL OF THE SIREN

1952 to November 1954

'I panicked then. I phoned Leo and said, "Look, what have I done? I've encouraged the birth of this monster!"'
BILL COLEY TO LEO VILLA, SUMMER 1952

Donald Campbell was not easy to live with when he was forced to return to civilian life. It was a wretched feeling knowing that Fate had written him out of the speed game. Reid Railton took to dropping in to keep him up to date with John Cobb's Crusader. Campbell was genuinely interested, but it must have taxed his sense of fairness not to have felt pangs at someone else's progress when his own attempt had come so close only to fail.

While Cobb moved steadily ahead in this strange race, Campbell no longer had any reason to rent the old stable at the Reigate Hill Hotel. In giving it up and disposing of the equipment, he knew he really was letting go. Bill Coley took the wrecked Bluebird into storage, and Campbell let her precious Rolls-Royce engines go for their scrap value. As a final recognition of his circumstances, he went back to full-time work at Kine Engineering. Typically, he found a job there for Villa, as chief inspector.

There were some happier changes in his personal life that year. In its early months his divorce from Daphne Harvey was made final, and he was free to marry Dorothy McKegg. Not too long after she had met Campbell at Coniston in the summer of 1950, Dorothy had stayed with Harry Leech and his wife in Southampton. 'She'd said, "Don't you dare come back after you've been to Ireland without coming to see us,"' Dottie recalled. 'And, funnily enough, Donald was down there staying with them while he was visiting the Admiralty. He took us out in Lyreen, his yacht. We had such a hoot.' Dottie suddenly realized how attracted she was to the dashing young adventurer. 'He might not have been anyone's oil painting, but, my God, he had charisma! And he was enormous fun.' Campbell began to call her in London and invited her down to Little Abbotts Cottage (or Abbotts, as Donald always referred to it) near Dorking in Surrey, the house he had bought in the autumn of 1950, where she met Jean Wales. 'She was my best friend. Do I remember those days! Jean and I in our tight little trews!' Before long, Dottie quit college and went to live with Campbell. It was an avant-garde thing to do in those strait-laced times. 'I was swept off my girlish feet,' she said. 'The greenest virgin you've ever seen. It was full voltage. Nobody could stand a chance with Don once all that was connected. When anyone mentions charisma to me, I know exactly what they mean. It goes with naturalness, fun, and then whoosh!, that sort of instant connection that some people have!' They were married at Kensington Register Office on 19 March 1952.

In the race for the water speed record, there was another twist of the knife on 7 July. In Seattle, Stan Sayres upped his own mark to 178.497mph on Lake Washington. Since its first record, Slo-mo-shun IV had continued to stun on-lookers and sceptics, and in doing so became the first boat of its kind to generate hydromania on America's Pacific coast.

Campbell's friends did what they could to cheer him up. Bill Coley understood what he was going through only too well. Coley Metals was based then in Brentford, and dealt mainly in aluminium. 'My father, Robert, was involved in the aircraft industry,' Coley revealed. 'I said we ought to set up, not a Society of British Aircraft Constructors, but a Society of British Aircraft Destructors! He broke up about ten thousand aircraft after the First World War.' Robert Coley had done business with Malcolm Campbell. 'Father had a spares place up in Kingston. Malcolm used to buy stuff. They were two of a kind, always arguing. Malcolm used to gather the stuff he wanted and put it on the floor, then say, "I'll give you ten pounds for it." My father would say, "Not bloody likely!" And Malcolm would storm out but come back and buy it half an hour later! The first real deal I did with Donald was to sell him four thousand ping-pong balls for Bluebird K4, for buoyancy. From then on we were buddies. I bought engines, all sorts of things from him. He was always hard up. He contacted me again in 1951 after his bad do when the boat broke up and sank.'

Coley had immediately been attracted to Campbell's character, though like many he found it difficult to express why in words. 'Ah, you couldn't help it,' he said. 'I don't know, it's hard to put a thing on a bloke like Donald, isn't it?' He pointed to an old painting on the wall, showing figures dressed like Thomas Becket sitting round a table. 'He gave me that. He said it was supposed to be one of our early board meetings at Coley Metals! We just got on over the years, and he got on very well with my wife.'

One day in the summer of 1952, Coley called Campbell and made him an offer calculated to help him regain his old sparkle. 'I originally wanted him to go for the Harmsworth Trophy, because the Americans had held it for so many years, and there had been that business in the thirties when some felt that Gar Wood had tricked Kaye Don out of his chance of winning with Miss England II. The idea got Donald going, but to be honest I think he was really just interested in the straight-line thing, the record breaking.' Campbell nevertheless started to give a Harmsworth speedboat serious consideration. It was the shot in the arm he needed. Never happy sitting behind a desk nine to five, he welcomed the new challenge. He and Villa began to discuss the possibilities. No longer constrained by the need to use an existing boat, they gave their imagination free rein.

But it was not a comforting time to be a record seeker, nor to live close to one. Early in September 1952 test pilot John Derry and navigator Tony Richardson crashed to their deaths at the Farnborough Air Show when their de Havilland DH110 broke up. Then, on the 29th, came the terrible news that Cobb had been killed on Loch Ness when Crusader exploded at 240mph. Campbell and Villa were deeply saddened. Cobb was universally admired not just for his skill – at the time of his death he held the lap record at Brooklands, numerous class records and had broken the land speed record three times; on his last try, in 1947, he had been the first man to reach 400mph on one leg of his 394.20mph mark – but also for his calm and gentlemanly behaviour. Villa had competed against him with Malcolm Campbell, and Donald Campbell had known Cobb since childhood.

Professionally they were appalled that such a carefully planned project could go so horribly wrong. Railton had studied countless configurations before choosing the most effective, a tricycle known as a reverse three-pointer with only one forward planing shoe and two outrigged at the rear. Bluebird K4 had been the world's first jet-powered hydroplane, but Crusader was the first to be built specifically around a jet engine, a de Havilland Ghost with 5,000lb of thrust. Railton and Peter Du Cane of Vosper, which built the 31ft monster, had experimented with powered scale models that had performed faultlessly while attaining speeds of almost 100mph. Nothing had been left to chance, and no expense had been spared. Yet still Crusader had crashed. Villa, however, had had his doubts. 'Reid showed us some photos of the near completed hull and I did not favour the idea, preferring two planing surfaces forward, as with Bluebird,' he admitted. 'The single forward planing shoe reduces the frontal area and promotes better streamline, but I thought it would be dicey in the event of severe pitching conditions.'

Cobb's accident touched Campbell deeply. 'John was one of the old school,' Villa explained. 'I knew him as a very modest person who always shunned the limelight despite his many racing conquests and his brilliant last land speed record. John's misfortune more or less mapped out Donald's future for the rest of his life. Donald's father had been unsuccessful using a jet engine. John had all but succeeded. Donald made up his mind that John's sacrifice should not have been made in vain.' Indeed, Campbell saw Cobb's death as a challenge. British prestige was at stake, something about which Campbell felt passionately. Somebody had to step forward and solve the stability problems that had shattered Crusader into silver fragments and thrown the burly Cobb to his death. Campbell resolved to carry on his work. And he knew there and then that if he was going to build a new boat, it would not be for the Harmsworth Trophy, but to challenge again for the water speed record.

'That was the start of it, after Cobb was killed,' Coley confirmed. 'Donald was very depressed. We had a long lunch at the Berkeley Arms in Cranford, either late in 1952 or very early in 1953. And I said, "OK, go ahead. We'll back you to some extent." We talked a bit of money, and he went away cock-a-hoop. I panicked then. I phoned Leo and said, "Look, what have I done? I've encouraged the birth of this monster!" Leo's words to me were: "Look, Bill, you've only given him a shove in the direction he was bound to go." Perhaps we just got him there quicker.'

After living for a while with his sister Jean and her husband Brian 'Buddy' Hulme (one of his old friends whom he had introduced to his sister), Campbell had moved into Abbotts after finding it during a short break from the waiting at Coniston. The moment he saw the place he was entranced. It had been a farm labourer's cottage for centuries and dated back to Elizabethan times. It had been modernized and extended in the thirties, and boasted oak beams and low ceilings. He lived there for a while with just Maxie the labradoodle – Donald's coinage: Maxie was a crossbreed Labrador and poodle – for company, and a housekeeper who came in daily. Abbotts also had another major asset, a large barn that he had converted into a garage and workshop, with an office upstairs. It was perfect for his new project.

The next step was to renew the association with two young and extraordinarily gifted brothers. Lew Norris had designed the new propshaft for the Bluebird K4 prop-rider; together with his elder brother Ken, he had worked at Kine but left in 1952 to set up Norris Brothers, consulting engineers, in Burgess Hill, Sussex.

Ken Norris was apprenticed to the Armstrong Whitworth aircraft company at Whitley, where he ended up at the age of twenty-three managing the mechanical testing department. 'It was a good job,' he said, 'and I had six men under me, all of them older.' He also taught at Coventry Technical College, which is where his trademark moustache first appeared. 'At one time I got up to give my lecture and all the students were laughing and nudging each other because they thought I was just another student larking around, pretending. I must have looked younger than most of them! So I grew the moustache.' In 1949, around the time that Campbell was making his decision to take over his late father's mantle, Norris made a decision of his own and headed for university to improve his education. He enrolled at Imperial College, where one of his lecturers was an Australian called Professor Tom Fink, who would play his own significant role in water speed record history. Norris took aeronautical engineering, while also studying business administration part-time at the London School of Economics. He got involved with a couple called Frank and Stella Hanning-Lee, who had water speed record aspirations of their own. They invited him to design their challenger, a jet-powered hydrofoil called White Hawk, but had such limited funds that payment was not always forthcoming.

Lew Norris, meanwhile, went to work as a workshop manager with brother Eric, who was the accountant at Kine, which was part-owned by their relatives, the Meldrum brothers. Campbell was managing director. Lew had been on assignment in Malaya, and the moment Campbell learned that he was a marine engineer he set him to work on the new shafting for K4.

Ken Norris had first met Donald via brother Lew when he was working on the shafting and props on K4.

I got interested when he got me to go and see it at the Reigate Hill Hotel. Leo was there, and he said, 'I can't understand it, Ken. This back's coming up. What's causing it? There's no reason for it to come up, and it goes faster.' It was the first era of prop-riding, of course.

We were in opposite camps in a way, because brother Lew was with Donald and I was with the Hanning-Lees on the White Hawk. But then we were both out of work on the record-breaking side, Lew after the K4 incident and me when the Hanning-Lees ran out of money. Then I got introduced to Donald again on New Year's Eve in 1952. We got together up at Abbotts. We raided the neighbour's hedge for holly. Donald just decided, 'Oh, he's got some and he won't mind.' We had a bit of a romp, had the music on, laughed around a bit. Then he talked to Lew and me. 'Now that you're together, how about designing me a boat?'

Ken Norris was the ideal man for the job. Jean Wales summed him up perfectly when she said of him, 'A brilliant brain. And he cared. There was simply nothing to dislike about him.'

Initially, Norris Brothers considered building another propeller boat. Campbell talked Saunders-Roe into helping with the manufacture and testing of a rocket-powered scale model. But the Norrises increasingly realized they were aiming too low with a craft that would hit 200mph, and that propeller propulsion would not be sufficient. 'When we did the sums,' Ken Norris said, 'we decided that horsepower converted to thrust is only 45 per cent efficient, at most. Then we rapidly went through the sums and various tests and finally decided that it had to be a jetboat. So that was it.'

By April 1953, Campbell had reached a crossroads. His course was set, and he quickly appreciated that the undertaking would demand his full-time attention and a lot of money: the budget to build a new Bluebird was £25,000 (£408,000 at today's values). He left Kine Engineering, taking Villa with him, and sold his 50 per cent shareholding to the Meldrums. The proceeds, and the remainder of the inheritance from his grandfather that he had not already spent on Bluebird K4, amounted to around £15,000 (£244,845). Later, Bill Coley gave him a cheque for £2,500 (£40,800). But money would continue to be a worry throughout the project.

One of the first tasks was to undertake a grisly analysis. Before they could design a boat capable of attaining 200mph safely, they had to know exactly what had killed John Cobb. The work melded Campbell, Villa and the Norrises into a tight-knit group. 'I got on with Donald straight off,' Ken Norris remembered. 'He was a friend more or less the whole way through, because I got to know him very well when we were analysing Crusader's crash. We worked overnight, in the dark in the office above the garage at Abbotts, and he would sit there smoking his pipe, watching every detail. He was working the projector, frame by frame, Lew was giving me some figures, I was writing them down.' Frame by unhappy frame, they measured the angles of the planes of Crusader as it porpoised at 240mph, just before the devastating lunge that killed its pilot. The sixteen-frame-per-second film revealed just how quickly Cobb had been going, and how he was being thrown up and down through an eighteen-inch arc six times every second. They took a ruler and drew lines on the wall and measured the angles so they were able to plot them on graph paper and calculate that the oscillations were gradually increasing.

'Suddenly,' Ken continued, 'there was a big bang on the door downstairs. Donald got up and looked over the balcony. There was a policeman standing there. He'd come to see why the lights were still on so late, I suppose. Donald could never resist a joke, so he shouted down to the man, "OK, Constable, they're up here. Take them away!" I got to know him pretty well from that point onwards. He had a fun side as well as a nervous side, as well as a determined side. I think the back trouble that he had during the subsequent record attempt could largely be due to the fact that he was pretty nervous. Quite highly strung.'

There were other memorable moments in their relationship:

Donald and I went out on his yacht with the fellow who owned Holts, the car care products company. Donald took the boat sideways over a sandbank, and we were the only people to get out to sea because of that. Everyone else was stuck in the harbour on the Solent. When we got out to sea it was really rough, and I was sent below to clear up after the fridge door had come open. To this day the smell of diesel fuel and eggs makes me feel sick!

On the road, Donald drove with Leo up front and me crammed in the back, and he liked a lark. He'd say to Leo, quite nonchalantly, 'Shall I pass him round the island?' looking at the driver in front. And he would overtake him on the wrong side of the traffic island, just for the hell of it.

Norris sought the advice of Tom Fink, his old tutor in aerodynamics at Imperial College who was still in charge of the faculty's wind tunnel. Serious testing would be essential to make sure that the new boat did not fly. Fink, who sadly died before the writing of this book was finished, soon found himself subjected to the full power of Campbell's charm.

I'd been at Imperial College for five or six years. I was a native Australian, a graduate of the University of Sydney. I first met Donald in 1953. I had worked at Boscombe Down Aircraft and Armament Experimental Establishment for a period, and I remember, on coming back, Ken having his preliminary chat with me and then saying, 'You've got to meet Donald Campbell.' Now, although I had lived in Britain for some time at that stage, I still hadn't got used to the upper-class way of meeting people. So I said, 'OK, come any time when you're not doing anything.' And Ken said, 'Oh, no. He wants to take you to lunch. And allow a fair bit of time. No question of you coming back for a two o'clock meeting.'

So I was invited to Rules restaurant, in the West End, quite a famous place. Donald collected me from Imperial College in his Aston Martin DB2/4, which was very snazzy. I remember the number was OYK 7. Ken was squashed in the back seat, such as it was.

During lunch, I looked at my watch every so often, because we talked about everything under the sun *except* record breaking. I remember that a very famous British radio comedian with a handlebar moustache, Jimmy Edwards, came and sat with us. Donald introduced us. The extraordinary thing is that I saw him again during a visit to Australia, it must have been twenty-three years later, long after Donald's death. We were at some social function in Adelaide, and this man looked at me and I said, 'Yes, we have met before.' And he said, 'You're the professor type Donald Campbell introduced me to in London, aren't you?' He had the most incredible memory.

Anyway, we had a lunch that lasted from twelve thirty to four thirty. And it wasn't until around about a quarter to four that we actually began to talk about wind tunnel tests. So far as Donald was concerned there was no question of him paying for them. And I found myself saying that we would fit him in. I think he was assuming all along that we would! I think he probably felt that a long lunch would help!

We talked then about the need for more than just wind tunnel tests, because there was the need to study simulated behaviour on water. We were interested in this oscillatory behaviour, after the films of Cobb's accident, so we persuaded him to make a model and tow that on the duckpond at his home. I used to go along on a Sunday morning, fetched in his Aston Martin. And his little seven-year-old daughter Gina and my five-year-old son had to play together inside while we dragged this boat across the duckpond.

Fink had the Australian's traditional reservations about English gentlemen, and was initially quite sceptical about what Campbell had to say.

All Australians tend not to take people in Britain with upper-class accents all that seriously. They think you are trying to put something over them. It takes a while to realize that Lord So and So really does speak that way. So I really tended not to believe what Donald was saying, but it didn't seem to worry him!

Once, when I was with him, he was asked by a journalist why he was doing it, and he said, 'I'm doing it for Britain, and for British trade. If we win this water speed record there will be more irons sold to the housewives of Argentina.' But as to whether he really believed that himself, I never really got to the bottom of it.

Campbell's team faced a fantastic challenge in the design

127

of what became known as Bluebird K7 (White Hawk had been K5, Crusader K6). But again, Fink was cautious as they progressed.

The first thing was that I wanted to hear a bit about John Cobb and other people. One just knew from newspaper reading that they tended to kill themselves doing this. And the answer always was, unfortunately, 'They hit a submerged log.' And then I heard about railway sleepers that would float just below the surface. It supposedly happened to Donald in 1951, but to me that all just seemed too good to be true. So they assembled for me the news films of the Cobb accident. I had it displayed on the wall of our laboratory, with the lights out, so that we could really see large pictures of the boat. It was quite obvious, frame after frame, that it was pitching heavily. And then there was just a little spout of water visible on the upper deck, just in front of the windscreen, which showed that the first break must have happened down at water level, letting water come up out of that hole. And that said to us that it might have been a structural failure associated with the oscillation period. So the main thing was that we were able to analyse it more clearly, and work out what the stresses must have been which had caused that breakage. Of course, it was mainly only a wooden structure.

Initially, Peter Du Cane had intended the front planing point to be made of wood, but finally aluminium was chosen. On previous runs, this had started to buckle slightly. Du Cane implored Cobb to let him take Crusader south and redesign the planing shoe at Vosper's expense, but Cobb already felt that they had kept too many people waiting too long, and instead absolved Vosper from liability and promised that he would try to keep the speed down and beat the record by just a small margin. The corrective work could be carried out prior to an all-out effort. The decision proved fatal.

After his own analysis, Fink was satisfied that Crusader's front planing point had collapsed as a result of the craft's violent porpoising and impacts at a crucial point with three small ripples set up when one of his support boats moved out of position just prior to the run. They now knew that the structure of Bluebird K7 had to be much stronger than Crusader's. Norris tackled the design as if he was drawing a fighter aircraft, not a boat, as Fink explained: 'The all-metal structure was stressed to twelve times normal g. So that made it easier to operate a boat under oscillatory loads, which we knew could be substantial. The period of oscillation would be quite short, but the frequency would be high, so that the loads would also be. I think it was six cycles a second at 200mph, which really is awfully fast. Our hope was to design it so that there would be enough damping so that it wouldn't excite too much oscillation.'

The other major concern was that the boat would go so fast that it would blow over onto its back. The loop-the-loop was not a new phenomenon. As unlimited hydroplanes in America went ever faster, the blowover became ever more prevalent. On one remarkable occasion at the Gold Cup race in Seattle, Lou Fageol had actually blown over in a complete 360-degree arc in Slo-mo-shun V. He had been thrown out of the open cockpit at the top of the loop and was injured so severely that his racing career ended, but the Slo-mo carried on running briefly as it landed back flat on the water. 'Of course, there is nothing to prescribe that you hit the water in a horizontal position and carry on,' Fink continued. 'On Donald's last run he came down at the wrong angle. Most do. The shape of the boat, with more of it forward than aft, was such that should the nose lift up a little, it would catch more wind and lift up more until she went over. The reason aeroplanes don't do that is that they've got tailplanes. Of course, I immediately prescribed fitting one, but that was not acceptable because the rules of the International Motorboating Union at that time forbade the use of them.'

Though critics called into question Campbell's understanding of the technicalities, he was very closely involved in the design process. As part of his training he was submerged in a mock-up cockpit to practise the evacuation drill in the event of an accident. At the Siebe Gorman tank in Tolworth, near Surbiton, watched by representatives of the press, he went through the eerie process as he was lowered some twenty-five feet below their sight, before releasing his safety harness and floating to the surface. He was certainly very well aware at all times of the potential risk that he alone would ultimately have to face. To continue in that knowledge was further indication of the extent to which he shared his father's much-praised courage.

Though it was Campbell who would take the life-threatening risk, the weight of responsibility was no easy burden for his designers. When Richard Noble and Andy Green were testing ThrustSSC in the Al Jafr Desert in Jordan in 1996, Ken Norris and I spent a lot of time together driving back and forth from Petra. On the road to Ma'an one morning, as we talked about those early days of the water speed record attempts, he admitted that he would frequently wake up in the middle of the night thinking, 'What the hell have you committed yourself to? I was always conscious of the terrible responsibility we had for taking every precaution possible to preserve Donald's life.'

Before the design of the new craft, which they codenamed

'C' boat, could be finalized, they had to know what engine it would use. Early on, Campbell had begun discussions with Captain E.D. Clarke, the managing director of Saunders-Roe, with a view to having the Cowes company build the new boat. The initial plan had been to use a Rolls-Royce Griffon twelve-cylinder piston engine, but once the idea of using a propeller had been abandoned in favour of a turbo-jet, Campbell had wined and dined old friend Geoffrey Verdon-Roe, the son of Sir Alliot Verdon-Roe, who had founded the original company from which Saunders-Roe had evolved. At the time the company was happy with the idea of creating a Griffon-powered craft, and was instru-mental in helping with the initial scale model testing. But things deteriorated when the matter of a suitable jet engine came up. Clarke favoured the Rolls-Royce Avon RA3 jet, a derivative of which Richard Noble would thirty years later take to a new land speed record. But this was a large, heavy engine. On the advice of Air Commodore Rod Banks, Campbell was persuaded to look at the smaller and less powerful Metropolitan-Vickers Beryl, which produced 3,750lb of thrust. According to Norris's figures, that was 750lb more than they needed to create a new record of 230mph. With Banks's help, Campbell located two Beryls at the Ministry of Supply in Woolwich.

An argument between Campbell and Saunders-Roe dragged on for much of 1953, the former convinced that the Beryl was fit for the job, the latter set on a bigger engine. Eventually, Campbell posed the hard question to Geoffrey Verdon-Roe: 'Are you prepared to build a boat around the Beryl?' The answer was no. Saunders-Roe did not believe that the small engine had the necessary power to create a record that would last, even though Bluebird was the only jet-propelled boat then under design in the world.

Subsequently, the Beryl would prove sufficient to power Bluebird K7 to speeds in excess of 280mph, but all that lay in the future. At this crucial point, Campbell's project was in serious trouble.

What he did next was completely in character. Rather than be backed into a corner and feel obliged to compromise, he reluctantly parted company with Saunders-Roe and prepared to go it alone. But because he had been brought up to play the game by the rules, he also wrote to Norman Elce, the helpful managing director of Metropolitan-Vickers. He believed it was incumbent on him to inform Elce of his changed circumstances, in case Metropolitan-Vickers wanted to reconsider its involvement. Elce was a strong character, however, and had no intention of going back on his word. The engine supply and maintenance side of the project, at least, was intact.

Subsequently, Campbell's smooth salesmanship persuaded Accles & Pollock to manufacture the tubular steel frame, and Salmesbury Engineering in Blackburn to complete construction. Wavell Wakefield was the chairman of Park Royal Vehicles and through him Salmesbury (a subsidiary of Lancashire Aircraft Corporation) agreed to help. Villa and his crew would then move north to Salmesbury's premises to complete the fitting out. Bill Coley remembered an evening at Abbotts with the BBC presenter Cliff Michelmore and Sir David Brown, who owned Aston Martin and had an interest in Salmesbury, and how Campbell turned on the charm to get him to agree to build the boat. Subsequently, however, Aston-owning Campbell fell out with the magnate when he tried to sue Brown for the standard of workmanship on the boat.

The Bluebird that emerged gradually through 1953 and 1954 bore no resemblance to any other craft. Its fuselage was like a jet aeroplane's, with the cockpit mounted ahead of the Beryl engine. Either side of the cockpit and the stubby nose, metal spars carried the outrigged sponsons that would give the boat its flotation and stability. Construction fell way behind schedule, but bit by bit Campbell found the remaining £10,000 (£163,200) he needed to finish the craft, even though the project received a massive setback in its early stages when the Wakefield company, which had backed so many record projects since the 1920s via its famous Castrol brand, withdrew an initial offer. Castrol's representative was Captain George Eyston, the former land speed record holder and a gentleman in the mould of John Cobb. Eyston was a friend of Captain Clarke at Saunders-Roe, and Campbell was dismayed to find that Castrol shared Clarke's views about the suitability of the Beryl. It was a body blow, not just because of Castrol's past relationship with the Campbell name, but because its rejection would send out the wrong signals to the rest of British industry. Subsequently, the company relented, but its actual contribution was lower than its original offer. Despite the financial assistance of the Coleys, and help from the electrical components company Lucas, Dunlop, and individuals who made contributions, Campbell had to mortgage Abbotts to make ends meet.

Villa had taken on new engineers, and before long Maurice 'Maurie' Parfitt and Ken Ritchie became indispensable members of the tight-knit team. One memorable day in the summer of 1954, they rigged up a test bench in the workshop at Abbotts, stuffed their ears with cotton wool and fired up the first Beryl jet. When the noise finally became too much and they shut it down, they discovered that they had singed two oak trees and blown most of the cinders on the drive onto the main road to Reigate.

On 26 November, the almost finished Bluebird K7 was

finally unveiled by Lady Wavell Wakefield at a formal ceremony at Salmesbury's factory, as company chairman Eric Rylands handed it over to Campbell. Resplendent in its sapphire paintwork, it resembled a large blue lobster. Two years of blood and sweat lay behind its construction, and every penny that Campbell possessed. But as he savoured the elation of the unveiling he was momentarily able to forget about the stress of the new boat's gestation. It was three years since he had driven the old Bluebird K4 at 170mph; all he could think of now was how soon he could get out onto a lake and open the throttle.

Shortly before the unveiling there was more bad news, further confirmation – as if it was needed – of the danger he faced. On 9 October, Mario Verga, the Italian champion against whom he had competed during the Oltranza Cup race in 1951, took his flame-red Laura 3a hydroplane out on Italy's Lake Iseo. Verga was in much the same position as Campbell had been with the Bluebird K4. Laura 3a, named after Verga's wife, was also a prop-riding boat faced with what was likely to be a final crack at the record as a jetboat of much greater potential was being prepared. Verga's boat was powered by two of the supercharged straight-eight Alfa Romeo engines that had taken Giuseppe Farina and Juan Manuel Fangio to the first motor racing world championships at the start of the decade. At only 22ft in length and with more than 750bhp, it presented the experienced Verga with a stimulating challenge. But, like Cobb, he was pushed into impatience by his desire to deliver for those who had supported him. Rather than wait for a local wind known as 'Il Tivano' to abate, or to change the angles of Laura 3a's planing shoes to cope with it, he made his attempt. He was travelling at 190mph, in excess of Sayres' record, when his boat lifted to an alarming degree, stood for agonizing moments on its tail, and then barrel-rolled to destruction. Verga, for whom Campbell and Villa had great admiration, did not survive. Another challenger had become a victim of the call of the siren.

Campbell was already far too advanced with Bluebird to consider pulling out, but such action never occurred to him. Like Cobb's death, Verga's acted as a spur. Their work remained uncompleted, and the finest tribute he could pay such men was to carry on the cause in their name.

8

THROUGH THE WATER BARRIER

February to July 1955

'He cursed himself because he was running short of money and he knew that having nearly got to 200mph, and having broken the record, would put him in a good position, somewhat later, to really go through 200 somewhere else, like America.'

TOM FINK, BLUEBIRD AERODYNAMIC CONSULTANT

The sky over the Lake District dawned clear and fine on 11 February 1955. It was a Friday, but for once Donald Campbell was prepared to put his superstitions to one side. He was raring to go, and nothing was going to stop him from trying his new boat for the first time.

Ullswater, one of the larger British lakes, had been chosen as the site for his new attempt on the American-held water speed record because of its associations with Ullswater Navigation Company. Sir Wavell Wakefield, MP for Kendal, was its chairman, and had agreed to provide a specially built boathouse and slipway on the south-western shore near Glenridding. Campbell didn't like Ullswater very much. There can be three or four conflicting winds to contend with, and several different varieties of current make it unpredictable. He had always wanted to go back to Coniston, but politically Ullswater made more sense.

The weather was cold, the lake initially calm, but a northerly wind picked up before the official christening ceremony could begin, whipping the surface into a chop. Both the christening and the proposed trial run were postponed until the afternoon. Watched by Donald, Leo, Buddy and Jean, Ken and Lew Norris, Maurie Parfitt and Ken Ritchie and other well-wishers, Dorothy Campbell sent the champagne bottle arcing into contact with a metal bar held above Bluebird. She then intoned the same sentiments her husband had voiced for his father's old boat some sixteen years earlier: 'I name this boat Bluebird. May God bless her, and her pilot, and all who work with her.'

Within moments, Bluebird's special transport cradle was winched down the custom-made slipway from the boathouse that Wakefield had constructed, and suddenly the blue craft was finally free, afloat for the first time, ready for the action that Campbell and Villa had dreamed of for two and a half years.

The press had turned out in force, for Campbell liked to play up contentious issues. After John Cobb's accident he had talked up a water barrier, similar to the sound barrier that held such fascination for schoolboys and their fathers alike in the early 1950s, which literally shook boats apart around 200mph. It made good copy, and it appealed to his sense of the dramatic. 'He liked all that,' Tom Fink said with the dismissive tone of the trained engineer to whom such things are merely fanciful. 'All that talk was simply journalese, because things get worse the faster you go. There never was a definite barrier. In those days everyone was talking about the sound barrier which, of course, wasn't a barrier either. I think it was all one of Donald's typical exaggerations, not that he meant any harm by it. But he liked to talk these things up, make them seem more dramatic perhaps than they really were. Mind you, I wouldn't like to have been in his shoes actually driving the boat.'

There was no talk of the water barrier when Campbell first tested Bluebird. By the time he reached the first leg of Ullswater, at Glenridding, there were white horses prancing on the surface of the lake. Bluebird wallowed unhappily on the end of a rope attached to one of the launches. In the cockpit, Campbell was warmer than he had been on the shore, but everyone else was huddled on the support boats, faces nipped with the cold. Villa beseeched him to call it a day and to try again the next morning, but Campbell would never quit in such situations. The plan was merely to try the boat to check flotation and manoeuvrability with the engine running, but all along Campbell was determined to try to get the boat up onto its planes.

There was a more sheltered spot on the north shore, and there he ordered Villa to slip the towline. At last he was running through the start-up procedure he had rehearsed over and over, and he was delighted when Bluebird responded to steering inputs. Low-speed manoeuvrability was excellent. But through the flat screen he could already see that the sponsons were too low in the water, indicating that the trim was not yet right.

When the great moment came and Campbell put his foot down for the first time, Bluebird floundered like a duck with oiled feathers. Every time he tried to accelerate the boat refused to rise. Instead, the nose dipped and water poured into the air intakes and flooded the engine. After fifteen minutes Bluebird was back at its dock, Campbell reporting few problems while manoeuvring it alongside the pier under its own power. It had been disappointing not being able to get K7 planing, but there was plenty to be satisfied with. 'The turbine, fuel, electrical and control systems functioned extremely well and without need for any modification whatsoever,' he noted. And the three gallons of water that had found their way into the hull had come in through the flap actuator slots. The only other drama concerned the radio. Campbell admitted, a trifle sheepishly, 'A loudspeaker had been inadvertently plugged into the shore monitor station, located at Pier House. A very considerable number of spectators and reporters were therefore able to hear the instructions and messages passed between Control, Launches and the Bluebird, all of which were out of sight during the run. This was unfortunate to say the least, for the language was of a distinctly nautical nature.'

The redistribution of Bluebird's weight was easy enough to accomplish; it required only removal of the aft buoyancy tanks and repositioning of specific components within the hull, such as the air bottle and the fire extinguishers, to move the centre of buoyancy forward. Campbell took Bluebird back out on the 18th and 19th for further tests, and found the trim better. But it was still proving difficult to get the boat to plane, and the weather was now so inclement that the flying spray was icing up three-quarters of the Beryl's inlet annulus, and also freezing over the sponsons, spars and cowlings. There was also a small risk of collision with floating icepacks.

It was 10 March before the big blue hydroplane reappeared, and for the first time it began planing. Campbell found that the transition from displacement to planing condition occurred at the gratifyingly low speed of 40mph, and he completed his first high-speed run at 120mph.

Subsequently he reached 'a long way over 100' – around 150mph – on half power, and repeated the performance the following day. But in order to get the boat to plane, Ken Norris had been forced to fill in the gaps between the sponsons and the hull with aluminium sheet, to protect the engine intake from flying spray. Campbell now had a boat that would get out of the water at low speed, but which ran the risk of flipping over backwards at the speeds he sought. They decided to put the eighth-scale model back in the wind tunnel to assess the effects of the temporary changes, and the Norrises prepared to make some far-reaching modifications that would significantly alter the boat's appearance. The redesign work would take months, but Campbell was astute enough to treat it as part of the game. There was not the slightest suggestion of giving up. He had come too far to turn back.

There was one consolation at this point: the US Navy had expressed an interest via the Admiralty in learning more about K7's behaviour. Campbell was flattered, and confirmed his willingness to comply as once again he waxed lyrical. 'On a matter of principle I am only too pleased to help. We believe it is probable that Bluebird can form the basis for a useful war weapon, and if the Americans want it they are welcome to have the information and the details with one end in view: to help in the defence of the free world.' Record breaking has always fundamentally been about the pursuit of a goal by a free spirit, but Campbell always liked to lend his endeavours greater credibility by hinting that they had loftier values above and beyond self-gratification, even if it was self-gratification of a most heroic kind.

Back at base, the aft buoyancy tanks were removed altogether, since the preliminary trials had indicated that weight distribution could more effectively be altered by shifting static weight rather than by adhering to the original plan of using the engine's compressor to move water around the hull via the tanks to adjust the trim while the boat was active. Removing the tanks was no small job, but the wind tunnel tests, allied to empirical data gathered during the trials at Ullswater, confirmed fears that Bluebird's aerodynamic trim had been compromised significantly. Before the temporary baffles had been fitted, Bluebird's ultimate aerodynamic safety point was 8° pitch at 250mph; now that had been reduced to only 4° at 200mph. 'Four degrees is a relatively high pitch angle,' Campbell admitted, 'and, in finality, would have been acceptable. In the circumstances, however, it was felt expedient to first of all seek an alternative solution to the problem of water entering the engine air intakes at speeds of around 10mph, a solution that would not drastically affect the high-speed aerodynamic factor of safety.'

Forty-seven different configurations were tested on a dynamically corrected eighth-scale waterborne model, and the results were analysed minutely on cine film. The outcome meant that Bluebird's front spar needed to be raised by ten inches, and on 10 May Leo Villa and Maurie Parfitt returned to Ullswater, where the boat had remained, to begin the work. At the same time, a new moulded Perspex cockpit canopy, made by Triplex, was fitted, enhancing visibility significantly.

To date, all of the information had been gathered by means of voice reports from the cockpit, tape recorder and cine film. It was intended to utilize the onboard telemetry system once the boat returned to the lake, but in the meantime Campbell had done a fine job of relaying feedback to his engineers, as Ken Norris recalled:

He called me the Professor. 'What does the Professor think?' He used to like to give hifalutin technical names to things. He liked to talk in technicalities and use words of his own concoction. We knew they were his concoctions, but he knew what he was talking about. He tended not to under-state things. And he embellished things further when he talked to the press. But during the runs he was good. He was the only one that could report the way he did. Richard Noble couldn't report like that, when I worked with him on Project Thrust in Nevada in the 1980s. Donald would tell you all the way through what he was doing. You could hear it: constant; precise; accurate. It certainly didn't sound like he was frightened or hyperventilating. In all the messy stuff at the start he was going through to get the boat on the top, he would simply tell you exactly what was happening. He was loud-voiced about it, which you'd be anyway having to speak audibly over the radio. You've got to speak high to get it all ashore with all that noise in the background. He was good at that. Better than Richard in that sense. He could describe it and tell you about it at the time. It was natural. He was very test pilotish.

Norris is, however, sure that Campbell had a fear of what he was doing even then, but a healthy fear was an essential safety valve for a man indulging in such a lonely and cold-blooded pastime. Craig Breedlove, who would later be a land-bound rival for both Campbell and Noble, always maintained, 'If you're not a little bit afraid of this thing, then you're not playing with a full deck.' 'I think Donald was frightened during the attempts,' Norris said. 'He had what I would call a safe fear. He had a safety fear, enough to say, "I've got to behave here or otherwise I might break my neck." But when it came to putting his foot down, he did it. But he did listen to you beforehand.' Fink, who would later play a pivotal role in fellow Australian Ken Warby's success in capturing the water speed record at 288.8mph in November 1977, and then raising it by the biggest increment in history to 317.596mph in October 1978, disagreed. He admitted that the thing he had enjoyed most about working with the bluff, no-nonsense Warby, in comparison to Campbell, was that Warby listened to what he had to say and acted upon it. Norris explained:

> To Tom, Donald was always a bit of a playboy. I think he was always slightly suspicious of him. The reason he joined in so much – and Tom joined in a lot – was because I'd been through college with him; he was my lecturer. And we really worked together. We got on fine, Tom, my brother Lew and I. Marvellous. And Donald, if you like, came in late because of that. Tom would talk to us rather than Donald, perhaps. But he was very sincere in his advice.
>
> As far as I could see, the biggest contrast between Donald and Ken Warby was probably the voice! And the attitudes! The difference of chalk and cheese, weren't they? Donald's was very much the parliamentary language, and of course Warby was cobber and all that. 'She'll be right,' you know? There was a terrific difference there.

Dorothy McKegg, though swept away by her man's charisma and the sheer excitement of living with a speed-king, was not blind to his failings. The 'parliamentary language', as Norris termed it, maddened her. Even she was exposed to the man with the mask, and far, far preferred the overgrown boy who hid behind it.

There were lots of things that used to drive me crazy. When he'd put on The Voice – 'My team and I'. That terribly upper-class British accent. I can't tell you what fun we used to have on the yachting holidays. And then we'd come into Southampton or Cowes, and on would go the cap. We'd all been arsing around, the skylight would be leaking and everyone would be getting wet, the stew would be boiling on the little Bunsen burner in the galley. Then all of a sudden we'd be approaching harbour and the whole thing would change. Ah! There'd be the cap and the pompous voice. Arf, arf, arf. Jean and I would go into hysterics whenever that happened.

Dottie described Donald Campbell's mask perfectly, all stiff upper lip, terribly British. A carapace born of his adoration for his father, and his inner fear of revealing too much of his real self to the world. Yet the real man, the one behind the mask, was an infinitely better person.

Campbell was a good engineer, with a solid grasp of engineering problems and a strong working knowledge of what made his boats and car tick. It was he who designed the quick release for the boat, as Norris pointed out.

Of course, we had to hold him back when he fired up the engine. He was towed out onto the lake at Ullswater, and we had a battery start in those days off the side of the Bluebird. We had to hold him still while we plugged in, otherwise when we let go he started to drift off. Donald designed the release so that when he was ready and fired up he could release the hook himself. He made the hook and he made the release. It was nothing much, but he could work with his hands. And he thoroughly understood everything about the project. He was very disciplined, and later he had a pilot's

144

licence. He was nothing like Richard [Noble] was when he started. Richard was terrible on discipline initially! But Donald wasn't. He always worked a checklist right from the start.

One of the people who knew Donald Campbell socially at this time was a young pilot called Norman Tebbit, now Lord Tebbit CH (Companion of Honour). He, too, noted Campbell's passion.

From late 1954 to early 1956 I and a fellow BOAC pilot, Mike Bull, had rooms at the Red Lion in the village of Betchworth in Surrey. It was there that we met Donald Campbell, and subsequently I met him from time to time at the Seven Stars too. I never knew him well, but always enjoyed his company. As a pilot I had something in common with him. It always seemed to me that he was driven by an urge not merely to compete and succeed in his chosen field of speed, but that he was in love with the addictive thrill of danger. I felt even then that that particular addiction, like so many others, would demand more and more of Campbell until it destroyed him. Was it an inheritance in the genes his father gave him, or acquired in childhood from the environment in which he lived?

Bluebird was finally ready to run again in July 1955. By then Campbell had not only been buoyed by the official request for information from the US Navy Department, but also by the fact that the American interest had sparked off a plan to run Bluebird in the States. With that in mind, he secretly planned to ease past Stan Sayres' 178mph record on Ullswater and save breaking through 200mph and the water barrier for an attempt in America later that year.

Soon the team was back into fourteen-hour days. The pressure of all the work took its toll on Campbell's back, which he had damaged as a result of his various motorcycle accidents years earlier. 'At Ullswater he was in terrible trouble,' Bill Coley recalled. 'In the end the only thing that helped was to let himself hang from the Coles crane.' It would not be the last time that the pain would influence one of his record attempts, but in later years greater significance would be attached to the treatment he received. There were also some restless nights. Once, Dottie awoke to find her husband kicking the hell out of her after a nightmare.

But despite such personal problems, it was a happy team. 'Donald put me in charge of the press,' Coley remembered. 'Well, I had no idea how to deal with them. Some of them, one or two photographers, were a real nuisance. One of them took a picture of him in bed! I mean, it was appalling. Geoff Hallawell [a local man who had been appointed the project photographer] was very kind to me, and the *Daily Express* man, Basil Cardew, he was very thick with Donald. We had a bit more trouble with another photographer. He came down to the boathouse and was on the jetty outside. That was enough for Tom Fink. He said to him, "You're press, trespassing," and kicked his camera into the water! That cost Donald something!' Ken Norris also had fond memories of those far-gone days. 'We used to play jokes on one another at dinner. Normally we'd have been at the same table as Donald, but on one occasion he had somebody with him, probably a sponsor or some dignitary. We left this plastic spider in Don's soup, and he was so busy talking away to this fellow that he didn't notice it until he was about to spoon it up! It was a real case of, "Waiter, there's a spider in my soup!" Heaven knows what Donald's guest made of it all.'

On 23 July, Campbell finally achieved his greatest ambition, setting a new record of 202.32mph to smash America's mark. Upon hobbling ashore, the first thing he did was to lean over a rail to stretch his aching back, then he dangled from the crane to ease it further. Soon he sought Villa's assurance that he had done well. 'The Old Man would have been proud, wouldn't he, Leo?' he asked. Still, the shadow engulfed him.

Campbell was delighted with his wonderful success after all the expense and heartache, but there was still the tinge of regret at having topped 200mph before he got to America. 'I'm almost embarrassed to have gone over 200,' he said. 'I really wanted to leave that for runs in America.' Fink confirmed the feeling. 'The record stood at 178 before he took it. He wanted to get a little below 200 but his first run was, I think, 220, something like that. He cursed himself because he was running short of money and he knew that having *nearly* got to 200mph, and having broken the record, would put him in a good position, somewhat later, to really go through 200 somewhere else, like America.'

Bill Coley recalled that even in his moment of triumph, Campbell remembered his team and the part they had played in his success.

Tom Fink was a dreadful man in a boat! We were on one during the run, down at one end of the course. Tom was in charge, and when Donald finished and we knew he'd got the record, we knew he would wait for us to get back. Tom was in a hell of a hurry, of course. He cut the corners, went onto some big rocks. Oh God! It was a complete flap. But all Tom worried about was my son, Christopher, who was five years old. 'Is the boy all right? Is the boy all right?' Typical Tom! He wasn't worried about anybody else. But we were all right.

I don't think the boat was very badly damaged, either. But Tom insisted on cutting across to save time, and hit these rocks. In the end we got back late, but Donald had waited for us. That was so nice of him. Lovely. We were very delighted that he'd waited for us, because of course everybody else was already waiting for him at the hotel. That was typical of him. Always a thoughtful man in those circumstances.

He was thoughtful in other ways, too. Four days after the record fell, the workforce at Denford Engineering, one of the many companies that had contributed to the project, received a telegram. Former employee Rod Booth still has a photograph of Campbell working a lathe there, complete with cigarette drooping in his mouth. It's accompanied by a telegram sent from Ullswater on 27 July to Denford Engineering, whose contribution had only amounted to supplying him with accessories for his Boxford lathe. The telegram congratulated them on the sterling service of their machine tool and thanked them for their help. Donald Campbell, the proficient engineer and now speedking, was not a man to forget those who helped him, no matter what their input had been. Other companies received similar expressions of gratitude.

The success was also a boost for Ken and Lew Norris. When they set up on their own, Ken drove an elderly Austin Ruby and Lew a Wolseley Hornet. While visiting potential clients they would park the cars round the back and then walk in the front door with their smart briefcases to see the managing directors. 'If they'd seen our cars, we'd never have been allowed in,' Ken admitted. Much later, as they prospered, came new Ford Consuls; Ken's was blue, but Lew opted for pink!

Ken Norris also recalled another extraordinary moment that was typical of Donald Campbell's character. 'Soon after he had set the Ullswater record he showed me round his Rolls-Royce. You know, sitting in the back with his cigar, puffing away, his eyes twinkling. I knew he was up to something. "How much will you give me for her, Ken?" he asked. "How much for what?" I replied. "For this," he said, indicating the car. Well, it was no good at all to me. I needed something which didn't use much petrol, to use with the business. But I honestly believe that if I'd offered him five bob for his Rolls he would have taken it that day!'

Subsequently, Campbell bought each of the brothers a new Austin saloon as a symbol of his gratitude for their work on K7. His gift to Leo Villa was a bright-red Triumph TR2.

9

SUBMERSION AT LAKE MEAD

October to November 1955

'Let's see those suckers get out of that.'
OBSERVER'S COMMENT OVERHEARD BY DONALD CAMPBELL, LAKE MEAD,
16 OCTOBER 1955

Even before he had broken the water speed record at Ullswater in July 1955, it was clear that Donald Campbell was not going to be content with just one success and had planned to keep some speed in hand for a follow-up attempt. Prior to that first success, an invitation had arrived from the Las Vegas Chamber of Commerce to visit Lake Mead in Nevada 'with a view to attempting the new world record under ideal water and weather conditions'. Campbell had agreed but was still mulling over the details in the afterglow when Leo Villa gave him the news that they already appeared to be firmly committed. An agent had agreed definite terms. Campbell flew to New York and found that the date of 16 October had been set and that the event was to be televised on NBC's *Wide, Wide World* for an estimated audience of sixty million. To have demurred would have reflected badly on British prestige, and though he had serious doubts that a record could be staged at any specific time, like a race, he went along with the plans. 'We feel that everyone associated with the project would welcome this invitation to "Show the Flag" in the United States,' he said. The team now had only three weeks in which to prepare Bluebird before it was flown out, but that was fine. America was the land that had made his father great.

There was another serious incentive: Mobil Oil was offering sponsorship. Given that Campbell subsequently entered into an arrangement with the company in 1956 that was worth a total of $32,500 for a successful outcome, it can safely be assumed that this was worth not less than $30,000. In today's money, that would be almost £122,800. After all the hardship and heartache, Campbell was finally beginning to get something back over and beyond the personal satisfaction of breaking the record.

Immediately after the success on Ullswater he had taken Bluebird out for a series of 100mph runs to pinpoint the spray patterns that continued to be problematic at low speed. Minor modifications were made before the boat was shipped to Lake Mead, a manmade body of deep-blue water thirty miles from the gambling town of Las Vegas, nestling in an otherwise arid desert. Campbell and his crew set up base camp at the Sahara Hotel in Vegas in October, but in the glitzy environment they soon came to feel that they were just another circus act. NBC's coast-to-coast hook-up via 160 stations soon made Donald Campbell a household name for enthusiastic Americans to whom television was still a novelty. Whenever word went out that Bluebird was due to make a run, hundreds of pleasure craft would assemble on the water. Villa came close to exploding on several occasions, especially after one side of the cockpit canopy shattered during one run, possibly through heat or fatigue.

On the 16th, Campbell was scheduled to make a run at exactly four minutes and twenty seconds past one o'clock in the afternoon, to satisfy the television schedules, but the situation was hopeless. The local Chamber of Commerce had boasted that Lake Mead offered ideal water and weather conditions, but the former were far from good. Far too many private spectator craft had been allowed onto the lake since ten o'clock. Some were only small rowing boats or speedboats, but others were medium-sized cruisers, and all were allowed to roam without supervision within minutes of the start of the first run, even though US rangers did their best to discourage it. They were simply outnumbered, and the errant traffic set up dangerous swells. Campbell reached the start of the course four seconds ahead of schedule to begin his first run, but already Bluebird was bucking and jumping around and he managed only 160mph in what amounted to just a demonstration. The refuelling point was seventeen miles from base, and while Campbell was there pleasure craft closer to base began to head for the harbour despite the strict order of the rangers.

He made his return run at a similar speed after hitting more swells, then slowed at the end of the course so that the television cameras could zoom in. The water was still heaving. Swells flooded the Beryl engine three times before he could finally trickle back towards base at 5mph. Before he got there, he ran out of fuel. Completely stricken, Bluebird was now at the mercy of the swells. A launch came alongside and took it under tow, but just as mechanic Don Woolley tried to fit the engine cover over the tailpipe to seal it off, Bluebird caught another swell. Woolley burned a hand on the jetpipe as he tried to balance himself, and dropped the cover.

Under the launch's full power, Bluebird edged close to safety under the full glare of the television cameras, but a mile out from shore a large cruiser, unaware of the hydroplane's plight, swept in to take a closer look, bringing with it a serious swell that lapped straight into Bluebird's unprotected jetpipe. For the second time in his career, Campbell found himself scrabbling out of a hydroplane just before it sank as Bluebird went down stern first, live on television. Woolley bravely jumped onto the front spars and attached a heavy rope, desperate to get a line on the boat so that its position could be identified. He was momentarily dragged beneath the surface, but freed himself just in time. While trying to go to his aid, Campbell discovered that his lifejacket inhibited the arm movements necessary to swim cleanly (subsequently, he would decide not to use one). Just as Campbell was dragged from the water, too stunned to speak, Bluebird momentarily broke the surface like some giant blue marine creature, its two sponsons pointing sky-wards, before settling back into the water and sinking to a depth of one hundred feet. It took divers eleven hours to attach ropes and chains to Bluebird and then inch it along the lake bed in the tow of two cruisers. They finished with the help of car headlights. Finally, at one thirty in the morning, just over twelve hours since the ill-fated runs had begun, the world's fastest boat was back on dry land. As Bluebird was stored in the tent that served as a base, Campbell was incensed to hear an American observer say in a loud, sneering voice, 'Let's see those suckers get out of that.'

Campbell's natural leadership qualities immediately came to the fore. There was a fair amount of damage to the boat, but it was relatively light and close inspection revealed nothing serious to be amiss. But the Beryl turbojet engine was full of silt from the lake bed. Initially he enrolled assistance from Lake Mead Marina, but Commanding General James E. Roberts lost no time in putting the full engineering facilities of the USAF Fighter School at Nellis Air Base, ten miles from Vegas, at the team's disposal. There they carried out what amounted to a complete strip-down and rebuild. While that work was being carried out, a new three-mile course was laid out on the western extremity of the lake to avoid problems with spectator control.

The rebuild was completed on 9 November, when Bluebird was finally ready to run again. But then, with the sort of ill fortune that frequently beset Campbell's efforts, the weather broke and kept the hydroplane off the water until the 16th. Very early that morning the team breakfasted in the Sahara Hotel's Casbah lounge, surrounded by all-night gamblers. As they were leaving for the lake, jazz musician Louis Prima stopped playing a Dixieland set and, to the astonishment of the weary blackjack and roulette players, wished the team the best of luck. Some of his audience hadn't got the slightest idea what he was talking about; others applauded heartily.

The early rising was wasted. Out on the lake there was a delay when one of the cables on the timekeepers' clocks was found to have been vandalized. Then it was discovered that one official hadn't even turned up. It was a while before he was located, drunk, at a gambling den in Vegas. Local police brought him out to Lake Mead, but he was not at his best. It was not until 10.27 that Campbell made his first run, south to north, in an elapsed time of 9.34 seconds and at 239.50mph. He described it as 'comparatively uneventful', but water conditions were still not ideal. He had used the full 7,200 feet available as a run-up for acceleration, entering the kilometre at 205mph and leaving it around 250mph, still accelerating. Bluebird certainly had more than enough power for the job, but Campbell found deceleration a little tricky where the mountains rose sheer from the lake at the northern end. Fortunately, the available width alleviated the problem as he was able to zigzag to lose speed.

After refuelling in seven minutes he was on his way again, reining himself in, partly to keep something up his sleeve and partly because the sun's glare made it difficult to pick out the marker buoys. Coming back took him 11.59 seconds and his speed dropped to 193mph. This time he encountered a severe ground swell, and K7 left the water altogether at one stage, forcing him to back off. 'The recorded vertical g was fractional of that which might have been expected, although my shoulders are very bruised from the effects of the harness, possibly because I was only wearing a light nylon shirt,' he reported. 'The ground swell cannot be accounted for: it was not caused by wind or by the movement of any vessel; it may have been due to the fact that very strong winds had been prevalent during the preceding five days.'

It didn't matter. Campbell and Bluebird now had a second record to celebrate – 216.2mph. And this time there had been no dramas with crowd control. Campbell smiled shyly at all the Americans who had suddenly become 'the Britisher's friends', looking relaxed and boyish, tanned, fit and muscular in his Aertex short-sleeved shirt. He was on top of the world again.

Dottie had not made the trip to Nevada with Campbell, for her own career was undergoing a dramatic development back in London. While Campbell was pursuing speed, her television career was beginning to take off. She had dolled herself up in furs and brooches and driven up to London in her red MG Magnette for an interview for a programme called *Quite Contrary*, directed by a well-known figure, Richard 'Dickie' Afton. 'Well, the guy running the auditions took one look at me and dismissed me as a rich bitch. He kept asking me to sing when I was ready, but all the time was letting the others have a go. Eventually I got my turn.' He was surprised by the result, and remarked to her, 'You can sing.' 'Of course I can,' Dottie replied. 'I've been on the stage since I was seven.' She was taken to see Afton, who didn't even look up as she entered his office. 'He ignored me completely. I had time to smoke a complete cigarette, then I'd had enough. Just as I was walking out the door, he said, "I gather you think you can front this show."'

Dottie Campbell was as feisty as her husband, and she got the job, but even she was surprised when Afton asked her to write her own script. Then one day, while she was on final run-through for the airing of the first show, she received a telegram that made her scream. It was from her husband in Nevada, telling her he had just broken the record. It was the first time any of her colleagues learned of her other role in life.

When Dickie found out, he said, 'Right! We'll beat the nine o'clock news!' And he took the telegram out of my hand and said, 'I don't want you to look at it, I don't want you to think about it, I just want you to do everything that we've been rehearsing today, OK? And when Michael Gillenny comes into camera shot he'll give you the telegram and you can do what you like. But I don't want you to think about it until then.'

So on we go, and there were these blasted Pearly Gates that used to open at the start of the programme and the theme song was 'Moonlight and Roses'. I chatted away – I'm Dorothy McKegg, I'm a New Zealander, blah, blah, blah – made my little intro and the various people on the show did their thing and the Television Toppers did their dance. I was well under way, on a roll. Then in comes Michael, thrusting this telegram at me and saying, 'Read it, read it!' And I can remember to this day my feeling. 'Oh God, I've gone and blown it! What have I done?' My face must have been a study, because the camera was right on me. And then I got it and remembered and was so excited. I read out: 'My husband Donald Campbell has broken the world water speed record at Lake Mead, and the speed is . . .' The entire studio erupted. And it was a big studio. They went berserk. What a way to start the series!

Yet behind the scenes things had already started to go wrong between Donald and Dottie. Their marriage would end the following year.

Despite the dramas, Campbell thoroughly enjoyed his time at Lake Mead. A friend of mine visited the place decades later and came back bearing tales of how Campbell had discovered the joys of call girls while staying in Vegas, told to him by some of the locals who remembered the speedking with affection. But Tonia Bern, Donald's third wife, subsequently cast doubts on the veracity of the stories. 'You know, I don't think they are true. I never heard those stories. And in our time Donald told me every story of every girl he'd been to bed with.'

On the night that he broke the record, Campbell was presented with a massive gold urn during a riotous party. But the icing on the cake came later in the form of a letter from the Information Policy Department of the Foreign Office back home in London. It read:

I expect you already have a complete set of cuttings regarding this event, but I thought you would like to know that the

Embassy sent them to us with the comment that your attempt had given a very good boost to Anglo-American relations in a very tough part of the United States which does not normally tend to throw its admiration away on people or things British.

I would only like to add that whenever you are in the U.S. and have time at your disposal, the British Information Services would very much like to use your presence to their advantage in the publicity fields of radio etc. Were you able to do this it would greatly add to the promotion of general British prestige in the U.S.A.

It was precisely the sort of boost Campbell loved. It flattered his strong sense of patriotism, and convinced him that what he was doing was valuable and right.

On his return to Britain, he told the media, 'It's one of those things you've sort of got to experience to really appreciate. If the water gets disturbed you could liken it to driving a car with no springs and flat tyres over a rough road covered in ice.

'Why do it? Why do anything in life? No doubt there is impending and very serious opposition coming up in America. If we are going to keep this record we are really going to have to go back to work, and I would like to hope that next year we might see the 250 mark come up.'

Speaking of the team that stood so firmly behind him, he added, 'I can pay them no greater tribute than to emphasize that Bluebird established a new world record exactly one month after being on the bottom of Lake Mead.' This was testament to the fortitude of men such as Leo Villa, Maurie Parfitt, Don Woolley and Ken Ritchie, and further endorsement of the job Ken and Lew Norris had done in designing and building Bluebird K7. It might not have been the first hydroplane to break a record after sinking (Miss England II achieved the feat in 1931 after Segrave's fatal accident in June 1930), but it was without question the fastest.

Norris Brothers would go on to further success in industry, its involvement with the Bluebird hydroplane acting as a springboard. Ken Norris said, 'That really opened doors for us that had hitherto been shut. We worked for Briggs Motorbodies, which did bodies for Ford and Rolls-Royce, who would never have used us without the record-breaking successes; Clarnico sweets, all sorts of companies.' But union problems with Rolls, which eventually curtailed a great deal of the brothers' work, decided them on a policy of never allowing any one client to be worth more than a third of the company's overall turnover. Before long, however, Donald Campbell would bring to the company a project that would be worth far, far more than even Bluebird K7.

10

'HERE'S TO THE LAND
SPEED RECORD!'

Winter 1955/56

'What are we going to do about the land speed record, then, lads?'
DONALD CAMPBELL TO KEN AND LEW NORRIS, LITTLE ABBOTTS,

DECEMBER 1955

Lake Mead was more than just the venue for Donald Campbell's new success with Bluebird K7, it was also where the dream of the land speed record really surfaced. The car to end all cars! A 500mph monster that would boost the record for Britain! What better way to banish his inner doubt that he was the man his father had been, and to prove himself to the world? But the glorious dream would ultimately turn into a nightmare. It would mire his career and sully his reputation. And unwittingly create the most expensive white elephant in land speed record history. In fact, the dream would almost kill him . . .

The origins of Campbell's land speed aspirations have become tangled by the passage of time. The adulation heaped upon him at Lake Mead certainly made a big impression, for now it was his turn to experience what his father had enjoyed so often at Daytona Beach and later at Bonneville. The giant gold urn Campbell had been given after the triumph bore the inscription: 'Recording the courage and scientific achievement of Donald Campbell in raising the world speed record to 216 miles an hour on the waters of Lake Mead, and so showing the possibilities of the lake as an area of aquatic recreation.' Then there was the congratulatory letter from the Foreign Office, which praised the effect his achievement would have on British prestige. Perhaps that really sparked off the dream. Or perhaps it merely put the match to a blue touchpaper that had always been there, its end crisply twisted in anticipation ever since he had watched his father break 300mph at Bonneville.

Whatever the truth, he was still at Lake Mead when he first enthusiastically mooted the idea of a car to Villa. 'What about it, Leo?' he said. 'We'll get the water speed record here at Lake Mead and then fly out to Utah and get the land speed record on the same day. Of course it would take a lot of organizing, and we'd certainly need two separate teams. But what about a go?'[18] Villa, who was used to Campbell's flights of fancy, had answered him with his habitual avuncular gentleness and reminded him that records didn't fall easily, before adding, 'And with your sort of luck, I don't think you'd stand a chance.'[19]

How very prescient the older man was. Campbell subsequently revised his ambition. Even he appreciated that two records in a day was pushing credibility. But right from the start he was dead set on breaking both marks in the same year. Just before Christmas 1955, Campbell invited the Norris brothers to dinner. 'We met up at Abbotts and he kidded us about it,' Ken Norris remembered. ' "What are we going to do about the land speed record, then, lads?" And then he toasted us, "Here's to the land speed record!" He was sounding us out. But I'm quite sure he'd got it in his mind already.'

Ken and Lew Norris jumped at the chance, savouring the project even more than the creation of Bluebird K7. They would have carte blanche to create whatever vehicle they deemed best suited to the challenge. It was any designer's dream. Campbell's sole stipulation was that the car should be powered by a gas turbine engine, something with which the Norrises agreed fully in any case. They settled on the Bristol-Siddeley Proteus, and Ken remembered going to see managing director Sir Stanley Hooker early on. 'He was an imposing man, and I began to outline what we wanted. There was some scepticism among his engineers, but I plunged on. I explained that we wanted an engine that had power output shafts either end, so we could drive both axles. Hooker listened intently. "So that's what you have in mind is it, young man?" he boomed. Then he looked round at his engineers and said, "I think we can manage that, can't we, gentlemen?"' The Proteus 705 came from the Bristol Britannia airliner and the Brave Class fast patrol boats operated by the Royal Navy. It was light and compact, produced more than 4,000hp at 11,000rpm, and would enable Norris to use a very simple four-wheel-drive transmission. Its efficiency and flexibility suited it perfectly to an automotive role.

Design work on the new car began in January 1956. Very early on in the process the Norrises received one piece of advice that was to have a far-reaching influence on the design of Bluebird CN7, and on its ultimate success. It came from the doyen of record car design, Reid Railton. 'He told us, "Look, you boys have got to run by the rules,"' Ken Norris recalled, 'and we took that to mean that we couldn't go for any kind of moving aerodynamic device, like a fin.' And also that they had to stick firmly with driving the car through its wheels. Back in 1956, when CN7's concept was first proposed, the pure-thrust jet car was still a few years into the future. The rules laid down by the governing body, the Fédération Internationale de l'Automobile (FIA), stated that any vehicle seeking to break the land speed record must be 'a land vehicle propelled by its own means, running on at least four wheels, not aligned, which must always be in contact with the ground; the steering must be assured by at least two of the wheels and the propulsion by at least two of the wheels'. Bluebird complied fully with these regulations. Its only grey area was in the exhaust system, where the Proteus's thrust augmented the power that went through the wheels. 'We used to avoid answering questions about any thrust the engine also developed,' Norris admitted. 'We'd just say it was an ordinary exhaust.'

The brothers spent the next two years formalizing their design, on paper and in exhaustive tests using scale wind tunnel models. Meanwhile, Dunlop took eighteen months to perfect the design of the wheels and tyres. It decreed that tyres with a 52in outer diameter, inflated at 200psi, would be necessary to withstand the speeds and loadings envisaged, and that had a huge influence on the shape of the car.

By June 1958, general arrangement drawings were circulated to the press, revealing the car's distinctive Railton-like elliptical shape and forward driving position. In August, Campbell held a major (and typically well-organized) press conference at the Department of Aeronautics at Imperial College in London to outline some of the problems associated with high speed on land and water. Press interest was stratospheric.

CN7's structure broke more new ground, for it was built

on aircraft principles using Ciba-Geigy 'Aeroweb' aluminium honeycomb to create an eggbox structure that was light, rigid and immensely strong. Four honeycomb sandwich longitudinals were held together by similar transverse frames, with the driver and machinery inserted into the boxes created. This monocoque was then sheathed in aluminium body panels. The suspension was fully independent via transverse wishbones and oleo-pneumatic nitrogen-filled spring/damper struts. Girling dual-circuit, air-operated, triple-calliper disc brakes were mounted inboard of each wheel, and there were auxiliary air brakes either side of the tail. When bringing Bluebird to rest from 400mph in three and a half miles, the braking system had to dissipate 75,000,000ftlb of energy in one minute. During the course of this the discs would glow red at temperatures of 1,700°F. Overall, this impressive new Bluebird weighed between 9,000 and 9,500lb, was 30ft long and 8ft wide, and had a wheelbase of 13ft 6in and equal front and rear tracks of 5ft 6in. The design speed was conservatively put at 475mph, though Campbell and the Norrises entertained hopes of more than 500 in the right conditions.

By the time the great car was finally finished, sixty-nine British companies had contributed services, products, money or, in many cases, a combination of all three. At Campbell's insistence, it was British right down to the last screw fastener. Besides BP and Dunlop, Lucas, brake manufacturers Ferodo, Smiths Motor Accessories and Tube Investments had also made significant contributions. But the greatest came from Alfred Owen (he had yet to be knighted), head of the Owen Organization. Its offshoot, Motor Panels, had overseen the construction of the car in Coventry.

If Bluebird CN7 was going to be the most complex car ever built to attack the record, running the project would be equally exacting. It would have to be done the right way. In his typically flamboyant way, Campbell set up a trust and a grandiose Steering Committee.

The Trustee Council was chaired by the Duke of Richmond and Gordon, and comprised the Duke of Argyll, Charles Forte, Eric Knight, Alfred Owen, the Hon. Greville Howard, Cyril Lord, Bill Coley, Victor Mishcon, and Peter Barker. Squadron Leaders Peter Carr and Neville Duke were nominated as reserve drivers. 'He asked me to be a trustee, and I agreed,' Baron Mishcon said. 'We did very little, really, because it was a nominal trust. It didn't do anything very active, except have a bank account somewhere, into which money was paid. And faithfully paid out, of course, in accordance with what the trust was all about, which was advancing motor racing and, through motor racing, Donald. There were infrequent meetings of the trustees, as I remember. I think because of the names of the trustees, if you accept my own, they were a reputable lot and it therefore commanded sufficient respect among those people who were asked to sponsor.'

The trust was a clever idea given that Campbell, unlike his father, was not using his own funds, those of friends such as Bill Coley or sponsors such as Charles Cheers Wakefield, as he had with Bluebird K7. Instead, because this was a much bigger project, he was appealing directly to British industry itself.

Peter Barker, whom Tonia Bern described as 'easily Donald's closest friend', acted as his manager for several years in the 1950s, and handled the trustees in his role as secretary to the Trustee Council. He explained:

They were really there to raise funds by their names, more than anything else. They were just a nominal bunch really, they met once or twice. The Duke of Edinburgh came to a meeting once, unless I'm mistaken. I think it was at the Dorchester.

I was at the Hulton Press at the time and got permission to manage Donald Campbell if they got the exclusive pictures for *Picture Post* of everything he did. I wasn't with him every day, but I think I did three of the water records up at Coniston. I used to go round with him a great deal, fundraising more than anything else. We'd scour the Midlands, and I don't know what we didn't used to do. He was always up against it, you know. He was awfully bad at money affairs, old Donald was. He never had enough!

But he did have a genuine talent for sourcing funding from industry, born of an ability to talk to people on their own level, no matter how high that might be. 'He had that charm, which got their support,' Barker confirmed. 'The main ones that succumbed to it were BP, Dunlop and Smiths.'

The Steering Committee comprised a senior executive from each group that was playing a major role, to advise on policy and planning: Alfred Owen (Owen Organization), Dr K. Ridler (BP), Evan Price (Dunlop), Nigel Breeze (Lucas), F. Hurn (Smiths), Sir Arnold Hall (Bristol-Siddeley), G. Sutcliffe (Ferodo), Ken Norris (Norris Brothers), Leslie Hackett (Tube Investments, British Aluminium Company and Accles & Pollock), and Squadron Leader Peter Carr. The committee guided an Advisory Council comprising representatives of each company.

Smiths engineer Ken Reaks worked with Campbell both on the K7 hydroplane and the CN7 car. He had first met him in 1953 after Leo Villa had contacted Smiths' marine division in search of a small gearbox that would help with speed measurement on the scale model of the prototype C boat on which they were working. 'It gravitated to my desk,' said Reaks. 'I called Donald, then met him for lunch at the RAC Club in Pall Mall. Smiths did the gearbox and supplied a hand tachometer, too. We hit it off, and I saw an awful lot of him, off and on, and attended some of the original C boat meetings as it progressed from the Griffon engine to the Beryl jet.' Reaks, a diminutive but outgoing man with a military moustache, was immediately attracted by Campbell's character.

He was amazingly enthusiastic, and he could stimulate that in other people. It was quite fantastic! I was a long way down the chain, a junior. One day, way after our involvement with the boat, my phone rang. It was our managing director Mr Hurn's secretary, who said he wanted to speak to me. That was odd. He would summon you if he wanted you, not call you on the phone. He mentioned a Steering Committee meeting on the land speed record project, at the Dorchester. 'You're familiar with it,' he said. 'I can't get up there. Will you go up there for me and sit in?' He was chairman of the meeting, and there were fifteen to twenty companies involved. 'I want to emphasize,' he added, 'that you are not to commit the company to any more expenditure. You have no authority to do that.'

Just before I left, somebody from another company called, and their MD wanted to speak to me. I didn't know him at all. This one said, 'I gather we are meeting up this morning at the Dorchester. I wanted to have a word before we go in. You know what this man Campbell's like. We should all be fully agreed: no more money, that's it. We should all go in, and we should all come out waving the bloody Union Jack!' That was all a back-handed tribute to Donald's powers of persuasion!

Time and again, reluctant managing and financial directors would find themselves swept away by the enthusiasm and charisma of the man in the pinstripe suit sitting on the opposite side of the office desk or opulent restaurant table. Donald Campbell knew that his only hope was to charm British industry the way his father had all those years before, and he set about the mission with all his customary energy.

'I really liked him,' Reaks continued. 'He was a great character. Infuriating at times, with his timekeeping. He had very little sense of it outside record breaking. You'd arrange something, particularly if you were having him meet senior personnel, and half an hour later he'd arrive. But he would simply charm them. I had several situations like that. He'd be off somewhere else, and just forget other appointments.' While he could be infuriating, Campbell was also spontaneously generous. Reaks had fond memories. 'I have one or two nice little souvenirs that he gave me, silver pencils, thoughtful presents like that.' He also admired Campbell's leadership qualities, and sense of fun.

> I always felt that, as far as this country was concerned, he would have made probably the best ambassador if he had gone into the diplomatic service. He had that ability, and he always pushed the British slogan ahead. There was one time when he let the side down slightly, and that was when he arrived at Coniston in a Porsche! But he was mad about cars and it was nearly always Astons, Jaguars or Bentleys. He was a good road driver, but I went out with him once in the Aston and that was a frightening experience. He drove fast, though he was very positive. He'd teach you how to go into corners, put your foot down and come out in a high-speed slide. He loved that.

At the launch of Bluebird CN7, Campbell made a speech thanking the many companies who had contributed to its design and creation, ending with another heartfelt recognition of the role of Leo Villa and his team. 'We are approaching the eve of a great adventure,' he concluded in typical fashion, 'one which we hope will further mankind's knowledge and contribute to British leadership and prestige.'

Thus did he commit himself to following in his father's wheeltracks as well as his hydroplane roostertails. But Bluebird CN7 was still a long way into the future at the beginning of 1956 as he contemplated more water speed records before the car to end all cars would be ready. The decision to go after the land speed record had notched his life up another gear. He was on top of the world. He knew just who he was, and precisely where he was going. He also had a shrewd idea who might help him finance the lifestyle that would go with it all.

11

SPEEDKING: THE BUTLIN YEARS

1956 to 1959

'Oh yes, he was doing it for money if he possibly could. His desk was always full of bills, they were sky-high. He used to live well, and he was a kind man. Over-generous to everybody.'

PETER BARKER, CAMPBELL'S MANAGER IN THE LATE 1950S

Donald Campbell's new success brought him into contact with a number of people who would influence the course of his life. One of the most important was a South African-born, London-domiciled entrepreneur whose four watchwords were money, ambition, power and women; a tough, uncompromising showman who reputedly carried a cut-throat razor in his top pocket, and whose rags-to-riches life had been dependent upon his staying two or three steps ahead of the rest. He started out as a huckster at fairgrounds, and his first fortune came from the UK rights to dodgem cars. Then he worked his way up from seaside amusement parks to create the holiday camps that would become world famous. Learning fast from pioneer Harry Warner, he took the concept a stage further and prospered dramatically.

His name was William 'Billy' Butlin, and he would make Donald Campbell a rich man.

They shared the common interests of speed and women, but other threads bound them, too. Butlin, like Campbell, was a control freak when it came to external appearances and what the media wrote about him. He was also publicity-conscious, and like Campbell had his heart firmly set on a knighthood. Butlin had negotiated favourable deals with the government, which took over his new camps as military training grounds during the war. They were then refurbished and sold back to him at a fraction of the cost when hostilities ceased, in time for him to cash in on the post-war boom in cheap family holidays.

By the time Donald Campbell was preparing to marry for the first time, Butlin was already an extremely rich man. By the mid-1950s he was offering a prize of £5,000 for every time the water speed record was broken. It was never clear whether this was Butlin's own idea or something that Campbell had cannily sowed in his mind as a patriotic gift that might serve both well. It didn't matter. At today's values, the four new marks that Campbell and Bluebird would set between 1956 and 1959 were each worth on average nearly £72,000. 'Oh yes, he was doing it for money if he possibly could,' Peter Barker confirmed. 'His desk was always full of bills, they were sky-high. He used to live well, and he was a kind man. Over-generous to everybody.' That was the problem.

As his great new car slowly took shape, Campbell remained the toast of Britain, the *Boy's Own* hero speedking of the 1950s. Each year he would carefully edge up his water speed record, always keeping something in hand, to earn Butlin's generous prize. These were his happiest years. As the dashing young man about town his stock was at its highest, and his exploits regularly attracted headlines. He was finally enjoying some of the recognition his father had basked in, and he unashamedly basked in it too. He was part of the fabric of the 1950s, one of the reasons for the country to hold its head high. A household name. He was comfortable in the spotlight and, perhaps for the first time in his turmoiled life, was truly at ease with his success. He had yet to become embittered by the disappointments that Bonneville and Lake Eyre held in store, or gripped by the fears both would arouse in him. In the days when Stirling Moss, Mike Hawthorn and Peter Collins were just breaking through to regular victories in Grand Prix racing that would lay the foundations for the country's domination of the sport, Campbell was Britain's most consistent and high-profile motorsport success story.

In 1956 he was awarded the first of his four Segrave Trophies, presented by the Marquis of Camden at the RAC Club in Pall Mall. Set up to honour the memory of Sir Henry Segrave, the prize was awarded annually to the British subject who, in the judgement of an awarding committee, accomplished the most outstanding demonstration of the possibilities of transport by land, air or water. The simple idea behind it was to stimulate others to uphold British prestige by demonstrating how the display of courage, initiative and skill – the spirit of adventure – could assist progress in mechanical development. In his acceptance speech, Campbell made it crystal clear that he was only on the first lap of his journey. 'This coming year I hope that we shall try and further this record again,' he said, and Dottie would have cringed at his clipped, almost aggressive use of The Voice. 'Only by doing that do I feel that we have any chance of keeping this particular record against mounting opposition, and at a time when once again this great country holds all three records [air, land and water].' He was, as usual, beating the drum of self-justification to some extent, but over in America, Slo-mo-shun designer Ted Jones had been making noises about building a 34ft jet-boat to challenge Bluebird. Though ultimately it came to nothing, it was an indication of why Campbell never felt able to relax for long. Getting onto the pedestal had been a gruelling fight; now he was finding that staying atop it would require similar stamina and commitment.

Both he and Butlin became the subjects of Eamonn Andrews' *This Is Your Life* television show. Butlin's appearance in 1959 came on his wedding day and was no surprise to him; he'd orchestrated it carefully with his new (yet already estranged) wife Nora. But when Campbell was caught by Andrews in 1956, he was taken unawares. And he didn't like it. Dottie and Lady Dorothy Campbell had handled it all in conjunction with Andrews, but though he smiled all the way through Campbell was secretly livid that such a thing had been done to him without his knowledge and permission. For the duration of the surprise show, he was not able to hide behind the mask.

Alongside this nationwide exposure came some lucrative deals. One of the most important was with Socony Mobil in New York. In July 1956, the oil company agreed to pay him a sum of $10,000 (£34,800 at today's values) for a certified new water speed record, and a further $6,666 (£24,500) if it was officially in excess of 250mph. The contract ran from 1 July 1956 to 15 May 1957. And on 6 August 1956 Bluebird went on a month-long display at the Festival Gardens in Battersea to raise funds for the new attempt, though the London Federation of Boys' Clubs also received 60 per cent of the revenue.

About this time, Campbell began a new relationship. His

marriage to Dottie was over and she had returned to New Zealand, though the official annulment would not come for another year. He was invited to the opening of a play, and became taken with a young girl who seemed aloof from the crowd. Her name was Dory Swann. 'I'd been invited along, I can't remember quite why,' she recalled. 'I was given a glass of champagne, and there were so many people I was really nervous, so I went to one side and leant against the wall. Donald Campbell came over and talked to me. I didn't know who he was. He said that he'd like to get together with me at some point. He gave me his telephone number to call. He didn't ask me mine. That was it. I was just so happy that somebody talked to me. You know what opening nights are like. He was really cool, casual. That's the reason why I called him a few days later.'

Dory, who was only twenty-one, would become his companion for the next two years.

After the Lake Mead effort there had been talk of a new attempt for 250mph at Eagle Mountain Lake in Fort Worth, Texas, but in September 1956 Campbell went back yet again to Coniston, the venue he preferred for his attempts. Besides the usual team, Gina went along for the first time with Dottie. This would be the venture that would frequently be raked up in the aftermath of the fatal effort that lay eleven years into the future.

The 19th dawned with a light mist. By the afternoon conditions were perfect and Campbell sped through the kilometre at a shattering 286.78mph on his first run. This was nearly 50mph faster than he had ever gone before and was certainly faster than he had intended. He had told Villa that the plan was to feel things out around 240mph and then go quicker on the return run to achieve an overall goal of

250mph. In view of the speeds Bluebird later achieved on the lake, it is interesting that initially he wondered if it was really long enough to allow sufficient distance either end to slow down from such speeds. When Villa informed him of his actual speed at the end of the run, Campbell refused to believe it. Villa also advised him that the port stabilizing fin had clearly been visible for the first time. It was a danger signal. Campbell's voice over the radio as he throttled back betrayed his surprise and dismay at the boat's wayward behaviour: 'I'm getting a hell of a shaking. Shipping water. Something's adrift. I'm taking a beating. I'm down to a hundred miles an hour. I don't know what happened.' Returning very quickly after refuelling, he came back at a much more sedate 164.48mph. It was still enough to achieve another new record, at 225.63mph.

Had he really had problems on both runs, or was he just so horrified at his speed on the first because it had threatened his capacity to bank Butlin's money by using up so much of his margin for future improvement? Had he deliberately backed off to preserve that lucrative margin? The air-speed indicator had malfunctioned on the outward run, which certainly influenced his performance. The most it had registered in Bluebird's cockpit was 240mph. Villa discovered subsequently that water had entered the pitot head, causing the indicator to register lower speeds than the boat was really attaining. Bluebird had behaved so alarmingly that Campbell feared a stabilizing fin might have been torn off, and he ordered an underwater inspection between runs. Don Woolley obliged, and found nothing amiss. On the return run Campbell was affected by fumes in the cockpit, whose new Perspex canopy had also misted up. 'Something must have gone wrong,' he insisted. 'The fumes were so bad that I nearly passed out and was just doing things automatically.' But the disparity in speeds was quite remarkable and, to some, suspicious.

'I think he gave himself a bit of a shock on that one, you know,' Ken Norris said years later. '286mph then was a phenomenal performance. And when I think of it now I still see those front fins absolutely out of the water. For a fairly long time, a second or so. A lot more than you'd want them to be visible.'

So was it genuine, or was Campbell sandbagging to preserve his future income? Habitually, he would make a quick first run and then come back slower, carefully gauging what the likely overall average would be, though on this occasion he had initially intended to go faster on the return. Certainly, Bluebird never went as fast again until 1964 on Lake Dumbleyung when the first run yielded 283mph. Nor was a second run ever so slow. The fumes were real enough, though, and were clearly visible in one remarkable photograph in which Campbell's face registers his disbelief at the ordeal he has just experienced. 'I was lucky to live through it,' he said. 'After we left the measured kilometre the boat snaked incredibly and went completely mad. The only description I can use is that it went into convulsions.'

The bottom line was the money. By backing off so much on the second run Campbell damaged his overall average so that he failed to achieve 250mph. It is unlikely that he would have done that voluntarily, when it cost him £38,000 at today's rates.

There was one other important aspect of this attempt that Campbell would not forget until 4 January 1967. By returning so soon after his first run he had a rough ride in the wake he had created.

Whatever the truth, the new record further cemented Campbell's status as a national hero. And he gave his public something else in October, when he officially announced his plans for the land speed record.

Off the water, he played hard and fast. Richard Noble, who would become the country's next speedking in the 1980s, once suggested that Campbell would go out and make something happen if he felt he wasn't getting enough publicity. But Baron Mishcon disagreed. 'I think that's cheapening Donald. If you asked me if there was a natural shyness when he was in a room with people, and on the other hand a desire to be in the public eye, which I suppose is a little paradoxical in a way but true enough, I would have said that was a correct picture. Donald wasn't awfully good at light conversation. I mean, he could hold a drink at a cocktail party, and chat away, but I don't think he was terribly comfortable when doing it.' He was much more at ease discussing turbine engines and planing angles. Many made the mistake of taking him purely for a playboy because of his lifestyle, but his engineering background was sound and he preferred conversing in such terms. Nevertheless, he lived both his professional and social lives at full throttle. Whatever he did, he did it standing on the gas.

When the Hulton Press was purchased by Newnes and Odhams in 1957, Peter Barker struck off on his own, working in public relations and licensed merchandising.

I kept up with Donald, of course, but I didn't really go on as his manager. He called me that, but it was a bit of a euphemism. I used to do most of the organizing up at Coniston, the odd jobs. The course markers, the time-keepers, the press and all that.

He was a lovable, marvellous man. Fun. He used to decide just to take off and would say to my wife Cherry and me:

'We're going down to the south of France tomorrow. Come down with us.' So Cherry and I would go down in his Jaguar, a Mark II I think. We were always doing things together. He regularly used to come round to our house in Kensington and spend the evenings with us. He was a most delightful man to be with. Generous in the extreme. He used to give everything away, and he hadn't got it to give, really. He was always putting his hand in his pocket, and you couldn't stop him.

Barker has no doubt that Campbell was impelled by some sort of need to live up to his father's reputation. 'Oh yes. I think Malcolm was the dominant factor in his life, the dominant character, and Donald came on as a sort of aftermath, almost. I can't ever say I thought that he enjoyed record breaking. I think he felt sort of forced to do it, because he didn't know how to do anything else. That's the answer I think, more than anything. I don't think he ever enjoyed going into that boat.'

Just before Christmas in 1956, Campbell received some news that thrilled him. He was to be made an ordinary Commander of the civil division of the most excellent order of the British Empire, for his services to speedboat development. It wasn't the knighthood that he craved, but a CBE was the next highest civilian order and a step in the right direction.

In 1957 he was ready to try for another new record, and this time there was significantly greater funding than he had enjoyed in 1956. On 21March he had negotiated a new deal with Socony Mobil, worth $30,000 (£170,714). This took the form of $17,500 (£99,014) by the time Bluebird arrived in America for a new attempt, and $12,500 (£71,700) on certification of a new record. Again, there was an incentive, this time of only $2,500 (£14,214) if he averaged more than

250mph. The deal would run from 21 March through to 30 September 1957.

He was invited by a group of entrepreneurs, who called themselves Canandaigua Lake Promotions (CLP), to challenge his own record on Lake Canandaigua, one of the beautiful Finger Lakes in New York State. On 20 June Bluebird sailed from Southampton on the liner United States. The previous day, Campbell and Dottie had finally been granted their decree absolute. By the 26th the advance party had reached New York State, and on Independence Day, 4 July, Campbell made his first trial run. But this time, through no fault of his own, the venture would be a financial disaster for his hosts. They had invested $30,000 (£170,714), hoping that crowds would also boost the local economy by spending in shops, restaurants and hotels. Profits would then be invested in a YMCA building fund. Ultimately, however, the revenue would barely cover Campbell's expenses.

Up to 14 August he had made few attempts, but that day he did two runs, at 175mph and 195mph, then two more at 201mph and 207mph. But Lake Canandaigua generated some unusual swells even when its surface appeared glass smooth, and the number of pleasure boats on the lake was as worrisome as it had been at Lake Mead. He could never reach full throttle within the safety envelope to which Leo Villa so strictly adhered. Campbell explained that the peculiar swell caused Bluebird to pitch violently, but promised to keep pushing. The promoters became progressively anxious. CLP president Howard J. Samuels said, 'People are simply not coming into Bluebird Park to see Don and his boat. It's as simple as that. We were wrong in our estimates of attendance. We probably will draw only 35,000, and many of these are complimentary.'

The following day Campbell was on the lake again, and this time Bluebird took off for 200ft after hitting a swell from an errant pleasure craft at 240mph. 'I was lucky to come through alive,' Campbell told reporters. He averaged 198.67mph on the first run, heading north into the wind. Despite having to lift off on the southern run when Bluebird took its leap, his speed for the run was 220.83mph, giving him an overall average of 209.5mph. Fast, but not fast enough.

In a desperate effort to recoup some of its losses, CLP resorted to shipping Bluebird and her pilot to Toronto for a two-week stint at the Canadian National Exposition. The contract with CLP expired on 7 September, but long before that Campbell knew the Lake Canandaigua venture was at an end. Rather than give up altogether, however, he began to seek an alternative venue. The Americans hoped he might be persuaded to visit Lake Mead again, and for a time there was speculation that he might run on Lake Picton in Ontario, which bordered the National Exposition grounds. This was where Art Asbury would shortly break the water speed record for propeller-driven boats with a Canadian un-limited hydroplane called Miss Supertest II. But Campbell said it was too rough. He and Villa were quoted as saying that Bluebird needed $40,000 (£227,714) of repairs to its hull and to rebuild its engine after the rigours of the Canandaigua attempt, but given all the other known figures this was clear hyperbole.

Determined not to go home empty-handed, they switched to another New York State venue, Onandago Lake up near Syracuse. It lacked a slipway, but the US Navy pro-vided a landing craft to act as a floating headquarters, launch facility and workshop. But this effort, too, was doomed. Sewage from Syracuse flowed into the lake, which possibly accounted for what Villa described as its dark and oily water. He thought the place ominous, and he was right. Bluebird tramped badly whenever Campbell opened it up. Its behaviour was so alarming that they even had a surveyor test the craft with a theodolite to check whether the adventures at Canandaigua had damaged anything. But it was the lake, not the boat. After several fruitless runs, they bowed to the inevitable and headed for home.

Asbury, already the Canadian speedboat champion, met Campbell while he was in Buffalo, New York. 'I only chatted with Donald for a few minutes,' he said, 'but found him to be the kind of person who makes you feel that you have known him all your life. He was indeed a fine gentleman of vision, and I was privileged to have known him for that short time.' Extraordinarily, Campbell then drove a prop-rider for the first time in six years when he took out the Miss Supertest II hydroplane with which Asbury would raise the propeller mark to 184.494mph at Picton Reach that November. 'When he came back ashore, he said, "Art, she's a bitch – she'll kill you,"' Asbury remembered. 'And he was right. But it wasn't me she killed, it was Bob Hayward.' Hayward, Canada's other great racer, died four years later when Miss Supertest II crashed during the Detroit Silver Cup race. Campbell spent a lot of time chatting with boat owner Gordon Thompson and his crew after he took his run. 'He also offered me a ride in the Bluebird,' Asbury added, 'but I'm sure he was just kidding!'

Campbell eventually got his record that year, but not before his deal with Mobil had officially expired. In October he went back to Coniston, and by November the project was operational. There was a setback when, in an eerie preview of what lay ahead, the first Beryl engine was damaged after it sucked some rivets out of the air intake and scarred its turbine blades, but on the 7th Campbell earned Butlin's money once again. As usual the first run, which began at 9.58 a.m., was the faster. He averaged 260.107mph, but on the radio Villa warned him that Bluebird was again showing too much daylight under the front planing points. This time he came back at 218.024mph for an average of 239.07mph and another pay-packet. His first move on stepping ashore was to kiss Dory on the forehead. 'Hello, Nonsense,' he said, and reached out to stroke Maxie the labradoodle's head. Dory told him she had never been happier in her life. But once again it had been no cakewalk. 'I had a really bloody pasting on that first run,' he told Maurie Parfitt. He had missed his avowed target of 250mph, but discretion had been the better part of valour. 'I drove at the limit of safety today,' he said. 'Leo's warning stopped me from making a faster run on the return. To have exceeded that would have been exceedingly foolish.' Later, the patriotism that drove him surfaced most clearly when he told reporters: 'Let us not forget that despite the activities of Sputnik [the Russians had launched the first two of these pioneering satellites in October and November 1957] we are the tops. We hold the world air, land and water records and we intend to see that we keep the lead. It seems to be the fashion of some people to run down the British and royalty. It makes me sick and nauseated to hear them.'

It was after this attempt that Campbell began to hint at a new boat, something radical codenamed Bluebird KX, by Ken Norris. At that stage he and the Norrises were toying with the idea of an amphibious vehicle capable of 500mph on land and 300mph on water. 'We have hopes for the future,' he said. 'Next year you may see a rather stranger-looking animal.' Interestingly, while guardedly alluding to this vehicle, he expressed the view that K7 'would never see 300mph in its current form'.

Away from record breaking, one of Campbell's great buddies was the Canadian-born entertainer Hughie Green, a pioneer of the television game show genre and himself a household name in the 1950s with his *Double Your Money* programme. Besides his love of performing, Green also had an abiding affection for aeroplanes, having flown them during the war. 'I knew Donald for many years, on and off; I saw him particularly at parties given by Billy Butlin. Later I got to know Tonia. Donald and I had a mutual interest in speed and planes. He was always fascinating for me because I had many hours on flying boats and knew a bit about speed on water.' Green told an anecdote that revealed Campbell's sense of humour and the delight he took in pricking balloons of pomposity, though that in itself was something of a paradox given his own penchant for The Voice.

I had a tremendous success with the first giveaway show in this country, *Double Your Money*. Out of *Double Your Money* I was asked to produce musical specials for ATV and for Rediffusion. They had a lot more light entertainment back then than they do now. The Palladium, that sort of thing. My interest was always in doing things that were different. I was always interested to see in magazines and papers famous personalities like Frank Sinatra and Ava Gardner, departing for America and waving goodbye. So I got an idea. It was to take the viewing public to America. To say to them in the previous show, 'Now, you've seen Frank Sinatra and Clark Gable waving goodbye, but has it ever occurred to you what it's like when they sit in that aeroplane and fly all the way back to America? Because next week, we're gonna show you . . .'

I discussed this with a lot of people who thought I was crazy, one of which of course was not Donald. One time we were talking about it and he asked which aeroplane I was gonna get. I tried to get El Al's Britannia, because I thought they could do with the publicity. 'That's a jolly good idea,' Donald said. 'Am I invited as a passenger?' That hadn't occurred to me. I said, 'You'd like to come?' And he said, 'Of course I would! Particularly as the engines in the Britannia are the same as I'm going to use in my car.' That was marvellous. I said to him, 'Donald, you're a passenger.'

El Al rejected the plan, but Green finally sold the idea to BEA. He worked at that time for impresario Jack Hylton, coincidentally a friend of Campbell's, but Hylton was dubious, especially as the Crazy Gang were also on the passenger list. 'They always do mad things, especially with Donald Campbell,' Hylton told Green. But when Green pulled off the BEA deal, Hylton decided that he too wanted a seat. 'And I bet he'll want to bring Rosie,' Donald told Green. He was right. Rosie was Rosalina Neary, Hylton's girl-friend. 'She had a huge bosom and used to call Jack her titty boy,' Green recalled. 'She was a singer. Jack said, "It'll be marvellous. Rosie'll come too and she'll sing."'

So there was Rosalina Neary, Jack Hylton, Laurence Harvey the actor and Paddy Stone, who arranged a spectacular dance around the plane in the hangar at Heathrow. And it ended with all the star names running up the stairs into the plane. I'm the last one up, and I say to the audience, 'I've got your tickets, do you wanna come? Let's go!' The camera goes in with me as the door closes.

So we get into the air, though it wasn't all quite as easy as that. Donald and I were sitting side by side and he was telling me all about the engines, which was a very natural way of him telling us all about his new car. That was the first time he made a national statement about that aspect of his new attempt. We'd taken out the last two rows of seats so we could get an upright piano aboard, and Winifred Attwell played it. She might not have been the greatest pianist, but she was certainly the *high*est pianist! She played at 35,000 feet. Donald got up and sang while Winnie played. Not very well, but he did it.

Now, Jack Hylton had a way of getting other people to let you know things he couldn't bring himself to tell you face to face. The director came up to me and said that Jack wanted Rosie to sing, but that she had to make an entrance. I said, 'We're at 35,000 feet. What's she gonna do, walk in off the wing?' We had limited time for shooting and it was scripted down to the last minute, and suddenly we get this thrown at us. Then Donald said, 'I've got a great idea,' and he whispered something in my ear. I said, 'Donald, you're a genius. You gonna tell Rosalina Neary?' He said, 'No, you go and tell her.'

So I went to Rosie and said, 'Jack is right. You must make an entrance! This is going to be one of the greatest entrances you're ever going to make and it will be one of the biggest laughs of the whole show.' She said, 'Oh, I'm so happy, but what do you mean?' I said, 'Well, you can't walk off the wing, darling. You'll come out of the shit-house at the back!'

She went over to Jack and gave him hell, and Donald and I just sat there laughing. That was the kind of guy he could be.

Campbell, in more serious vein, was back at Coniston again in 1958, but still with K7 rather than a new craft. The old boat boasted further subtle changes to its appearance thanks to smoother cowlings on the sponsons and a smart truncated tail fin intended to house a parachute. This was rarely used, however, since it tended not to open fully in tests up to 150mph. 'All it did was get wet and fail to open properly,' Norris reported. Below the waterline there was another key change that proved much more effective: Villa had added a water fin on the transom that projected four inches below the rear planing shoe. It was intended to cure K7's tendency to oversteer, but also exerted further downE load on the bows and therefore enhanced the safety margin. Behind the scenes, the most important change was significant but undisclosed sponsorship from BP, which was also going to be a key part of the land speed record project.

Once again the attempt took place in November. BP's presence was everywhere, not least in the form of an opulent new boatshed. The Bluebird team had now got its act finely honed, but there were to be a few dramas before it was able to celebrate yet another triumph. On the 10th, Campbell warmed up with runs at 188mph. His first pukka run was at 243.41mph, but as he started his return too much water came over the front spars and drowned the Beryl. When the onboard starter failed to revive the jet he had to summon the starting launch, but that wouldn't start either. After a plug change and further hesitation it finally drew alongside the stricken hydroplane with fewer than ten minutes of the allotted hour remaining. Campbell remained calm, and for once the return run was quicker, at 253.83mph. The new record was 248.62mph, and now he was confident that the boat could eventually push for 275mph. That became his avowed goal for the following season.

Campbell's hairline was receding, but movie footage shows his locks falling over his eyes and giving him a boyish look as he is greeted by Dory Swann. They seemed very happy together as they celebrated his fifth record, yet within days their relationship would be doomed, for he crowned this latest achievement by meeting the woman with whom he would spend the rest of his life. How Donald Campbell met Tonia Bern has become one of those mysteries deepened by the passage of time and the whim of whoever happens to be telling the story. This is how Peter Barker remembered it:

> After we'd beaten the record, Donald said, 'Come on, we'll go back to London now.' So we jumped into his Bentley, and we drove down to London that evening. We went to his flat in Dolphin Square and then he said, 'Come on, we're off to the Embassy Club.' And that is where he met Tonia. She was doing cabaret there.
>
> They clicked almost at once, it was quite extraordinary. She sang two songs there, and there was another act there with a knife thrower, throwing knives at a girl and trans-fixing her with them all round her. The manager asked us if we would say good evening to them and we said of course, so they came over to the table where we were and that is where they met.

In her book *Bluebirds*, Gina Campbell suggested a rather different version in which Tonia was a relatively sophisti-cated stripper. 'What Gina said about how Donald and I met in her book was absolute rubbish,' Tonia riposted, before laughing dismissively. 'My stepdaughter says I was a stripper when we met. Well, I never had that kind of a figure! I'd love to have had, darling, but I didn't. I'm flattered!' A photo-graph of Tonia Bern in a bikini, taken from the front cover of the 1950s magazine *Picturegoer* and used in her own book *My Speed King*, suggests that she sold herself short with that self-deprecating comment. Certainly Gina's account had come from her father's own words, in his early draft of *The Eternal Challenge*:

I met Tonia, my present wife, in the strangest way. I went to a bachelor party at the Embassy Club. Seated in a glass cage on the floor during the cabaret was a beautiful blonde. Men in the audience were supplied with toy guns that they could fire at her. Wherever the bullets hit the glass cage, they stuck by the rubber suction pellets at the end. Wherever they hit, the girl in the cage had to take off the nearest piece of clothing until she sat naked but for a G-string. It was amazing how shaky one's hand became when there were only about two garments left.

The girl came and had a drink at our table afterwards, and we exchanged telephone numbers. The following morning she phoned me at my Dolphin Square flat and asked me to a party that night.

The party was at the Savoy, which struck me as strange, but I arrived pretty late to be greeted at the door by a beautiful, statuesque blonde who bore no resemblance whatever to the girl I had met the night before. She said icily, 'You are more than an hour late.' It was Tonia Bern, and the party was publicity for her opening at the Savoy. I was so late that I missed all the pressmen.

I took her out to dinner to make amends, and two weeks later we were married at Caxton Hall, but a rather quieter affair than my first marriage to Daphne Harvey.

Over to Tonia. 'We met at a press reception at the Savoy,' she countered. 'I was coming from Paris to appear at the Savoy. I was a star at the Savoy, and that can be checked. This was 1958, November. He was in the Savoy. Our group were having a lunch there and Donald met a press guy and they chatted because he'd photographed him on his record attempts, and he'd just broken the water speed record again. And Donald said, "Where are you off to?" and the press guy said, "I'm interviewing Tonia Bern."'

Campbell did attend a Variety Club lunch at the Savoy at that time, to receive his third Butlin Water Speed Record Challenge Trophy and the ever-useful £5,000 cheque that went with it before an audience that included the actor James Stewart, boxer Henry Cooper, golfer Dai Rees, tennis star Christine Truman and newly crowned world champion racing driver Mike Hawthorn. Butlin was that year's Variety Club president, so it made sense to make the presentation part of the luncheon's activities. Again, Campbell made a patriotic and aggressive acceptance speech, jaw thrust out, The Voice modulating his every syllable. 'This year – and thank God – has been a wonderful year for Britain politically,' he boomed in full Churchillian mode, 'ditto economically, ditto industrially. And beyond that it has been a wonderful year for British sport. A world record perhaps has one meaning above all others. If you today achieve a new record then yesterday's unknown becomes today's known. And above all what you are trying to do is shed light on darkness and to further human knowledge. We are going – God willing – to press on.'

According to Tonia, they met as he left. 'I had been front page when I arrived from Paris. You know in those days it was so easy to be front page; all you had to wear was an exciting dress and you were it. And I wore a zebra-crossing dress and it was in all the papers. So the press guy Donald had bumped into told him to come along when he interviewed me, and Donald did. And that was it. But I was actually starring at the Savoy. I've never been a stripper in my life.'

* * *

In the early months of 1959, as he began a new chapter in his personal life with Tonia Bern, Donald Campbell could now see 300mph on the horizon. He had attacked the water barrier, he said, 'because the barrier was there ... all mankind's efforts are like that – a series of barriers that have to be knocked down'. And he kept on breaking his records because each represented, quite simply, 'more barriers'. With CN7 taking shape after all the months of research and development, he had his sights set on two records. For 1960, he finally revealed to reporters, the plan was to hit 300mph in K7 and 400mph in CN7. It was the first time he publicly admitted to the ambition to break the land and water speed records in the same year. Then, he said, he would retire, because at forty he would be 'too old for this sort of thing'.

In the meantime, there was the matter of 275mph to resolve. Yet again the team returned to Coniston, in May 1959. Despite the date, he took Bluebird out on the 13th and quickly worked up to 265mph in test runs. He was delighted with the boat's performance, and remarked, 'She really wants to go.' Peter Barker remembers those far-off days with a mixture of fondness and fear. 'I've stood by Coniston with Tonia many a day, in fear and trepidation. About the only times I've been frightened in my life, I think. You never really knew what was going to happen. They all came off all right, thank goodness . . .'

The following day, Campbell again made the business of record breaking seem easy. He got his 275mph, but only on the first run when he hit 275.15mph. He came back at 245.55mph to his apparent disappointment, having encountered disturbed water, but that was still good for a new record of 260.35mph. It was his sixth. Tonia greeted him as he stepped ashore and several times they kissed, like hungry teens. He told reporters, 'We have learned a great deal about the boat from these runs, and we now have the information that will enable us to take the final step in the story of this boat.'

Before then, however, there was a different horizon to scan, a fresh barrier to breach. Construction of the great new Bluebird CN7 car finally began in October that year, and it would be ready to run in America in 1960 as another dramatic new chapter opened in his life.

It would very nearly be the last.

12

A VERY NAUGHTY BOY

1940 to 1967

*'He came in and I saw his eyes, and that was it. Three hours later we
were in bed together!'*
TONIA BERN CAMPBELL

Donald Campbell always maintained that the experience as
a young boy of walking round the corner of the tennis court
at Headley Grove and finding his father in the throes of
passion with his governess gave him quite the wrong outlook on relations with the opposite sex. Women would
always mean trouble for him. But if Campbell was an in-
corrigible flirt and a dedicated skirt-chaser, he never lost his
basic respect for them.

'Dad and Donald both had charisma,' Jean Wales said.
'Not that they were women mad. But women just threw
themselves at them. Donald was about nineteen when he
had his first girlfriend, Moira Jo, who ended up in an iron
lung and died of polio. Women went for Dad possibly
because he was a famous person, but women chased Donald
anyway, before he made his name. They could both get me

mad, and I'd think, "You rotter!" And then suddenly the charm just oozed and I would melt. I adored Dad. I adored Don.'

David Wynne-Morgan, one of Campbell's various managers, said, 'Donald was a great womanizer, and very attractive to women. That slight little-boy look, combined with the sort of hero image . . . a very difficult man, but an exciting man.'

Campbell's own account of an early coupling at the Kit-Kat Hotel in London's Jermyn Street in 1940 bore all the hallmarks of both his appetite and his innate sense of humour.

The time was two o'clock in the morning. The setting was pretty hellish. Bombs were falling, guns were blasting and the walls were visibly shaking.

The scene in one of the double rooms was almost as dramatic. I was a twenty-year-old aircraftman. Life was for living. There was no point in planning for tomorrow because no-one knew if there was going to be one. Life was for living today, and I was living it.

The girl was beautiful. That night I loved her to a background of noise that was unbelievable. Suddenly there was a deafening crash. I felt a violent blow on the back of my head. The bed collapsed and I rolled on the floor. So this was the end. I thought we had had a direct hit, and faced the inevitable with equanimity. Five minutes later, I realized I had a very sore head, but otherwise I was very much alive. I picked myself gingerly off the floor. The girl was lying beside me, and then I saw what had happened. The double bed had a large wooden bed-head which had broken apart from the bed. As the top half of the bed had collapsed, the bed-head fell and hit me on the back of the head. It was a terrible anti-climax.

Just after the war ended, Lady Dorothy Campbell suggested that her son invite a school friend of Jean's to a birthday celebration. She came from a Jewish family, and her name was Daphne Harvey. 'It was a very gay evening, and I found I had eyes only for her,' Campbell admitted. The following Sunday he drove with Daphne, her mother and her stepfather Andrew Harvey to their opulent home at Locke, in two thousand acres near Partridge Green in Sussex. Harvey owned stables and bred horses. Daphne was an accomplished rider and joint master of the local hunt. She and Campbell soon found themselves head over heels in love, but their parents did not approve. Undeterred, the couple planned to become engaged, and were initially given blessing provided they waited a year. But when they got together just before the Harveys went on holiday to Minehead, Daphne told Donald she had been forbidden to see him again. 'We just sat in the car, parked at the edge of the Serpentine, and for some time not a word was spoken. Quite suddenly our eyes met, and with one accord, and quite simultaneously, we said, "Why don't we?" Daphne was twenty-one and I was twenty-four. We drove straight to Caxton Hall and applied for a special licence.'

The Harveys were leaving from Claridge's the following morning, so the couple drove there to inform them prior to driving to Horsham, where Daphne would spend the night with Jean. But they got a rough reception. Harvey was an imposing man, and an argument soon developed in the hotel foyer.

In a booming voice he told me exactly what sort of character he thought I was. He was a Scot, and his temper was really roused; his adjectives were of a really colourful nature. For a moment it was all I could do to avoid standing at attention, and taking the firmest hand I knew how, I tried hard to remain calm. By this time the place was in uproar; managers, guests, footmen, porters, all looking on as the scene moved towards the front door. As we reached the street we changed corners: Andrew Harvey was remonstrating with his stepdaughter whilst Mrs Harvey was pleading with me. They were tense moments. We were young and not a little headstrong. Whilst we were convinced that the family would never agree to our marriage, we were in love and our minds were made up.

Harvey summoned a policeman and told him that 'this heinous fellow' was trying to steal his little girl. Campbell countered that Harvey was trying to obstruct him, and showed the officer their birth certificates to prove that they were old enough to do as they wished. It was a civil matter, beyond the policeman's remit. But Harvey refused to move as Campbell tried to drive off, and though Campbell subsequently managed to dodge round him, Harvey made a vain grab for one of the car's door handles as they drove down Brook Street.

That evening there were further adventures as Campbell drove to Locke so that Daphne could collect her MG, only to find that Harvey's chauffeur had been ordered to remove its rotor arm. Borrowing one from the family Rover parked alongside, Campbell got the car going in time for them to slip by the distraught man.

The following morning they stood in the chief registrar's room at Caxton Hall. Neither Malcolm nor Dorothy, long divorced, was present. Like Daphne's parents, they disapproved. But Andrew Harvey was there to stage a last-minute attempt to dissuade his stepdaughter. Pressured for a decision by the registrar, Donald and Daphne went ahead, leaving Harvey to depart in an agitated state. 'Although it is always sad to see people upset at a solemn moment, I had to fight hard to suppress my wretched sense of humour,' Campbell wrote, 'for it all seemed so much like a shotgun wedding in reverse.'

They honeymooned in Devon, and returned to the three-bedroomed house he had bought in Kingswood. He settled into a routine as an insurance broker, commuting to the City, then within a year their daughter Georgina arrived. She was to have been born in a private wing of a London hospital, but when the moment came no room was available. Gina eventually made her debut at home, delivered by Dr Binney, the family's physician. Many events in her colourful life would bear the traditional Campbell mark of controversy, but her birth had the therapeutic benefit of effecting a reconciliation between the young Campbells and their respective parents.

Gina and her father had a formal relationship which was obvious even to outsiders. Louis Stanley, a member of the Owen family that built Bluebird CN7 (he was Sir Alfred Owen's brother-in-law), remembered meeting Gina when she was seventeen. 'A very nice girl,' he said. 'She was about to take her driving test. Afterwards she was sent off to bed at ten o'clock. Donald was very strict. She wasn't allowed any lipstick. No make-up. He was really hard on her.'

Still, Andrew Harvey was right to be concerned about the longevity of a marriage between his beloved Daphne and Donald Campbell, but not, it would transpire, for the reasons that might most obviously occur to a doting step-father. More than half a century later, the memory of her former friend was still enough to light Jean Wales' blue touchpaper. 'I didn't see her from the time she and Donald split up until the day she died, and I was happy with that.

She wasn't with Donald very long, but she led him a merry dance.' Jean and her first husband, Brian 'Buddy' Hulme, were living at Bottle Cottage in Reigate at the time. Campbell arrived suddenly with his beloved labradoodle, Maxie. Buddy had discovered Daphne in bed with a local veterinary surgeon, whom Jean described as 'an awful-looking man!' Within the Campbell family Daphne forever after was known as 'The Vet's Pet'.

Campbell would live with the Hulmes for the best part of a year. His divorce came through early in 1952. For a variety of reasons, mainly his desperation for a knighthood, he ignored Daphne's memory altogether. On the way back from the attempt at Coniston in 1949, she'd been travelling in a car driven by Harry Leech. It was involved in a very unpleasant accident as a result of which he was thrown through the windscreen. Campbell covered the incident in great detail in his autobiography *Into the Water Barrier*, published in 1955, but though his narrative was full of concern for Leech's welfare, not once did he make the slightest mention that his first wife had also been injured.

Daphne married twice more but continued to ignore her daughter, only once expressing a wish to have Gina spend time with her. Campbell was opposed to the idea, but agreed to let Gina go after a close friend suggested that refusing her permission might be even more confusing for her. She was curious, because so many other people had told her that her mother was very beautiful, and she herself didn't know. Campbell finally relented, but according to the close friend Gina came back ahead of schedule and said, 'I don't want to see her again, thank you.'

Campbell was a strict but often caring father, but rarely did he make the time Gina might have wanted him to spend with her. And he had serious problems showing her his true feelings. 'As a result of his unreliable love life,' one friend said, 'Gina was pretty insecure at school. I was once asked by Donald to go down and plead with the headmistress that she shouldn't be expelled because she'd played truant. She was always in love with horses, and she'd escaped with hers.'

It did not take long for Campbell's growing friendship with Dorothy McKegg to blossom into romance. 'She was the best of the lot. A lovely person,' Jean said, the fondness still evident in her voice more than forty years later. 'But I don't think Donald really should ever have been married, quite honestly, because of his lifestyle.'

The 1950s was not a time when social mores embraced the idea of people living together in sin. Campbell had already eloped with Daphne Harvey, albeit to make an honest woman of her. Then he embarked on an adventurous and rebellious relationship with Dottie. Flouting social etiquette, they began living together in 1951, long before his divorce had come through. They had fun, and she adored the record attempts, as she recalled:

One day when we were up at Coniston he'd been going like a bat out of hell and told me to get hold of Basil Cardew at the *Daily Express* and tell him that we had unofficially broken the world record. 'Go and ring him, right now! Go, go, go!' I didn't know if we'd really broken the record at that stage, but it was desperately important to Donald. Basil was terribly excited and wrote a good piece, and all of a sudden a bit of money started coming in.

Donald had all that youthful energy. And he was a very good, natural driver. He worried, though, in the days before he was a success. He had an almost naive belief in things, and great respect for women and women's opinions. He'd say, 'Tell me what you think about this. You'll probably come up with something I'd never think of.' He'd talk it over with me. He never excluded me.

During her trip to Ireland in 1950, she'd had an unnerving experience with a gipsy fortune teller.

She told me incredible things. All I wanted to hear was that I would be in the West End within, oh, two years at the most, but no such thing! She said I'd be getting married, and of course I knew that because I was engaged then to someone else. She told me I had met the man I was going to marry, but it wasn't the one I expected. And that it would end very suddenly. I was relating this story once to Donald, and he said to me, 'Ah, yes. Just my bloody luck, Dottie! It'll be me and the boat.' I said, 'Oh no, she didn't mean that!' But he would turn everything round that way. He really thought that he had the world's worst luck.

Aside from The Voice, there was a side to her husband that Dottie always found embarrassing, and that was his talent for self-promotion. 'It wasn't my nature at all,' she said. 'We would have people to dinner at Abbotts and I would be there to do the entertaining and cooking. To make it look more than it was, I would get Mrs B – Mrs Botting, our housekeeper – and one of her daughters to play maid. We would put on a great spread, entertaining everyone from royalty to I don't know what.'

Life was full of excitement, but sometimes Campbell got very depressed – 'blue' as Dottie called it. When they were married he drank little but smoked a lot and liked the odd night out with the boys. Eventually his continual worries over money gave him a duodenal ulcer. 'He had very bad twinges with that. That's why we never had any aluminium

[pans] in the house [for cooking], otherwise he would get ghastly ulcer pains. I think it was just from worry and stress. He used to internalize things so much.'

Dottie had the right stuff to cope. Not all wives would be happy with the idea of their partner building a high-speed boat when previous challengers had died as spectacularly as John Cobb and Mario Verga. Especially when they had been there watching him and his designers conducting their own scientific post-mortem. Some might quietly have entertained the hope that his venture would fail at an early stage so that they could return to normal life. Not Dottie. She understood. 'Absolutely not! That was what he wanted. His job. That was what he loved. Asking him to stop would have been like someone asking me not to go on stage. I was not frightened, ever. He was so thorough! He and Ken and Lew and Leo, they would sit there and go over every angle, everything they could discuss, everything that could possibly go wrong. He would never go out unless everything was absolutely right.'

Some of her fondest memories were from the days when they had no money and rented a cottage in the Lake District. 'I had to cook for the whole crew, with no electricity. Lady Campbell pitched in, give her her due. We took morning tea down to the boys, and lunch.' It was the excitement of seeing the project come alive, of seeing Villa bustling around, and Maurie Parfitt, quiet and unobtrusive, ever the loyal assistant. 'Donald's team adored him. I never heard any team member have any problem with him.' He once discovered that a young man on the fringe had stolen some tools, but rather than expose and banish him Campbell gave him a private dressing-down and let him learn from that.

There was another incident recalled by Dottie, even more poignant in light of Campbell's own fate, which again illustrated his true nature. 'One time at Coniston we were waiting for the weather and there was a huge crowd. Then the news came that a young man had drowned. He'd gone swimming after lunch and got into difficulties. Donald was wonderful. He took over, cancelled everything with the boat and helped to find the body and to look after the parents. He was at his absolute best in those situations.'

Dottie saw firsthand the obstacles her husband had to overcome, and his courage, too. 'The whole time I knew Donald it was one ghastly struggle to get money. I could see it on his face just before he was killed. He was only in his forties, but at the time he looked so old. And lonely. His last marriage had gone to pot, the money had gone. Life was passing him by, and I think he sensed that. He was the bravest man I ever met. And yet at the same time, physical pain was anathema to him. When he got chickenpox, I've never seen anybody cry so much! He blamed it all on Gina.'

There was the mixture of amusement and wrath that was all too familiar, too. 'Donald taught me to drive in his Aston Martin. I drove everything from a Bradford van to the Aston. Every morning in those days it was up with the bonnet and check the oil. And if ever there was a slammed door, dear God, did I get it!' The Aston was the car that Tom Fink remembered, and just like the Australian, Dottie found herself eating at Rules the first time she and Donald Campbell went out in London. 'Then I said I'd never been to a nightclub, so he took me to one. Then we went out to the East End to some sort of pie cart. It was wonderful. There we were, late at night, sipping lovely hot tea. Afterwards he said to me, "I like that, Dottie. You can mix with one and fit in with the other, and that suits me." That was Don, too. He was absolutely brilliant at that, and he wasn't slumming at all. It was absolutely natural. Gina's got the same gift, though she doesn't realize it.'

Dottie was less enamoured of his friendship with the Crazy Gang, which she believed sowed the seeds that blossomed into their divorce. 'They led him astray. Dear God! That's when it started with me, those constant nights out with them. And we went to a Butlin's camp once. Billy Butlin would have these parties. Awful! People stripping off and swimming naked in the pool! Too much booze, too much everything. I said to Donald, "This is not my thing," and he admitted that it wasn't his either, but of course he had to be friendly with Billy.'

Though Campbell respected the opinions of women, the woman in question was not always his wife. Eventually, Dottie had had enough.

Donald was a kid who never grew up. He was still a school-boy in one way. He could never say no to a sexy woman. But not just so he could take her to bed, but so that he could talk to her, have fun with her. Let's go motor racing, let's do something exciting!

I remember trying to leave him once before I finally did it. I don't know where I was going, but I had all my gear piled up. And there was Gina, leaning against the fence into the paddock at Abbotts, crying her little eyes out. I went over and said, 'Now what's all this for?' And she said, 'You're leaving. You're cross with Daddy.' And I said yes, I was cross with him. And she said, 'Please, Mummy, I'll give you all the money in my moneybox if you'll stay.' So I just said, 'Well, I don't want the money in your moneybox. I've been cross, but I'm not cross any more. So you can help me take all my stuff back in.' She just cried, 'Yes, yes!' And we unpacked together.

But before long Campbell's infidelities became too much. 'He would never tell me about other women,' Dottie said. 'I just knew.' Dottie even had an affair of her own, a fact to which Campbell's medium Marjorie Staves had alluded during an interview with me, when she said, 'I remember she came here, looking glamorous, and made a confession to me, about a personal matter . . .' 'I tried that, and it wasn't me,' Dottie admitted. 'I just knew the first time. I hated it. I felt terrible. I felt like a slut.' Campbell wanted her to stay, but his terms were just too much for a wife who craved monogamy. 'He wanted us to live our own lives. It sounds awful, but it's true. He wanted to be as good as his father. He wanted to have a knighthood. He would really have loved one. He told me, "I did the gentlemanly thing and let Daphne divorce me. I cannot survive another divorce." In all my innocence I said I understood that. "You can divorce me, I don't mind. I'm going back to New Zealand." I can still see him sitting at the dining table at Abbotts, saying, "Oh, I'll never marry again." I said, "Yes you will. Women are your big thing in life." And that's how we left it.'

The parting, just before Campbell took Gina to Canandaigua, was amicable, but Dottie discovered more than one sting in the tail. She received no settlement, just her fare home to New Zealand where she prepared to resume her singing career on radio.

I was walking to Broadcasting, and there was a horrible newspaper called *Truth*, our version of the *National Enquirer*. Yuk! It's carved on my memory. This big billboard for *Truth* which said: HOW SPEEDKING FINDS NEW ZEALAND WIFE ERRING. The old-fashioned language! I thought, 'Shit!' I walked on and passed another shop with the same thing, and I thought, 'Dear God, that's me . . ' By the third shop I had enough courage to go in and buy a copy. And it was awful. *Awful.* They'd made up a really good story. As if the divorce was all my fault.

I walked into Broadcasting for my nine o'clock call, and everyone in the Green Room shut up, just like that. And my dear friend, Dottie Toogood, gave me a love [a hug]. Everyone else just shut up. Then the head of drama came over and said, 'I'd like to see you in my office, please.' In I went, and he said, 'I don't know about this rubbish in the paper, but we couldn't care less. I just want you to know that everybody here is behind you a hundred per cent and we are going to work you hard.' And they did. Work in the morning, work in the afternoon, work in the evening. I'll never forget that. I was starting all over again.

That all happened on a Wednesday, and on the Saturday I opened in the Skyline, a cabaret. It was very, very hard. I was immediately given a name. I was a scarlet woman. But I really found my friends. Dottie was my best friend until she died, but a lot of others thought I was only good for one thing, and I got a lot of people thinking that, believe me. I didn't worry so much for myself, but for my family. We lived in a hypocritical society, so that story in the paper was so desperately hard on them. Even now I get people saying in that way, 'Oh yes, you were married to Donald Campbell.' *That* story. And I get the old poker up my backside. 'Excuse me?'

And all because she let Donald Campbell divorce her.

Jean Wales became very fond of her brother's next amour, the young teacher from Wallsend near Newcastle called Doreen Swann. 'She was very nice, and they were very fond of each other. I think she ended up with an American. She was very good to Don. She was attractive. They were quite well suited.'

'I thought of using the name Daurene, then Dory Gil-Swann, before I finally settled on Dory Swann,' Dory admitted. Like Dottie, she didn't find Campbell necessarily handsome: 'his father was frightfully good-looking, Donald wasn't'. What really attracted her were his personality and charisma. She moved down to London to share a house with a friend once she had finished at teachers' training college in the north-east. She was teaching when they met, but gave up her career to be with him, though they still lived their separate lives. 'He had a large flat in Dolphin Square, I had a small one,' she explained. 'At some points he was in America, and I was in Britain.'

They liked to play games with newspaper reporters, who usually described her as an ash-blonde model who acted as his secretary. 'That was all the press, the ash-blonde secretary thing,' she said dismissively, but they were amused by it. They used to enjoy saying nothing and letting the press speculate. It became the all-purpose Dory Swann description. When we met, she snorted with self-deprecating derision at the headlines: DASHING DORY DARING DONALD'S DOG HANDLER, or BLONDE WHO SMOOTHS WAY FOR SPEEDKING. Whenever reporters asked her what her role was, she would simply reply, 'I look after Mr Campbell's dog.' And there was no question that she, like Campbell, adored Maxie the labradoodle. When the reporter in turn would ask Campbell what Dory Swann did, he too would respond, deadpan, 'She looks after my dog.' One newspaper article mentioned that her hair might be pink one day, lavender the next. But during our interview, Dory snorted again. 'Baloney. I went to a hairdresser in London for a shampoo and cut and the owner came over and asked would I consider going blonde? He did it for nothing, like an experiment.'

So if the newspapers of the day got so much wrong, what

was the truth of their friendship? 'We were lovers, of course,' she explained brusquely when we finally met up in New York in April 2002. Then, touchingly, a hard-bitten woman approaching her seventies, sitting in a sleazy bar sipping vodka and smoking heavily, became the twentysomething young girl she had been during one of the most exciting times of her life. 'I was young,' she said. 'He was very important. I was impressed with myself. And I worshipped him. He was very good to me. He didn't act like a celebrity whatsoever. Caring, loving, kind, gentle, considerate.' Momentarily she had gone far, far away.

She went to Coniston in 1957 and 1958. 'Of course, it was exciting,' she said, 'but you worried in case anything went wrong. I admired his courage. And I always felt he was trying to do what his father had done.'

It was either on the evening of his 1958 record or very shortly afterwards (depending on whose version of events you believe) that Donald Campbell met Tonia Bern and his relationship with Dory Swann approached its conclusion. But just to complicate matters, Dory had a different version of what happened. She says that she wasn't at Coniston in 1958 (although film shows her there). 'Apparently, Tonia and a few friends were up there, and he met her . . . that's what Don told me. I wasn't there when he met her. Our relationship was reaching its end by then in any case. I guess things had drifted apart. He told me that he had met her at Coniston, and that was it.'

She left England bound for San Francisco in 1961, but was persuaded by a friend to stop over in Manhattan. 'I never did make it to San Francisco,' she concluded with a smile. 'I discovered New York and fell in love with the place.' Later, she had a long relationship with a prominent dietician who bought her the loft in Soho which she admitted she hated back in 1978 when it was a printing and manufacturing area. Now it is a very trendy residential part of Manhattan.

On the other side of the United States, Oak Tree Cottage nestles into the woods up by Big Bear Lake, a two-hour drive from Los Angeles that spends its final fifty miles weaving and winding up through the wooded mountains like a rollercoaster. It could have been the setting for Raymond Chandler's novel *The Lady in the Lake*. This is one of Tonia Bern Campbell's American homes. We sat there talking after she had finally agreed to an interview in 1992, with Crumpet the dog leaping around. 'I called her Crumpet after the way Donald always used to be looking at it!' she said.

With the tang of wood smoke in our nostrils, Tonia was remarkably open after her initial reluctance, as if her barriers had been some sort of test you had to pass. She held nothing back, even when the questions got very personal, and volunteered much. I was reminded of Gina's remark. 'She was a striking woman, she still is, and she exuded sex. She is extraordinary. Much nicer than she gives away.' She was good company, jumping up and down like Crumpet every so often to answer the phone, chatting to her agent, delighted that her part in an American soap called *Santa Barbara* was going down well.

On one wall there was the portrait of Donald by Vasco Lazzolo from Douglas Young-James's book. 'I love that,' she said. 'It is so dignified. I've always had it in my home, regardless of boyfriends. If they don't like it they can lump it. They have to accept the fact that I'm Donald's Tonia. Some do, some don't. There are a lot of things that I would never part with, that are very special. I'd go and sweep the streets before I'd part with them.' There was also a studio shot of Campbell, a silver salver, and a Donald and Tonia candlestick on the table, the latter a gift from Adams Transport. Lower down on a shelf was a wonderfully uninhibited photo of them embracing after the successful 1964 assault on the water speed record, looking young and attractive, happy and successful. I thought it poignant that this was the photo she appeared to have treasured most.

The years had been kind to her. She retained her vitality – vibrant is one word that immediately leaps to mind when you meet her. An elfin figure, dressed then in slacks, loose-fitting overshirt and pointed green pixie boots whose toes curled up. From being so aloof on the phone, she had become a different person, engagingly garrulous. It wasn't hard to believe she made her living on stage.

Tonia Bern Campbell *was* an actress, but she was no diva. She wasn't afraid to tell stories against herself. When the singer Larrae Desmond did a show for the team out at Lake Eyre in 1963, team member Carl Noble remarked afterwards how pleased he was to have seen a real woman in the outback. 'I said, "What about me, Carl?" And he just said, "Oh you, you're just Fred!"' 'Fred' was the nickname Noble had given Tonia, who by that time had come to be accepted as just another of the lads on the Bluebird team.

She was happy, working, reading scripts, still plugging away at her own book. At that time it was still entitled *Bluebirds & Windmills*, as it had been since she had started work on it back in 1968. In 2002, it finally emerged as *My Speed King*. 'I have this cottage here which I had built,' she said with an air of satisfaction, 'and I have a lovely home in the Hollywood Hills. No mortgages. They're both paid for and I'm proud that I've done it all on my own.' She was careful about publicity regarding Campbell; though she was proud of him and was no shrinking violet, she wanted to be recognized in her own right. The novelty of being Mrs

Donald Campbell appeared to have worn off a long time ago, yet paradoxically she threw herself wholeheartedly into promoting *My Speed King*.

Outside the cottage sat a white Nissan 240ZX, licence plate LA BERN. She had just sweet-talked a judge into letting her off a speeding charge. The citation said 95mph . . .

The controversy over how Campbell and Bern met was not the first time that Gina and Tonia had crossed swords, and until 2001, when Donald's funeral provided some sort of watershed, theirs was an uneasy relationship. Both are independent, feisty women. 'Donald always said Gina took after her mother,' Tonia said, 'and I was always frightened of this because I wanted harmony in her life. I did love her, and I had no children. But whenever there was trouble, she was just like her mother. She did things afterwards . . . but I don't hate her. I will always have a part of me that will love her. I wish her the very best. When I read her book, I was on a plane. And I was very hurt. I was this blonde in a cage, and every time they shoved money through I took off my garments. I mean, that is so undignified. God forbid . . . I had a photograph taken [in a skimpy bikini, for the magazine *Picturegoer*] but that was about as naked as I ever was.' That and the time she was presented to Lord Mountbatten at a Royal Yacht Club dinner wearing a diaphanous black dress she had bought in Paris. 'The night before I met Donald he had been to the Embassy Club, and there had been a story like that, about a girl called Tuesday Next. She was a very strange girl, went into a convent later. And he told that story very often, because as I say, he liked boasting about me. They took that story and made up the one in the cage.'

One of the first things Tonia said when the subject of this book was raised was, 'You'd better have a good lawyer, because Donald was a very naughty boy! He liked the girls. He was a very healthy man! And he loved sex.' Campbell's close friend David Benson agreed. 'I'm not surprised Tonia said that. He was a rounded man. Of course he liked women.' Tonia never forgot that moment *she* says they met at the Savoy. 'Donald had come with the pressman, and he came in and I saw his eyes, and that was it.' She broke off with a laugh. 'Three hours later we were in bed together! A few weeks later we were married! My mum said they'd never respect me if I was easy!' Tonia also recalled that after first meeting Campbell, he whisked her off to Rules, his favourite restaurant for such matters, and ordered her steak and kidney pie, which she hated.

Tonia replaced Dory Swann in Campbell's affections, but it was not long before she realized that he wanted what might be termed today an open marriage. After the initial infatuation, she wrote that she was incensed to learn of Dory's existence when a newspaper article was illustrated with a photograph of Campbell and Dory on a visit to Austria. (Dory insisted that was incorrect: 'It isn't true. It never happened.') But Tonia admitted that she knew Donald had other women. Once, in 1966, they stopped at a pub in Manchester on the way back from Coniston, and while being served their drinks she noticed the publican say something jokey to Campbell and nod in her direction. 'Donald told me, "He made a joke that you were better than the usual standard I brought here."'

'Donald was the kind of guy who probably had a girlfriend in every port,' believed Craig Douglas, a well-known singer in the 1950s and a close friend of the Campbells. 'Wherever he went he had a friend he would call up. He loved to go to nightclubs and so forth, but he wasn't really into the call-girl thing at all. And he always treated these "friends" with respect. He was very good in that way.' But though he loved women and treated them with respect, Campbell had difficulty expressing himself, either to his lovers or to his daughter. It was not just in his courage and addiction to speed that he so closely resembled his father. In many ways he was more comfortable with men, where he didn't have to venture into such ticklish territory. 'We'd go to places and he'd seem to know a lady there and I wasn't quite sure why,' Ken Norris remembered. 'I'd be in one room and he'd be in another, and I was never sure what the hell he was up to. I remember once Leo showed me some slides of all of Donald's girlfriends. There were quite a few. We set off early one morning to go up to Coventry, and he said to me, "You know, Ken, I think the company of men is much better than women, don't you?" Right out of the blue. I think he'd just had an argument with Tonia!'

'Donald wasn't the type to cry,' Tonia asserted, 'but his eyes would well up with tears. He kept his emotions like that to himself, but every now and then he'd open up in strange places, usually in public. One time we were at a party with the Duke of Argyll who said something very complimentary about me to Donald. Later, Donald stared across the room at me, and when he caught my eye he mouthed "I love you". He told me once that if I knew how much he loved me, I'd walk all over him. He was right! But he was rarely demonstrative.'

In his book *The Record Breakers*, Leo Villa remembered how he was recuperating from trouble with his right eye when Donald called on him and Joan, accompanied by Tonia. 'I could see that she was something special,' he wrote, 'and I wasn't altogether surprised when he invited Joan and me to be present at their wedding on 24 December 1958.' When Campbell had proposed to Tonia, she told him she'd make a rotten wife. He told her he'd tried two supposedly good ones, and wanted to give a rotten one a go, and certainly the first year of their marriage was very tough on both of them. They fought, but somehow they survived. Perhaps *because* they fought. Campbell quickly got bored with acquiescent people, and it was only when Tonia began to give as good as she got and deliberately set out to develop her own life and make her own friends that their relationship really began to gel. It didn't help that early on in the marriage she didn't get on with Campbell's secretary, an older woman called Joan Maskell. Subsequently she enjoyed a warmer relationship with her successor, Rosemary Pielow.

In public they made a dramatic, good-looking couple. Louis Stanley will never forget the first time he met Tonia. 'Donald and I were having drinks at the Dorchester, and as she came over I said to him, "Who on earth is *that*?" And he said very cheerfully, "That's my wife!" Very embarrassing! She was good company. A nice girl. And she wasn't blameless. She wasn't blameless.' Bill Coley knew most of the women in Campbell's life, apart from Daphne. 'Dorothy was a pretty uncomplicated person,' he said. 'And I liked Dory. She was a very nice woman. But perhaps Tonia was the best for Donald. She understood him, from a woman's point of view. I think they were very honest together. I first met her at the Fairmile at Cobham. Donald turned up there with her, and I was having lunch with my family. I think she was pretty good for him at that time.'

But there was one area in which their marriage did not gel. In an earlier relationship of Tonia's with a man called Michael Aptaker, a child had been stillborn. When Tonia fell pregnant by Campbell, she was unable to carry to full term. After her miscarriage while they were at Dumbleyung in December 1964, they both believed they had lost the son he so desperately craved. Despite this, his relationship with Tonia was perhaps the least complicated Donald Campbell ever enjoyed long-term with a woman, his daughter Gina included. On that sad occasion he bought her a small dog called Bobs, and told her she was his one true mascot.

13

A SUPERSTITIOUS AND
MYSTICAL FELLOW

1921 to 1967

'I think he liked to come and talk to me as a form of escape. Perhaps nobody else would listen to him.'

MARJORIE STAVES, MEDIUM

Dorothy McKegg was far more of a mother to Gina than Daphne Campbell ever was, and was perfectly placed to assess the relationship between father and daughter. 'Gina's relationship with Donald was like Donald's with his father,' she observed. 'Donald was very hard with her, though I think she might exaggerate at times, or else Donald got a lot harder after I left. He was firm, but I was used to that from having a firm and loving father myself. But had he done some of the things that Gina subsequently claimed he did, I truly would not have stood for it.'

Before their marriage, Dottie had not even been aware that Campbell had a daughter. 'He never talked of her. Then one day he finally mentioned Georgina. I asked who she was and where she was – was she with Daphne? "Oh no," he said, "she's at High Trees." It was a boarding school, a few hundred yards from Abbotts. I asked how old she was and why she was there. He had been working at Kine Engineering in Crawley and was using his yacht to demonstrate the equipment to the Portuguese government. Daphne wanted to go too, so they put Gina in the school. When the marriage broke up, Gina was left where she was.'

'That's where my mother and father put me, for the best part of three years,' Gina said. 'But it gave me tremendous loyalty. I consider to this day I can be the best friend anyone could ever have because I can be totally loyal. That comes from High Trees.

'People are horrified when I tell them about all that. But it's like battery hens. The last thing a hen will do if it's unhappy is lay an egg, but battery hens pop eggs out all day, every day, because they're content. They don't know there's a life out there in a green field, clucking away, with a fox about to snap their neck.' It took Dottie to show Gina the green field. 'I asked Gina once to give me a cuddle, and she said, "What's that?" I explained it to her but it wasn't so good the first time we tried. So we left it. But one day we were outside Buckingham Palace and she suddenly hugged my legs, wouldn't let go, and just said in this tight little voice, "I love you, Mummy!"'

Gina never came to terms with why her biological mother, Daphne, rejected her.

My mother bought a stud farm five miles from us with her second husband, Tony Turner. Dad gave me a rather scruffy little pony for my eleventh birthday. I loved it to bits, but it was nothing fantastic. Then suddenly my mother bought me this big horse, a thoroughbred pony, shining, sleek. It was going from a Thelwell pony to a Derby winner. 'He's here for you, dear, whenever you want,' she said to me. 'There are grooms; you don't have to fight your father to get new shoes for him.' And this caused problems. There was my little scruffy pony – I had to go and clean my father's car to get a quid so I could get it horseshoes – and now she had put this enormous birthday cake in front of me.

My father was rather clever. He told me to hold the extension line and then he rang my mother. He said, 'Daphne, Donald here. I'm going to the States for ten days. Seeing as Gina has got a new pony with you, why don't you have her?' Well, she backtracked so fast. And Father looked at me and said, 'There you are.'

God rest her soul, she died suddenly in 2000. I had begged her to talk to me about why she didn't want me. The circumstances that led her to that position. Because it's not natural for a mother not to want her child. I just wanted to try and understand. I was fifty years old and I didn't think it was much to ask for. But even then she couldn't tell me the truth, and say, 'I'm so sorry. I did something wrong, I made a mistake.' She just would never speak to me about it. You can't say that you don't like a child when it's only a year old, because that child is barely beginning to form a personality. She'd got a new man who probably didn't want any baggage. She was as unfaithful as my father was. As Tonia was. As I've been. But I did try very, very hard to love my mother.

As for her father, she thought him a mellower version of his father.

There were elements of Dad that were part of his father, his upbringing. Life was not normal for any of the Campbell kids. We were picked up and put down. The picking up was

216

wonderful, and the putting down was very painful. But each putting down made the next picking up even better. My life is a series of plus columns and minuses, but the bottom line is so heavily weighted with pluses that the minuses are, to me, seriously character-building. I'm conceited enough to look in the mirror and to like myself, because I have one thing in my personality: truthfulness. It was beaten into me as a child by my father: 'Have the courage of your convictions, woman, otherwise you are a dead loss.'

When I was a teenager at college I had flu and was really sick, in bed. On the Saturday night it was my friend Cherry's birthday party. I said I must go, she's my best friend. Dad said, 'You can't bloody go, you've been in bed all week and you've missed your studies. I forbid you. If you go, your schooling will finish now, young lady.'

I went, and my studies did finish, there and then. He called my bluff, and I went out to work. I think that secretly he really admired me, but it was never discussed again.

Gina was just out of her teens when Campbell died. In all their years together they had never sat down and talked together. 'I used to semi-avoid him,' she said. 'He was a moody man, and for sure I was going to get told off for something. I used to try and sneak away. I had to go down and say goodnight. He used to be livid if I didn't. But I used to be nervous. If you wanted to go into his office, you had to knock. It was always a relief if he called me "Old Lady". The best I would get from him was a kiss on my forehead.' When she was a child being fractious about eating, he would threaten to give her food to the dog and the dog's to her. Once, when she wet herself after he smacked her bottom, he simply said, 'Go to the toilet.'

But the acid test is whether Gina Campbell loved and

217

revered her father, which clearly she did. Just as he had loved and revered Sir Malcolm Campbell.

But it's a fine balance. I was terrified of Dad because I respected him. As a child I was always doing things. Throwing sticks in the pond for the dog, because it pleased me to see the dog swim. I knew I was going to get a damn good spanking for it, but which did I prefer? It gave me so much pleasure to see the dog jump in the pond that I was prepared to accept that I was probably going to get a spanking for it.

I wouldn't say that I was an unwanted child, but I was a total bloody inconvenience, and I was made to feel that. Certainly record breaking came first and everything else came after that.

I was fiercely competitive and did well in local gymkhanas. Father and Tonia would embarrass me. He was flamboyant. Turned up in a Bentley, with picnic hamper and champagne, and all the other kids had mouldy sandwiches and a flask of tea. He did things in style, even if he might not have been able to afford it. Tonia told me he said to her on the way home, 'She was bloody marvellous on that horse. Bloody marvellous. Fantastic! That's my girl!' And Tonia said to him, 'You should tell her, Donald. You should tell her how proud you are of her.' 'No, no, no,' he said. 'I can't possibly do that. Us Campbells aren't too good at giving praise.' And that's something I do resent him for. He was very quick to tell me I was a bloody fool and I was useless, but he never put the balance back the other way, to tell me about it when I did something well.

It was precisely the way Malcolm Campbell had been with him ('You're a bloody fool, boy. You'll never amount to anything!'). The wheel turned full circle. Donald Campbell didn't want to beat his father, but he wanted to prove to himself that he was worthy of his respect. For Gina, it was just the same. 'But I'm still left with this feeling that I've never really proved myself.'

This was untrue, though Gina Campbell didn't realize it. She did prove herself, in different ways, notably with her safety lectures for the New Zealand Water Council, but the thing that mattered to her was record breaking. She, too, had a successful career racing AGFA Bluebird powerboats. In October 1984 she survived flipping a catamaran at Holme Pierrepont shortly after setting an unofficial women's water speed record of 122.86mph. On 1 April 1990 she set a new women's mark of 146.49mph on Lake Karapiro in New Zealand, driving a Lauterbach three-point hydroplane powered by a big-block Chevrolet V8 engine and sponsored, appositely, by Bluebird Foods. It was not the sort of boat you climb into by mistake.

Gina was still just a young girl when her surrogate mother departed the scene. In April 1958, Dottie married a Swiss accountant called Hans Wenk. They had three children, Max, Lisa and David. But Dottie never forgot Gina. In the mid-1980s Dottie and Hans travelled to Europe. 'I told him that I wanted to look for Gina. He said that if that's what I felt, I really should do that. I hadn't heard a word from her.' Dottie never got to the bottom of it, but she believed that because the split with Donald had been so traumatic her parents, with whom she lived for a few years, had inter-cepted mail from both Gina and Jean. Both wrote to her, but she never received their letters. 'For years I didn't think or talk about the whole Campbell thing,' Dottie continued. 'The fifties was a bad period, all the hypocrisy. And I've always been an incredibly private person. But then I did see

Gina again. And Hans was so good about it, such a good man. My family always knew all about Gina because she was like my first child. My kids always knew that they had got a big half-sister over in England.'

The story of their reunion is poignant. 'I'd written to anyone I could think of, trying to find Gina, and finally through Buddy Hulme I got contact numbers. I rang her. "Gina," I said, "I don't know if you will remember me. It's Dorothy . . ." I was about to go on and say I used to be married to your father when she let out a great scream. "Dottie! Where are you? Don't move! I'm coming up." And she was there, within the hour. I opened the door and there was this little girl's face that I so remembered, on a young woman's body. And we cried, and then we talked and talked.'

Besides his wives and daughter, Campbell also had a complicated relationship with his mother, Lady Dorothy. 'Dorothy was a very difficult woman,' Bill Coley said enigmatically. 'She took Donald for a ride, you know. But they were very thick too, in the friendly sense, and she could be really charming.'

Dolly Campbell always had a firm idea of her position in society. She preferred Mayfair to the country, and there is a telling little vignette in a 1950s out-take from Pathé News. Campbell has just done his piece to camera, looking smooth and suave in a camelhair coat and as debonair as television heart-throb actor Roger Moore, with whom he shared the ability to raise one sardonic eyebrow. Then it is Dolly's turn to be interviewed by the terribly well-spoken girl with the cut-glass BBC accent. She begins, 'Mrs Campbell . . .' Dolly mutters something, but the frame is completed. Moments later, the scene is shot again, but this time the girl begins, 'Lady Campbell . . .'

Mother and son were wary of each other, despite her oft-espoused belief that he was a better man than his father had been. One of Campbell's close friends confirmed that they were 'a little uncertain of each other. I don't think there was a deep understanding of what the other was really like.' Gina firmly believed that Dorothy was instrumental in Campbell's marriage to Dottie breaking up, and in Dottie finding that many of her possessions had gone missing when a trunk finally arrived for her in New Zealand after her divorce.

In later life, Dolly became susceptible to attempts to befriend her. On one occasion Campbell believed that a couple had invited her to stay at their home for an ulterior motive. It was not unusual for her to turn up on doorsteps seeking shelter, but this time he had got it into his head that they were intent on getting her to sign a new will in their favour. With a couple of friends he made a dash to the countryside to 'rescue' Dolly in the early hours of the morning.

'Lady Campbell would just home in on someone and stay with them,' Ken Norris confirmed. 'She was lonely, I guess. My sister knew Jean through her relationship with chauffeur Reg Whiteman. His wife Ivy had died of cancer and he eventually married my sister. Dorothy would gravitate towards Jean's place. She landed on us once. She must have lost another big anchor when Donald was killed. She turned into a recluse.' After her son's death, Dolly stayed for some time with Norman Buckley and his wife Betty at Windermere. She cut a tragic figure. 'I went back to Coniston a few times, and often saw her,' Peter Barker recalled. 'She stayed up there for years afterwards. She always had the feeling that Donald would emerge one day from the water. They were a mystical family . . .'

Mystical indeed, for there was one other very important woman in Donald Campbell's tangled life. Her name was Marjorie Staves. Besides being a medium of some renown, she was his Mother Confessor.

Campbell had little time for conventional religion. He was raised as a Christian, but Jean remembered her brother as a little devil when they went to church every Sunday with their governess. 'He used to put buttons in the collection box, and keep the sixpence,' she recalled. 'Once, he put a banana skin down the aisle. We used to hate church. None of us was religious. I think if you can look at yourself at the end of the day and say, "I haven't really done anything I shouldn't have done, or upset anybody," then that's better than just going to church. Donald thought the same thing.' Spiritualism became the substitute. 'On that boat trip that he made to Portugal [in 1948] there was a guy who spoke in tongues, went into trances,' Dottie said. 'I think that was where Donald's interest started. He was very swayed by things like that.' As was Jean. 'We were both very interested,' she confirmed. 'We went to several séances together.'

Campbell frequently wrote about his belief in and experiences of the paranormal in revealing features in Sunday newspapers. Having developed an unshakeable conviction that his dead father was watching over him, on several occasions he claimed that he had saved him from seemingly inevitable accidents. Early on with Bluebird K4 he decelerated too quickly after becoming mesmerized by a sliver of oil smoke and was suddenly showered in hot lubricant. He claimed that some supernatural force – his father's spirit – took control of the boat until he recovered. A year later he claimed that a friend's motor cruiser refused to react to his steering inputs and was headed for a pier at Coniston until miraculously the throttle opened wide and the boat finally responded just as a crash seemed inevitable. Five years after that, coming into shore after a run in Bluebird K7 on Ullswater, he narrowly escaped running into rocks. Water getting into the pitot head had made the speedometer under-read. Again, he put his deliverance down not to his own wit in zigzagging the boat to scrub off speed, but to the intervention of his father.

He had first sceptically discussed spiritualism with milkman Peter White, who had convinced him to maintain an open mind. He liked to tell the story of how he once heard White, a man of no great education, speak fluent French during a trance. Lady Campbell also became a convert. Several times during 1956 Campbell tried to contact his father. He and Dolly took to visiting mediums, usually letting none of them know their true identities or their wish to contact Sir Malcolm. First they visited Tom Redwood, then Elsie Hardwick, Bess Hewitson and Harold Sharp, and then White. Hewitson told Campbell that his father had been very angry when he died but was pleased to see his son taking up his work. Campbell was particularly impressed with one Jean Thompson, who spoke of speed and water and a father figure without knowing his identity. This all made good newspaper copy, but there was no doubt that Campbell was a devout believer and was not merely making up newsworthy stories. He concluded one series of investigations for the *Sunday Pictorial* (now the *Sunday Mirror*) with the comment: 'If you are born with a curiosity to probe the unknown, then you must do it.'

He was introduced to Staves by Fred Archer, the editor of *Psychic News*. One of her principal claims to fame was that she had told Richard Nixon he would be the next President of the United States. She had also foreseen the death of a woman called Dolly Goodman, a close friend of the novelist

Nancy Spain who perished with her in a plane crash at Aintree racecourse near Liverpool. Staves found Campbell very nervous when he consulted her in the early days of the K7 project.

He was a little shy because he'd never talked to a clairvoyant before. He rang me one day and said could he bring his mechanic. They were surprised at what I was picking up, and that helped them to build it more securely. I had to describe to them what I felt. I told this guy who came with him, Leo Villa, 'I'm not happy enough to let you walk out of here, and me say it's OK.'

Donald went up to the Lake District and phoned me, about the trials. He came in frequently, just for that huge joy of knowing he was doing the right thing. But at the same time I said, 'I have to be quite frank with you, Donald. That's what I'm here for. I'm not happy at the result. There's something about it that doesn't give me the joy of saying this is it.' And again they went into doing all sorts of things with the engine or whatever. So consequently there were more trials. I remember him phoning one Sunday and racing over to see me, because things were so bad.

Staves had a quirky manner of speaking that sometimes made her conversation tricky to follow, and she cheerfully admitted that she knew nothing of technology. But Campbell certainly drew something from his visits. 'It was with me that he was able to let his hair down. To tell me various things. He came so often, to tell me matters that he couldn't talk about to anybody else. He wanted to outdo his father, and he was in the neighbourhood of wanting to prove his worth. But at the same time he was very nervous and very shy. What it was really, I think, he didn't have that support that he wanted. Some people put him in Promise Street, but never came over.' Staves detected unhappiness behind the superficial glamour of Campbell's image as a world-famous record breaker. 'Let me say this. Besides all the aggro with the boat, he was not very happy in his personal life. Not that he confessed a lot to me, but he wasn't as free as he'd have liked to have been. That may have been in an impersonal way, it may have been money, or whatever. I don't know. There was always a big confusion with money.' In fact, Staves' role with Campbell was less that of a medium and more that of a psychotherapist. 'I got to know him so well that I didn't have to impress him. He was along with me. I suppose, really, he developed a psychic attraction in his own way. I think he liked to come and talk to me as a form of escape. Perhaps nobody else would listen to him. The whole emphasis was a genuine need to be successful and to prove a point, and he did all he could do towards that. He allowed his father's image to be the image he wanted it to be.'

Tonia recounted tales of how Campbell refused to leave her alone after his death. She said that his spirit would appear to her, indicating his disapproval if he didn't like her latest suitor. Once he appeared before her as she lay in bed worrying about a lost manuscript that she wanted to refer to for her book. He indicated an attaché case, but after a search of it had proved fruitless he reappeared, pointing out that he had not meant his own initials – DMC – but MDC, his father's. In Sir Malcolm's case she claimed that she found what she was looking for. Another night she lay worrying about money when Campbell appeared to show her where £250 lay in a sealed airmail envelope. In a trunk full of his old clothes, she found it with her name written on the front.

Campbell was also famously superstitious. 'The number

thirteen is, of course, another unlucky thing for me,' he admitted. 'Many times things have gone wrong and I have found the date was the thirteenth. And I am superstitious about Friday – it is a day I find unlucky.' He would never run on a Friday if he could possibly help it, though he did, and was successful, on several occasions. He also detested the colour green. 'I really don't know why, because Dad was never superstitious of it,' Jean Wales reflected. 'I had a green MG once, and he said, "What the hell did you get that for?" But Dad was superstitious. He wouldn't have thirteen at dinner one Christmas. We had to split up the table.'

Grahame Ferrett, one of Campbell's managers in 1964, had little time for such things.

You'd go to a restaurant and the knives and forks were crossed, and he'd cancel them all out. And he was so anti-green. I have an Australian cricket cap that belonged to the great cricketer Wally Grout, and in 1964 I decided we'd hold a cricket match on the salt [on Lake Eyre]. Australia playing the Poms, naturally. I got the green cap, and I made him wear it. Amazingly, he wore it, and it was never mentioned at all. He never referred to that cricket cap or the Australian colours.

According to him, the Lake Bonney water record attempt failed because we arrived on a Friday. But he got the record on a Friday at Lake Eyre and then again at Dumbleyung, so that blew that away! But he used to admit to being super-stitious in the extreme, and we used to joke about it. He could laugh at himself. He wasn't uptight about it.

'Being in the forces, of course, I was in green uniform,' said Corporal Paul Evans, who handled radio communi-cations for Campbell on the final attempt at Coniston. 'I had

226

a blue pullover. Every time I went into the boathouse I used to have to wear that. Sometimes I would forget and Louis Goosens [Donald's butler] would look up and cough, then nod at my uniform. I'd have to go out and put my pullover on. Green was definitely a no-no. Which is funny, because though Donald didn't know it, the radio set in Bluebird was green! When it was installed, Leo made the comment, "Wait until the Old Man sees that!" There was some hasty manoeuvring going on at seven o'clock one night making up this box for it, and painting the box blue.'

Campbell also hated being wished good luck prior to an attempt, ever since boatman Goffey Thwaites had said those words to him before he and Villa set off on the fateful run at Coniston in 1951. He had a Polynesian doll called Tiki that he stroked for luck, and of course there was the fearless teddy bear Mr Whoppit, the magic talisman. Whoppit was a gift from the tolerant Peter Barker. 'His father was always having an "influence" over him,' Barker said. 'Whoppit was mine. I used to be on the edge of the toy trade when I was at Hulton's, because we used to do what was called licensed merchandise for children's comics. Whoppit was a sample from a firm called Merrythought. I had it for a long time on my desk, and in 1956, I think, I said, "Don, you ought to have a mascot. I think this one is very appropriate." And he said, "Oh, fine, fine." After that Whoppit was always there.'

Despite his idiosyncrasies, Campbell collected friends easily. Always a generous host, he set his guests at ease with extraordinary charm and grace. Craig Douglas remembered fondly the parties Campbell threw that made Roundwood famous.

He was the greatest guy I've ever known. When you'd go down there for dinner, ten or so of us, he was always very generous with the drinks. Always had the greatest firework display. He used to set them all up, and it was always wonderful. And dear old Louis, his butler, and Louis's missus, they were a lovely couple.

He'd get the latest film. 'Look, old boy, shall we go and watch it?' And we'd all go into his study and he'd have this button behind the desk, the screen came down, all very impressive. He was fanatical about gadgets. He also loved cartoons. Occasionally he'd say, 'I've got this wonderful cartoon!' and then he'd stick something on like a blue film, and after two minutes or so he'd say, 'God, sorry, old boy!' and put the cartoon on. A lovely sense of humour.

But he was restless. It was never long before he started to get fidgety.

You'd be down there, say, for the weekend, and maybe the girls, Tonia and my girlfriend, had gone off shopping in Reigate. And he'd pick something up and say, 'I don't know how the hell this works, old boy. It's going wrong and I've got to sort it out.' And whatever it was, he'd sit there for hours until he fixed whatever the problem was. And then all of a sudden he'd say, 'Come on, old boy!' And we'd get all his guns out, and go onto this range that he had out the back. He was just like a child, a Boy Scout. And he might ask Louis to bring some coffee out, and Louis would look at me as much as to say, 'Oh, God, here we go.' We'd be out there only half an hour, and then Louis would have to pick all the guns up, clean them all and then put them away, just for Donald's brief amusement. Then on the way back into the house he might get on the lawnmower, start it up, and as he was going across the lawn the gardener would come and stand in front of it and growl, 'Get off of that!' And Donald would say, 'Oh, sorry, Harry.' So then it was sort of, 'Oh, what else can we do?' He was a restless kid. Very, very restless.

One of the few memories Don Wales has of his uncle dates from when he was six years old and also illustrates Campbell's impish restlessness. 'Donald waved me over as he set light to this pile of rubbish, and there was this great big bang. It turned out he'd put gunpowder on the heap. He roared with laughter, and beamed at me. "Fantastic!" he said, before striding away.'

Campbell once invited Douglas to bring his mother and father to Roundwood. As they swept up the drive, his father's attention was attracted by the petrol pump.

'By God,' my dad said, 'that can't be bad, can it? His own pump?' Donald was absolutely smashing to them. Absolutely super. When we left, he came out onto the driveway to say goodbye, but suddenly disappeared. No sign of him. He just said, 'Won't be a minute, darling!' to Tonia. And we looked around for him, Mother included, and suddenly there he is up against a tree, having a piss.

My father went back to work on the Monday. I remember him saying how his friends had been asking him all about coming up to see me in London. 'Yeah, and we met Donald Campbell.' 'What, the speed ace? You didn't . . .' 'Yeah, nice guy, Donald . . .' And it was a lovely thing. He treated them superbly. He would treat everybody absolutely the same. He was very good like that.

14

THE GREAT CONFRONTATION

August to September 1960

*'It was quite a show. Donald Campbell went up the far end of the salt
along with his trucks, fire trucks, and I don't know how many Rovers
he had. He went up one end and down the other end. It looked just
like the Indy parade.'*

AMERICAN OBSERVER, BONNEVILLE SALT FLATS, SEPTEMBER 1960

By 1960, John Cobb's 394.196mph benchmark had stood for
thirteen years. Two American challengers had reached
speeds close to 350mph the previous year, but 1960 was to
be open season on the land speed record. Campbell showed
off Bluebird CN7 at the Goodwood racing circuit in Sussex
in July, lapping at idling speed with the brakes firmly on.
Among the racing celebrities who turned out to watch were
reigning Formula One world champion Jack Brabham and
sportscar ace and flying aficionado Ron Flockhart.

As a relaxation prior to the American challenge,
Campbell took Tonia and Gina on holiday to Majorca with
Bill and Betty Coley and their family. Just before he left,
while he had been seeing off the advance Bluebird party as

it left London bound for Utah, he felt an uneasy pang about the outcome of the project. Being deeply superstitious, he did not ignore the feeling but fretted for days about it. Even when he got to their Spanish villa, it persisted. Peter Carr, the Bluebird project manager, called him one morning from Utah, and when Campbell put the phone down the feeling hit him harder than ever – a deep premonition that he wouldn't be coming back from Bonneville. There was no rational explanation for it, but he couldn't shake off the certainty he suddenly felt that something was going to go badly wrong. It was so strong that he sought out Coley to tell him about it. 'He told me that he'd been feeling that way for a week or more,' Coley said. 'I was horrified, but I couldn't agree with him, could I? I did my best to keep things light and to try to persuade him differently. I told him he was just too wound up after all the stress and strain of getting the car finished, the flying lessons he'd been taking, all the last-minute things. I told him to forget it, and he smiled. But neither of us was fooled; he was deeply apprehensive, and we both knew it.' Campbell liked and respected Coley because he was one of the people who would stand up to him, who wouldn't be walked over. But they didn't live in each other's pockets. 'We wouldn't hear from him for three months, then suddenly he'd phone up. Betty would say, "Donald's in trouble!" And he'd come along. He was very fond of my wife. And my boy, Christopher. And we looked after Gina a bit.'

Campbell had an involvement with Dowty Marine, and he took two of its JetStar jetboats out with him to Majorca aboard a ship that gave Coley little peace of mind.

It leaked, and it was a terrible trip. We nearly sank. Donald took over from the captain. We heard afterwards that the guy was nearly blind. They had no radio and they'd sold everything, all the maps. We got to Majorca, anyhow, and Bob Sharples, the musician bloke who was an orchestra leader, looked after us when we got there.

The two Dowty boats were always in trouble. I mean, they were promising, and he took them out to show what they could do. And we took photographs underwater. One time he even drove one onto the beach just to show off, to show how safe it was. We had a great time out there, but it wasn't very successful. The boats kept on getting clogged up, the intakes kept on getting blocked. Eventually they would break down.

I remember one time at Coniston with K7 when he drove it straight at us. Frightened the life out of us. I didn't think he could see where he was going, but of course he knew where he was. He did that to me in Majorca, too. Suddenly the lights went out on the lake; we were left high and dry in the middle. He had one of the Jetstar boats and I was looking after the other, with my son. Donald was just creeping along in the dark, could hear what we were saying, and suddenly there he was. We had to wait for the lights to come on before we knew where we were!

Another time the American fleet was in the harbour there. Donald used to go and dump the rubbish, and there was a lot of smuggling going on then. The authorities were after the smugglers. Donald got knocked up once; he was caught dumping the rubbish. Then he tried to frighten the Americans, getting hold of a pumpkin and tipping it into the sea so they'd think it was a mine! He used to laugh at the Americans. Dear, oh dear. That was a good time there.

There was, however, another difficult moment that Coley never forgot. 'I think Donald had a healthy regard for the water at all times. He got very, very cross with people who didn't abide by the rules. I remember taking Tonia out waterskiing while we were in Majorca, and she fell off. And because I didn't go right around straight away and pick her up – which is the right thing to do of course, I realize now – God, he gave me one hell of a bollocking! He really did. I remember that to this day!'

The night before Campbell left for Utah on 2 September, he was given a final send-off at London's Café Royal. Among the celebrities were friends Hughie Green and Jack Brabham, who was also sponsored by BP. The world champion made a speech, but he was not the only one, as Ken Reaks recalled.

The party was held in a private room, with a smattering of aristocracy. There were all sorts of speeches and things. And that blighter Campbell suddenly, out of the blue, said, 'I think we should hear a little from Ken Reaks.' I hadn't got a clue what to say! But then I suddenly thought of the problems we'd had initially with Bird being too wet up at Ullswater and putting the light out when Donald tried to get it up on the plane. I said that one of the problems with Donald was that he always travelled so fast and was always pushing water down the pitot head so that the air-speed indicator became a problem. We were having to clean it out every trip. I was just waffling, literally, because I hadn't got a clue what to say. A terrible situation! Anyway, I finally sat down and Donald immediately leapt to his feet and said, 'Gentlemen, the moral of that story is always keep your pitot clean!'

A more sombre note was also struck that night that Campbell was careful to keep hidden. During the course of the evening, Victor Mishcon had two members of the Crazy Gang, Teddy Knox and Jimmy Nervo, witness Campbell's will. Nervo teased him for worrying about old age; Campbell joked that he had asked for them in particular because he was going to cut them out of the will.

The Americans had been out of the land speed record race since Lee Bible's death in the White Triplex at Daytona Beach in 1929. Now they were back in force, and no fewer than four cars were ready for battle with Bluebird. But when Donald Campbell's entourage finally arrived on the white, open salt wastes of Bonneville, the American challengers were open-mouthed. 'It was quite a show,' one observer noted. 'Donald Campbell went up the far end of the salt along with his trucks, fire trucks, and I don't know how many Rovers he had. He went up one end and down the other end. It looked just like the Indy parade.'

But if the Americans were impressed, Campbell in turn blanched when he saw the depth of his competition. Never before had so many projectiles gathered in one place to attempt the record.

A Mormon preacher called Athol Graham had a two-wheel-drive car he had built himself. His flame-red City of Salt Lake cost him $2,500 ($15,000/£9,400 at today's values) and was powered by an Allison aero-engine from industrialist Bill Boeing's potent Miss Wahoo unlimited hydroplane. Californian hot-rodder Mickey Thompson had a beautiful little machine called Challenger 1, which was powered by four Pontiac V8 car engines and drove through all four wheels. The ingenious Thompson had designed and built it himself, with the help of a small but dedicated crew, running his operation in a similar way to Campbell during most of his water speed attempts. Graham had reached

344mph in 1959, Thompson 362mph. Now Thompson had added superchargers to his engines, and would clearly pose a very serious threat. Then there was Art Arfons with his Green Monster 'Anteater', another teardrop-shaped, piston aero-engined, two-wheel-drive machine. Perhaps the most threatening of them all was Dr Nathan Ostich's Flying Caduceus, which trod where Campbell and Norris had been warned not to tread by the FIA and ushered in the pure turbojet age for cars just as Sir Malcolm Campbell's Bluebird K4 had for boats. Named after the American symbol for medics, Caduceus used a 6,000lb thrust General Electric J47 turbojet engine and, like Bluebird, it was designed with 500mph in mind.

Graham was the first to try, convinced that he was ready for the big numbers, but on 1 August he lost control when he accelerated too harshly and was killed as City of Salt Lake went tumbling down the salt at around 350mph. Possibly something broke in the crude suspension. The structural integrity of the homebuilt special was light years away from Bluebird's sophistication, and in the cockpit Graham suffered a broken neck when the firewall collapsed as the car rolled and slid upside down. Arfons soon realized that his Green Monster was not up to the task and withdrew. His day would come. Ostich experienced myriad mechanical problems with the engine's intake ducting, suspension and steering, and never looked dangerous.

Thompson emerged as the real threat. He was a contro-versial figure, a brash, determined man who never backed down from a fight and was never afraid to speak his mind, but who also appreciated fight in others. Against the expectations of those who saw irreconcilable differences between the down-to-earth hot-rodder and the English gent, he and Donald Campbell liked each other immediately.

In part, this had its roots in the kinship felt by men out on the edge, isolated from their less adventurous fellows, but it was also founded on mutual respect. Theirs was a bond of friendship that was not always understood by observers, but Campbell did not bother with what Dottie Campbell called The Voice when fraternizing with Thompson. Nevertheless, each liked to indulge in good-natured needle. Thompson never lost a chance to try to outpsyche his British rival, and Campbell responded in kind. They enjoyed their jocular verbal jousting. Thompson's speedy performance was undoubtedly one of the factors that put pressure on Campbell to push with his multi-thousand-pound juggernaut, even though he had less need than Thompson to move ahead in a hurry. Bluebird had far more potential. As far as the Bonneville regulars were concerned, it was not a matter of if Bluebird broke the record, but simply by how much.

Campbell's arrival at Bonneville brought his own personal wheel full circle, for it was here a quarter of a century earlier that he had watched his father break 300mph and establish the venue as the world's capital of speed. His own performances in the K7 hydroplane had already taken him well beyond Sir Malcolm's efforts on water, but the Old Man had forged his reputation on land, and Campbell regarded everything that he had done before as mere practice for this moment. Now he could at last achieve something that would help him to live up to his own image of his father – and, by definition, his own image of himself.

Partisan Americans had come to dislike British speed-kings tripping over to Bonneville and rubbing their noses in it. First there had been Sir Malcolm, then George Eyston and John Cobb. Gentlemen all, but there was a small faction at Bonneville in 1960 that just couldn't wait to see Sir

Malcolm's son stumble. Athol Graham's efforts had, to some heartless minds, merely endorsed the Americans' reputation as make-do backyard hot-rod also-rans, but Thompson gave them pride with an upper-case P. Challenger 1 was not just any hot-rod, it was the *ultimate* hot-rod. It was the car that many believed without question was going to put Uncle Sam back on top. It had cost an awful lot less than Bluebird, and there were many who were quick to point this out. American writer Griff Borgeson, a close friend of Thompson's who would ghost his autobiography, led the cheerleading.

Campbell was always gracious and humble in his dealings with the Americans, be they friendly or critical. He was smart enough, and hardened enough, to regard criticism as part of the game. Richard Dixon, who owns the Museum of Speed in Wendover, the closest town to the salt flats, met Campbell during that attempt and was impressed. 'I was only twenty-one at the time, but we shook hands. I remember him as a distinguished gentleman. He was cordial. The thing I most remember is that despite what he was trying to do, he had time for everyone.'

All the razzmatazz of the Bluebird Project was nevertheless too much for some American observers who, though frequently poorly informed themselves, could not resist a snipe. 'He didn't know his equipment too well,' said one. 'I thought he should have known it a little bit better. On his first run he started to move out and drove down the course about fifty or sixty yards, and all at once he stopped and got up. They had a red light on the dashboard which I believe was his emergency brake, and he had forgotten to release it, but he didn't know what it was and had to ask one of his chief people.'

This was the sort of nonsense that abounds when people

observe record attempts without being closely enough involved to get their facts straight. Campbell knew every inch of the car, having been closely involved with the Norris brothers all the way through its design stages. But the red light, which had nothing to do with the emergency brake, had been fitted without Campbell's knowledge. Those who should have informed him of it forgot to. The way Campbell liked to tell the story, somebody shouted 'Fire!' just as he was about to start rolling, and when he went to switch off the Proteus engine nothing happened. Mindful that it was only supposed to idle for two minutes before the risk of bearing damage arose, he opened the canopy to ask Villa for advice. Then he decided to let the car coast fifty yards before applying the brakes and trying to switch it off again, only to discover that the brakes weren't working. He was toying with the idea of driving Bluebird into a shallow lake a mile down the course when finally the brakes came on and Ken Reaks arrived to tell him about a rotating switch down on the left side of his seat. According to Campbell, it had been installed by a stand-in fitter from Joseph Lucas after George Burrell, who had supervised the installation of the electrical system, had been struck down with a duodenal ulcer and had to miss the trip. Once Campbell operated the switch, the engine could be turned off.

This, however, was a rather more dramatic version than the one told by Ken Norris and Reaks himself, and may be an indication of how Campbell liked to embroider things. 'Donald didn't know about it because Ken Reaks had fitted that thing overnight,' Norris insisted. 'I didn't even know it was damn well there.' Reaks explained what had happened:

We had a problem on Bird as far as batteries were concerned, and had a limited amount of electrical power. So we had batteries which were also used for the transducers, which were giving us things such as vertical wheel motion, steering angle and the data recorder. As a result of this we used to limit the switching-on till the last moment. My job as the car started to move was to reach through a flap in the side and switch the recorder on. This limited the drain on the battery. As a result of all this, there was a fuel solenoid valve on the main fuel supply to the engine, a rotary valve. When the power was switched on the valve opened, allowing fuel to flow. But if the power was switched off, the valve would stay in the position in which it was last set. And what happened was that a little extra 'idiot' light was put in, unfortunately red, but at the time we used what we had. This showed when the power was off.

Donald got into the cockpit and the engine was started. We don't know exactly why what happened next actually happened, but the main switch was down by his left foot, a round knob with a little lever. From the outside you had to lean over the cockpit, put your hand down, and operate the switch. What I think happened is that after he started the engine Donald must have adjusted his harness and knocked this switch to the off position, and that held the fuel solenoid valve in the on position so the red light came on. Or maybe someone had knocked it when they were in and out of the cockpit prior to the run, polishing the glass or whatever. Anyway, Donald called to Leo, 'What's this bloody red light?' Which is what that chap overheard. Subsequently we put a manual switch on the solenoid valve. It became a joke, actually, because whenever we wanted to annoy Donald, we used to shout out, 'Leo, what's this bloody red light?' He didn't know that we had rigged up this red warning light the day before. But I know for a fact that the car hadn't actually moved at all before he spotted it.

Reaks also learned to be canny when dealing with another of Bluebird CN7's advanced systems that tested its pilot's superstitious nature. This was the head-up display unit, the HUD, which was true pioneering technology by the speed record contender standards of the day. The system enhanced safety by projecting figures far ahead onto the salt so that Campbell did not have to keep looking down into the cockpit and then readjusting his vision every time he looked back up. Green was the middle of the spectrum and therefore the best colour for the HUD figures, but of course Campbell hated it and refused to use the system. 'I thought I'd got over the problem,' Reaks admitted. 'He was certainly very anti-green, but I changed the filter and told him it was cyan, which is blue, and he accepted that. But the problem with the HUD was that it was not gyro-stabilized. It was projected thirty yards out onto the salt so he didn't have to change the focus of his eyes. But any slight motion of the car made the image move up and down. He found that distracting. But, oh, he was superstitious, no doubt about that!' It was part of the mask that, in all his writings, Campbell quite happily described how he would flick on the switch to activate the HUD.

The first runs were made on the 11.9-mile National course rather than Bonneville's Record course, which was in inferior condition. Experts said it was in any case a poor year for the salt, and Villa in particular was most perturbed that it had changed so much since 1935. Back then it had been hard and white; now, relentless mining of the salt's potash content, in one of the most scandalous legalized acts of environmental piracy, had left it brackish and wet.

The first five runs seemed tentative and pitifully slow to some of the gung-ho American hot-rodders used to the jump-in-and-floor-it mentality of Graham and Thompson.

Left: One of Gina's favourite photos, taken on her birthday in 1956 complete with Maxie, the day Campbell broke the water speed record on Coniston. GINA CAMPBELL

Below: Riding the knife edge: on Coniston Water, 19 September 1956, Bluebird K7 rides balletically on her three planing points as Campbell heads to his third record at 225.60 mph.

Above: Proof of Bluebird's cockpit problems at Coniston in 1956: a shaken Campbell gesticulates as smoke rises from K7. GINA CAMPBELL

Best Wishes
Geoff Hallawell

Left: The greatest team in record-breaking? Leo and Donald celebrate their latest triumph. GEOFF HALLAWELL

Right: Another of Gina's favourites. Taken at Canandaigua in 1957, it goes some way to explaining Campbell's appeal to women.

LIFE MAGAZINE

Below: On 10 November 1958, her shape subtly enhanced, Bluebird won her fifth record at 248.62 mph. That evening, according to Campbell, he first met third-wife-to-be Tonia Bern after driving down to London.

GEOFF HALLAWELL

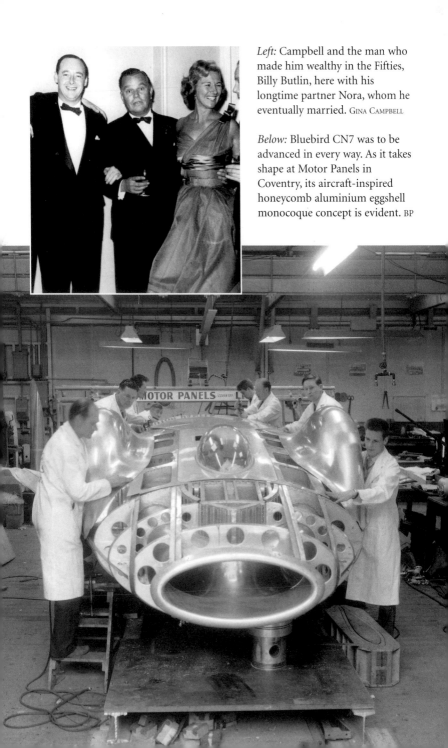

Left: Campbell and the man who made him wealthy in the Fifties, Billy Butlin, here with his longtime partner Nora, whom he eventually married. GINA CAMPBELL

Below: Bluebird CN7 was to be advanced in every way. As it takes shape at Motor Panels in Coventry, its aircraft-inspired honeycomb aluminium eggshell monocoque concept is evident. BP

Above: Two of the most influential men in British record-breaking history were the architects of Bluebirds K7 and CN7: Lew and Ken Norris. BP

Right: Relaxing during the Goodwood launch, Motor Panels' Maurice Britton found Campbell a hard man to get along with, and their clash of personalities would have far-reaching effects in 1963. BP

Left: Young love 3: Donald and Tonia at Bonneville before the accident that changed everything. BP

Far left and below: When Bluebird CN7 finally arrived at the Bonneville Salt Flats, its elegant streamlined shape was the perfect complement to the lunar quality of the landscape, but American critics savaged the apparent opulence of Campbell's record attempt. BP

ILLUSTRATED SPEEDWAY NEWS

PICTORIAL SECTION   ISSUE SEPT 27 '960

NO RACING LEADING PUBLICATION

THE BLUEBIRD CRASHES!

THE BRITISH SPEED KING, DONALD CAMPBELL, ESCAPED CRITICAL INJURY WHEN HE LOST CONTROL OF HIS $4 MILLION CAR AT 300 MPH AT THE SALT FLATS, UTAH. BLUEBIRD DARE-DEVIL, WARMING UP FOR A CRACK AT THE WORLD'S AUTO SPEED RECORD, WAS MAKING HIS 4TH RUN ON THE SALT. WAY FROM HIS SPEED KING. CHUCK OF TIRES. HE AND CHANGED THE RUN AND DISASTER THEN STRUCK. THE ROYAL BLUE CAR VEERED AND THEN SPUN AND START TO ROLL OVER IN A CLOUD OF SALT DUST. THE CAR ROLLED OVER AND OVER COMING TO REST ON ITS TORN TWO WHEELS WERE EXTENSIVE DAMAGE TO THE CAR. PETER CARR, CHIEF OF THE PROJECT SAID THE 4,860 HORSE-POWER BLUEBIRD WAS A TOTAL LOSS. "IT IS CHEAPER TO BUILD A NEW CAR THAN TO REPAIR THIS ONE," SAID CARR. THE BLUEBIRD WAS A DE TOOK NINE MONTHS TO BUILDS SECONDS, CAMPBELL SAID HIS EXPERIENCE WILL NOT SHAKE HIS DETERMINATION TO PUSH THE LAND SPEED RECORD PAST THE 400 MILES PER HOUR. TOP PHOTO AT RIGHT SHOWS CHIEF MECHANIC LEO VILLA PEERING INSIDE WRECKED BLUEBIRD. PHOTO BELOW SHOWS DON CAMPBELL EN-TERING THE LOCAL HOSPITAL WITH AMBULANCE AT-...GILLETTE.

Above: The disaster at Bonneville in September 1960 left Bluebird a shattered hulk, but the fact that Campbell survived the 300 mph accident was testament to the design ability of the Norris brothers. BP

Left: Campbell had a phobia about being seen to be incapacitated. Despite his ordeal on the salt, he insisted on walking into Tooele Hospital, with only the assistance of ambulance driver Ted Gillette.
WORLD WIDE PHOTOS

But that was precisely what had killed Graham, who had declared to Thompson prior to his final run that he had nothing more to learn below 400mph even though he had no previous experience of the locked differential he had fitted to City of Salt Lake. But Ken Norris was insistent that Campbell make a prescribed number of slow-speed runs prior to building up speed, just to obtain data and to test the car's numerous systems. This was not merely his own academic bent coming into play; the sponsors and companies that had provided support were determined to learn as much as they could from their expensive investments so that in the future they could make better products. Bluebird was a rolling laboratory, as Campbell so often liked to point out, and had to justify itself as a data-gathering device while it tried to break the land speed record.

Alfred Owen's brother-in-law, Louis Stanley, who would later run the BRM Grand Prix team, travelled to Utah with Campbell and during these test sessions witnessed the paranormal side to his complex character. 'I remember one test when he was ready to go, early, about six in the morning,' he recalled. 'It was all clear. I said, "OK. That's it." No sign. So I tapped his helmet. Nothing. I said, "What's the trouble?" And he said, "Well, I've been in touch with my father, and he says we mustn't go today." And I said, "Are you sure? You probably got a wrong line." And he said, very seriously, "Oh no, he told me." What was the point of arguing?'

The first run was made at 5.35 in the evening on Monday, 5 September. Running north, Campbell averaged 120mph over the mile. Norris wanted him to run at a constant throttle opening and constant compressor rpm on these early runs, and that first run was made with the engine merely idling. Campbell later joked with newsmen that driving his Mercedes 300SL Gullwing felt quicker. The idling compressor rpm was only 4,000, so Campbell was permitted to use some throttle and made the return run just over an hour later at 170mph. The timing was done unofficially, and later the team would merely rely on the car's onboard telemetry. Both methods were cheaper than having the timekeepers from the United States Auto Club (USAC) on hand to time every early sortie. Campbell described the acceleration as 'fantastic!', but complained that the steering ratio was wrong. At 25:1 it was too direct, making his progress erratic as the big blue car darted down the salt, its direction at the whim of the slightest steering input. The wheels were also out of alignment, a problem that took Dunlop the best part of two days to rectify. But it was the steering ratio change that really took the time since it entailed removal of the instrument panel to facilitate access to the steering box. At the same time, screening was added on the advice of Bell Laboratories, after static interference on the salt flats had threatened to negate all of Bluebird's copious radio and telemetry systems.

Four days after Campbell's first outing, Thompson achieved a one-way speed of 406.6mph in Challenger 1. Campbell was there to see it. He had sportingly offered the American his own time on the salt as Bluebird was not ready to run, and was one of the first to offer Thompson spontaneous congratulations during his turnaround. This was entirely in keeping with his personality. A 12mph increment on Cobb's record was not enough to cause either Campbell or his engineers to lose any sleep, given Bluebird's design target. Instead there was genuine pleasure in the achievement of another. Like his father, Campbell believed implacably that records were made to be broken. He wished Thompson Godspeed for the return run, then sympathized with the Californian's bitter disappointment when

Challenger 1 failed before it could cement a new record. At the time, Thompson put it out that a driveshaft had broken during his return run, rather than rub salt into the wounds of his engine supplier after one of his supercharged Pontiac V8s had actually exploded. Nobody could have known it at the time, but the failure that forced him to return to Los Angeles to make repairs effectively wrote him out of the race for outright land speed record honours.

Campbell did not run again until the 15th, when the steering ratio had been changed to 100:1. He made two more runs, and his speeds on the onboard telemetry were 175mph and then 240mph. He reported that the car had a tendency to wander, which might have been due to a 10mph crosswind, but critics cut him little slack. They were irritated by the team's apparent opulence and its sole occupancy of a hangar on the old USAF Air Force Base at Wendover from which Colonel Paul Tibbetts and the Enola Gay had flown on the mission to drop the H-bomb on Hiroshima. There was continual criticism of the way in which Campbell was approaching things, though many of Thompson's admirers omitted to mention that, like Graham, Thompson had run at Bonneville the previous season and therefore had a considerable advantage over his British rival. In 1959, even before the construction of CN7 had begun, Thompson had taken Challenger 1 to 362mph. He had been able to iron out many of the bugs, and to identify areas that required modification. He was significantly more advanced on the learning curve.

It was already obvious – and would become even more so twenty years later when Richard Noble arrived at Bonneville with his Project Thrust jetcar – that the days when the British could simply breeze across the Atlantic, raise the record and go home within a month were as far into the past as the Charleston and Prohibition. The Bluebird team was a long way from home with a car that more closely resembled a fighter aircraft. That was why it needed so much back-up, and plenty of testing before it was ready to run at anything like full power.

Bluebird came out again on Friday the 16th. Campbell had already been pushing Norris for permission to make an early attempt on the record. He wanted to crack 300mph on run five and reach for 400mph on the sixth. He began talking of making his official attempt on Saturday morning. Norris was seriously alarmed, and considered this far too premature. He told Campbell as much with, for him, unusually unrestrained vehemence.

At 6.24 a.m. on Friday, Campbell was again on the startline. This time he had permission to wind up the thrust before releasing the brakes, and he peaked at 300mph within three miles. He was happier with Bluebird's directional stability now that the steering ratio had been changed, though the car still displayed a tendency to wander in the 6mph crosswind. 'In general,' Norris reported in his logbook, 'everyone was very happy with the run.' But there was one jarring note in the harmony. Campbell had talked of seeing a truck out on the track, which had turned out just to be a course marker. Tonia was slightly surprised when her husband spoke volubly of the experience immediately after bringing Bluebird to a halt. It was uncharacteristic of him to be so garrulous right after a run, when normally he was clipped and precise in his observations of the machine's behaviour. It was another pointer to what lay ahead that went unnoticed.

At 7.10, the engine was fired again for another run. This one would change everything about the remaining seven years of Donald Campbell's life.

15

DISASTER AT 360MPH

16 September 1960

'Your husband is sending you a message. He says to tell you that the family jewels are all right.'

UTAHAN HIGHWAY PATROLMAN HOWARD COOPER TO TONIA CAMPBELL

Donald Campbell was impatient to run hard and fast at Bonneville, even though he was only on his sixth run in Bluebird CN7. He wanted to try to accelerate the car rather than use constant compressor ratings, and then to try the brakes in earnest at the other end of the course. Ken Norris, who wasn't at all keen on that idea, finally agreed to discuss it with Leo Villa and Dunlop technician Don Badger, who reminded Campbell that the test tyres on which he was running were only rated to 300mph. But Campbell was insistent and persuasive and, ultimately, it was his project. They agreed to let him have his way, provided he did not exceed that speed. Campbell agreed, but then made the sort of error that had killed Athol Graham just over a month earlier.

He accelerated rapidly away from the turnaround. He wanted to hit 300mph within two miles, something he would have to do on the record run itself. And he wanted to give a film crew something worthwhile to film. 'I don't think there is any doubt about it,' Ken Reaks recalled. 'We had been there for a while and he was getting a little impatient. We used to send him off, then we'd hurtle down the track after him in the various Rovers to service him at the far end. Everyone was under pressure and it was costing £1,000 a day, or something like that, to rent the salt. I suppose that instead of working up to maximum via a number of test runs, he decided that he'd come back a little faster than he had gone down. The only thing I remember at the time was thinking that I had never heard the engine make that noise on the salt. He brought the revs right up before taking the brakes off, and he went down the track like a dose of salts.'

In action at real speed for the first time, the giant car looked like a ski jumper with his arms swept back for streamlining, the image enhanced by the large humps over the wheels. The fact that CN7 was at last operating in its true element lent it a unique and peerless beauty. Campbell reached 300mph quickly, but after 1.6 miles Bluebird began to veer off track in a long slide to the left that continued to the 1.9-mile mark. In the softer salt, it slipped ever more sideways as it lost traction. In the cockpit, Campbell appeared to be doing little to try to regain control. As Bluebird reached the critical yaw angle it presented its aerofoil-shaped side section to the wind and the inevitable happened. It took off, and suddenly it was flipping, fluttering like a sycamore leaf for 200 yards. It bounced several times on the wet salt before slithering along on its belly and finally coming to rest a further 500 yards down the left-hand side of the course. It was still the right way up, its engine emitting a futile scream. Campbell lolled in the cockpit. His skull had been fractured, but it had been a truly miraculous escape. Nobody had ever survived an accident on land at such speed. Athol Graham had died, and two years later Glenn Leasher would also perish after crashing his Infinity at over 250mph. Only the structural integrity of Bluebird had saved Campbell from a similar fate.

It was a Friday. The day the deeply superstitious record breaker would normally avoid like the plague.

Norris and Villa were the first at the scene. Legend has it that Villa was sucked into the open intake, landing painfully with a leg either side of its air splitter, but Norris admitted that he could not remember it for sure. 'We were chasing him along, and we saw it go up into the sky and come crashing down in the wake of salt,' he said. 'The wheels came off and it bounced and rolled before skimming sideways and landing on its bottom. The engine was still running, and we switched everything off.' Reaks added, 'Just as we went over to the telemetry van, I saw the speedo suddenly fall back to zero. There was an American on the end of a land-line, and he said, "Oh gee, he's flipped!" We didn't know at the time what he meant by "flipped"; it was an Americanism. We got in our car and went down the course, and there was Bird.'

CN7 lay like a blue whale that had been butchered on some vast saline beach, its hydraulic lifeblood leaving a red stain that was rendered all the more dramatic by the crisp white surface on which its terrifying progress had scored deep and jagged gouges. Both right-hand wheels had been torn off, along with the wheel covers and some tail panelling, but the left-hand wheels were still in place and the Dunlop tyres retained their full pressure. The car was junk, but considering the fantastic speed at which the crash had occurred, there was actually remarkably little major structural damage. 'The engine was off by then, but a shaft was still going round – chonk, chonk, chonk,' Reaks continued. 'You could see big blue patches on the salt where it had hit, and somebody said it had been up about thirty feet in the air. I think what happened is that if you take the section of the car it was elliptical, and when it had started veering she had become airborne. There was nothing Donald could do.'

Campbell sat in the cockpit, staring sightlessly. Blood streamed down his face. He was shocked and shaken but still conscious. In a faraway voice he told his stunned crew members, 'I seem to have clouted my ear.' Highway Patrolman Howard Cooper and veteran Bonneville ambulance drivers Ted Gillette and Neil Bishop helped Villa and Norris to lift him out. Just after they had done this, Peter Carr arrived with Tonia. Campbell was then taken in Gillette's ambulance for twenty-four hours' observation at Tooele Hospital, an hour's drive away. On the way, two incidents occurred that Tonia never forgot. 'He looked at me, winked, and whispered something to the highway patrolman,' she remembered. 'I learned later that he said, "Don't let Tonia come in the back of the ambulance on the way." He was frightened he was going to die, or he didn't want me to see him like that. He was like a rag as they lifted him out of the cockpit. I was pushed into the front of the ambulance, and we set off on the drive to Tooele. A bit later on there was a knock on the glass partition that separated the front of the ambulance from the back, and then it opened. The highway patrolman and the nurse said, "Your husband is sending you a message. He says to tell you that the family jewels are all right." Even then, you know? Unbelievable!'

Campbell had an absolute horror of being seen to be incapacitated in public. Perhaps that went back to an incident in his youth, when he had been abandoned in an intoxicated state by friends during a riotous evening on the town. In an act of considerable courage, he insisted on walking from the ambulance into the hospital entrance under his own steam, assisted by Gillette and the nurse. He winked at reporters and managed to say, 'Good morning!'

It was glorious, inspired, bloody-minded bravado.

After X-rays, his injuries were initially diagnosed as severe concussion, a ruptured eardrum and middle ear, a cut right ear and abrasions to his face, neck, arms and legs. The basal skull fracture he'd also sustained was linear, and had not been detected by the X-ray. It was only when a surgeon walked in, saw the blood and cerebral fluid trickling out of Campbell's right ear and said, 'Good God, this man has got a severe fracture at the base of his skull,' that he was put back to bed.

Campbell wanted to leave hospital that day, but was told very firmly, 'You're not the doctor – you're staying here.' When he first confronted the press, he smiled broadly and was more concerned about the car than himself. Sounding punch-drunk, he told reporters, 'The wind caught me when I was accelerating to just over 300mph. I lost it in the recovery.' When asked how he felt, he replied, 'Bloody awful, you know. I don't feel exactly happy about it. But as soon as I get the car back on the track again, I'll go.' It was some time before he could be persuaded that Bluebird had actually flipped. Tonia also faced the press. 'Certainly, he'll do it,' she answered loyally when asked if her husband would ever break the record. 'This is a setback, but he'll do it. That's why he is the man he is – he's a marvellous man. I admire him a little bit more after this. He just keeps asking about the car. He wants to drive it again, and his only concern is about how badly damaged it is.'

The switchboard was jammed with calls from all over

the world. Mickey Thompson was among the first visitors the Campbells received in hospital. Just after the accident, Campbell had wired Thompson: 'Having now experienced a high-speed angular rotation like your good self [Thompson had once spun his car during testing at California's Muroc Dry Lake] I am thankful for good cockpit protection. My injuries were nothing serious, except to my pride.' Thompson had replied: 'Very kind of you to crash your car. Have you thought about our publicity?'

But why had Campbell crashed? Why, when Bluebird began to veer to the left, away from the course, had he not done more to recover control? Had he simply deviated too much from the flight plan? 'He only really did that on that last run at Coniston when he didn't refuel,' Norris said.

Normally he wouldn't go outside the flight plan. He'd be very keen to get Leo's advice. You see, when he lost it up in Bonneville, he said to me, 'How about accelerating this run? Can I put my foot down?' And I said, 'For God's sake, watch it,' because we weren't sure of the thing yet. We'd now got the new steering ratio, which was still wrong. But he could use just pressure steering, not make big movements of the wheel. You know, just sort of nudge the car into a change of direction, rather than out and out steer it. So he scoots off, and the next thing is Leo and I are chasing after him. We could see this cloud of salt, of course, and then we see this blue flash emerging through the top of the cloud. Obviously he'd gone off and taken off sideways-on, like a wing.

Let's face it, we didn't have a fin. Now, for an aerodynamic fin to work properly you've got to get going so fast and get some good stability out of it. We would have got some good stability out of it that run. I think he simply lost all four wheels, spun them, and off he went. He just put too much power through.

So it was a driving error, caused by accelerating too hard? 'It could have been,' Norris replied. 'It could have been a combination of the bad salt and that factor. That was the first run on which he'd wanted to accelerate. I said, "Well, just take it up to 200, 300, something like that. But don't push it down too hard." That was my advice, just get a feel for running it.'

In his logbook, Norris summarized the reason for the accident quite succinctly: 'Because the limiting tyre co-efficient was exceeded!' Why that had happened was due to several factors. One was the low grip of the salt that season, particularly close to the black oil guideline; then the output torque of the Proteus engine was higher than anticipated, partly due to the peculiar torque characteristic of CN7's exhaust arrangement, the temperature and general in-experience with the unit. 'Indeed,' Norris noted, 'the driver must have been surprised to find after selection of the throttle position that the torque "followed" up and hit him so hard!'

Campbell estimated his speed at the time of the accident as 360mph. Norris reckoned it was closer to 225–250mph, according to the telemetry, but reported that the onboard black box, though severely damaged, indicated 365mph as the maximum the car had reached. Possibly, like John Cobb on his final run with Crusader, Campbell had got caught out by the throttle lag of a turbojet and then the sudden rush of thrust, reaching a higher speed than intended.

'Bluebird drifted to the right, I tried to correct it, and then it went sideways,' Campbell said initially, stressing that that was all he could remember. But he told interviewer John Pett at Coniston in 1966 that 'Utah was an accident where there was no sense of fear whatever, or reality, for that matter, because it was caused by oxygen poisoning. And this has the effect on you of nitrous oxide. You think you are doing a wonderful job, and in fact you're five cycles behind the game. You see the crash coming and you think, "Too bad." '[20]

Campbell had already discussed the matter with entertainer Hughie Green, who spent time with his friend in America during Campbell's recuperation.

He went to convalesce at Palm Springs. He'd just had one hell of an experience, and he and I discussed the technical reasons for what happened. He was of the opinion that you can get drunk on oxygen. He had an oxygen system based on demand. We had it in the B-17s and B-24s I used to ferry during the war. It was always great because if you got pissed the night before and you went out to the field with a bloody hangover, you went straight up in the aeroplane and the first thing you did was put the mask on. You pushed the button to override the system and you got pure oxygen. Whoops! And away you went and drove the aeroplane! You didn't feel that good, but you felt a bloody sight better! Donald's opinion was that somehow something had gone wrong with that and he had got pure oxygen. And with getting pure oxygen, oh boy! He was gonna make that thing fly! And every time there's an accident, there's trauma. I would say that he was all right. But you couldn't expect him to be jumping up after that.

Campbell came to suspect that he was one of those people to whom pure oxygen, inhaled at sea level, did some odd things, but the theory that he made it even worse by hyperventilating – to the point where he became almost drunk –

would not surface for a long time. For her part, Tonia clung to the belief that he had seen a mirage, after his experience on run five. 'I think that was it, he had an eye problem . . . he saw something. Or he thought he saw something on the track. A mirage. I think he definitely had that.'

All Donald Campbell had to show for his first attack on the land speed record was physical and psychological injury, damage to his pride, and a wrecked car, not to mention severely depleted finances: just the Utah operation alone had cost his backers £38,000 (£520,000 at today's values). Still, by the grace of God he was alive, and would recover in time.

16

THE LEGACY OF BONNEVILLE

1960 to 1962

*'The act of dying? That most certainly worries me. I enjoy this life far
too much. But you can be just as frightened of failure.'*
DONALD CAMPBELL TO JOURNALIST GEOFFREY MATHER

The newsreel films that showed Donald Campbell walking
unaided into Tooele Hospital, despite his basal skull
fracture, went all round the world. And when he spoke of
another attempt before he had given himself the time to
recover from the shock of his accident, let alone to ponder
the situation, his courage impressed Alfred Owen. The
industrialist immediately communicated his willingness to
build a new machine. 'If Campbell has the guts to have
another go at the record, I'll build him another car,' he said.
So, even before he had started to recuperate, Campbell felt
morally obliged to go ahead, and cabled acceptance. He left
himself no option. The die was cast.

The skull fracture mended quickly. What took much longer
were the psychological injuries, which would trouble
Campbell on and off for the rest of his life. Nursed by Tonia,

he gently played himself back to health through 1961 before choosing once again to immerse himself midway through 1962 in the logistics of the new project. Gradually he was drawing closer to a new moment of truth. Around him, his loved ones did the best they could to help.

'When Donald crashed at Utah, I was about to have our Donald,' Campbell's sister Jean Wales recalled. 'Tonia rang and said, "Don't worry, you'll hear the Old Boy's had a terrible crash. But he's OK." The shock sent me into hospital with my Donald! So I was in Epsom Hospital, and he was in hospital in America! A crash like that must have an effect. I don't think he changed much; mind you, I didn't see all that much of Don. He was always here, there and everywhere else. He was never in one place more than five minutes. He loved life, and he lived it to the hilt.'

It was Tonia who had to bear the brunt of the aftermath, though for a wife used to the wayward behaviour of her husband, the Utah accident was to have a silver lining. 'That was the difficult part about being his wife, all the other women,' she admitted, 'because if they were a secret, he didn't enjoy it. It was all in the open. He never lied to me, ever. All the stories of ladies, I know them well.' But she denied that they had an open marriage. 'Not really. It was a *solid* marriage. Honest. An open marriage means he can play around and she can play around. That was not the kind of marriage we had. Don't forget, the first year we were married was very difficult. I was very naughty, too. I mean, I'm not a one-man woman. Never have been. That first year was very difficult for both of us and we had a very bad time. But after that Donald didn't have any affairs for years. Not any. I would have known, and there weren't any. We were always together, and we were very strong.'

She had learned how to fight back, goaded into it by Leo

Villa early on in the marriage when she was about to admit defeat. Aided by her friend Vera Henderson, she had learned how to play her husband at his own game, and had won through. But now she no longer had a man who wanted to play around, or even one who felt relaxed and content in his relationship with her. Instead, she had one who needed her with naked desperation. 'After the crash at Utah, Donald had problems, but he didn't fool around,' Tonia said. 'He had health problems. He leant on me, night and day. Donald had a very, very difficult time. I enjoyed those two years. I did not enjoy seeing him ill, but I enjoyed being very needed. Like any woman does.'

Campbell's new vulnerability kept him close to home. The first sign manifested itself five weeks after the crash, while he was still recuperating in Palm Springs. He woke in a sweat one night with a physical sensation of something sharp creeping up his back and over his scalp. A doctor suggested that the thalamus area of his brain – the part that governs the nervous system's control of things such as breathing and fear – had been injured in the accident. That could trigger panic attacks at a moment's notice, unless he learned to relax and let nature take its course. The doctor recommended six months of complete rest, but there was no way the Bluebird schedule would ever allow that. On one occasion in Palm Springs, General Motors lent the Campbells a Cadillac, but when he tried to drive it Campbell found himself creeping along in the inside lane, terrified by each passing car. When he and Tonia stopped at a restaurant, he was embarrassed when a middle-aged woman, who happened to come from Lancashire, asked him if he was Donald Campbell, and had he seen the bronze Cadillac she had passed earlier on which had been holding up all the traffic. She told him it had been driven by a dithering idiot, and that she had been surprised to see the driver wasn't a day over sixty.

The attacks continued when the Campbells returned to England in November, but he put on a good show when he and Tonia stepped off a BOAC flight at London airport. 'Bluebird is the most fantastic car ever built, from every standpoint,' he told reporters.

When you realize that it accelerated from rest to nearly 400mph in a mile and a half . . . brakes, stability, everything about it was equally fantastic. The accident was a tragedy, it shouldn't have happened. It was simply caused by the fact that we were running on a track which we now know, but which we didn't know then, was too narrow. It was only a hundred feet wide. We were drifted by a wind – a very light wind – to the side of the course and the car licked the rough salt whilst it was under tremendously high thrust, and of course the left-hand pair of wheels spun slightly and the right-hand pair was biting into hard salt, and it was rather like braking the track of a tank in slow motion. It went round and I was instantly blacked out. It took off. It was airborne for a thousand feet and during that time it rolled over three times. It hit the ground, came back, it went skywards for sixty feet, it came down on the tail, it took off again, and did that I think three more times before finally coming back down sideways on, shearing off two wheels and sliding another hundred yards. In all, it covered much more than half a mile.

But I don't think any of us can wait to get back on with the job. And I hope and pray that we shall be back on the salt flats next year and that we shall successfully achieve the goal that we set out to achieve in September.

It was a wonderful performance, but an interview with *Daily Express* journalist Geoffrey Mather provided dramatic illumination of the psychological problems that lay behind it, and just what he had to cope with. 'The act of dying?' he reflected. 'That most certainly worries me. I enjoy this life far too much. But you can be just as frightened of failure.' And he went on to describe just how the accident had affected him.

We were on run six with Bluebird in Utah. I slammed the throttle to the boards. The tail went haywire. I did not take the slightest notice. It did it again. Perfectly obvious what was going to happen. I saw it coming, and I thought, 'Oh well, nice morning, not to worry – bang.' The curtain came down. I had a good dose of oxygen poisoning. I woke up – I do not know how much later – and there was a great blur across my head, and out of the darkness, I thought, 'I'm upside down.' Well, for quite a long time after this incident things went wild. You could sit just like this, talking, then suddenly you could be very frightened. Your hands would start to shake and your brow would pour with sweat. Driving in traffic might bring it out; telephone ringing. It wasn't a fear of getting back into the car. For a time I was desperately worried it might have been.

It was a purely nervous psychological reaction, something that fighter pilots in the war often went through after a crash or a close shave. But Campbell had little time for doctors or psychiatrists, who might have been able to help. Instead, he took to visiting medium Marjorie Staves again.

He came to see me because I'd got to know him so well. He really confessed to me that the fault was partly due to

258

himself. Lack of control. He couldn't put the blame too much on anybody else, that's what he was telling me. It was all due to having disappointment all along the line, and not being able to have the success he was after. And of course, he didn't have much money, you know. Quite honestly and truthfully, I can't remember him ever giving me anything, moneywise. I don't think he ever thought he could put a fee down and pay me. Not even from the first visit. In the general coming and going, when he'd have a cup of coffee or whatever, I can honestly say I never received any money from him.

In her own way, this remarkable lady, with her quaint pattern of speech and her quiet understanding, became quite attached to Donald Campbell. She became his Mother Confessor, his high priestess, somebody with whom he could be completely relaxed and open, to whom he could bare his deepest feelings without fear of ridicule or public exposure.

I didn't say I felt sorry for him, but I felt it was worth him trying to maintain his cause. What I was trying to help him with was that he was after something that was right in its context. He wasn't going to try and be a big guy at something he was no good at. His purpose was to prove his worth, that's what he was after.

He was always like a little boy at school, you know. Try and help me. That's the guy I had. He wasn't coming in and showing off, or throwing his weight about. By jingo, no! I can remember when he phoned me once from Cumberland and he was a bit delighted that a trial had gone well. He was so excited, to pick up a phone and tell me. I was pleased that he'd got something at last. But by the same token, there was something that would always be in the way of him getting off to a good start. Psychologically, too, that must have affected him. And he could talk to me with a confidence in which he couldn't talk to anybody else. He could be the natural guy. From that I could feel that, somehow, there was a continuation of interruptions for him.

Gina remembered one incident when his nerves played up. 'There was one poignant moment when the three of us were driving on the Leatherhead bypass, going to a lunch, and he came over all sweaty and pale and pulled into a lay-by and said, "I just can't go." The Campbells can live with a lot of things in life, but not failure. He blamed himself for Utah. Not to be cruel, but there was human error involved. He knew he had let himself and his team down there, and it really got to him.'

Eventually, Tonia and Villa persuaded him to take up flying with ex-RAF pilot Tim Williams at Redhill. The aerial therapy helped him overcome the panic attacks, and by September 1961 Campbell believed they were finally over. His back was still painful, though. It had affected him at Ullswater, and now Utah had made it worse. But he could cope with that, and he cautiously hoped that the absence of panic attacks meant that he was finally healing. But then he suffered another, which prompted him finally to seek fresh medical advice. He and Tonia headed off to Guy's Hospital. After assimilating all the facts and studying encephalographs of Campbell's brain, one doctor pointblank advised him that he should never make another record attempt. At the very least, he counselled, take a complete break. The Campbells headed for the south of France.

Tonia continued to play Florence Nightingale for another year, but eventually Campbell's clinginess drove her into an affair. 'I was very young and very wild, and I had been playing live-in nurse,' she explained. 'He was leaning on me night and day. I had to massage his back every night before he could sleep. We had to make love just to relax, not to enjoy it. It was about 1963, and I had an affair, not Donald. I went to Belgium, finally went to visit my father, and I had an affair while I was there. And it's what made me understand why Donald did it too. Later on, he had an affair too. Whether he broke that fidelity spell because I had broken it, I don't know. I'll never know.'

Ken Reaks hadn't noticed too many outward changes, but for those he had seen he had a different suggestion. 'I just don't think he was happy with the car. He wasn't quite so carefree with it. I think the actual accident did leave its mark on him, but on the other hand he didn't seem to have the same reaction with the boat. I think he always felt more comfortable with the boat.'

But it was the car in which Campbell eventually returned to the record-breaking arena, and for that he needed money. He was all ears in the autumn of 1960 when Hughie Green visited him in Palm Springs during his convalescence, for the entertainer-aviator had a business proposition for him.

I was in the aviation business in those days as well as in television. I had the job of selling the Grumman Gulfstream throughout the whole of Europe. When I sold it, it was selling for anything between one million seven and two million one dollars. The agency was held by Henry DuPont, the head of the DuPont family, DuPont Nemours, General Motors, American Aviation, probably one of the wealthiest men in the world. I went out to Palm Springs to see Donald, and I made him an offer that we would write letters, and Donald would sign his name to them, to leading industrialists throughout the world, on behalf of DuPont.

He was such a famous and wonderful guy. And Mr DuPont knew exactly what I was doing, because I had told him that he could be selling gold, but unless he had an entrée to the head of ICI, he wasn't going to get to see him. My idea was that Donald was very pro-American and knew a lot of people, and those he didn't know, knew him. And I do stress that these were letters that were going out to the captains of world industry. This wasn't any sort of gimmick. A letter from Donald Campbell, in my estimation, was a letter that could not be ignored. 'Dear Mr So and so, I realize that your business is reliant on the latest in business aviation, and consequently I would like to recommend to you an aeroplane which I have indeed flown in, the Grumman Gulfstream. This excellent aeroplane . . .' and so on. 'I would like you to take a ride in it, and if I may be so bold I will have one of our representatives contact you . . .' It was one of those letters.

Mr DuPont said, 'Well, if you could persuade him to do this, we'll pay him for each letter and give him a cut on every aeroplane we sell.' All Donald had to do was sign each letter. So Donald said, 'Great. I know the Gulfstream, I've flown in it.' So I said, 'OK, what do you want to do now?' And Donald said, 'Well, I never do anything without my lawyer.'

So I flew back to England and I saw his lawyer. He said, 'Why should he do this?' And I said, 'It's an awful lot of money per aeroplane, and he doesn't have to do anything.' And then this lawyer just shattered me. I had taken a violent dislike to him right then, as he had probably taken a violent dislike to me. I suddenly found myself selling to Donald's lawyer something that Donald needed from a financial standpoint. I found myself having to battle with this man. Already in those days I was known in this country, and he certainly knew that I knew Donald. But he just said,

'Well, who's behind it?' And I felt like some pokey little guy. I said, 'Well, I'll tell you who's behind it. Mr Henry DuPont, the head of the DuPont family.' And he just said back to me, 'And what do they do, Mr Green?' So then I said, 'Well, I don't think I can do any more for Donald because I realize that you look after all his business, and you certainly looked after this for him. We can't do business.' And I left. It was extraordinary! Ridiculous! The people we were writing to came straight out of Mr DuPont's blue book, you understand?

That cost Donald a lot of money, let me tell you. I sold planes to [ship-owners Aristotle] Onassis, [Stavros] Niarchos, and probably one of the greatest industrialists in the world, [Fiat boss] Gianni Agnelli. He had a bedroom in the back of his. And then I sold four to Shell. Don't by any means take it away from Donald, but I got the impression that he didn't piss without his lawyer's say-so. And it would have been such a wonderful thing for Donald that, out of the two hundred letters, about twelve aeroplanes were sold. If you take twelve aeroplanes being sold at a million and a half dollars each, you are talking eighteen million dollars. Back in the sixties. So figure the cut he might have had . . .

Later, Campbell did do a significantly less lucrative deal, however, with a man called David Wynne-Morgan, who at that time wrote the William Hickey column in the *Daily Express*. Their paths crossed frequently after Wynne-Morgan had given up journalism and set up a public relations company that also did some management for celebrities such as world squash champion Geoff Hunt.

I'd been motoring editor for a newspaper which died, the *Sunday Dispatch*, and someone said to Donald, 'Why don't you get in touch with David, he may be able to help.' When he came to me it was 1962, and he was really in very bad shape. He was broke, and he was having a lot of trouble raising the money to continue. So he came to me and said would I be prepared to help. He said, 'I can't afford it, but I will pay you 25 per cent of all the money you raise on the sponsorship, but you will have to pay your own expenses and I can't pay you anything else. And we want to look at all the possible ways of raising money.'

So I spent about two weeks making a few enquiries around town, talking to people, measuring up my chances of being successful. My PR business wasn't mega, but it would really mean making this my number one activity, so that was a fairly significant change of direction. I finally decided it was a goer. The situation at that time, frankly, was that all the sponsors really didn't want to do it. But this was regarded as a patriotic British venture, and from the PR point of view they didn't want to look as if they were dumping him.

The problem was that after Campbell had spoken from his hospital bed of having another go and Alfred Owen had promptly offered to build another car, everybody had effectively become committed to something that, subsequently, many of them came to realize they would rather not be involved with.

The wreckage of Bluebird CN7 had arrived back at Motor Panels in Coventry on 29 October 1960. Owen did not build a brand-new car, however. Though the original was severely knocked about, Ken and Lew Norris examined it minutely and decided that they could salvage the basic structure. Work began in December 1960 and was finished a year later. 'We used a lot of the original car, around 75 per cent,' Ken

Norris said. 'The basic framework was all right, the longitudinal and transverse honeycomb panels and all that sort of stuff. In fact, I was amazed how well it had stood up. Apart from the skin, most of the middle section seemed perfect. The basic structure was marvellous. So we used that, and repaired the other damaged areas.' The original engine was also reused, but ultimately a more powerful version of the Bristol-Siddeley Proteus engine was fitted, a type 755, following Leo Villa's time-honoured dictum that however much power you thought you would need, you always needed more. The 'new' car incorporated a glass-fibre cockpit cover in place of the previous Perspex bubble, stressed to more than fifty tons. To encourage the new car to run straight at all times, the Norrises had not only strengthened the suspension and locked both differentials to minimize wheelspin, but also incorporated a large tail fin that was built in sections, so its overall height was adjustable. Other changes included upgrading the onboard telemetry, changing the steering ratio to a final thirty 33:1, and changing the fuel tankage. The rebuilt car now weighed in at 9,500lb.

The new Bluebird ran for the first time at RAF Tangmere in Sussex on 9 July 1962, prior to a demonstration run at Goodwood racing circuit. But there was speculation that the attempt would not go ahead after all. 'Donald was certainly committed. It was his life, because there was nothing else,' Wynne-Morgan said. 'He lived off it, that was the whole thing.' But some of Campbell's backers were looking for a way out. Even at this stage, his relations with Owen weren't good. By the time Wynne-Morgan became involved, they were horrific. And the situation was never fully resolved. Owen took the view that if his companies were building the new car, it was his project and he would control it. This was a red rag to Campbell. Bluebird was his idea, and he had commissioned its design; it was *his* project and *he* would control it. It was a case of two British gentlemen, each with enormous egos, going head to head. Neither would back down.

With Campbell, Wynne-Morgan hatched a plan.

I reckoned that if we pressed ahead and did it, these companies *had* to take part. What they were hoping was that we *wouldn't* do it. So they were just deliberately delaying, not saying yes, not saying no. I've no doubt they were hoping it wouldn't happen.

In the autumn of 1962 we called a press conference at the Dorchester to announce that the project was on. But all the sponsors were still hoping it wasn't going to happen. So I wrote to them and said that we *were* doing it and that we would announce the names of all the people who were with us and all the people who had pulled out. I told them they had to make their minds up before that press conference. Even the day before, I think that the only people who had come in were Dunlop. Everybody else finally came in that morning, because they realized that it really was a brinkmanship exercise. At the end of the day it wasn't all that big an amount of money. I felt sure they would say yes, because they couldn't afford to let it go at that stage.

The plan was risky, but it worked perfectly. Certain individual representatives remained incredibly committed, but many of the sponsoring companies came in only with great reluctance. Wynne-Morgan and Campbell had won the first round of the new battle, but they knew that a desperate war lay ahead.

17

MUST I DIE FOR SIR ALFRED?

1962 to May 1963

*'I am not suggesting that Donald Campbell is incompetent, but
I still think his record attempt at Lake Eyre was not pushed with
sufficient urgency.'*

SIR ALFRED OWEN, AUGUST 1963

Donald Campbell refused pointblank to countenance a
return to Bonneville when the Bluebird project spooled up
again. He believed that the salt flats were jinxed, and with
the assistance of BP, he undertook an intensive worldwide
search for an alternative. Impressed by a report from
explorer and geologist Warren Bonython and the promise of
significant help from Australian Prime Minister Sir Robert
Menzies and South Australia Premier Sir Thomas Playford,
he settled on a salt bed in the Madigan Gulf, part of the
huge Lake Eyre. It was a primeval place, arid and barren,
located close to the country's scorched, dead heart. It was in-
hospitable to man, unless he was a twentieth-century
swashbuckler seeking a seventeen-mile race track somewhere in its 4,000 square miles of rock-hard salt. It

had not rained seriously there since 1955.

Like Bluebird CN7 itself, the vast salt lake seemed a great idea at the time, but its appeal would be cruelly diminished by events beyond anyone's reasonable expectations, the first of which David Wynne-Morgan recalled:

> We spent months going all over Australia, trying to find somewhere. One of the most frightening moments of my life was when we were crossing the Nullabor Plain and had almost given up, and somebody told us about this dried-up salt bed, Lake Eyre. Donald was a very keen pilot, and we had this Piper Aztec. We land on the lake and Donald gets terribly excited. 'This is absolutely right!' Then he says, 'I've got to go and get some more equipment for measuring the depth of the crust and load-bearing ability. I shan't be long.' He took some stuff out of the plane, said, 'Look after this,' got back in, and flew off. I was left on my own, and I didn't have any water. I thought, 'Shit, what happens if anything happens to him?' He was only away about an hour, but I've never been so pleased in my life as when I saw that plane come back.
>
> We only realized the full extent of the dangers later. The typical Aussie would say, 'Let's go and see Donald Campbell's Bluebird this week,' and they would pile into their cars and just drive across the bush. There was one whole family, their car broke down miles from anywhere. Died of starvation and thirst.

The new Lake Eyre course was named after Warren Bonython, but his association with Campbell didn't get off to the best of starts in Australia. Grahame Ferrett, who became Campbell's manager in June 1964, remembered a function at the Bonythons'. 'He and his wife were very much Establishment people, more British than British types,' he recalled. 'Warren Bonython's put a party on in Adelaide, a typical Establishment party, dull and boring! Everyone's on their best behaviour. He's decorated the place, Bluebird-wise, with whatever memorabilia he can pick up. And there, as you walked in, was a photo of Mr and Mrs Campbell – but it was the wrong Mrs Campbell! It was number two, Dorothy, the New Zealand girl.'

Nevertheless, Campbell's project was now up and running full-bore. There was assistance from the army and state police, not just to help Dunlop's representative Andrew Mustard to prepare the track itself, but to build the mile-long causeway that facilitated access to the lake. An analysis of meteorological records revealed that April, May and June were the calmest months of Lake Eyre's year. Plans were therefore laid for the attempt to be made in April or May 1963, with June as the fallback.

But even before Campbell left for Australia, there were storms. His poor relationship with newly knighted Sir Alfred Owen was not improved when he learned that the industrialist had asked Tony Rudd, chief designer and team manager of the Owen Organization-owned BRM Grand Prix team, to manage the Bluebird project. Rudd had far too much work on his plate and turned Owen down, but a fundamental difference arose between Campbell and Owen over the way in which the new project should be managed. It soon degenerated into acrimony. At the same time, Campbell was further angered that some of the sponsors who had been dragging their heels throughout 1962 in the hope that he would give up were now accusing *him* of procrastination.

It was not all doom and gloom, though. Wynne-Morgan had been busy on the public relations front. 'Having got the sponsors on board we were in business, and it was a case of making as much money as we could. So the next thing I tackled was the journalistic rights. I did deals, with Old Man [Sir Frank] Packer, that we would do daily reports for the Packer media from Lake Eyre. And I did Donald's life story, which we sold to one of the magazines out there. I did Tonia's life story too, which we sold to *Woman's Weekly* in Australia. And it all initially went very well. We got good money in, and it was turning out to be a worthwhile venture.'

In February 1963, Campbell flew out to inspect the progress of his great new track. It was surveyed in the middle of the month, at a time when the Bluebird car and boat were proving to be hugely popular attractions in the British Pavilion at the Melbourne International Trade Fair. Campbell tested a Jaguar XK150 at speeds over 100mph and was delighted to find that the surface of the lake was hard and dry, though rough. He set up his main base at a sheep station called Muloorina, owned by Elliot Price. It was thirty-seven miles south of the track, and getting to the lake was an ordeal on the scrub track that had been roughly graded by the government. When team members finally reached the lake they faced the mile of causeway, which later had to be extended when the salt at its far end began to get dangerously soft, and then a further nine-mile trek out to base camp. But the facilities offered by the Muloorina outpost far offset any geographical disadvantages.

The track itself was located to the west in the most consistently dry area of the Madigan Gulf, where sand mixed with the salt and became baked by the midday sun into a very hard surface ideal for record breaking. The best coefficient of adhesion measured at Bonneville was 0.65; the new course, the Bonython Run, yielded 0.85. This was crucially important, not just because a harder run would help to prevent the wheelspin that had caused Campbell to crash at Bonneville, but also because it would give Bluebird greater grip in the high-speed range as its tyres sought the purchase necessary to overcome increasing drag beyond 400mph. Preparation work began early in March, but the payback for the adhesion factor was that a number of salt islands had to be removed along the plotted line for the intended seventeen-mile run. They built up around the bodies of birds or animals that had perished in the harsh environment, and the best way to remove them was to tow a rotary milling cutter slowly down the course behind a tractor. It was painstaking work. Typically, one island would comprise fifty tons of salt that would take two days to remove.

All sorts of visitors turned up. 'People would just arrive to watch, and they were really not allowed to do so,' Wynne-Morgan remembered. 'Donald had leased the place. Once, I remember him driving his grader right up to a party of three Australians and saying something like, "Get off my land!" in this terribly aristocratic English accent.'

Fifteen miles of the Bonython Run had been graded when it rained on 17 March, flooding Madigan Gulf to a depth of seven inches. It was a bad omen. Salt tends to be self-healing, however, and after absorbing the water like a sponge the surface was suitable for work to recommence on 5 April. Bluebird arrived on the 13th, but then course preparation was delayed again when a grader broke through the still-soft surface at the northern end of the run. Since the grader weighed less than Bluebird, it was another bad omen. The rain, and removal of the salt islands, had severely compromised the track's load-bearing capacity. It was beginning to dawn on Campbell that the salt crust was thinner than everyone had expected.

On the 24th, a Wednesday, Elliot Price's old 4x4 Ford truck, known affectionately as the Blitz, set off to tow CN7 from Muloorina to the lake. But the journey was delayed when the Blitz's fuel pump failed after only a mile and an army wrecker had to stand in. The journey, some of it through sand eight inches deep, took five hours. That night heavy rain fell, forcing an abandonment of the first trial run, which had been scheduled for the 25th. Further rainfall that night left large areas of the course submerged, and in the early hours of the 27th Campbell was obliged to drive Bluebird back over the causeway under its own power. After another day of work on the car, flash floods cut off the road from Marree to Muloorina and left the track in an unstable condition. Further plans for a run the next day were again frustrated, and two more vehicles had to be rescued after breaking through the salt. The situation had suddenly become critical. The Madigan Gulf was a catchment area for floodwater from Queensland and New South Wales. The threat of flooding, so unthinkable and unlikely when Lake Eyre had first been chosen, had suddenly become very real. Bonython predicted that they had fewer than three weeks' grace before the floodwaters arrived. All the carefully laid plans to make sixty trial runs in a calculated and gradual build-up to the record had to be reconfigured rapidly.

Upon this harsh fact was piled another: the Bonython Run, all £50,000 (£632,000 at today's values) of it, was ruined. Work switched to another course, nicknamed Hobson's Choice by Ken Norris. It was the one piece of desert through which a course centreline could be laid without encountering salt islands. It was fifteen miles long, but at little more than twenty feet wide, safety width margins had to be more than cut in half. Now they had to achieve in days what had taken weeks with the Bonython Run. Because the surface had been softened so much by the rain, they could prepare the course the way they had in Bonneville by towing large girders slowly behind tractors. But the unspoken understanding was that this new course would not, even in its prime state, be as hard as the Bonython Run had promised to be, negating many of the factors that had been in Lake Eyre's favour. Campbell probably had nothing bigger than a five- to nine-day margin in which to set his record once the timekeepers from the Confederation of Australian Motor Sport (CAMS) had been called up. It was an impossible task.

Conditions improved sufficiently for him to drive Bluebird back onto the lake on 30 April, and on 1 May he was finally able to try it out on the improvised course. It was only a slow sortie, at 110mph in each direction, but the project had at last begun. Spirits lifted.

Bluebird ran again on Friday the 3rd, at speeds of '175 to 200', but the day was curtailed when salt created a short circuit in the braking system. Gradually, though, Campbell began to work the speed up. He found that the tail fin, locked differentials and 33:1 steering ratio made the car handle far better than it had at Bonneville. It now had 'hands-off' directional stability. On only 25 per cent power it could reach 175mph in one mile and 260mph by the third, even on damp salt. This was comfortably in line with the sort of performance it would need to establish a new record well in excess of 400mph.

Then a new problem arose. Maurice Britton, the chief designer for Motor Panels, a Rubery Owen company, removed one of Bluebird's circuit breakers on Sir Alfred Owen's orders so that the vehicle could not run. It was one of the few times when Campbell's argument with the industrialist actually spilled onto the salt. 'Maurice was so

273

proud of what he had done when Motor Panels built the car, and they did a damn good job. A beautiful job. No doubt about it,' Norris recalled. 'And he certainly didn't ever forgive Donald for damaging his baby [at Bonneville].' The problem with the circuit breaker was only resolved when Campbell threatened legal action against Britton, who was summoned back to the lake from Adelaide to replace the component. Subsequently, Campbell refused to have him on site.

Campbell got another run in above 200mph on Thursday the 9th, and on the 11th he achieved his best speed yet, 220mph. He let engineer Ken Burville drive the car back at 100mph, then did another brace of runs that saw a peak of 240mph. Spirits were rising again, but there were still problems with the Hobson's Choice track and the decision was taken to widen it in an attempt to avoid a weak spot created by one of the many salt islands. Campbell managed 170mph and 240mph on the Sunday, and after overnight rain had left pools six inches deep in places he did two more runs on Monday the 13th. On the first he hit 220mph by mile two, and then 180mph by mile one on the return. But that night it rained yet again. Tuesday night's downpour was heavier still. 'Since we'd arrived they'd had their first serious rain in fifteen years,' Wynne-Morgan said. 'And I remember that night, it was absolutely belching down. Suddenly, around midnight, Donald, who loved such gestures, said, "We've got to go and rescue Bluebird." It was all very tense. So we drove all the way out to the lake, and under the lights of the Land Rovers he drove Bluebird off the lake. He loved being dramatic, and he said, "She goes off under her own steam."'

Ken Reaks also had good reason to remember events that night.

We were having dinner at the sheep station at Muloorina when an Australian army major rushed in and said he was getting his troops back from the lake, which was likely to flood. Donald stood straight up and said, 'Volunteers, chaps. We've got to get Bluebird off the lake.'

Suddenly we realized we had thousands of miles of lake with seven major rivers feeding into it. Visions of a great wall of water coming down from the top end.

We strapped together all the torches we could find, and when we got out to the lake Donald sat on the bonnet of the Land Rover with this giant torch. You couldn't cut straight across to base camp. With all the salt islands and the thin bits you could have gone straight through the surface. You had to go in a big arc. It was belting down with this tropical rain. But he sat there calling out directions. We got out to base camp, and by that time the water was well over our ankles. It was really frightening.

We hadn't got enough vehicles to make a flare path for Donald as he drove Bird back that time, so we lined up all the vehicles we'd got and literally pointed the headlamps in the direction he was to go. Then we were supposed to leapfrog until we got to the causeway.

I had a little Commer van that certainly wasn't suited to getting wet. I was the first one on the little trot and I was on my own. Donald went by, and I followed him to the next stage, where all the other boys leapfrogged by. Then my engine suddenly stopped, and when I went to switch on the ignition again, nothing happened! I tried to dry off the plugs with whatever came to hand and eventually I was down to my vest and underpants! The amazing thing was that against the expectations of some, Donald had got Bird onto the peninsula and suddenly thought, 'Where the hell's Reaks got to?' I was pretty chuffed that he came back out to get me.

Army Corporal Paul Evans, who would oversee communications during the final attempt at Coniston in 1966/67, had no doubt that Campbell would have made good officer material. There was something about crisis that brought out the absolute best in him. He had all the qualities of a natural leader.

As salvage operations continued on Wednesday, and another cloudburst over the lake marred the evening, the first hints came of postponement. Clerk of the course Kenneth Walker and stewards Ken Archibald and Donald Hoffman were due to arrive on Thursday the 16th, together with timekeepers from the Melbourne University Car Club, but Campbell advised them not to bother making the trip.

Talk of a water speed attack, possibly at Lake Eucumbene, south of Canberra, began to filter round the unhappy camp as a final decision on the land effort hung in the balance. Then, on Saturday, 18 May, Campbell announced that it was over, probably for twelve months. Out on his track the water was already half a mile wide and, in the centre, ten feet deep.

It was a nightmare. Not only was there the pressure of the massive assistance that had been afforded him by the Australian federal and Southern Australian governments, but also the expectations of his reluctant sponsors. Campbell was accused of stringing things out, either for his own financial gain or because he was frightened after the Bonneville incident. Everyone was impatient. Carpet magnate Cyril Lord, one of the Bluebird trustees, demanded to know why it wasn't possible to go back to Utah. He cabled Campbell and Wynne-Morgan with the information that a decent twelve-and-a-half-mile course was ready and waiting. But, in addition to his hatred of Bonneville, Campbell was too far indebted to the Australians. Instead he decided, with their assistance, to undertake another survey to seek an alternative site in the southern hemisphere.

Thousands of miles away, on a remote desert lake without the communications that are taken for granted today, it was difficult for him to explain to impatient businessmen back home just how much of a bitch Mother Nature had been. He had been the fifties speedking, but now, six water records notwithstanding, the old doubts about him were resurfacing. His critics said he had bitten off more than a frightened man could chew. That he was, after all, only the son of a speedking. But Norris resolutely denied that Campbell was a worse driver after the experience at Bonneville. 'He was a bit more cautious or apprehensive, because he'd had this very nasty one, and who's to say what had caused it? It's all very well telling him, "You've got a fin on now so it's OK," but he still had to take the risk. If anything, I think he was a *wiser* driver.'

Still, Campbell was on the cross, a target for anyone with a grievance as he waited vainly for his lake to improve. At no time in his latest attempt had Bluebird ever run on a dry surface. The coefficient of friction never exceeded the 0.7 minimum Norris considered necessary to break the record. The track was bumpy, its level varying in places by as much as an inch despite Norris's requirement for a flatness tolerance of a quarter of an inch in every hundred feet. Not much for businessmen in their chauffeur-driven Rolls-Royces on London streets, perhaps, but yet another perilous obstacle for a man in a 400mph car.

Campbell, together with Bill Coley's young son Christopher, undertook exhaustive investigations of the Eucla region of the Nullabor Plains, looking at Lake Cowan, then Lefroy, Carnegie, Ballard, Disappointment, Eighty Mile Beach and the Derby flats, and reviewing Lake Eyre yet again. Lake Lefroy, east of Perth, seemed promising on several fronts, particularly the lack of salt islands and the proximity of suitable accommodation facilities, but again flooding was the problem. It appeared to be Lake Eyre or nothing.

Then, just as it seemed that things could not get worse, two events conspired to make Campbell's situation even more untenable. The first occurred when Sir Alfred Owen, who had arrived in Canberra at the beginning of August, immediately became embroiled in a slanging match with Campbell after the media had bushwhacked him into making public his private thoughts. The controversy rapidly escalated the already tense situation between Campbell and Owen, which now degenerated into an unseemly clash of egos.

'You can't race cars in an amateur fashion,' Owen told a press conference in Canberra. 'We in England were bitterly disappointed. Far too much time was spent on publicity and displaying the car. By the time Mr Campbell got down to the job, conditions were unsuitable for the attempt.' This was manifestly unfair, especially as the project had had to wait after the demise of the Bonython Run until government graders became available again after they had been called back to repair flood damage on the road to Marree. 'My outlook differs from Mr Campbell's,' Owen added. 'Correspondence between us does get heated at times.'

One technical representative suggested that Owen was 'barking up the wrong side of the right tree', but others pointed out that the aggravation between Owen and Campbell had been brewing long before it had been exacerbated by the circuit-breaker incident with Maurice Britton, whom Owen had defended. In a statement issued by Motor Panels, Owen had claimed that Britton had acted in the company's interest. 'This was done entirely as a measure of protection against a risk that, without Britton to maintain a watching brief, the driver could in ignorance damage the car,' he stated. 'But this small component, as we all know, could have had no effect on the performance.' This was a ludicrous, specious defence. The removal of the circuit breaker certainly didn't compromise the *performance* of Bluebird, but nonetheless it couldn't run without it. Moreover, Leo Villa and Ken Norris watched over Campbell's every move, not Britton, no matter how good a job he and his team had made of building and rebuilding the car. And the suggestion that a man who had already won six water speed records with a turbojet hydroplane might damage an equally complex car was laughable. Wynne-Morgan dismissed the Motor Panels statement as 'almost totally and completely inaccurate'.

Louis Stanley remembered the fiasco. 'Donald was such a curious mixture,' he said. 'When he was out in Australia there was a lot of discussion about all the delays. Sir Alfred had dinner with us before he went out there, and I said to him, "Now look, you've had plenty of press interviews, just don't say anything." So what happened was that Alfred fell into a trap. He was asked a question, and later he said to me, "I only said yes or no." So I said, "Yes, but the man asked you a question and you said yes, so it became your quotation. It came from you because you said yes to it." So there were lawsuits.'

Campbell responded vigorously to Owen's attack. 'I am afraid of death. Does Sir Alfred think that I should commit suicide?' he asked an interviewer, prompting the next day's headline: MUST I DIE FOR SIR ALFRED?

Did he really expect me to make a go at the record when he and everyone else knew conditions were unsuitable? He has accused me of wasting time exhibiting Bluebird, yet he has been happy to put his organization's products on show with the car. He doesn't appreciate all the factors connected with a record attempt, and apparently does not realize that one could not have made an attempt before the beginning of April because the heat was too strong and the winds too great. We have exactly the same team working here that was responsible for the design and operation of the Bluebird hydroplane, which has held the world record six times, and if this is an amateurish approach, I intend to stick to it. I have some very pointed questions I want to ask him.

This comment was made on 6 August. He and Owen had been invited to a dinner at Adelaide's Southern Australian Hotel the following week, and by then (on 9 August) Campbell had angrily instructed Mishcon to issue a slander writ, via the Supreme Court of South Australia, to go with one for defamation issued by the New South Wales Supreme Court. He sought damages of £80,000 (£1,011,000). Both writs led to further legal argument over who exactly owned Bluebird. Owen claimed that he did, since his companies had built it; Campbell claimed that Owen was merely a sponsor and that he was the owner. 'Donald didn't like Owen. I don't think they got on from the very beginning,' Baron Mishcon said years later. 'In my opinion, Owen was a buccaneer.' Later, the bitter dispute was settled out of court. Campbell and Owen patched things up publicly, on television. 'When two gentlemen shake hands, that is the end of the matter,' Campbell said. But beneath the surface the rift never healed.

Remaining raw too were his feelings for Stirling Moss, who got drawn into the controversy during a holiday in Melbourne. 'I might be sticking my neck out,' Moss was quoted as saying, 'but I believe a racing driver would have a better chance than a professional record breaker. Campbell carries the image of being a motor racing driver, and this is unfortunate for the motor racing industry. He is a professional record breaker, not a racing driver. I do not think he has ever driven a racing car in his life. A racing driver has more experience in handling deceleration gravities and cornering gravities and would be in a better position should any mishap occur.' Moss was then asked if former champion Jack Brabham would be a good choice, as Owen had suggested. 'He would be as good a bet as any,' Moss replied.

Moss's criticism stung Campbell deeply. 'I'll move over when my doctor tells me that I am unfit to drive,' he retorted. 'Until then I shall carry on. I have just about had enough of this argument. It is meaningless, and purely academic.

'I repeat what I have said before. Of course any top-rank racing driver could do it. So could a top-flight test pilot. But they would have to have suitable training in the use of turbines. The driver is the least important factor in any world land speed record attempt. I don't mean that any "rabbit" could get behind the wheel, but the top-notchers in the racing world would be quite capable of having a go, once they had been trained.'

The second event that soured the project occurred on 5 August on the Bonneville Salt Flats, and came only two months after Wynne-Morgan had told reporters, 'It would be a very sick joke indeed, costing two million pounds, if somebody beat us to it.' Somebody did. A relatively unknown hot-rod racer called Craig Breedlove smashed John Cobb's long-standing record with a speed of 407.45mph. He was driving a pure-thrust jetcar called Spirit of America, which he had largely designed and built himself.

He was sponsored by Shell, at that time one of BP's biggest rivals. It was a devastating blow for Campbell, whose only consolation was the minor one that Breedlove's speed was not recognized officially by the FIA, the sport's governing body, because his car did not comply with the rule that it should drive through four wheels and was therefore not an automobile. It was the automotive equivalent of the Bluebird K7, the first successful application in its field of the turbojet engine. In some ways, Campbell could hardly complain about Breedlove's concept, even though the Norris brothers had played by the rules of the day when they started drawing up the big blue streamliner back in 1956. But the world has never had much time for semantics. An American in a three-wheeled jetcar was now the fastest man on wheels. What more did anyone need to know? Campbell found himself in the position he had put Stanley Sayres in back in 1955.

In Australia, *Pix* magazine's 7 September issue said it all in the headline to its story on Breedlove's remarkable achievement: NEXT TIME . . . 500MPH. The subheading read: 'Whether it's called a car or not, it's still the fastest thing on wheels.' And there *was* somebody who thought that Breedlove's record was official: the FIM, the governing body of motorcycle racing, ratified it as a motorcycle and sidecar in deference to its three wheels. Doc Ostich had spray-painted the first graffiti on the wall back in 1960 with the unsuccessful Flying Caduceus; now Breedlove had created a stunning mural. For sixteen years Cobb's record had withstood allcomers. Within a year, however, an explosion of speed would render Bluebird CN7, the spiritual successor to Cobb's Railton Special, a very expensive white elephant.

Few situations speak so eloquently of Campbell's inner character than the way he dealt with the whole Breedlove situation. Forty years later, the American still remembered him with genuine affection.

> I loved Donald. He was cool. We had a lot of fun. I have a cartoon character in mind when I think of him. It's a kind one. I never told him this, but Donald reminded me of Thaddeus Toad in the *Ichabod Crane* series, when he first got the motor car. He had this horse that first rode with him and they used to go and raise hell with the buggy, and then they got the motor car and they were off! Donald was very charming in that way. He was almost like a child who had been held down all his childhood, and then when the Old Man died, boy!
>
> I have very fond memories of him. I met him in London and then at his home in Surrey, where he actually hosted a reception for me after we had set the 400mph record.

It must have been terribly hard for Campbell to do that, but his genuine generosity shone through. Here was an upstart Californian who had ridden a coach and horses through the international regulations and beaten his multi-million-pound wondercar to the magic 400mph. A man whose achievements had created yet another storm of controversy around his own, and put him under even greater pressure to perform despite wholly unsuitable circumstances. Yet Campbell was prepared not only to meet with his rival during Breedlove's victorious tour of Europe, but to welcome and entertain him without reservation in his own home. It happened on 19 October, when the Bluebird Project for 1963 had been mothballed, and Campbell handled a potentially explosive situation with tremendous panache, as Breedlove recalled:

I can remember that the press was very excited because they viewed this as some kind of confrontation between Campbell and myself. And he was so polite and charming. I mean, I had no idea what to expect. I was this twenty-five-year-old kid. I didn't know anything from anything. All I knew about was driving Bonneville cars and building them, and I was very naive to the political aspects of the situation. I knew of Donald's efforts and I really didn't know what to expect, frankly. Shell and Goodyear had me on this tour and England was part of it for a week on my way to Australia. It was just one of the things on a list of things to do. There was this reception at Donald Campbell's house, Roundwood.

My first awareness that there might be something going on was riding out to his house with all the press guys. They were all excited about it. I didn't know what all the fuss was about. But they were expecting some fireworks, I think. Well, I'd say within five minutes that Donald had all the press guys just following him all over this house. He just had a very charming way with him, a lot of charisma, a lot of polish, and, I think, stature from the Campbell name. In reality he controlled the whole thing. It came off just like he wanted it to. He was real good at it.

He was really a funny speaker. Very, very good. Very charming. I have a little more perspective now that I'm older and I can see how skilled he was, and how talented. How he would be able to go out and raise the money. I think Richard Noble is pretty good at that, too. He also does very well in promotions.

(Ironically, in 1969 Breedlove and Tonia Bern Campbell hatched a plan for Bluebird CN7 to be taken out of mothballs for a fresh attack on the wheeldriven record. The Californian planned to relocate the cockpit in the tail and to call the car Bluebird America, though interestingly, in reply to a question about why he located Campbell's cockpit in the nose, Ken Norris had once said, 'We can hardly sit him between the exhausts, can we?' Breedlove's new idea never really gained momentum and was subsequently overtaken by his plans for a rocket-powered challenger for the outright record when he lost that to Gary Gabelich and the Blue Flame in October 1970. Unconfirmed reports also suggested that Breedlove and Tonia became more than just friends for a while.)

If Breedlove and Campbell respected each other, there remained much less warmth in the relationship between Campbell and Moss. 'Donald Campbell had one saving grace, I think,' the racing driver ventured many years later. 'He was a brave man. And I respect him for that. I quite liked him. As a person he was a likeable scallywag, I suppose you might put it politely. What I didn't like was that he brought the name of racing driver into disrepute, because he would go along to an oil company, the lifeblood of racing, and he would get some money to go for an attempt. And he would do whatever speed he would do, on water or whatever, and then within a few weeks, or maybe even a week later, he would say, "Look, I reckon I can go a little bit faster than that, and I want the same money again."' Moss, an unquestionably honest man, thought that was unethical. 'It wasn't necessary to have that sort of money. And I just thought that sort of thing wasn't very nice. I was in a boat with him somewhere and he did something and said it was me, which wasn't true. I can't remember what it was, it wasn't anything very important, but I just thought there were a couple of things where he wasn't a gentleman.' It should be noted that Moss's family found the money to pay for the Maserati 250F that gave him his pukka entrée to

Grand Prix racing, but thereafter he was a professional works racing driver. He did not have to find the financial resources to have his vehicles designed, built and operated. Campbell did. But comparing the requirements of a record breaker and a racing driver has always been fraught.

As Tonia Bern Campbell recalled, an appearance together on television once did nothing to improve their relationship. 'We were all on *The Jimmy Young Show*, and I had a real go at Moss because he had said something nasty about Donald earlier on,' Tonia said, her eyes flashing. 'He tried to deny it, but I really kept at him and pinned him down. I would always defend my man!'

Moss, of course, had been one of the nominated drivers for Bluebird CN7, together with star test pilot Neville Duke, Squadron Leader Peter Carr, world champion racing driver Mike Hawthorn (who was killed in a road accident early in 1959, long before the car was even built) and Leo Villa. Tonia alleged that while the others kept it the secret it was intended to be, Moss leaked it to the press. Moss remembered things differently.

Yes, he nominated me. But the reason for that was publicity. No way would I have driven the thing. I don't know if he'd even bothered to ask me. But I'm not a record breaker, really. I enjoyed driving the experimental MG at Bonneville because it was a new experience, something I'd never done, and I now know more about it than the normal person. In its own way it's an interesting challenge – special tyres, the aerodynamics, the lift and the braking. I enjoyed it for that, but as an achievement it isn't that gratifying. There's no other person you're doing it against, really, just yourself. I've nothing against that, but . . .

Both men were contracted to BP.

This is why I know a bit more about it, because I knew some of the BP people quite well. And although, thank God, it didn't reflect back on me, I could see how it could have. I don't blame Donald for pushing the record up a bit each year to make a living at it, but he just didn't do it in the way that I felt he should have done. And I do think he was frightened. I think he was brave because he overcame that fear. He was not a foolish man by any means, and I think it took a lot of courage. But, you see, bravery and stupidity are very closely related to my mind, and it's difficult to say whether he was brave or stupid. But he certainly had a lot of bravery.

Tony Robinson, at whose parents' Lakeland hotel the Campbells had stayed many times over the years, took a different view when recalling the bitterness of the dispute with Sir Alfred Owen and Moss's role in it. 'I always remember Stirling getting tied up. I'd always been an admirer of his until then, but I always felt that was a stab in the back. I could never understand why a man like Moss, who must have been in the same position in many ways, got involved in that way. I never understood why he said what he did, because he and Donald were at the extremes of their particular niches in the racing world and he must have been aware of the dangers Donald faced. Maybe he was put up to saying it. From that moment he went down in my estimation.'

Brabham, the world champion of 1959 and 1960, also got dragged into the controversy. But Black Jack never did drive the Bluebird. The closest he got was sitting in the car at a show, making a farewell speech to Campbell at the send-off party at the Café Royal in the summer of 1960, and taking cine film of the demonstration at Goodwood that year. 'I think that when my name was mentioned the whole thing was a ruse to get Campbell moving,' he said. 'I was approached by Rubery Owen and asked if I wanted to drive the car. I said that I would. I was never really nominated as a reserve driver. I think it was all just a bit of publicity for me, and to stop Campbell dithering about a bit. He was dragging his feet.

'I was never quite sure that he was capable of achieving what he was trying to do. He never appeared to be a confident enough person who really wanted to do it. I guess he was happier when he was in the boat.'

There was another racing driver of note whose view had greater relevance than either Moss's or Brabham's because he actually drove Bluebird on Lake Eyre. But by the time the late Lex Davison got to experience the jetcar in 1964, Campbell had also fallen out with David Wynne-Morgan. The Bluebird land speed record project had been alive for eight years and the latest chapter in the ongoing story had cost £46,000 (£581,500), and still nobody had anything tangible to show for it.

18

'WHO'S THAT BASTARD WEARING GREEN?'

May to June 1964

'He was pretty useless as far as we were concerned, an utter idiot.'
KEN ARCHIBALD, CAMS STEWARD

The tensions that riddled the Bluebird Project went undiminished and unresolved into 1964, as Donald Campbell prepared to return to Lake Eyre. BP had finally withdrawn its backing. The company had offered to defray the cost of the new attempt, estimated between £30,000 and £50,000 (£367,200 and £612,000 at today's values), and to make a grant of £27,500 (£336,500) to Campbell himself as salary. It was a good offer, but a conditional one: BP wanted Campbell to relinquish managerial control. This was completely unacceptable to Campbell, and he turned his back on the deal rather than compromise. 'An administrative chain was proposed which could only have led to certain failure, due to the highly specialized nature of the enterprise and to harsh, tense conditions imposed on personnel by the cruel nature of the Australian desert,' he said.

It was not a decision he took lightly, as it obliged him once again to shoulder the financial burden. But then he and David Wynne-Morgan – with whom Campbell was, at the time, still on good terms – succeeded, against the odds, in attracting another oil company. 'Raising the money was a great deal more difficult, because there was a lack of confidence in Donald,' Wynne-Morgan admitted.

> The Seven Sisters, as we called them, really closed ranks after the postponement. None of the seven top companies would have anything to do with it, because BP had told them not to. So it was a question of trying to find another oil company. I looked up those in Australia that were independent. The most aggressive was Ampol. I wrote to them just before Christmas in 1963. I had a message back saying we don't deal with documents, we deal with people, and if you come out here we'll discuss it. I said fine, I'm prepared to come out and discuss the terms on which you'll do it, but I'm not prepared to come out to discuss *whether* you'll do it. Tell me you want to do it and we're just discussing the terms, and I'll come out.

He got the deal: half the money up front, the rest on completion of a successful record challenge. Dunlop was Campbell's only backer that season not to employ similar tactics. Wynne-Morgan and Campbell raised just enough money to proceed.

Unfortunately, the relationship between the two men did not last, to Wynne-Morgan's regret, and he was largely replaced as project controller in 1964 by two Australians. The first was journalist Evan Green, the second a car salesman from Adelaide called Grahame Ferrett. Ferrett had first met the Campbells the previous year, during an endeavour in Adelaide called the Miss Australia Quest which was run as a charity to benefit the local Spastic Centre. Ferrett recalled:

We had a super girl called Jenny Christmas. But we just couldn't give her fifty quid and send her off, we had to do something. Just out of Adelaide, on the Anzac Highway, was the Lido Night Club and Restaurant. It was run by Florence Allvay, who used to bring over the very best artistes for her shows. One of them was called Larrae Desmond. Florence suggested I go and see Tonia Campbell, who was a great friend of Larrae's, to see if she would join in a charitable do. I knocked on the door of the house they leased on the fore-shore and asked to speak to Mrs Campbell, and out she came. I put it to her that this would be a great thing for her to do. I'm still trying to do the sell, and all she's trying to say is yes, I'll do it! She was busting to get up and sing. So we sold a hundred tickets at ten quid a ticket – big bucks back in 1963 – and thanks to Tonia we made six hundred quid for this girl.

After Lake Eyre was washed out, Donald was planning to go outback in their Land Rovers. I'd spent quite a number of years in the bush, so I said I'd help him. He was there that night Tonia performed, that's how I met him.

Anyhow, he comes back in 1964 without the Rootes Group, that's another one that's dropped off. So he's got no vehicles. He's come to me at Yorke Motors, and he's purchased three Valiants; one he kept down in Adelaide and two he sent up to Lake Eyre. I became the Adelaide depot. I'd go to the butcher's and send up four hundred t-bone steaks, I'd go to the gunsmiths when they wanted some lead to put in the nose of the car. Do the running around. I enjoyed it.

Evan Green didn't have quite such a good time. 'Donald had a habit of really taking to people,' Tonia revealed. 'Evan had tremendous faith in Donald. But Donald would get bored with people and sort of back off. He needed them to be a challenge. If they ran around hurt like Evan did, then Donald lost interest. If they fought back and gave him a hard time, the relationship kept going. Evan was like a spurned lover after he and Donald grew apart.' When Campbell tried similar tactics with Ferrett, a no-nonsense character, Ferrett simply didn't allow it to happen. And he handled well a tricky situation of Campbell's making in which he effectively took over from Green. Later, Green would write an excellent series of features for *Motor* magazine in which his affection for, but exasperation with, Campbell came across loud and clear. One of the questions he raised was whether Campbell justified the DINGO DON and DON THE CON headlines he got from some other Australian writers.

'I guess there's a bit of con in everyone, but you couldn't call Donald that, never,' Ferrett said, denying that Campbell was an overly complex character whom you either loved or hated. 'I really didn't think he was complicated. I've got a fairly direct approach with people, and I had no problem getting to know him and getting his confidence. And there were very few of us. Evan was one of them. He was in that inner sanctum. But then, you see, I just wonder whether people whose profession is writing wanted to make something out of something that wasn't there . . .'

Perhaps, then, Campbell was just naive, easily taken in? The type to see the best in people and then be disappointed?

'I would think he believed people. Why wouldn't he? Of course some of the people he became involved with became greedy in their own right.'

Record attempts, of course, attract all kinds of people, but it's only when trouble strikes and problems arise that shake off the hangers-on that you can determine who are the ones who will stick with you.

According to Ferrett, there was nothing naive about Campbell when it came to television or radio interviews. 'He always wanted to know the questions. And if anyone strayed from them, he would walk away. He'd want to rehearse, to know what he was going to say so he could sound completely professional and knowledgeable. I guess his ego said that he never wanted to be caught out, and so many people in interviews do want to do that. He told me, "Make sure you know the questions. Otherwise just say fuck. They can't really print that."'

By 1964, Bluebird was deemed an embarrassment to British industry, and it was not just Sir Alfred Owen who was becoming increasingly angry and impatient. To some, the attempt had all the hallmarks of failure as more good money was thrown after bad. Campbell was under massive pressure to deliver, and plenty more problems lay in store.

For the first time since white settlers came to the lake, it rained heavily for the second consecutive year. In March, the weather threatened to ruin the five months of gruelling effort that had seen workers toiling in 140° temperatures to prepare a smooth new track. But in April, while Californian Lee Taylor was at Lake Havasu on the California/Arizona border preparing for his preliminary trials with his water speed record challenger Hustler, Campbell went back to Lake Eyre.

It was not until 1 May that Bluebird finally made its first trial run. That night it rained again, flooding the track with four inches of water. Campbell tried again on the 5th, and on the 9th he reached 200mph on only 20 per cent power, but even that was too much. The blue monster had torn four-mile-long ruts. All the effort that went into the £6,000 (£73,500) worth of track was wasted in that one outing. It was 1963 all over again. Once more Campbell seemed doomed to failure, the victim of elements that cared nothing about the man they were tormenting. He had to find yet another new track, and to prepare it in days, not months.

It seemed impossible, yet within days the beleaguered team had plotted an eleven-mile stretch of salt that might just be suitable, though it was another Hobson's Choice, with only twenty feet of safety margin either side. Still, Campbell had the conditions he needed to work Bluebird up to 300mph, but suddenly the emphasis of the problems switched. Up until this point it had been the weather that was troublesome; now it was the car. It was beset by violent vibrations that affected Campbell's vision and threatened to send him out of control. The sceptics had a field day. He was still suffering from fighter pilot syndrome. The ghost of Bonneville was still haunting him, and the problem was getting worse the closer he got to the speed at which he had crashed there. He was inventing reasons not to put his foot down. In short, he was scared stiff. And on this occasion, the black box was unable to back up Campbell's claims.

Villa and the team stripped the entire suspension down in a fruitless search for the cause of the vibrations. Outside the team, scepticism increased. The work was completed in time for another run on the 27th, with the same unnerving result. It was as if the wheels were out of balance, yet Dunlop representative Andrew Mustard was adamant that could not be the case. They were always painstakingly balanced. Nevertheless, Campbell insisted on changing all four wheels and made a return run at 286mph without a recurrence of the problem. This time the black box showed how horrifying the vibrations had been. The traces wrote their staccato message all over the graphs that Norris studied. It was the designer who eventually figured out that wet salt was pooling at the bottom of the wheel rims between runs, then hardening, putting them out of balance. Campbell was vindicated. Bluebird had been on the very edge of control.

The following day, Campbell achieved 352mph, and by the 29th preparations were underway for an immediate attempt on the record. But when the CAMS officials, stewards Ken Archibald and Geoff Berry and scrutineers Max Bowden and Roly Forss, arrived, they brought the rain with them. Campbell's relationship with them got off to a bad start. 'I went to Lake Eyre wearing what I considered to be suitable clothing,' Forss said. 'I knew it got freezing cold, so I brought wool clothing and light clothing. We got flown up there, and I was wearing warm trousers and jacket. Both green. I was told by a bystander who was with the Campbell group that when I got off the plane, Donald had said, "Who's that bastard wearing green?" Of course, he hated green; wouldn't have a green car, green anything. And I got off wearing green trousers and a green jacket because they were the warmest clothes I had! I don't think Campbell ever spoke to me from that day onwards.' Campbell's colour phobia was so bad that he would even jokingly refer to Evan Green as Evan Turquoise. Geoff Berry was also once caught wearing the dreaded colour. 'He hated my dark green jumper. He said to me once, "That is a dark blue jumper, isn't it?"' Forss admitted that he laughed about it. 'The Bluebird people all had these lovely blue jackets and blue trousers,' he continued. 'They all had Campbell's Bluebird Project and Ampol and everything written on them. All he had to do was offer me a pair of trousers and an Ampol jacket and I would have been absolutely anonymous. And I wouldn't have minded, even though I was a CAMS official. You know, sponsor's logo and all that. But this guy said to me, "Course, you arrived wearing green that day, you were on the out from that point onwards!"'

Campbell eventually made another run, hitting an average 360mph on 85 per cent power. Four years on, he had just reached his peak speed from Bonneville. But Bluebird was still cutting dangerously deep ruts in its course. He could no longer use the same track for return runs because of the danger of tramlining. He complained bitterly that the ruts robbed the car of speed, but it was subsequently discovered that there was a problem with the hydraulic throttle linkage. Campbell had gone for broke on that run, but following consultation with Norris and Villa he chose to regard the throttle problem as divine intervention that had saved him from getting into the ruts and crashing again.

As usual, he made a commentary: 'Bluebird to Control – check recorders running, brakes at 8,000, rolling now, increasing to 100 per cent power. Compressor 12,000, acceleration .65[g], speed 150 – three miles to go – speed 350. Maintaining full power – 360 – accelerating, 370 – 380 – track's collapsing – wheels spinning, sliding, I'm out of control – OK, back now on the centreline, full power again. Speed 350 – one mile to go – accelerating again – 360 – 370 – vibrating – 380 – vibrating severe, still accelerating – 390 – clear – can't hold her, parachute now.'

The attempt on Cobb's official record failed by just 6mph, but in any case he was outside his allotted hour between runs.

The delays and the disappointing speeds, heaped upon the ennui that is part of any record-breaking attempt, continued to create tensions. Many people were packed into a small area, some in better accommodation than others. Many were journalists who quickly became bored sitting around waiting with the pressure of having to justify their presence to their editors. For much of the time nothing happened, but they still had to write something. Stories were often blown out of proportion. People would come back from the lake, have a few beers, shoot some pool, and then go and add a little topspin away from the table. Record breaking creates situations which become a microcosm of all the worst human traits. Yet Ferrett was adamant that Campbell was a good mixer, and that it was not him that was the source of friction. 'I don't think there's any doubt that Donald could get along with most people. I think there were times when he wasn't tough enough in his negotiations, but there was no reason why people shouldn't get on with him. There were people involved with him who were impatient, and this showed up in 1964 because so many had pulled out. But he got on with people.'

One of the primary problems was Campbell's relationship with Andrew Mustard, the small, bearded man from Dunlop who tackled his work with intensity and passion. He had a small Elfin single-seater racing car, shod with smaller tyres made to the same design as Bluebird's so that he could test the adhesive properties of the track. He was an academic who took a calculated approach to every problem; Campbell had an instinctive reaction to situations and tended to do things on the spur of the moment. As the delays mounted, Mustard found it progressively harder to disguise his impatience with Campbell, Campbell to hide his complete disdain for Mustard. Interestingly, Mustard was one of the few people for whom Norris did not care. 'He wanted to give his left ball to drive the car, he told me. And he was against Donald. In a team you usually get one who's a sod like that.

He just wouldn't have it that the wheels and tyres could be out of alignment, when Donald experienced the vibrations. In the end Dunlop pulled him back, and Don Badger, who'd been with us at Bonneville, came out to take charge of the final effort. It was much better with him.'

This mutual antipathy fomented an argument between Campbell and the stewards, who got it into their heads that he was no longer fit to drive the car he had spent the past eight years creating and running. When Campbell brought a chiropractor, Roy Charles, up to the lake, they worried even more and eventually took it upon themselves to issue him with an ultimatum: 'You are not allowed to drive the car until you have had a full medical by Dr Denis Burke.'

The situation had been building since 31 May, when Campbell had annoyed the stewards by not waiting for an all-clear before starting a run. Then, after Campbell had hit 389mph, his best speed yet, on 1 June, he'd had a disagreement with clerk of the course Stuart Dibben over the state of the track and wind conditions. These were factors he was far more used to discussing with Leo Villa, who had experience of them from all their previous attempts together. Later that day Burke, an RAAF doctor who was on site, brought to the stewards' attention *his* feelings about Campbell's level of fitness; possibly his nose had been put out of joint by Campbell choosing to bring in Charles. The stewards' reaction was to request a private meeting with Campbell. Thus far they had been on site for four days and had seen the car run twice, yet they were prepared to make serious allegations about his suitability to drive it. Mustard was a frequent visitor to their part of the camp.

Campbell was already up to his neck in problems, and did not need any more from people who were supposedly there to help. But the stewards were taking their role very seriously and he handled the situation with them badly as he allowed it to escalate into confrontation. But the stewards themselves did him no favours. By their own admission they were motor racing men, used to races starting at scheduled times and drivers putting their right foot down on the loud pedal come hell or high water. They seemed ignorant of the sort of delays that are an intrinsic part of record breaking. They were impatient, and unforgiving, with a collective streak of Australian machismo of the 'go for it, she'll be right' variety. Campbell himself had been like that at Bonneville, but had learned the hard way the lesson that every record breaker must learn: patience is a life-preserving virtue.

Ferrett recalled how the situation developed:

Burke wasn't the most popular guy there. And when Donald got the ultimatum, he said, 'Hmm, I don't like this very much.' In fact he said it stronger than that! He didn't like it at all. Cliff Brebner, the local sheriff, had come down and forewarned him that a bit of an ugly scene was going to pop up. There was Mustard, Burke, the stewards, Archibald and Berry, and the scrutineers, Bowden and Forss. You got this feeling that Mustard badly wanted to be put in the driver's seat of Bluebird, and because he lived in the camp with all these guys, he'd been undermining Donald. Suggesting that he wasn't fit to drive. Mustard wanted to drive the bloody car.

So Donald picks up the phone and rings Donald Thompson, who was the CAMS secretary in Melbourne, and tells him what's going on. So they've had their conversation and Thompson's obviously cleared it. And then Donald's pre-empted the stewards by calling a meeting with them in the lounge room at Muloorina.

Campbell tackled the situation head-on, fronting up the stewards. The atmosphere during the meeting was electric, as Ferrett remembered:

Evan was there, with me, Mustard and Brebner, and some other journos including Wally Parr from the *News*, and the stewards, Archibald and Berry, of course. It didn't take long, this meeting. Don sacked them all. They were incredulous and insisted on phoning Thompson, and he of course verified that they were relieved. Then Don told Mustard that he could stay on in his capacity with Dunlop, but relieved him of the job as project manager that he had sort of inherited from Wynne-Morgan.

So I'm sitting in the corner of the room, and Don is making these announcements to the press that Mustard is off. And then he says, 'And might I announce that Mr Grahame Ferrett is now the new Australian director of Bluebird Projects.' And that's the first I've heard of it. So I wasn't sweet-talked into it. I smiled, and then they all went out. And then I said, 'What have you fucking done? I know nothing.' And Don just smiled and said, 'You were there, old chap, you were there. And now you've got the job.'

The problem was, Ferrett already had one, at Yorke Motors. 'I'd just gone up to the lake with Donald, Tonia and Roy Charles. And now my new appointment would be reported in the following day's newspapers!' Campbell offered to do a deal that would placate Ferrett's employer. The fee for Ferrett's work was that Yorke Motors would get the exclusive viewing rights and exposure with Bluebird when the record was achieved.

Though Campbell won the battle with the stewards, he was persuaded to reinstate them, in the interests of the project, on 2 June. On the 3rd he made it clear in a press conference that he had no intention of taking a second medical. The only grounds the stewards had for seeking one appeared to be Burke's suggestion that Campbell suffered from hyperventilation when he breathed oxygen. Some people who hyperventilate do so because of stress or emotional upset, and literally breathe too much. Their level of carbon dioxide falls dramatically, sometimes inducing drunkenness. Burke convinced Campbell that this was why he had crashed at Bonneville; he had watched Bluebird slip out of his control with the detachment of an isolated observer. Burke believed this would no longer affect Campbell provided he took a whiff of carbon dioxide before a run. That same day, at 10.10 p.m., Dr Simpson Newland of the RAAF gave the stewards a copy of a medical certificate which proved that Campbell had recently been passed fit for his Australian pilot's licence by a medic in Adelaide, Dr Michael D'Arcy Stanton Hicks. The matter was thus eventually resolved in the simplest of ways, but because of the characters of the parties on both sides, it left bad feelings all round.

Years later, orchardist Ken Archibald, the senior steward who had borne the brunt of the argument with Campbell at Muloorina, remained bitter. 'He was a very peculiar fellow. He got up to all sorts of tricks. He was pretty useless as far as we were concerned, an utter idiot. I'd rather forget about all that.' Roly Forss was of the opinion that Archibald had probably upset Campbell.

Ken was something of a wit. Ken had a long grey beard, but he had a joke wig at Lake Eyre that was about the same colour as his beard. He had this in his pocket, and when he put it on he looked like a caveman. I don't think that went

301

down too well. But that had nothing to do with Campbell; that was just Ken Archibald being a little arrogant. I can still remember that Brebner walked into our tent one night. I forget what he said but I don't really agree with John Pearson's account of it in his book [*Bluebird and the Dead Lake*]. Ken was wearing his wig, which didn't go down too well with Brebner, who was a bit straitlaced.

Then Campbell discovered that Geoff Berry was an undertaker. So what? Geoff was one hell of a nice bloke. He didn't walk around in a black overcoat and a top hat. He'd got a big walrus moustache, looked like a RAAF pilot. Big bloke. Big shoulders. Big moustache. Very hearty manner. Not at all like an undertaker. And it was kept from Campbell only because there wasn't any point in telling him one of the stewards was an undertaker. Course, Geoff'd tell jokes about it, but that was it.

Berry, who was present at that decisive meeting with Archibald, was more forthcoming about the details of the furore.

Denis Burke was quite concerned that Donald was hyperventilating. He said that Donald thought he'd seen a truck on the course at Bonneville and had swerved to avoid it. I can't imagine Donald doing that. Denis was concerned that the track headed towards base camp, and that if a similar thing happened Donald might drive right through it at a couple of hundred miles an hour.

On Denis's advice, we had a meeting and he persuaded us as the CAMS stewards that he would be happy only if Donald had another medical. Well, we had very little power as stewards. We were really there to observe and answer questions. We met with Donald and Andrew Mustard. Now, he was an unusual fellow, but he was on our side. But then Mustard backtracked and the writing was on the wall [this was when Campbell relieved Mustard of his duties]. That left us with no support. It all blew up for a while. In it all, poor old Donald said, 'Why do I need another medical?' What had happened was that he'd had the chiropractor [Roy Charles] out from Adelaide. That upset Denis, which is why he wanted a second medical. John Pearson's book *Bluebird and the Dead Lake* was very accurate.

I was pacing up and down, thumping the floor with this carved walking stick, and Dick Mason, from Ampol, took it away from me because it was an Aborigine artefact and worth quite a bit! I then had to speak to Donald Thompson in Melbourne. Campbell was sitting there with a glass of brandy, happy as Larry. I told Thompson that he really needed to be there to see it for himself, the situation, but he told us to keep out of it. Not to get into an argument.

I was a bit like a bull at a gate, I admit. The Bluebird team was all for doing it properly, but all the time the car was running it was leaving furrows in the salt. We got on famously with Ken Norris, but we opened our mouths in a way and upset them. We said that we could declare the track unsafe if they were looking for a way out without upsetting their sponsors. We took the view that Donald's safety was his own pigeon, but that we had to concern ourselves with the safety of others. All the time Mustard was saying that he'd take over, but of course there was this big Bluebird dynasty thing. The meeting went on until eleven o'clock that night, and we said we were sorry but we couldn't do anything. We were acting on what we considered to be medical advice, from Burke, but in fact Donald had been cleared by another doctor. Dr Newland said he was perfectly OK to drive, and we accepted that. All we had asked for is that Donald submit himself to another medical, but he had flatly refused. He'd dug in, and that was when it all blew up.

May and June 1964. Strike a light! It was fun while it lasted. At the same time, while I was at Lake Eyre, my wife had taken the kids on a train journey, and while we were both away some young offenders escaped from a local detention centre and broke into our house. Really messed it up. So I had all this to worry about as well. We were only supposed to have been at Lake Eyre for forty-eight hours!

I had the greatest admiration for Donald. He was a peculiar fellow. Pale, worried, scared stiff, every time. You could see his mind working whenever he sat in the car. But he was one of the bravest men I ever met. I've done a fair few speeches since, and that was what I always said. He lived in the shadow of his father and he tried to emulate him. He tried to do today what his father had done in the past. I wasn't the least bit surprised when he was killed at Coniston.

I can't be sued for libel now, but to put it in Denis Burke's words, during the meeting with us, 'I would put him in the category of an alcoholic. Anyone who can drink a bottle of Napoleon brandy a day isn't doing any good to himself or anyone else.' Well, I'm not saying he had all that, but he did give it a very heavy nudge. He and three others were there, so you never knew how much they each had of it and how much he'd had to drink. But the police and the army – he had a huge amount of assistance up there – were getting very cross, very cheesed off. It was almost as if they were deliberately dragging it out, to make it last as long as they possibly could. But they were running out of money and sponsors, and they knew there wasn't much chance of coming back again.

Roly Forss's recollections were laced with irony, and what he said, and the way in which he said it, gives a telling insight into why the confrontation arose.

We had a certain amount of trouble with *Mr* Campbell, because *Mr* Campbell was very autocratic. I think we got on the wrong foot early. I think he decided he was going to treat us like servants, not gentlemen, which was rather a shame. We didn't want to be treated like gentlemen, just as officials of the meeting.

Denis Burke was actually my GP in Adelaide. He was a curious bloke, very believable. He was a young, with-it, bouncing, fairly aggressive sort of bloke. I guess he'd have been in his thirties. In retrospect, some might have called him a crackpot. He fastened onto the latest, almost way-out theories, so I can look back on Lake Eyre and say that Denis was practising one of his theories at the time and he was believable, because he was a medico and he knew all the right words. And he, of course, got this idea that *Mr* Campbell was hyperventilating. Denis could produce the effects of hyperventilation in a few minutes. He could sit there, convincing us that this was what Campbell was suffering from.

My impression of Campbell after a few days – and that's all we really knew him for – was that he was very nervous. He was *highly* superstitious. I don't know what the best word for it is, but I think he'd been promoted beyond his capabilities by his demands to do what his father did. His father was probably a fairly good driver and he became a fairly good land speed driver, in the times when you had to be fairly heroic. I think Donald was brought up in this atmosphere. Father was obviously close to God, Leo Villa was his attendant, whatever. And I think as a kid

305

Donald grew up in this atmosphere, and decided that he would go on and sort of fulfil his father's inheritance. And I don't think to this day that he had quite the capabilities of his father. I don't think that because you're your father's son that in any way you inherit some of the capabilities necessary for conducting high-speed vehicles, boats or cars. I'm not saying he was incompetent, but I don't think he had the capabilities he probably needed. I think he'd gone a bit far, because he wasn't a racing driver.

But in the record-breaking arena there was nothing new in that. Neither Richard Noble nor Andy Green, Campbell's successors, had any race car experience, though Green was an RAF squadron leader. Nor did Art Arfons, Craig Breedlove or Gary Gabelich, though they'd driven dragsters. And Campbell had, of course, proved himself to have the right stuff time and again in the Bluebird hydroplanes. And his 'fairly good' father broke the land speed record nine times and the water record four.

'We stewards and scrutineers,' Forss continued, 'used to have long discussions up at Lake Eyre, because there was nothing else to do. You sat in an army tent, if it was raining, or you sat in a car on the lake, or you stood around and you wasted time and talked about things. We talked about Campbell, and we were blokes who'd been mixed up in motorsport competitions for some years. We all reckoned that, looking at what Campbell did and what he had done in America at Utah, it was perhaps the mark of a guy who was a bit over the limit. He was doing things he really oughtn't to have been doing.'

All this insight in just three days!

This didn't affect our relationship with him, but when Burke came along and said, 'Oh, I think one of the things that's wrong with him is that he's hyperventilating,' we went along with it.

The business of the chiropractor was blown out of all proportion. I remember it as being a very quiet sort of approach, but Campbell wanted it to be a big deal. There was no way it could be anything like a big deal. He went off in a huff. He said, 'If you want to have a meeting, all right, we'll have a meeting. We'll line everybody up.' Some of it's in our report. We said, 'Look, in land speed record attempts, CAMS doesn't take a very big part. We just measure how fast you go and see that everything's being done properly.' If there was a crowd there, we set it back. We were administrators doing what the rulebook said we had to do. We started asking questions, and the thing went off at a bit of a tangent. We were pretty unpopular.

Forss found Campbell autocratic, and believed he was afraid of the car. 'You certainly got the impression some days that just about the last thing he wanted to do was to get into it. And the impression you got was that he *suddenly* decided that he was going to get into it and do it. There were some days when he wouldn't drive it under any circumstances; the wind was too high, the salt wasn't right. We used to go up there every morning at dawn and wait for him to arrive. We could see that the course was all right, the wind was reasonable; it was going to be a good day. Donald would arrive and say, "No. Nothing doing." And go home again.'

None of the various stewards who oversaw this Lake Eyre attempt appeared to appreciate the degree to which Leo Villa and Ken Norris called the shots during runs. And when assimilating their views it is important to remember again just how short a time they were on site, that they only saw the car run on 31 May, 1 June and 7 June. Ultimately, they submitted an eighteen-point report to CAMS which contained a little sting in its tail. The brevity of their spell on the salt did not discourage them from recommending that Campbell should not be issued with a permit until he had agreed to a new medical examination by Denis Burke, and it ended with an astonishingly spiteful conclusion. They doubted, they said, whether Donald Campbell was a 'fit and proper person to hold an International Licence'.

In the weeks ahead, he would prove them embarrassingly inaccurate in their snap judgement.

19

CODE 'D'

July 1964

'... *all of a sudden, about a mile down the road, we're looking out onto the track and we've seen all this black stuff. So we've gone over to it, and it's all the rubber off the tyres. We had handfuls of it. Not just the odd piece, we had bloody handfuls of it.*'

GRAHAME FERRETT, LAKE EYRE, 17 JULY 1964

During all the hoopla surrounding Donald Campbell's 1964 attempt at Lake Eyre, one subject for debate was bandied about with little concern for truth and accuracy: Australian racing driver Lex Davison's performance on the occasion when he drove Bluebird. This was compounded by the gung-ho nature of men such as Roly Forss, who erroneously used it as a means of strengthening the argument against Campbell continuing as the official driver. 'It's probably fairly well documented that another bloke got in that motor car and drove it a damn sight faster than Campbell had been driving it,' Forss remarked, before amending his comment when it was pointed out that this was not actually the case. 'Lex didn't go that quickly, but the fact is that he drove it far

309

more capably than Campbell. I can't tell you very much about it, but he just went out and drove it. And Campbell wouldn't let him drive it any more. Lex in effect kept offering. "Would you like me to drive it?" And that's all I know about it, because we were fairly distant. We got the impression that Campbell got him out of the car.'

Hearsay and distant, contradictory impressions – damaging factors in any endeavour, let alone a land speed attempt. The scrutineer's version was certainly not the way either Davison or his widow Diana (now Diana Gaze) remembered things.

Davison and fellow racer and Gold Star champion Bib Stilwell visited Lake Eyre in the middle of the fight between Campbell and the stewards. Davo, as the former was known, was well respected by all those who were so critical of Campbell, but if Campbell had any sort of plan in mind it was a subtle one. Initially, he simply invited Stilwell and Davison to have a look at the great car, as Diana Gaze confirmed.

I don't think that originally we were invited there for Lex to drive it. Lex was intensely interested in what was happening, and Campbell had got very bad publicity. It was very thoughtless really. The press and lots of people connected with the land speed record really had no idea how difficult it was to drive on the salt pan. Our thought was for Lex to go up there and perhaps try and smooth things out between the oil company and the various sponsors and the press, really. That was my impression. Possibly driving the car briefly was what they had in mind for him, but I don't think that had been spelt out to Lex at the time. He thought he *might* be asked to drive it, but it was mainly to pour a little oil on the water.

The Davisons went up to Muloorina with three of their children, but as far as social timing was concerned it could not have been a less apposite moment to try to befriend the beleaguered Campbells. 'It wasn't a happy scene when we arrived there,' Diana remembered. 'There seemed to be a tremendous amount of tension. That struck me as soon as we got there, because Campbell had received very bad press. Everybody was saying, "Is he a wimp? What's wrong with him? Why doesn't he make the attempt?" But when we got there we realized that the salt pan had to be absolutely correct, because if he got in his own wheeltracks on the return run, well, it would have been curtains.'

Campbell and Tonia kept themselves to themselves, though Diana was surprised and honoured when she and Lex were housed in the homestead with owner Elliot Price and his family. The Davison children were quite content to be quartered at the army camp, and the family stayed four or five days. Diana added, 'I said, "I can't believe it, I've even got pink rosebuds on the pillow cases!" And we'd brought all our own camping gear ...' Campbell, unusually, did not go out of his way to make her feel welcome. This was further indication of the strain he was under, for Diana is the sort of attractive woman that would undoubtedly have appealed to him in normal circumstances, when he would always go out of his way to make somebody feel relaxed and comfortable in his company.

We didn't talk to Donald or Tonia a great deal. I found him unapproachable, and I was probably a little apprehensive. Tonia was a very vivacious girl, but she had her own friends around there. She didn't talk a great deal, although I do remember she told me she would never wish him good luck. She always said '*Merde*', but at that stage I didn't know what

311

that meant! Donald wasn't friendly. I think he was just terribly nervous, really apprehensive. That was my impression, and I think it was Lex's, too. Lex got on very well with him, though.

As you know, when people are working during a motor race, they're concentrating on what they have to do. I felt Campbell was not happy with the job he'd undertaken, but he knew he had to do it. We had a few meals together, but I can't say it was all, you know, a ball of fire. I can't say we ever became friends. I think Tonia and I corresponded once or twice after the event, but that was it.

Just as Diana Gaze's recollections paint a vivid picture of what the normally outgoing Donald and Tonia Campbell were going through behind the scenes at Muloorina, so Lex Davison's account of his drive provided a graphic image of what Campbell really faced out on the lonely salt.

Davison's invitation to climb into the cockpit came on 4 June when it was too windy to push for really high speeds. Campbell planned to accelerate at maximum power before braking and deploying the parachute in the measured mile, just to amuse some of the visiting guests who were getting impatient to see some action. 'Then he turned to me,' Davison remembered, 'and said, "I'd be obliged if you would drive it back."' To Diana, Bluebird was 'a pretty terrifying monster, but really, all Lex was terrified about was what would happen if he bent it, with all the millions of dollars that were involved. It was a difficult situation, just to pop in it cold and have a cockpit drill that probably lasted ten or fifteen minutes. But it was an interesting thing for him to do. Totally different to anything he'd raced. But I don't think you could ever say he *raced* Bluebird. I think he drove it, as he would have said himself, like a flannel-footed curate! If

312

the surface had been perfect, Campbell would have been driving the car himself in any case. Not that I'm saying they put Lex in it when things were not safe, but the surface there was never right to do the speeds that were required for the record.'

When Davison first lifted off the throttle, he discovered that Bluebird's aerodynamics were so effective that nothing happened. The car barely slowed down. Even with the engine on idle there was sufficient power to push it over 200mph. But with the turbine switched off, the giant car slowed quickly. Davison also discovered that there was no similarity whatsoever between driving Bluebird and driving the powerful single-seater racing cars with which he had established his reputation as one of Australia's leading lights. It was a machine, he figured, that had to be aimed and trimmed rather than steered. 'Controlling it above 300mph would call for specialized training and practice, and complete familiarity with its complex controls,' he said. 'The car strayed off the course several times because I was so busy watching the instruments, but there was no difficulty in trimming it.'

Ferrett put things into perspective.

Donald was absolutely right when he said that if breaking world records was easy, everybody would be doing it. It didn't happen that way. What you don't quite realize is that if you are going to break a world record, you are going into areas no-one has ever been before. If the world record is, say, 360mph, what's going to happen at 370mph? Does the whole car fall apart? You don't know until someone actually does it.

I was given the job of going down and lifting the lid off after Lex'd done his seven miles or so. I've got down the end

313

and I've lifted the canopy off, and all we'd done was leave the engine on idle, so he's gone 220 max, possibly a fair bit less than that. I lifted the lid off, and the bloke's in there, white. All he said was, 'All this power coming from behind me!' It was as if it was going to envelop him.

Most pertinently, Davison's conclusions were at complete variance with those of the stewards and the scrutineers. He figured that, more than anything, driving Bluebird to a land speed record in excess of 400mph would require cold, hard courage. 'In my book,' he said, 'Donald Campbell has all of these and is the only man fitted to drive the car at this stage.' But Davison, like many men who haunted that desolate camp on Lake Eyre, doubted that Bluebird would ever break the record on the terrible salt. With full steam up, he believed, the car would become a 5,000hp trench digger, 'and a rather dangerous one at that'.

Gradually, the run-in with the stewards faded into history, but still Campbell seemed no closer to his record. On Saturday, 6 June, three new CAMS men – Donald Hoffman, Alex Hawkins and Reid – arrived to replace the departed Berry and Forss. The following day, after Campbell had run the car again briefly, three timekeepers and two other officials left. On the Monday, the attempt was post-poned yet again.

Even before the Bonneville catastrophe the land speed record had been a tightrope walk. Now, as the horrible and deadly game continued, Donald Campbell became increasingly convinced that there could be no turning back. That was why he returned to Lake Eyre several weeks later, in July, against wiser counsel to quit while he was still in one piece. He had no alternative. To have stopped at this stage would have been to surrender his very being, for the land speed record encapsulated every last thing he believed in. And a record breaker who fails or, worse still, who gives up, is no longer seen to be a record breaker at all. In accordance with the tenets by which he lived his unusual life, he had to proceed along the taut-stretched wire, and to do so at a run if he was to beat the weather. And this time, on this treacherous track, he could not even see the other end of the wire, let alone be sure he would ever reach it.

It went without saying that there was no safety net.

On Monday, 13 July, only days after they had returned, it rained yet again, flooding two miles of the southern part of the track. But somehow the rain missed the precious centre section. It was an omen, the first good one for a long time. Moreover, the forecast for the next few days promised calm weather. With more rain predicted after that, Campbell realized this four- or five-day window might be his last chance, especially as on the 14th, across the world in Geneva on a whistle-stop tour, Craig Breedlove announced his intention to try to break 500mph later in the year. However you looked at it, the pressure on Campbell was mounting. That night there was more rain on Lake Eyre, and it continued into Wednesday morning, but apart from the southern end, which was under water, the rest of the course, miraculously, was fine. On Thursday, 16 July, as fellow countryman Screaming Lord Sutch was entertaining fans on his arrival in Sydney, Campbell took Bluebird out and used three short bursts of full power to hit 300mph, but he was mindful of the need to preserve the track as much as possible. The following day would prove that he was right not to squander what little it had to offer.

Meanwhile, stewards Hoffman and Reid had returned. Geoff Berry could not resist voicing a memory. 'Shortly after they arrived they said to the team, "Right, today's the day. Go for it, or we go home and call Ken Archibald and Geoff Berry back as stewards!" They really were there only about forty-eight hours. The whole attempt was run by a very long and laborious method, but then they gave their ultimatum. And bang! That's when he did the record! And he did it on the wrong day, on a Friday.' Grahame Ferrett put the situation into more accurate perspective, however. The decision to 'go for it' had nothing whatsoever to do with ultimatums from fringe players. 'Outwardly, Donald was still trying to keep everything on an even keel. He never initiated this shit with Mustard and the stewards. They had to do it on *his* terms, and it was going to take a fair while. He wasn't going to go out there and kill himself, if he could avoid it. They were still learning. Ken wanted loads of runs, and had to settle for half what he wanted.'

The 17th dawned calm and dry. Somehow, everyone knew that the attempt was on. 'One of the things that was pushing him was that the track was getting shorter and shorter,' Ferrett revealed. 'Originally, in 1963, he'd had nineteen miles. Eventually he ran on a track ten miles long, running in a different direction. That gave five miles in, measured mile, four miles out, and vice versa on the return run.' The harder Campbell had to accelerate on the shortened track, the closer he would come to risking a repeat of Bonneville. 'Actually, we were worse off than at Bonneville, as far as the track was concerned,' Ferrett added. 'It was like the same thing but on a much worse surface. Donald realized this was going to be it. Tonia told me about the restless night they had in bed. She felt the pressure too. What was going to happen in the morning? Because it was like, if the wind is down, it's on. And it *was* different that morning. I couldn't put it into that many words, but it was quiet. There was an atmosphere that was not morbid so much as pregnant. It was a good feeling. You know, we'd drawn up our plans. I was going to follow down in the car with one of the new stewards, Alex Hawkins. And we all just went out and did our thing.'

Some observers were subsequently surprised when the record actually fell, because Campbell had seemed so calm as he smoked a cigarette and talked quietly to Tonia before stepping aboard the big blue streamliner. But he knew that he faced a harrowing fight between his own natural desire to push to the limit and his wish to avoid the damaging wheel-spin that would churn up his flaky course, push the 9,500lb monster through the surface, and make the return run even more dangerous. After all the years of frustration, fear and disappointment, it amounted to this: he was facing a desperate and solitary game of high-speed Russian roulette. Campbell had once said of his obsession with record breaking, 'There is something attractive to me in venturing into a hell for no reason whatever other than it being a hell, and struggling with it.' But before the run that day Lake Eyre seemed like a hell from which there was no escape.

The Proteus engine was fired at seventeen minutes past seven that morning, and Campbell left the northern end of the course, heading south. Two miles into the run, three short of the measured distance, and still accelerating under full power, he felt the wheels again break through the pitifully fragile surface. The turbine was set to overrun at 110 per cent, to squeeze out every drop of power, but still it felt like a giant brake was being applied. He was approaching the most hazardous part of the course, where the new and old tracks intersected, but he knew that even a momentary lift from the throttle would generate a massive penalty in elapsed time and speed. In the mile, he fleetingly glimpsed a peak speed of 440mph – 50mph quicker than his previous best. But Bluebird began to hum and vibrate beyond his control as its belly scraped the deck, and the sharp ruts it was cutting in the salt retaliated by tearing matchbox-sized chunks of thin rubber from the Dunlop tyres. Still Campbell kept his foot planted to the floor, in an act of stupendous courage that was the ultimate riposte to all his critics. Then, suddenly, he was through the mile, able to ease back. The ordeal was over, but there was no time for elation as he coasted to a halt at the service depot at the southern end, for he knew that the return run would be even worse. Tyre adhesion is crucial to any wheeldriven land speed attempt, but few people, especially his impatient sponsors back in England, understood that he now had far, far less than he needed to operate Bluebird with any margin of safety.

'Donald had gone bolting down the track on his first run, following the dye markers,' Ferrett recalled, 'and we've gone along behind him, myself and Alex Hawkins. We tried to plot it with the various markers, so we could tell him at the end which line gave him the best run into the mile. So he's gone down there, and it's 403.1mph. Everyone is sort of itchy-toey. No-one is gung-ho. It's Code "D", the first time over 400, but nobody is code whatever you want to call it because of course he's got to do it both ways.'

On that first run, Campbell had indeed averaged 403.1mph through the mile, but he also knew just how awful it had been and how close to the edge Bluebird had been because of the ruts it was ploughing. Now he had to go back through them, and risk even more. On that first run, his lead-in to the measured mile had been five miles; this time it was only four, meaning that he would have to accelerate harder still on a surface that had deteriorated.

Knowing how close he was to the record made the torture all the more exquisite, but there could be no turning back, no second thoughts. No abandonment. Only he, of the hundred people on the salt that day, knew just how close to disaster he had come. And how intolerable the odds were for his return run.

In all his life, Campbell had never faced quite such peril, for the accident at Bonneville had been unexpected, and the oxygen poisoning that might have caused it had rendered him relaxed and immune to worry. But this time, the whiff of carbon dioxide he took before each run at Denis Burke's suggestion left him clear-headed. This was altogether different. This was a deadly and cold-blooded poker game.

Campbell later claimed that as he sat alone in the cockpit between those two runs, he saw the ghost of his father reflected in the raised screen of the cockpit canopy. He remembered how he had felt watching his father deal with his own fear at Bonneville back in 1935, when one of Bluebird's front tyres had burst and caught fire on the first run and Sir Malcolm had faced the prospect of a repeat on his return. He claimed that his father said to him, 'Now you know how I felt back then,' before adding, 'But it'll be all right, boy.' Ken Norris was used to seeing the Skipper sitting quietly by himself in the cockpit, particularly on the turn-arounds when he was waiting for the team to change the wheels. 'He'd be sitting there ready, and he'd sort of retire into his shell. The canopy would still be up. I'd go over and have a little chat with him, and he'd say, "What do I do this time, Professor?" or something. But this particular time when I leant over and said, "How are you, Donald?" or something like that, he was just staring straight ahead, and he continued to do that. He didn't seem to acknowledge me at all. Leo had felt the same thing, and had left him quietly in the cockpit. Yeah ... he could have been communing with his dad.'

Grahame Ferrett was struck by the incident, too.

I saw the same thing. I don't know what he was doing, but we pulled up and I said, 'What's the speed?' But nothing, nothing. He was sitting there like a dummy, his head tilted back. He didn't tell me then what had transpired, or supposedly transpired, and I certainly saw no vision of anybody, let alone Sir Malcolm Campbell sitting there, but he was definitely in a trance-like state. But not for long. Maybe thirty seconds. Then he was into the conversation. And what used to amaze me about it was that at the end of any run, he could read those instruments like you wouldn't believe. He could give all those guys what everything was about at practically any stage of the run. Way beyond my comprehension that somebody could do that.

Ferrett's observation put into perspective the Bonneville slurs about Campbell's knowledge and ability. The Australian agreed with Norris that Campbell's feedback was of test pilot standard. 'It was unbelievable. I saw it happen. Not just once or twice. We had a lot of runs, and each time that information was required, or he would volunteer it, it was accepted as gospel by Ken and Leo and all these guys.' And it was borne out by all the telemetry on the car. 'Oh yeah, they had enough of that to either verify or negate it. And what a lot of people didn't know is that he'd get to the end of a run and say what the gauges had been reading – bom, bom, bom. The full test pilot bit. You can't do that if you're shit frightened.'

Now, as the minutes tiptoed by, everyone grew nervous about the return run, which had to be made within the hour. Bluebird was ready to run again at five minutes past eight; the engine was fired five minutes later. The wind had risen slightly to 2mph, the maximum permissible.

This time the track disintegrated at the third mile, but still Campbell kept the throttle wide open even as the salt scraped the tread from the tyres again and the fantastic torque of the Proteus engine drove the 52in wheels right through the thin crust. In places, Bluebird was literally tobogganing down the course on its belly, on the very edge of control. The slightest excess of steering input could have sent it careering over that edge and into another nightmare of Bonneville proportions, perhaps worse. The chances of surviving another inversion at such speed were remote, yet Campbell kept his nerve and never lifted his foot as Bluebird ploughed and planed through the measured mile. In an incredible coincidence, the mean speeds in both directions were identical, 403.1mph, but on the second run the telemetry revealed that the last third of the mile had been covered at 429.5mph. Bluebird was still accelerating as it seared out of the measured distance, peaking again at 440mph.

Donald Campbell was the holder of the official land speed record at 403.1mph, while his kilometre speeds were 388.7mph running south, 400.5mph running north. He was too exhausted emotionally to feel elated.

Ferrett recalled that final run:

. We knew that with four miles' run-up instead of five, he'd got to let out a bit of shaft, and there wasn't any left. Away he went with a roar and a bang like you've never heard before, so Alex and I got into our car again to track him back; Leo and Ken had already gone ahead before they'd let him go. So we're tootling down this ten-mile strip, and all of a sudden, about a mile down the road, we're looking out onto the track and we've seen all this black stuff. So we've gone over to it, and it's all the rubber off the tyres. We had handfuls of it. Not just the odd piece, we had bloody handfuls of it. As we got up, we looked up to the horizon and there was this big blob right in the middle of the track. Of course, our hearts went right into our mouths. 'It's gone in, the car's gone in!' We hopped back in the car and got there as quick as we could, and all of a sudden the big blob became a narrow blob and disappeared from us. It was Ken and Leo. They'd gone into the middle of the track to see how far he was cutting into the salt.

So we've got up to the other end, and the car is turned round again and he's getting ready to go back on a third run, because he's done the same speed both ways. There was a little jubilation, like everyone was on a little bit of a high, but we had to have this one extra run because he wanted to go better than 403.1mph average. I said, 'You'd better come and have a look at this.' They hadn't changed the wheels yet. I showed him the chunks of rubber and said, 'That's off there.' The biggest bits of rubber were the size of a human hand.

The debris was spread over seven miles. The right rear tyre had no tread left at all. 'It was all kept fairly quiet, because of Dunlop,' Ferrett continued. 'The intention was to go back, but whether they were going to do it, I'm not sure. I think they were running pretty short of tyres at this stage anyway. But I'll never forget what happened if I live to be 109. Donald said to Mustard, who'd come back, "How do you explain this?" And Mustard's reply was, "Oh, it never happened in the laboratory!" To which I said, "Well, we're not in the laboratory now, we're out here!" '

The state of the tyres and the course finally persuaded

Campbell – who had not been aware during the nightmare runs just how much rubber the tyres were losing – Norris and Villa that a third run would be tempting Fate too much. There simply wasn't any point in putting Campbell's neck on the line again. 'He would have had to go back yet again through the ruts,' Ferrett said. 'He was going into the salt three or four inches in some places, and it only had a four-inch ground clearance. And it was like razor blades, the crystals at the side. That's what was shredding the stuff off the tyres, particularly when he had to go gung-ho with only the four-mile run-up on the second run. It was just incredible that both runs were identical. The only time it had ever happened. As if somebody was telling him that was as fast as he would be allowed to go. He was pretty calm and cool about it all. So it was decided that that was it.'

The nightmare was finally over. Even Campbell himself did not seem to understand it, or really to appreciate that it was finished. It was as if it had dragged on so long that the tribulations and the acrimony, the sheer nervous effort, had ultimately overshadowed the impact of the final triumph. He hugged Tonia and, tellingly, said, 'Darling, we've made it.' Not *done* it, but *made* it, as if he had survived when he had never thought he would. He also said that he was heart-broken not to have bettered Breedlove's speed, even though he now had the official record. There were three cheers from spectators as he was borne away from the car on the shoulders of his crew.

Later, he began to react to the long-awaited success. 'The vibrations were terrific, but stopped soon after we were through the measured mile,' he recalled.

My first reaction is a prayer of thanksgiving. Second is one of tremendous admiration for the machine, that it was controllable and that the tyres stood up to this terrifying treatment. Thirdly, I feel disappointed that the length of the track and perhaps even more the condition of the track took 40mph off what the machine would achieve on a surface that was hard and firm. This track is ruined for the present. Frankly, I don't think we could get a better speed in the present conditions. Fourthly, I feel gratitude to Australia, for the tremendous sportsmanship and support that has been given to us. Finally, I offer my thanks to all concerned with the Bluebird team, who are delighted that the two Bluebirds now hold the official world land and water speed records.

Back in England, Sir Alfred Owen said, 'I am absolutely thrilled that he has achieved it at last.'

'The speed was disappointing,' Campbell continued, sounding, as *News* reporter Wally Parr described it, half-happy, half-sorry, 'but in the circumstances it was a fantastic performance.' He added that the track had hampered that second run disastrously. 'On the run from south to north, 4,400hp was going through the wheels, but it was like driving through bulldust – just like a huge hand holding me back. The course is ruined for weeks ahead. The short track and the surface robbed us of a speed far in excess of Breedlove's unofficial mark.' But Norris praised Campbell, confident that he had obtained the utmost from the car. 'We could not get a better speed on the track as it is,' he said.

Australia gave Campbell his moment in the sun, the *Adelaide Advertiser* and the *News* in particular doing him proud. Both had him as front-page headline news: WORLD TRIBUTES TO U.K. DRIVER said the former's headline, while the latter declared CAMPBELL DOES IT: NEW RECORD. The *Advertiser* also lived up to its name by carrying large ads inside for

Mayne Nickless (in charge of transport), Dunlop, Ampol and Lucas. Telegrams came in from all over the world. There were so many that special arrangements had to be made to deliver them all to Muloorina. The *News*' editorial was particularly enthusiastic:

> Hurrah for Donald Campbell. He has done it at last. On the salty, treacherous surface of remote Lake Eyre, to which he has contributed his own salty tears over the past year, he has broken the world land speed record for this kind of vehicle.
>
> The applause for Mr Campbell's achievement will now be all the louder and longer for his having had so many disappointments and setbacks.
>
> It has been rather like the circus juggler or the acrobat who attempts some difficult feat. He fails and fumbles at first. We feel for him. Then, triumphantly, he does the trick, and we all clap hard.
>
> We are clapping now. Campbell has done what he set out to do. He has shown admirable doggedness in the face of uncanny setbacks. Even Nature seemed to be against him. Lake Eyre had repeated rains the like of which had not been known at Muloorina Station for years.
>
> Now Campbell has focused the spotlight of world fame on the flat, lonely Lake Eyre in a way that nothing else could have done. Whether everyone agrees that the speed record is important or not, it was certainly important to him. He deserves his moment of triumph.

Opposite this glowing tribute was a cartoon showing Campbell being fêted around a cooling Bluebird as an old local sage stood by and said, 'But this run only took 8.9 seconds ... what has all the durned fuss been about all along?'

The *News* gave Campbell the sort of laudatory copy he was due, but others would not be so charitable. Back home, in the land of his birth, the specialist magazine *Motor Sport* denied him the accolades his fabulous effort deserved. The self-styled 'voice of racing' at that time dismissed it with a stingy editorial laced with cheap shots and headed AT LAST!

Out in Australia Donald Campbell has at long last broken the motor-car speed record, by a few mph. His Bristol Proteus gas-turbine Bluebird is the first car officially to exceed 400mph. But, in view of the enormous expenditure and the time which has elapsed since Bluebird was publicly demonstrated at Goodwood, the speed is unsatisfactory. It is disappointing that the 5,000hp monster didn't go faster than Breedlove's American jet-thrust tricycle and settle the controversy as to who is entitled to land speed record laurels.

Early reports quote Campbell as blaming the Dunlop tyres, which, if true, is poor repayment to a vital sponsor.

This long-drawn-out record bid heightens our admiration for John Cobb, who so nearly did 400mph in his comparatively inexpensive, piston-engined Railton Mobil eighteen years ago, and for Segrave, who broke the record in 1927 and again in 1929 with minimum delay and fuss.

Few leaders have ever been as pompous, spiteful, damning and downright misinformed.

After all the heartache, all the effort and agony, though, cruel Lake Eyre had only granted Donald Campbell a qualified success. Even in defeat, it could not bring itself to give him a speed that would have bettered Breedlove's damned 407.45mph. And that, as history would reveal, was only scratching the surface of the potential of the pure jetcar. Though a gritty product of raw courage and bloody-minded determination allied to superb engineering, human endeavour and resilience, the record was an anti-climax. But even as he prepared to leave Lake Eyre for Adelaide to start the celebrations, Campbell knew precisely what he was going to do for an encore.

20

THE FINEST HOURS

July to December 1964

Ever since he had first planned to challenge for land speed
honours, Donald Campbell had been determined to break
both the land and water speed records in the same year, but
he had also said that if he set a record that was faster than
John Cobb's 394.2mph but failed to beat Breedlove's unofficial 407.45mph, it would be a failure. And that was what
he continued to believe, deep within himself.

Bluebird CN7, the car to end all cars, was a white
elephant. It wasn't Campbell's fault, nor the Norris brothers'.
They had tackled the project the only way they knew how,
with fantastic attention to detail, ingenuity, total commitment and the desire to take every step that needed to be
taken to create the fastest, safest automobile in history. But
circumstance had damned them. The gestation period was

essential for the vehicle Ken and Lew Norris had in mind, and it should not be overlooked that the aim was 500mph, a speed that wheeldriven cars have yet to breach today. 'It was a good job that brother Lew and I worked fast,' Ken Norris said. 'Sometimes I look back and just don't understand how we did so much in the time available.' But then came the setback at Bonneville, the prolonged rebuild and Campbell's own lengthy recovery; then the weather-induced fiascos on Lake Eyre. Nobody doubted that CN7 could have set a record much, much closer to 500mph on the right sort of track, but even before the Bluebird Project left Lake Eyre, Campbell knew that the CN7 programme was effectively finished.

He alluded to the supersonic car again when Wally Parr stole a march on the competition in the *News* on 18 July 1964, which ran the headline CAMPBELL PARADE IN CITY – SECRET CAR. Campbell spoke for the first time of the rocket car project, telling Parr it had been under development at Norris Brothers for the past two years. He talked of the supersonic region, saying, 'Totally unknown problems would be met at that speed. The next barrier to be encountered will be the speed of sound. So far we have crawled over the top of 400. I think now possibly that it is within economic grounds to lay down an artificial track. This would have the great advantage that wherever that course might be laid down it would automatically become the world centre for this type of activity.' It was bold talk, but it was just that. Ultimately, nobody would be interested.

There had been plenty of time at the lake to consider the future, though until the nightmare was over he had not been at all sure that he had one. The day after his 403mph record, both the *Adelaide Advertiser* and the *News* reported his plan to go for the water speed record. Lake Albacutya in Victoria was mentioned, though the *News* quoted David Wynne-

Morgan in London as saying that the attempt would take place at a neighbouring lake, Hindmarsh.

Before plans could be developed, there was a victory parade through the streets of Adelaide on Saturday, 25 July. If Campbell's dogged triumph met with only lukewarm headlines in his own country, the reception he received in the Australian city of churches was completely gratifying. More than 200,000 Australians turned out to greet the man who had just made the country famous. In a comment to reporters that was typically proper and stilted (The Voice again), Campbell said, 'My wife and I have become attached to Adelaide and I am looking into the prospect of obtaining a permanent interest here.' But they weren't planning to emigrate, just to lease a property.

The plan was for Campbell to drive CN7 (with the cockpit cover removed) at very low speed from Torrens Parade Ground, down King William Street to the town hall, where he and Tonia would be received by Lord Mayor Irwin in a small celebration in the Queen Adelaide Room. During that break, Villa would refuel Bluebird, then Campbell would drive the car again to Yorke Motors in Angas Street where, as part of his agreement with Grahame Ferrett, it would go on show prior to further exhibition duty in Sydney. 'That was a real hoot,' Ferrett recalled.

Donald's at his very best, wearing the blue overalls, nearly tailor-made jobs. The whole Bluebird team and support vehicles were lined up at the Torrens Parade Ground. The day before this is gonna happen, we've gone for a drive, done the course to the town hall. Then we're gonna drive on, into the middle of Victoria Square, hang a left, and go three hundred yards down Angas Street, to Yorke Motors. My part's done.

Bluebird has five degrees of steering, so it's important that we get the right angle to start turning out of one street onto the other, especially into Angas Street. Oh look, there's a NO PARKING sign there. That's the marker. I'll walk alongside the car, you start turning there. That's one problem. The second was that he can only drive it with the brakes on, because at full idle it's 270mph, isn't it? The third problem is that the fuel tank only holds sixteen gallons, because normally it's only got to run ten or eleven miles. Now it's going only one mile but it's going to take five or six minutes and there's every chance that it's going to run out of fuel between the parade ground and the town hall. Turned out it took fifteen and a half gallons at the town hall, so it was mighty close!

On the big day it's all gone off perfectly, and then we've set off to turn into Angas Street, but what we didn't take into consideration was the crowd. According to the police, there were more people there than there were for the Beatles. You're talking over two hundred thousand. And of course, all of them stand in front of this NO PARKING sign! So we finished up facing the Adelaide Police Court, actually on the steps of the law courts! The car's hot, so we've got to cool it down and back it out with the help of the police and thousands of willing pushers. Eventually, there it is in Yorke Motors. Then it went off to Sydney to the David Jones store. They paid £5,000 for a week's exhibition.

Over lunch in the town hall, Lord Mayor Irwin made a short speech: 'A project such as this needs courage and enlightened leadership. It had both. But I don't know why you didn't use the Adelaide measured mile for your attempt. The salt seemed to stand up pretty well this morning . . .' Campbell made a brief reply. 'The question is always asked, what good do these record attempts do? Well, if the human

331

race no longer wants to better the four-minute mile, conquer Mount Everest, the skies and the oceans, then it will stagnate.'

One little vignette from the day stands out as an indication of what the Campbells were really like as people, rather than the icons they had suddenly become to Australians. While Bluebird was at rest outside the town hall, Tonia asked the police to let the hundreds of children come forward to get a closer view. Campbell, clearly enjoying himself immensely and greatly amused, shook hands with most of them before setting off again.

Once the Adelaide parade was out of the way, work could begin on definitive planning for the water speed record attempt. Ampol and tobacco company W.D. and H.O. Wills remained as backers, as they had been at Lake Eyre, but by this time Campbell and Wynne-Morgan had finally fallen out for good, over money.

Donald refused to pay me the 50 per cent that was payable after the record. He said, 'Look, David, you've made a fortune out of this, I'm not going to pay.' I said, 'Donald, we had an agreement. I don't happen to have made a fortune; you might remember I've had to pay all my own expenses. I've spent a great deal of money, it's a gamble that has come off, and I expect you to honour it.' But he wouldn't. It was sad in a way. The one thing he obsessed about was getting the world water speed record and the world land speed record in the same year, the one thing that his father had never done. And he *did* have this sort of father complex. Both love, and trying to beat him. So I said, 'Well, if you're not going to pay me, I will leave and I'm going to sue you, Donald. It's cut and dried, we had an absolute agreement, and I worked for it. And I will do it with great regret.' He was very obstinate, so I went. And I knew that he didn't need me to anything like the same extent for the water record. For the land record, first of all we had to find somewhere we could do it and prepare the track, whereas with the boat, frankly, it was either the conditions were right and it was fast enough, or not. All you had to do was find a stretch of water.

I put things in the hands of my solicitors. Despite it all, I was still very fond of Donald, though of course I was angry. He was an extraordinarily complex man. I mean, half of him was so nice and so exciting, and the other half, over money, not good. His business relationships almost always ended in tears.

Wynne-Morgan never would receive his money. 'Subsequent to all our arguments he came back to England, went up to Coniston, and got killed. Now, suing Donald Campbell was one thing; suing the widow's estate was quite another. I had a word with my lawyer and he said again that it was absolutely cut and dried, but I really couldn't do that. So I didn't, and that was that.'

Campbell and Wynne-Morgan seemed to attract trouble. 'Another person who refused to pay up was Sir Frank Packer,' David recalled.

When we got washed out at Lake Eyre, he just said to me, 'Well, that's it, I'm not going to pay any more.' And I said, 'We had a contract, and you used the material, all the reports, Tonia's life story, and Donald's.' But he just said, 'Do what you like about it, but fuck off.' So again I decided to sue Packer. In Sydney I had to go to seven different firms of solicitors before I could find one that would issue the writ. He didn't have a leg to stand on, and he paid. Then I was at a party in Sydney and Old Man Packer was there, and he was a very big man, a former professional boxer or wrestler. People were very frightened of him. And I must say, I was very nervous. He looked across at me and said, 'Come here, young man.' So, very nervously, I went over, and he said, 'You were very brave.' I laughed, and said, 'I'm not brave, Mr Packer, just desperate.' 'You must have had a bit of trouble,' he said, 'serving that writ on me.' I said, 'Yes, it wasn't easy.' 'Oh well,' he said, 'I take my hat off to you. I'd have done the same!' And that was that. But it was typical of the sort of piracy that operated in Australia then.

Lake Bonney, four miles long, three miles wide and only eighteen feet deep, was eventually chosen for the water speed attempt. It was 150 miles south-east of Adelaide, on the coast near Mount Gambier. The weather could be unpredictable, but the local authorities were very enthusiastic to have the man all Australia was talking about running on their lake and offered to build all the necessary facilities: boathouse, slipway and even accommodation. Villa, Ferrett and Green had first visited the area on 14 September, and they called Campbell the following day. Villa had also flown out to Victoria to view Lake Albacutya. It was longer than Bonney but not as suitable since access was very difficult. Time was running short, so they settled on Bonney.

The new Bluebird Project left Adelaide by road on 6 November to set up camp. Campbell arrived on the 12th, and the following day the Beryl turbojet was given a static test. On the 14th, Campbell took Bluebird K7 out for the first time since his run at Coniston in 1959, a world away. After all that had gone wrong in the intervening years, he found it oddly comforting to be back in the familiar surroundings of the tight little cockpit. He reached 210mph.

'We could have got the record second day out,' Ferrett said. 'To make it profitable, the quicker, the better. But of course that's not easy. All the Longines timing equipment had been sent down after Lake Eyre to be overhauled because of the salt. We went out on the Saturday morning for the first run, and it was fine. All set to go for the record on the Sunday. But that second day the timing equipment malfunctioned. We were all feeling pretty happy after that 210mph, thinking it was all going to be over in a matter of days . . .'

By the time Bluebird ran again, local floods were starting to roll in and Campbell started to get a pounding. He couldn't get over 200mph without risking serious damage. 'It took us two or three weeks to figure out what was causing it,' Ferrett continued. 'You've got to remember that the local people didn't want him to go! There were thousands of people going to Lake Bonney because Donald Campbell was there, so the last thing they were going to warn us about was the local weather effects.' Snow melting on the Australian Alps was sending thousands of gallons of freezing water into the warm lake, creating unseen disturbances. Campbell persisted, but always the result was the same: he could not push Bluebird anywhere near its maximum. Frustration replaced the optimism with which they had all embarked on the venture. It was Canandaigua all over again. But Campbell still found time for some fun and games, as Ferrett recalled:

We had a boatshed, just by the jetty. Ampol had a very, very nice bloke, Reg Moroney. A bit full of himself, perhaps, but they were Ampol, the main sponsor. The rules were that no-one, but *no-one*, was allowed in the compound other than the team. So they're going to give the boat a static engine run, and they've got a bloody great cable on it, straight through the shed, and round a bloody great gum tree. In comes Moroney through the compound with all these journos. I said, 'Reg, you're going to have to get these guys out of here, they're not allowed.' And he said, 'Whaddya mean? I'm Ampol, we've got this tour, and we need the pictures and this story.' And I said, 'Sorry, pal, out.' And so it developed into a big argument, and I'm not doing too well. He's got the numbers, hasn't he? Up turns Donald. I thought, 'Thank Christ he's here, he'll put it to rights.' 'Oh,' he said, 'what's the problem?' I told him. So he said to Reg, 'What do you want to do?' And Reg said, 'I just want these people in here to take some pictures.' And Donald said, 'Oh, that's quite all right. That's not a problem.' I'm thinking, 'That's a putdown.' Then Donald said, 'Of course, what Grahame's done is quite right, because we are not secured for the crew, but providing that you are here at your own risk and you bear all the responsibility for all these people, it's quite all right.' And he spoke very nicely to all these blokes. 'Just please don't have anyone in front of or behind the boat.'

Well, I'm really pissed off. I've stormed up into the bloody boatshed, and Fred's [Tonia Bern Campbell] there, and I've said, 'Your fucking husband, I've had a gutful of him.' She said, 'What's wrong? Come with me.' So we've gone over and sat in the car, because I've really spat the dummy. Just her and me. And I blew one.

All these guys are up at the jetty. Donald has a grin on his face, gets in the boat, they crank the engine up and away it goes. The amount of water that gets whipped up is unbelievable. It's come over the boatshed, like a roostertail. Two of these guys fell in the water. And of course at the end of the static test Fred and I have stepped out, we're bone dry, all the crew are dry, and all these journos and Reg are soaked! And Donald came out of the cockpit and said to them, deadpan, 'Did you get the shots you wanted?'

Eventually it became apparent that they were never going to be able to reach a record speed on Lake Bonney. On 8 December, with time running perilously short, they began to look for another lake. Ferrett was sent off to view alternatives. First he went back to Lake Hindmarsh and Lake Tyrrell, both east of Adelaide, then Lake Eucumbene, a lot further east, south of Canberra in New South Wales. But in the middle of the recce, on 10 December, Villa called him to say that they had received an offer from Lake Dumbleyung, 140 miles south-east of Perth. 'There was a fellow called David Brand who was the Premier of Western Australia,' Ferrett explained, 'and he saw the promotional advantage of this thing happening in the west, so I got sent over to Dumbleyung. I rang Donald and said, "Well, it's long enough." It was about six miles long and three miles wide. Not ideal. Too long and too wide. You really needed something about five miles long and half a mile wide. But it was right for depth. Only fifteen, sixteen feet. So I came back to Melbourne to find that Donald had already made the decision to go to Dumbleyung!'

The new venue had a drawback: it was visited by a daily wind called the Albany Doctor, which would hit around three or four o'clock in the afternoon. But Campbell had few options and the clock was ticking loudly. Western Australia was very friendly, and the people wanted him there. Little over ten days later, the team had upped sticks from Lake Bonney and relocated 1,600 miles further west. Campbell had his first run at Dumbleyung on 22 December, but, agonizingly, it seemed likely that he was going to be denied the two-in-a-year record.

337

Almost immediately, Ferrett found himself embroiled in local politics. There were too many rotting gum trees in the area where ideally he wanted to set up base camp, and the Dumbleyung council wasn't about to uproot them.

I know I've got to go to either one end of the lake or the other, and they're taking me all round the bottom end, the Dumbleyung Shire end, and up as far as their ski club, about mid-lake. There was a nice clubhouse there, and I could see where, if you pulled up a dozen trees, you'd have a chance to get the boat out. But when they said the thing with the trees wasn't going to happen, I said OK, we need another launch site. And everything went quiet. The local inspector of police had come up from Albany, and I said to him, 'I don't think that's gone over too well.' He said, 'No, it hasn't. You've put your project now in the Wagin Shire council area.' There was tremendous competitiveness between the two local councils because the territorial fence went bang through the middle of the lake. And I only made the choice because the Dumbleyung people had too many trees their end and wouldn't move any.

Campbell and the Bluebird team actually got on famously with the locals, though the duck hunters had their noses put out of joint. The project arrived in the middle of the hunting season so the hunters were refused permission to go out on the lake. This pleased Campbell no end. 'He never shot anything live in his life,' Ferrett said. 'He'd have a go at a target or a tin on a post, but not creatures. That wasn't his bag at all.' The only problem was that it didn't take the ducks long to figure out that Lake Dumbleyung had become a haven. The team had to send people out in the course boats to discharge shotguns to clear them. On one run, a duck actually hit Bluebird's windscreen, and narrowly missed going down the intake.

Campbell's choice of watering hole for his team also spoke volumes about his character. 'Dumbleyung was like a lot of country towns,' Ferrett explained. 'You had the pub people, in this wheat-growing area, then you had the club people. There were two pubs in Dumbleyung, and all the good people went to one pub and all the others went to the other run by a guy called George Moore. George was a pisspot, but a lovely bloke. He showed Donald a friendship that was genuine, whereas the others wanted to know Donald Campbell for what he was, not for *who* he was. So we finished up making George Moore's place our headquarters. It was just another side to Donald. He could have had the club, but he just liked George.'

For days, high winds kept Bluebird moored in her boathouse. Christmas Day came and went without any sign of a let-up. It was as if the weather gods of Lake Eyre had followed the project west. A cruel chimera appeared on Boxing Day when the wind suddenly dropped at five thirty in the morning. A panic call summoned the timekeepers from Perth, only for the wind to return, complete with a thin, choking dust, just as they arrived after making the journey in record time.

In the days that followed, the routine became familiar: check the forecast the previous night; rise at three thirty only to watch white-capped waves disturbing the lake. It was soul-destroying. The battle of Lake Eyre could never be fought again; registering the land and water speed records in the same year could never be repeated. Yet here it was, slipping inexorably away. It was as if some malignant destiny hung over Campbell, set on denying him his place in history. To alleviate things, he once persuaded Villa to drive

Bluebird, sending him on his way with a cheery, 'Goodbye, Old Man, it's been nice knowing you.'

Finally, the last day of the year arrived, a Friday. Still Campbell hadn't got his record, and still the fifteen-knot south-easterly wind was too high. Spirits reached an all-time low. Eventually, Campbell and Ferrett prepared to inspect other venues. In such moments he could spring into action of any kind. It helped to take his mind off the bitter disappointment, and anything was better than simply sitting there, staring defeat in the face. Action at least created the illusion that he was not beholden to factors beyond his control, and it postponed having to acknowledge that, after all he had been through at Lake Eyre, the great opportunity had been snatched away. He was already airborne when Villa realized that the wind had finally dropped, but Campbell and Ferrett too had noticed the change and came circling back. 'We'd taken off in the Aero Commander not long after two o'clock,' Ferrett recalled. 'We were headed out over the coast to look at some skinny lakes, just up from Bunbury.' These were Lake Clifton and Lake Preston, salt-water lakes. 'You didn't want to run on salt water, but at that stage the desperation was there, so Donald said, "Stuff it, if the boat's gonna rust out it's gonna rust out. We've got to find a lake." So we got up in the air, but just then we could see that Dumbleyung was flattening off. We landed back again, in a fair hurry, around three o'clock.'

They were in such a race against the Albany Doctor that Campbell didn't even have time to change into his blue coveralls. He left Tonia holding his crash helmet, and Mr Whoppit, and leapt into the cockpit wearing shorts, a short-sleeved sports shirt and his radio helmet. He was desperate to take advantage of the sudden windfall. Yet despite the need for speed, there was also the habitual need for caution, as Villa monitored the dying swell. The wait was nerve-racking. The longer the delay, the greater the risk the Albany Doctor would arrive. But the decision could not be hurried. In Bluebird's cockpit, sweltering in 143°, Campbell dozed.

At fourteen minutes past three, Villa finally gave him the signal he was waiting for. 'I think it's worth a try, Skipper. Conditions are pretty damned good: flat calm, speed unlimited. Let's go.'

Watched by only a few hundred people, Bluebird sped down the lake, entering the measured kilometre at 275mph and leaving it with the air-speed indicator flicking close to 300mph. He averaged 283mph, well above his existing record, but the wind was already showing signs of picking up. 'I don't know whether to refuel or to restart,' Campbell reported. He actually began to do the former, but then changed his mind and started back. Then he nearly ran into fresh disaster when he applied a fraction too much power in an effort to get Bluebird back up on plane, and drowned the Beryl. Usually, at 30 to 40mph he would crank the boat in one direction to help get the front planing, a knack of driving he had long mastered. The start boat would be following him, monitoring his radio transmissions. At 70mph he'd crank the boat again to keep it on the plane until the fantastic acceleration kept it there, and the moment he felt it biting he would tell his crew, 'I'm going,' so that the men in the start boat knew there was no need to worry about a possible restart. Now he had to wait agonizing moments for the start boat to catch up and attach the starter before the engine fired again. Things were beginning to get out of control, and he knew that he was going to have to take a chance.

At last, the Beryl whined into life again, and this time

Campbell got Bluebird on the plane without drama. But he was not out of the woods yet. The wind was fast gathering strength. Foot to the floor, he shot back down the lake, literally outrunning the Albany Doctor. 'When he came back,' Ferrett revealed, 'the Albany Doctor was coming in behind him, and there are photographs showing the water roughed up on the lake.' When he cleared the end of the measured kilometre, after averaging 269mph, he had only five seconds' fuel left. It was forty-three minutes past three.

Campbell had succeeded, on the sixteenth anniversary of his father's death, on the last day of the year. Bizarrely, given his intensely superstitious nature, this latest record, like his previous triumph on Lake Eyre, had been set on a Friday, the day he so detested. And it had been won literally only moments before the water conditions would have prevented further runs. The conditions during the runs were '95 per cent perfect', according to Villa, but there were only three hours of daylight left. Yet when the timekeeper gave Campbell his speed, his response was typically muted: 'Much obliged, old boy.' He had set his seventh water speed record – an unprecedented feat in itself – at 276.33mph, and he had become the only man in history to break both the land and water records in the same year. An ecstatic Tonia braved the dank water and swam out to Bluebird to share the moment. When they returned to the jetty, Campbell asked spectators to bow their heads in memory of his father.

Later that night, while celebrating round the camp fire that kept away the scorpions and the snakes, he looked at Bluebird, resting on its cradle. Later, he wrote:

She looked rather as an old warhorse who has heard the last bugle call, battle scarred, proud and lonely. Rivets were going in her hull, there were pinholes in the engine combustion chamber casing, her skin still showed marks from the sinking on Lake Mead. I looked at Leo Villa and the men who had maintained Bluebird, thought of Ken and Lew Norris who had designed her in 1954 for a maximum life of two years. Now, ten years later, she still defied the sporting might of America – after all those years, still the only craft to have safely exceeded 250mph. Now she was at the end of the trail.[21]

It wasn't long before Campbell received a telegram from David Wynne-Morgan in England. It amused him greatly. 'I knew how thrilled Donald would be to get the record,' he said, 'so I spent most of the evening trying to think what I was going to say. Finally I was very pleased with myself, because I devised a cable which I sent – or initially *tried* to send – saying: "Congratulations. You are now not only the biggest but the fastest bastard on earth. David." Initially they wouldn't send it because of the language, but then they called me back and said they had been able to. I asked why the change of heart, and they said, "We discovered the word was in common use in Australia."'

During his efforts in Australia, Campbell deliberately never tried to claim the national water speed record. Paradoxically, that allowed those who followed to claim the national mark with lower speeds. His activities became the inspiration for a young man in Sydney called Ken Warby. When he designed and built his own jet-powered boat, Spirit of Australia, being able to claim the national mark as his own efforts increased gave him valuable publicity mileage which finally helped him to establish a new world record of 288.8mph in November 1977. A year later, in October 1978, he went back again to Blowering Dam in New South Wales to break that by the biggest margin in history, at 317.596mph. He is still the fastest man on water. Years later, on two separate visits to Coniston Water, Warby laid a wreath as a tribute to a man he much admired.

On 1 January 1965, Donald and Tonia Campbell were in Perth, ready to stay a couple of weeks before visiting every other Australian capital prior to settling down to finish off their film, *How Long a Mile.* 'We plan to spend four months or so a year in Australia,' Campbell said. 'We have made a lot of friends and business associations. I intend to set up a headquarters in Adelaide.' They lunched with Governor Sir Douglas Kendrew, then went to the Perth Cup with him. They were young and successful, and once again the world was at their feet. Only Sir Henry Segrave had ever held the land and water records at the same time, via his efforts with the Golden Arrow in 1929 and Miss England II in 1930, though he did not live to savour the achievement. But nobody had ever broken both records in the same year. Campbell's achievements were a mere five months apart. He had bounced back from the disappointment, frustration and qualified success at Lake Eyre; he had overcome the false start at Lake Bonney and pulled off one of the most remarkable feats in the history of record breaking.

These were his finest hours.

21

SUPERSONIC BOOMS

1965 to 1966

'There is no doubt that if I was the first man to go through the sound barrier on land in a British-built car, it would boost practically every product Britain sells abroad.'

DONALD CAMPBELL, 1965

While Donald Campbell was busy in Adelaide working on *How Long a Mile*, Ken Norris was at his drawing board continuing design work on the car that would come to be known as the Bluebird CN8. They had talked about it for months before formalizing the arrangement in October 1964, calculating that a speed of 840mph, or Mach 1.1, was feasible.

It was not enough for Campbell to consider a mere jetcar; this would be something so special that it would achieve a giant leap – the world's first supersonic land speed record. It would be totally different to its predecessor. Norris liked Craig Breedlove's tricycle *Spirit of America* jetcar and envisaged something similar: a cigar-shaped fuselage to contain driver and engine, with outrigged rear wheels to maintain roll stability. CN8 would be considerably smaller than CN7. It would measure 22ft from the tip of the air-speed indicator in the nose to the trailing edge of its rear-wheel spats, with a maximum width of 11ft. It would also be much lighter, at 4,000lb. And where CN7 had a frontal area of $23.5ft^2$, it would measure only $9.5ft^2$.

Dunlop had been a major backer of CN7, but CN8 would break new ground. Norris planned to do away with tyres altogether and run the car on solid metal wheels. It was the simplest way around the problem of centrifugal force at 840mph, the car's design speed, ripping tyres apart.

Norris also opted for two Bristol-Siddeley BS 605 rocket-assisted take-off (RATO) engines mounted one above the other in the tail. Campbell acquired four of them. Various power figures were mooted, but Norris calculated that 10,000lb of thrust would be sufficient, given the small frontal area. 'The Bluebird investigation emphasized the great advantage offered by the rocket motor in comparison to the jet turbine,' Campbell wrote. 'The former is light and very compact with similar thrust, permitting the design of an extremely small, simple vehicle of very high density and low frontal area. Further, being of the bi-fuel type (burning a mixture of hydrogen peroxide and kerosene) it entirely dispenses with the intricate problems of supersonic air intakes.' He calculated that on a ten-mile course, each run could be over in a minute.

Norris Brothers created a full-scale mock-up of the car as a means of raising the finances to build the real thing. By the time Campbell put it on display at Roundwood with Bluebird CN7 and K7, in September 1965, Norris had opted for two front wheels mounted closely side by side. Campbell invited the media to view his new project, but was bitterly disappointed by the lukewarm reception. Grahame Ferrett recalled Campbell's passion for CN8 from conversations he'd had with Leo Villa at Lake Eyre. 'People were close to putting men on the moon, but the speed of sound was up there in the spotlight. That was definitely one of Donald's main ambitions with the new car. It wasn't just to break Breedlove's record. He wanted more than that. He wanted to do something that would be significant.'

In November, reacting at the London Publicity Club showing of *How Long a Mile* to Craig Breedlove's newly minted 600mph record in Spirit of America Sonic 1, Campbell urged Britain to fight back. 'We must get after those chaps,' he insisted, adding, 'So little driving effort would be required at 700mph plus that I could almost do it no-hands. In fact, if I turn Bluebird's wheel at all I will crash.' He wanted to carry on competing with the Americans for the record because 'There is no doubt that if I was the first man to go through the sound barrier on land in a British-built car, it would boost practically every product Britain sells abroad.'

The following month, an underrated journalist called Dennis May conducted an interview in *CAR* magazine with Campbell, eliciting written replies to a number of questions. Campbell told him:

The FIA's decision regarding jet propulsion was inevitable and should have been taken in 1946. At that time the Union of International Motorboating, which controls the water speed record, immediately realized the potential of the turbojet and admitted its use.

There is considerable popular misconception on this subject of propulsion, particularly in relation to constant thrust versus ground horsepower. A natural phenomenon limits a propeller-propelled craft to an approximate maximum speed of 475mph, a wheel-propelled land vehicle to 500mph, a screw-propelled boat to 200mph. This situation was as well known in 1946 as it is today. If you wish to go fast in any of the mediums mentioned the use of the jet or rocket is mandatory.

Last October, having for years steadfastly refused to recognize the inevitability of the jet on land, the FIA suddenly altered the regulations overnight, making them retrospective to admit this medium. The FIA is currently in discussion with the FIM (motor cycling's international governing body) to frame rules to cover the land speed record in future. It seems they now contemplate recognizing any manned vehicle supported by the ground.

This means that it is now entirely feasible to contemplate speeds in excess of sound. The critical problem of adhesion is almost eliminated and, at this stage, it is difficult even to say whether or not the pneumatic tyre would provide the best medium of ground support. Inflation pressure would have to be so high that any tyre would be virtually solid.

On a hard, dry track there is absolutely no doubt the machine [Bluebird CN7] would have reached the 500mph for which it was designed. This is the considered opinion of her designers, Norris Brothers Ltd, in consultation with Bristol-Siddeley, who designed the Proteus engine.

When related to the appalling track conditions under which the car was running at Lake Eyre, its performance was little short of fantastic. The surface was wet and soggy from continual rain and at 400mph the tyres were wearing two-inch ruts in the surface – ruts which ran for the best part of six miles.

Attaining the speed of sound will be a major technical and human achievement, and in promotional terms something which could have significance throughout the world.

By the same token, it can be well argued that the entire

endeavour is totally absurd and will have no meaning whatever. The same argument can equally be applied to the climbing of Mount Everest or the Olympic Games, which cost so many millions to organize, where men and women are striving to run a little faster or jump a little higher. In terms of productivity, such activity has no meaning. The subject was concisely summed up by the late John Rhodes Cobb, who said: 'When man ceases to try to do better he will have reached a time of decadence.'[22]

Progress continued despite the feeble press reaction, Campbell believing that Bluebird CN8 would cost considerably less than CN7 because it was a simpler design. According to his own figures, he calculated that CN7 had cost £219,000 (£2,680,580 at today's values) against receipts of £242,000 (£2,962,105). He estimated that the new project could be achieved for £125,000 (£1,407,460). He broke this down as £50,000 (£562,985) for detailed design and drawing, final supersonic wind tunnel tests, and the construction of the mock-up and the final vehicle; £25,000 (£281,490) for administration, technical co-ordination and operational planning, including maintenance and transport of the nucleus of the operational team; £35,000 (£394,000) for the trials and record attempt; and a contingency of £15,000 (£168,895). Against that, he calculated a potential income of £115,000 (£1,294,860), comprising £50,000 (£562,985) for advertising rights to an oil company; £15,000 (£168,895) for advertising rights to Joseph Lucas; £15,000 (£168,895) for basic material supplier rights for either Tube Investments or Kaiser Aluminium Company; £10,000 (£112,600) for newspaper rights; £10,000 (£112,600) for insurance promotion; and £25,000 (£281,490) for exclusive television rights. On top of that came film and book rights, merchandising of models, and exhibitions, all of which would be dependent on the scale of promotion. He claimed that the American Broadcasting Corporation had expressed great interest in the supersonic attempt, and had made active enquiries into securing the television rights. Interestingly, he was also prepared to let an individual syndicate or company undertake the entire commercial management of the project in return for underwriting its cost, leaving him free to concentrate on engineering and operation.

At one stage he spoke of plans for the Jamaican government to construct a bespoke twelve- to fourteen-mile track on which he could not only realize the full potential of CN8, but also wind up CN7 to a speed closer to 475mph; there was even a supplementary idea to run CN7 for a standing-start record. But subsequently those plans failed to reach fruition, and instead he reverted to a schedule embracing running trials on Lake Eyre in May 1967. He remained convinced, despite his terrible experiences there, that in a normal season it offered considerable advantages over Bonneville. Later in 1966 there was talk of the CN8 mock-up going on display at the Silverstone circuit, but that, too, came to nothing.

Nevertheless, though the outside world was left to wonder if the project had been stillborn, it was still forging ahead behind the scenes. It was one of the fundamental reasons why Campbell decided on his final throw of the dice with Bluebird K7 at Coniston Water, for he figured that the 300mph mark would be the perfect publicity to generate greater interest in a new land speed record attempt. While he was in the Lake District awaiting the right conditions, on 29 December 1966 John Stollery, a professor of aeronautics at Imperial College who had been involved with K7 and

350

CN7, showed off the first designs for the car and explained the thinking behind them. The project was very much alive.

While initial work on the CN8 was progressing, Campbell had some other pressing matters to attend to in Australia. The taxman was on his trail, as Grahame Ferrett explained.

I'd not long come off the payroll, at three and a half thousand quid or whatever it was, at Yorke Motors, and Donald and I were going to see his accountant in Adelaide, a fellow called Dudley Pickering. So we've got there, and his face is about this long. We've got an appointment with the deputy commissioner of taxation. Now, the taxation office in Australia has a commissioner, but in each state they have a deputy commissioner who is the real head honcho. He's got a galashee [a lien] on all Donald's bank accounts; we can't get any money out. He's not satisfied that Donald won't be skipping the country without paying his right whack of tax. So I've just got a new job, and no bastard can pay me! I can't get my money!

So round we've gone, seventh floor, the deputy commissioner's name was Bagland. He had an assistant whose name was Pollard, who had been delving into all the Bluebird Project stuff. He'd decided that Campbell was dunning the system, and Bagland believed him. So there we were, typical bloody bureaucrat's office. Donald and I were sitting back on a couch and Dudley Pickering's at the desk with Bagland, arguing. You know, here's this man who's just become a hero, and he's driven through the streets of the city, and you're going to do this and chop that off. Bagland is sitting there, Pollard is standing alongside; they couldn't give a damn what this bloke Pickering is saying. They'd made up their minds!

I'm not too comfortable, not used to this sort of

high-level bureaucratic nonsense. Donald, blue suit, the gold watch chain into the pocket, is playing with this little mail knife, whistling to himself. And this is going on for maybe half an hour, and Pickering is saying all the nice things, and it's just not registering. So eventually Donald said, 'Excuse me, Mr Commissioner, I guess what you'd really like to do is have this matter resolved one way or another.' And Deputy Commissioner Bagland said, 'Yes, I certainly would, Mr Campbell, and I'm far from satisfied.' So Donald said, 'My arrangements to bring the Bluebird Project to Australia were made with the Prime Minister, Sir Robert Menzies, and the arrangement as laid down was that nothing in relation to the Bluebird Project would be taxable in relation to income. Likewise, there would be no reductions or allowances.' And Bagland said, 'That's not good enough.' Donald said, 'I do presume that you want to clear this matter up?' Bagland replied, 'Certainly.' 'Well,' Donald said, 'do you think I might make a phone call to expedite this?' And the answer, effectively, was ring who the hell you like, we're not changing our minds! So Donald said, 'Would you please have your secretary get Sir Robert Menzies on the phone?' Bagland and Pollard effectively said that they weren't going to worry the Prime Minister with something like this, but Donald said, 'I insist. You said I can make a phone call. Now I want you to get your secretary to get Sir Robert Menzies on the phone, and I insist you do it.'

Bagland has lost the high ground now. The call's put in, and the message comes back: there's a fifteen-minute delay on calls to Canberra. So Donald said, 'Come on, Dudley. We'll go back to your office and we'll take the call there, and I dare say' – he was very confident – 'that there'll be a message coming through very shortly.'

So we've come out of the commissioner's office in King

William Street, and we've only got to walk to the next street to Pickering's office. We get there in, what, five minutes? Up in his office, Pickering's secretary said, 'Oh, there's a message for you from Mr Bagland at the Taxation Department.' Effectively it said not to worry about talking to the Prime Minister, help yourself to all the money you like!

Donald knew what he was doing. Later, he got Menzies to help move all the stuff to Dumbleyung, and then there was the army, the South Australia Police Force – they were all involved. It was absolutely typical of him that when it came to sorting out such things he always dealt with the top bloke.

Mixing in such company always reminded Campbell of the other thing he longed for in his life: the knighthood his father had received after setting his 246.09mph land speed record in 1931. Denial of the ultimate honour was something neither Campbell nor his supporters could understand – or forgive. He had set seven water speed records and one land speed record, and was the only man ever to break the land and water speed records in the same year. And he had achieved this remarkable success in vehicles he had commissioned and in which he had invested significant amounts of his own money. All of these successes boosted British prestige, and that was always one of his primary goals. Looking back from the present day, when pop stars and even horse racing commentators apparently qualify at a time when men such as Richard Noble and Andy Green do not, it seems not only ludicrous but downright spiteful that Campbell did not get the ultimate reward his courage so clearly merited. The most apposite time would have been the Queen's Birthday Honours List in 1965, to mark setting the land and water speed records in 1964.

But the fifties, and to an extent even the swinging sixties, were prudent times where matters such as personal relationships were concerned, and Campbell's tangled love life was almost certainly the deciding factor. Bill Coley certainly thought so. 'He didn't get a knighthood ... that was his private life, I think!' he said. 'Nothing to do with his achievements, which were marvellous!' He never spoke about it, but he must have been very disappointed. He was well enough connected, after all, with the Duke of Richmond and Gordon and the Duke of Argyll as trustees, and the Duke of Edinburgh going to one of his meetings. Campbell's divorce from Daphne would not have helped, neither would the parting from Dottie, even though she sportingly allowed him to divorce her to preserve his waning chances. 'The mid-sixties were a time when things were changing over,' Craig Douglas observed. 'You know, rules on divorce and things. Captains of industry got knighthoods for no bloody reason whatsoever. It would have been very interesting, had Donald been awarded a knighthood, to see whether he would have accepted it or not. I think with his sense of humour he would have enjoyed them offering one and then saying no. I suppose on the other hand he would have taken it. He'd have mentioned it to Tonia and she'd have said he had to take it. Business-wise it would have been good for him, because he'd probably have got onto a couple of boards. He would probably have started making money then.'

It would have been particularly galling for Campbell that in 1964 his old sponsor Billy Butlin received a knighthood, for he too had been married several times, and his love life was far more complex. It has been alleged that he worked his way through most of his first wife Dolly's nine sisters, before finally settling down to marry her. Like Campbell, he was unable to resist an attractive woman. He had a twenty-year relationship with Nora, his wife's niece, and had two

354

daughters by her. Then Sheila became his mistress. Dolly and Nora slumped into alcoholism. When Dolly died, Butlin married Nora rather than Sheila, who was pregnant. But as they left Caxton Hall, he was with Sheila, and Nora was with her own boyfriend. Butlin had married Nora merely to legitimize his children and to clear the way to receive a knighthood. Butlin was smart, and made much of his Church and charity work, which were the reasons cited for his honour. Ten years later, he divorced Nora and finally married Sheila. In comparison with his former mentor, Campbell's life appeared saintly. Just to add insult to injury, when Butlin sold his camps to the Rank Organization, its accountant discovered that wherever there was a Butlin camp there was a house, and in that house lived a woman. Every time Butlin went to visit one of his camps, he went to stay in the house he had bought for each of his extra-curricular amours.

Campbell maintained a sense of humour about the situation, though. Tony Robinson remembered him popping his head round the door at the time of Lord Jellicoe's fall from grace, when the politician lost his job with the government for getting caught while misbehaving. 'He winked at Mum and said, "You see, I'm not the only naughty boy!"'

Unlike Craig Douglas, David Wynne-Morgan had no doubt whatsoever that Campbell would have accepted a knighthood with alacrity, and that he was desperate to match the one achievement of his father's that had so far escaped him. 'The knighthood thing was the one thing that illustrated the childishness of Donald,' he said. 'That was the one thing his father got that he never got, and it was incredibly important to him. He was never going to get it. If you'd been divorced, you didn't get one. And he'd been divorced twice.

'The Dorchester was his great watering hole. I remember how incredibly embarrassed I used to be going into the Grill Room. The head waiter would always come over very ostentatiously to greet him and take him to his table. It was always, 'Good morning, Sir Donald. Nice to see you, Sir Donald.' The hairs on the back of your neck used to twitch. Donald almost twittered. He never bothered to correct him. It really was a very sort of strange, Walter Mitty-like existence.'

22

RETURN TO CONISTON

November to December 1966

'Probably you'll say I haven't grown up, and if that's so I'm quite prepared to accept it, and I'm in no hurry. There's too much time to grow up and grow old.'

DONALD CAMPBELL TO JOHN PETT DURING A BORDER TV INTERVIEW

After the success at Lake Dumbleyung, Donald Campbell believed that Bluebird K7's working life was over. 'It has reached its absolute limit,' he told friends. 'The hull is twelve years old, the engine fifteen. The least I would have to do to get more speed would be to install a new engine and modify the hull.' In 1966 he still entertained high hopes for the new rocket car project, but it was the wrong time to try to sell it. He had stayed too long in Australia, and had failed to capitalize back home on his new successes. By May, Campbell was saying, 'Whether we proceed with the supersonic vehicle is a matter of speculation. But the speed of sound would be very good publicity for Great Britain and a considerable engineering achievement.' Before that, he needed something high profile to boost *his* publicity ratings as well as the Bluebird CN8 project, and give commercial plans to market the JetStar jetboat fresh impetus. There was an inevitability in the way Fate arranged the final scene shifts of his life as his thoughts turned yet again to K7, the faithful old warhorse.

He decided on one last throw of the dice, a final push to break 300mph on water. That was 50mph over the design limit of the ageing craft, but Ken Norris was confident, and so was Campbell. Leo Villa, however, had serious reservations, and he wasn't the only one. At this distance it is difficult to be certain whether people genuinely felt that Campbell was sticking his neck out, or whether the ensuing tragedy simply placed a gloomy retrospective cast on their views, but certainly the late Dennis Druitt, another ally from the BP days, agreed with Villa. 'The boat won't do it, Don boy,' he said.

But Campbell was on the record breaker's treadmill. He wouldn't be going back, even though his wife was also fervently against another attempt, especially after he had promised her that the Dumbleyung record would be the last. 'I felt that the boat was too old and had gone as far as it could,' Tonia said. His decision to go ahead anyway placed further strain on their marriage, which some believed had almost run its course.

Back at Coniston in 1959, she had relied heavily on Peter and Cherry Barker to provide her with emotional support as the strain and sheer terror of it all gripped her. But things got better. 'After the first one I became much more excited than nervous. I was also extremely proud to be included in the team. At the start, Donald had said it wasn't a place for a woman, but he soon saw that I could take it.' She was, after all, Fred. But now they were moving apart: Campbell to Coniston, Tonia to Bristol and more cabaret. Her career had given her independence at a time when she needed it to stand up to a husband who paradoxically wanted her to be both a homebody and a somebody. It had provided her with the means to save her marriage, but now he had become very friendly with Lady Violet Aitken, the wife of his friend, newspaper baron Sir Maxwell Aitken. Tonia chose to avoid Coniston, but Vi did not. Team members saw her there frequently, nipping around in her white Alfa Romeo. Their friendship was an open secret. She was there celebrating with the team when Campbell threw a fancy dress party on New Year's Eve. It was evident how fond they were of each other.

Hughie Green, however, believed Donald and Tonia would have lasted.

There was one thing with Donald; his dear wife made that very clear: they stood up to each other. It was quite a stormy relationship, but I think they loved each other a great deal in their own way. And their own way is the way people run their lives. You had two extremely fascinating and volatile people. They were real characters. He was totally fascinated by her, and she by him.

We used to laugh a lot. Got pissed together a couple of times. He was a great crumpet chaser, but then so were many. And I think that was one of the attractions between him and Tonia. In many ways they were well matched. She gave him as good as she got. Oh yes. They were ideal for each other, if you wanted to live that kind of life. They both had their careers, and she was a very, very good artiste.

Jean Wales disagreed. 'I got married in September 1958, and Donald married Tonia in December. I'm not being conceited, but I think because I got married, *he* got married.

The biggest mistake he ever made. I told him at the time, and he told Tonia as well! They weren't suited, they'd got nothing in common. She was theatrical, he wasn't.' Many of his friends said that Campbell was precisely that, however. And Tonia certainly managed to last longer than Daphne and Dottie. 'I don't think she would have lasted much longer if he had lived,' Jean continued. 'Their marriage was on the rocks. I don't think she was really interested in Donald, in his achievements. I used to go there for dinner with my husband Charles, and champagne was flowing and all this lot was coming down from London that I wouldn't have given house room to. Theatrical types. Donald was quite influential with some of her friends, discussing what he was doing. She wasn't interested in that. She was doing her thing. Fair enough in a way, but things were iffy towards the end.'

Ken Norris shared this view, pointing out the accurately portrayed scene in the BBC docu-drama film *Across the Lake* in which Tonia turns up unexpectedly at Coniston to find Campbell partying happily with Vi Aitken and other team members. They argue publicly, and he then has to chase after Tonia as she storms out. 'Donald was dancing on the table when she came in, and he didn't know she was coming. They had a big row that night, and he shot out after her and was gone for quite some time. I don't know how strong that was, but I don't think they would have lasted. My wife Marjorie summarizes women, and she didn't think it would last. Donald once made some remark to Marjorie along the lines of "She's going to be out as soon as I can do it." Marjorie thought that he seemed determined.'

Craig Douglas agreed with Norris.

I remember going down to Leatherhead one Saturday, and Donald came back on the Sunday morning. Tonia had told me he'd gone to Poole because someone was thinking of buying the yacht. He told her when she asked that the person hadn't turned up till seven o'clock, but how can you see a boat when it's damned dark outside? Donald just looked at me with a wink . . .

The truth is that Tonia, in the latter years, was also dying to get back into showbusiness, and I don't think that Donald was really into showbusiness, although he was a showman. Tonia loved it. She wanted to pick it up again. Hence, when he was at Coniston, she was working. And if she was away working for a couple of weeks, that gave Donald a bit of leeway. It was good for both of them. But in the last couple of years the relationship was going.

Gina, too, had her doubts. 'I could see him just saying to himself, "That's it, finished, no going back." And Vi Aitken and my dad, I think, absolutely worshipped each other. Vi was very much my father's type of woman. She didn't mind getting her hands dirty, she loved speed, car racing and boat racing. And Max [Aitken] himself had a lady friend called Rosie.'

Sadly, Vi Aitken modestly believed she could add nothing of value to this story.

On Wednesday, 15 June 1966, Campbell suffered a new setback. A friend, racing driver Peter Bolton, crashed Bluebird CN7 during a practice run at RAF Debden near Saffron Walden in Essex. Bolton, who had driven at Le Mans every year since 1956, actually crossed the Saffron Walden to Chelmsford road.

The RAF Benevolent Association was staging a charity event at the Debden Air Tattoo the following weekend, and Campbell was due to make demonstration runs with CN7.

He had constantly badgered BP for support. In the end, he'd been reduced to asking the oil company that had benefited so much from his previous efforts to supply fuel and oil as a charitable donation, but it had declined even that. Midweek, Campbell had begun to feel unwell and had asked Bolton to do a run in preparation for driving at the weekend as well. Bolton claimed in an interview in 1993 that Leo Villa had been struggling all morning with a sticking throttle, though this seemed unlikely since Bluebird had just undergone a major rebuild after its eighteen-month sojourn in Australia. 'By the time we got there Leo was going on about this and said he thought it was all right but it wasn't a hundred per cent. It wasn't shutting off every time,' Bolton said.

Bluebird was not an easy car to drive; even at idle it could exceed 250mph. But the Proteus took its time to spool up. By the time Bolton was ready to apply the brakes at the end of his run, Bluebird was ready for flight. Bolton likened driving it to a big kart, with its two-pedal control, but was unable to pull up at the end of the runway and made a spectacular trip through a fence and over the main A130 road before landing heavily in a barley field. This is how he remembered it at the time: 'I never want to experience anything like that again! I set off down the runway very gently, then I could not make the car stop. I might have put two feet on one pedal or just lost control, never having driven such a powerful car before.' Bluebird missed a passing car by fifty yards. Its driver, a television engineer called Alan Howe from Newmarket, said, 'It flew over ten feet up at an incredible speed. I thought it was an aircraft.'

Villa and Campbell confirmed that the brakes and throttle were working perfectly after the accident. 'Peter is a highly competent racing and rally driver,' Campbell said, 'but compared to racing cars, Bluebird is like a lion to a lamb. It's a deceptive car because when you first put your foot on the throttle nothing happens, and then suddenly you are over the blue horizon.'

Years later, Bolton remembered things differently.

They told me to use the throttle until I got to the first set of runway marker barrels, then coast through the trap, and at the end of the next set of barrels take my foot off and brake before the end of the runway. And of course, one of the most unfortunate things for me, the throttle didn't shut off. By the time I'd got the flame out, after I'd realized what was happening, I was halfway through the trap. So I hit the flame-out switch later than intended, and that's when I went off the end of the runway, did a sort of ski jump like off the end of an aircraft carrier, and went across the road. There was a wonderful cartoon in the *Daily Mail*. Bluebird was up in the air with a Mini going underneath it and a wife saying to her husband, 'Look, darling, a Bluebird.'

The car landed on its wheels, but bent one of its front suspension legs, the air intake and underbelly. But Campbell's claim that it would take £50,000 (£563,000 at today's values) to put the car into running condition again was another of his famous exaggerations; he drove the patched-up car himself in the demonstration days later. He was depressed by the damage but saw an opportunity, Bolton claimed, to generate more publicity as he tried to persuade him to open up a war of words in the press. Bolton said that when he declined, Campbell tried to sue him. 'He hadn't a leg to stand on. It never got to a hearing stage. He tried to claim on my motor trade policy, he tried everything. He was desperate for money. The lad was clutching at straws.'

During the course of the research for this stage of Donald Campbell's life, it was suggested by one interviewee that Campbell had reached such a low point that he had resorted to drugs. Purple hearts were suggested, but drugs were completely out of keeping with a character that loved to live life to the full, with speed, sex and the occasional drink and cigar as the priorities. No evidence ever came to light to support such allegations, and Gina Campbell maintained vehemently that her father would never have taken drugs. 'I doubt my father would know what purple hearts were. He was just not into that at all!'

By July, with or without Tonia's approval, his new plans for Bluebird K7 were progressing. He had already acquired one Bristol-Siddeley Orpheus engine (number 709), and on the 20th his secretary Pam Cripps wrote to the Ministry of Defence to make a formal offer of £200 (£2,250) for a Folland Gnat aircraft (registered as XN1 691) complete with Orpheus engine (number 711) lying at Dunsfold Aerodrome in Surrey. Soon the aircraft and both engines were at Norris Brothers, where Tony James drew up the conversion to replace the Beryl with the lighter and more powerful unit. To increase directional stability, he also incorporated the Gnat's tail fin to give K7 its final shape, and the boat was repainted.

At the end of September, the 30th, Campbell dropped in on his sister in Ashstead to tell her that he would be going back to Coniston. 'He was just his normal self,' Jean recalled. 'He didn't stop long. He had to be in London, and he'd obviously just been somewhere. He came in and had a drink, sat down by the fire and chatted, then said he must be going.'

It was the last time she ever saw him.

In October, BP firmly rejected his pleas for financial

support. 'Some months ago you explained your Company's view of this endeavour,' he wrote to R. B. Dummett at BP in a letter dated the 13th. 'Since that time, the National Economic situation has deteriorated and I feel deeply that anything that can be done to bolster morale at home and boost British prestige overseas should be done and done now. These reasons prompt me to write to you and ask if BP would simply like to supply the fuel and lubricants which are limited in quantity and to standard specifications. If success is achieved I would be happy for the Company to make such promotional and advertising use of it as you might decide in that event, and leave it entirely to you as to whether or not you wished to contribute towards the cost of the endeavour.' Bearing in mind what he had achieved in his career, and for BP, this was desperate stuff that must have stung his pride. He was clearly aware of factions within BP that had no time for his aspirations, for he added:

You may remember in times gone by I spoke of internal lack of confidence of my determination or ability to achieve the records we were after. You were always kind enough to say that there was no lack of confidence in this direction. Perhaps at this moment I should tell you that in 1963, twice to my face it was inferred and, I am told, on a number of occasions openly stated at meetings, 'that Campbell had no intention of attacking the record, but only of taking money out of the Company and another driver must be insisted upon'. It was from this approach that all my own fears stemmed. I hope I have proved that success of the record has, and always will be, the first and dominant consideration.

My present suggestion is made in the hope that we may achieve unity on what is very possibly my last record attempt, and in appreciation of something [BP director] Ronnie Tritton described as 'an arrangement that has not been without advantage to both sides'.

It was a poignant communication, but it fell on deaf ears. The company declined even his request for product support. It no longer suited it to have its name associated with his. Archive letters reveal the feeling at BP that Campbell would not be satisfied until he had 'killed himself'.

Campbell soldiered on, financing the attempt largely from his own pocket. His back was very much against the wall this time. He was gambling everything: the boat, his little remaining money, his reputation. The new attempt was much less lavish, with reduced facilities and manpower. Leo Villa, as ever, was there, together with the indefatigable Maurie Parfitt. Campbell's butler Louis Goosens turned his capable hand to anything, while his wife Julie continued her usual role as housekeeper, but now in the bungalow Campbell had rented from Connie Robinson.

Campbell did his best to ignore the financial situation. 'It was terribly rocky! We were so broke!' Tonia admitted. But the television drama *Across the Lake* attempted to portray things in a manner both Tonia and Bill Coley found offensive and inaccurate. In one scene, Campbell visits a friend, fictitiously called Jack Stanley, and in a roundabout way asks him for money. In the nicest possible way, Stanley turns him down, whereupon Campbell tersely cuts him off by telling him, 'I shall never ask you for money again.' The Jack Stanley character was supposed to be Coley, but Tonia was angrily adamant that Campbell would never have spoken to his old friend in that way. 'That never happened. To speak to a friend like Bill in such a manner was just not in Donald's character.' Coley himself just smiled. 'I objected to that and wanted it out. That conversation never took place. I've no idea why they put that in, or where they got it from. They sent me the script, and I think I upset them very much by deleting it. It was nonsense, just not true. Donald wouldn't have said that to me anyhow. I think they misunderstood the relationship between us.'

But, as Campbell himself admitted, the meter was running, and staying at Coniston was a serious financial drain. He had even considered going back to Ullswater, in the hope that Sir Wavell Wakefield and Ullswater Navigation Company might be persuaded to help with some funding, but the company showed little interest. Campbell had an income from his insurance business in Ewell, but it was not limitless. 'He was very desperate,' Coley said. 'He was out of time, out of money. Out of everything.' Every photo and every newsreel showed the strain on Campbell's face. He was old beyond his years. Where he had been boyish on his last attempt at Coniston, seven years earlier, now he was haggard. The efforts with the Bluebird car had taken their toll. Now, when he donned his radio headphone set and then his silver crash helmet, he had the beleaguered look of a battle-weary fighter pilot on one early-morning scramble too many.

In addition to his regular team, Campbell had another staunch ally: Connie Robinson's young son Tony, whom he affectionately called Robbie. 'I only really knew Donald well on that last attempt. With others, I was often away at school or only a very young teenager, so I wasn't really in a responsible enough position to be involved. On the final attempt we became much closer. For years prior to that I sort of knew him as Uncle Donald.' Their relationship matured as he became a young man.

I suppose whatever it was, he was responsible for. He obviously realized, probably quicker than I did, that I wasn't sort of a little thirteen-, fourteen-year-old. He treated me as a grown-up. We'd talk about things. One occasion – and it may be what put us on a more equal footing – came quite early on in the 1966 attempt. The Longines timekeepers had set their equipment up on the wrong side of the lake. I'd told them that they were on the opposite side to normal. They said, 'We know what we're doing.' Fair enough. But there was no access by road on the west side. The only way was by boat, so if you had to rush the timers down you churned the lake up. As it turned out they were wrong and I was right. It all had to be changed over.

During this period they'd gone down the lake and the weather got up very stormy. They hadn't come back, and darkness was approaching quickly, so I'd gone down in another boat to see what had happened to them. I thought they might have broken down and been drifting. When I got down there they were still on the shore. It was extremely rough and quite difficult to get to them. I managed to snap the locking pin on the outboard because the boat was bouncing up and down so much that I hit the bottom, sheared it off and damaged the steering. I eventually set off back with them, trying to steer this thing holding the tiller with one arm round it. I was keeping my eye on car head-lights at the end of the lake, because it was black dark by this time. Fortunately the blowing gale blew us back up the lake. This went on for about three hours, and poor old Donald was apparently getting a bit frantic. He didn't know how he was going to tell my mother I was missing! Eventually I'd had enough and just beached the boat. I appeared out of the trees, and Donald thought he'd seen a ghost! He was very relieved.

That incident formed a more adult bond between us. But I certainly don't claim any sort of special relationship over and above lots of other people.

Campbell, of course, had got into similar scrapes himself at the same age. He admired the fact that Robbie had braved it out, and that he had been right all along about the timekeepers.

Robinson subsequently joined forces with the slightly older Clive Glynn, a twenty-two-year-old mechanic who worked in a local garage in Ditchling. For Glynn, it would be a bittersweet experience of a lifetime, and one that he remembers with the fierce pride of a soldier who has fought with honour in an historic battle. 'My father had a garage, and Ken Norris was a customer,' he said. 'He was looking for extra helpers. I had an interview with Donald Campbell at Bluebird House [Campbell's insurance business premises] in Ewell, Surrey. He told me it might not be suitable for me, but he said he was looking forward to seeing me. Just like that. The following day, 6 November, a Sunday, around half past eight, I went to Priors Ford, left my car there, and went up to Coniston. Louis and I followed each other up, he in a Morris Traveller, me in a Land Rover.' Glynn and Robbie swept the lake for driftwood. Glynn pulled out half a tree at one stage. 'It needed the two of us. It was especially bad after the poor weather.'

Bluebird had arrived in Coniston on Wednesday, 2 November. The first bad omen came when it became stuck in the mud as its transporter driver avoided a tree on the route leading to the Bluebird Café. Two days later, the boat was launched there for the first time in seven years, and Campbell made a successful slow-speed test. But disaster struck the day before Glynn's arrival. During a static engine test, the 709 Orpheus sucked rivets out of the air intakes and sustained internal damage. Campbell, retorting to a journalist's question in the aftermath of the drama, claimed that redesigning the intakes would have cost £10,000 (£112,600). This, of course, was nonsense. 'It would have cost next to nothing,' Norris said. 'Some rivets were sucked out but that was about all. We worked flat out, and redid them with glass-fibre, and they were ready within twenty-four hours. It was just one of those things. We hadn't allowed for the Orpheus having greater suction than the Beryl.' Robbie remembered the incident well. 'That was another thing about Donald: he had this ability to get people to work all night and all day, probably because he would do it himself. He led by example. The lads went off to get this spare engine. In order to get it back in the shortest possible time they had to set off at around ten o'clock at night and drive overnight down to London, then have just a short rest before bringing it back.'

While Glynn and Goosens were convoying up to Coniston, Campbell was already taking the damaged intakes to London for modifications. No sooner had Glynn arrived than he found himself heading back to London, aboard a truck with one of Bill Coley's men, to fetch the replacement Orpheus, 711. On the 10th, Villa and Parfitt checked that one over and patched up 709 to test the revised intakes. But on the 14th and 15th gale-force winds threatened to destroy the boathouse, which was constructed from scaffold poles and blue plastic sheeting. Campbell came back with the modified intakes on the 16th and, true to his sense of theatre, told anyone who would listen that they had 'crammed three weeks' work into one'. Two days later, after a successful static test with 709, Bluebird made a disappointing low-speed test with 711 installed.

Two days after that, revised intake spray guards had been fitted, but still Bluebird refused to plane during low-speed runs. Robinson was now responsible for using a small dory to pull K7 away from the boathouse prior to each run. 'When Bluebird was having its problems with weight distribution and wouldn't come up on the plane, I did a lot of work driving very close by,' he recalled. 'Looking back on it, I'm quite proud of it, really! We'd literally less than a foot between our boat and the sponsons, trying to film it so that they could see what was happening. But at only 30, 40mph, the dory couldn't keep up with the Bluebird, even though at that stage it wasn't up out of the water. We'd just get covered in paraffin vapour. At home I'd be banned from the house and have to get changed outside!'

A minor change of engine position altered the boat's centre of gravity, and after experimentation with sandbags on the transom, Norris and Villa finally trimmed the boat and then made the modifications permanent with lead blocks. 'Initially it probably seemed a bit Heath Robinson,' Robinson said, 'but it worked.' Bluebird was once again the boat it had always been, rising out of the water and streaking along on the surface. Campbell was elated, and the mood of the camp lifted. He promised reporters '250 by the weekend'.

Over the following days he made five runs between 100 and 120mph, but on one of them hit a submerged log, slightly damaging Bluebird. It was not until 10 December that he averaged 200mph. On the 12th he upped that to 250mph, and the following day he improved that to 264.5mph, with runs of 267mph and 262mph, but had a lucky escape after striking a seagull at 250mph. This time one of the outrigger spars was damaged.

Bluebird would now plane, and was approaching its own

record speeds, but Campbell felt that he was not getting full power. Two engineers from Bristol Siddeley arrived on the 14th and quickly added a booster pump to enhance the fuel flow. It would make a dramatic difference, but not for a while. Bad weather kept Bluebird in the boathouse until 20 December. The downtime was damaging, just as it had been at Lake Eyre. David Benson, Campbell's close friend who wrote for the *Daily Express*, recalled that 'To while away the boredom we used to play poker for ridiculous stakes. And Donald was training me as his reserve driver. You know, he was having a lot of trouble with his back still. There was never anything serious in it all, but he would tell me how to start Bluebird, how to get her up on the plane. I mentioned it once to my editor, and he said, "There's no way you're going near that bloody thing!" But he needn't have worried. It was all just fantasy. Just a way of getting through the boredom.'

Glynn remembered Campbell as moody at this desperate time of his life, 'but he was fine to me, most of the time. He had his moments, but that was no more than usual for anybody. He was under a lot of pressure. He was just a moody person, that's the way he was. A good mood, or a bad mood. When he was in the latter he was just snappy; when he was in a good mood he was just the opposite. It was best just to ignore it, once you knew his ways. I liked him, got on very well with him. One night he showed me all the photographs in the Crown Hotel, bought me a drink. Mostly, he drank beer. The moods were nothing personal.'

Geoffrey Mather, of the *Daily Express*, was one of the few journalists to interview Campbell one on one. He formed the impression that he was fighting the Battle of Britain twenty-seven years late, and would subsequently write that his death reunited him 'with all those who had plunged from the skies'. He'd first seen Campbell at the edge of

Coniston Water, and thought him 'a darting man in every sense, physically and in the mind; affable, absorbed, hopeful, and, I thought, a little sad. Seldom in creation can there have been a bigger jingoist than Donald Campbell. He was the good chap in a wizard show. He alone had retained the jargon of the war long after its end.' Mather suggested that, had he been born a century earlier, Campbell would have been an explorer. 'No,' Campbell replied, 'I'd have been burned at the stake as a witch.'

They talked huddled in the warmth of his caravan. Mather noted his clipped tones – The Voice again – and felt, like many others had before him, he exuded a deep psychological need to prove himself to his dead father, who had humiliated him in his childhood, and that his 'curiously dated' words were laced with foreboding. 'This weather is driving one through the roof,' Campbell admitted. 'You know damn well that sooner or later you are likely to take a thoroughly unjustified risk. And what can you do?'

Mather also spoke with Tonia, who was struggling to control her misgivings and would eventually depart for her performances in Bristol to escape from the emotional torment. 'When Donald started speaking about this record I was not enthusiastic,' she told him. 'This is my seventh record attempt, and for the first time I am terribly worried. I kept telling him, "I wish you weren't doing it. I wish it were all over," and I have never before allowed myself to say that. I can't explain it. Maybe because it wasn't supposed to be lucky. Maybe because of this weather. I don't know why. I still feel it.'

But Campbell was insistent. He told Mather:

You've got to believe what you are doing, no matter what that is. Money is sugar in the tea. But no amount of money can make a man do something he hasn't got within himself. You know the old story: before the curtain goes up or the bell rings, the old stomach is turning over at a rate of knots, the adrenalin is pumping through the system. You know — well, we've all got this fright process. There are days when you are at a low ebb and days when you are high. I can get frightened during an attempt and before it. You need to be frightened. It is like a curve, if you could plot it. If you are not frightened you are a dead duck. And if you are too frightened then you slip down the other side. The act of dying? That most certainly worries me. I enjoy this life far too much. But you can be just as frightened of failure.

He also opened up to Mather about the financial problems. 'We are virtually on our own in this one. Something like £10,000 [£112,600] was needed to get the venture under way. Dear old Monty Berman (the theatre man) and I were having lunch one day and he said, "I'd love to be a part of this. It is so exciting. Would you be offended if I offered £1,000 [£11,260] towards it?" And I said, "Offended? That is 10 per cent of the total cost. You have just bought our new engine installation."' Hughie Green understood how hard the financial burden was for Campbell to bear this time. 'Donald knew Billy Butlin, of course, but he also knew that I knew him very well. He asked me if I could help him. I at that time was not in a financial position to help personally, and he was asking for big money. So he asked me would I go and see certain people. I gave up a week of my life, cancelled everything I had on. And I ask you to accept the fact that I am not going to give you the names of those people. It wouldn't be fair to Donald, and it wouldn't be fair to them. But I came back empty-handed.' Many of them were people who had been burned by the CN7 experience.

The 20th brought a calm lake for the first time in five days, but in a bitter irony Bluebird was trapped in the boathouse after overnight gales. The weight of melting snow on the plastic roof had distorted a scaffolding pole which had bent down behind the tail fin, preventing the boat from moving down the slipway. Somehow, the adversity merely drew the little team closer together. Whatever personality problems stalked Campbell at Coniston lay outside the team.

The bad weather continued on the 21st, when an argument broke out between Campbell and the Swiss timekeepers as they began preparing to go home to their families for Christmas. For Campbell this was tantamount to treason, but it was not unreasonable given the time of year. Eventually others, including the reporters, followed suit. 'All the timekeepers went back, and then it snowballed,' Glynn remembered. 'I think he was probably hoping that everyone would stay, but then he realized that he had to give in.' Even the Goosenses went south, Glynn travelling with them in the Morris accompanied by the poodle Cockle. Campbell stayed with the Robinsons at the Sun. Even Villa departed, for Derby and wife Joan's Christmas dinner, when Campbell finally yielded to the inevitable. But he would not be denied. On Christmas Day, while the rest of the country was tucking into turkey and mince pies and donning silly hats and pulling crackers, Campbell took Bluebird out on Coniston Water. Opinions vary, but according to one of his helpers he hit more than 250mph. Robbie recalled that day's events:

Donald was quite put out that everyone went home. He somehow felt a bit deserted. He came up to the Sun [having been down to the lake to assess conditions] about ten o'clock on Christmas morning and hung around a bit. In hindsight, he obviously wasn't sure how he was going to broach the subject. And then he sort of said, very non-chalantly, 'What do you think, Robbie, should we take the boat out on our own this morning?' And I sort of said, 'Well, I don't know, you're the Skipper!' And he said, 'I tell you what I'll do. Can I use your telephone? I'll call Stephen Darbishire [Campbell's doctor and confidant, who lived locally].' Then he said, 'Paul Evans is still here, isn't he? And Arthur Wilson at Pier Cottage [at the northern end of Coniston] will give us a hand. He'll probably be there Christmas morning, won't he?'

So Stephen arrived and the three of us went down and met up with Paul and Arthur. We winched the boat out, got the Bluebird off her cradle and towed her round the pier until she was pointing out into the lake. Then I took one of the big cruisers out. Donald used the Bluebird's self-starter, out he went, and up and away. He disappeared down the lake for a couple of miles, turned around and came back again, and we put it away. He'd achieved what he wanted to. He only went halfway down the lake. I think he just wanted to show that, because everyone else had gone home for Christmas, he could do it on his own anyway.

Corporal Paul Evans, an army radio technician, had been called in when Campbell fell out with the company that was providing his communications. A difficult situation was smoothed over when the Ministry of Defence pointed Campbell in the direction of Catterick Camp, ninety miles to the east over near Darlington. Evans, an instructor at the base who had not long returned from duties as an acting sergeant in Bahrain, was seconded to the project. He has never forgotten his first meeting with Campbell. 'The first words he said to me were, "Right, I expect the best." And being a smart-arse, I said something like, "Well, you've got it." And he just gave me a long, hard look and said, "Right, we shall see." The next time I saw him he'd just come in from a run and there was a problem with the radio equipment.' The moment was perfectly captured in a photo in Arthur Knowles' seminal book *With Campbell at Coniston* (now *The Bluebird Years*). Bluebird is back at the jetty and Campbell is standing in the cockpit, handing the equipment to an unseen person, a look of complete disdain on his face. 'That was me,' Evans chuckled.

The only thing he said was, 'It doesn't fucking work.' He very rarely swore; it was bloody this and bloody that normally. This time it was just the way he handed it to me. I knew I was in for a rollicking, because the transmission was breaking up.

I was there at two in the morning because there wasn't any other time you could fix it. At five o'clock he'd be looking at the water, and at six he'd receive the phone call and would come down to the lake. I don't know what he was doing there at two, but I heard this car door slam. Next thing, he came in and went through me like a dose of salts. Why was I still working? It had been snowing, and I know it was bloody freezing. At that time I was sleeping in the caravan that was parked alongside the workshop. 'Right, we'll get some coffee on,' he said. 'Don't you ever let me catch you doing this again.' I said that it was no good me turning round the next morning and telling him it still didn't work, and he gave me that look which said 'Keep your mouth shut'.

The next thing he said was, 'Right, tomorrow morning get

your gear and get up to the Sun.' When I asked him if he was sure, he just gave me the look again. Later, Connie Robinson came down and told me they had got me into the top room, and I said I was all right in the caravan. She said, 'Hey, don't argue with him. He's decided, and that's what's happening.'

Campbell was always forthright. A spade was always a spade. But the sense of humour was never far away, even if the laugh was sometimes on him. Evans's one-ton Austin army truck was full of radio equipment and recording gear. The safety convention in the forces was that whenever appliances were running in a vehicle, visitors had to touch the door with the back of their hand. That way, if the vehicle was for any reason live, as they recoiled they would be thrown off the steps rather than grabbing hold of the vehicle if their hand clenched involuntarily when they touched it in the normal way. Evans explained the convention to Campbell. 'You mean that you want me to knock?' he asked, ironically. 'Every time after that he would knock on that door and ask if he could come in. The first time, without thinking, I said yes, and came off the stool and opened the door. Of course, the door opened outwards and Donald was stood on the steps . . . He saw the funny side of that.'

There was another incident that amused him a great deal. Bill Jordan was an RAC man with a bushy moustache and an officious manner who saw his job as keeping the unwanted and the unwelcome out of the Bluebird camp. One night, his motorcycle refused to start. Unbeknown to him, Evans called out the AA, and when its representative arrived there were the two bikes, one in RAC insignia, the other in the AA's. Jordan was highly embarrassed. When he heard the story, Campbell thought it was hilarious. Jordan was never allowed to live it down. It was typical of the humour in record camps; the ennui fans something moderately amusing into something hilarious.

Evans had good reason to remember that Christmas Day run. The remnants from the team had enjoyed 'one hell of a night' in the Sun on Christmas Eve. Like the others, he had turned in around five or six on Christmas morning. 'Robbie came banging on my door to tell me that Donald was on the prowl. Talking about having a run. He warned me to make myself scarce.' Evans thought the day was the smoothest of the entire operation. 'The water was perfect. It was just as if somebody had thrown a cloak over the lake. It was completely flat, like glass. A mirror. If anyone had taken a photo, it would have been the same either way up. He went down to the lake and there wasn't a hitch. And he was quick. We timed him by stopwatch and he did about 250mph.'

Campbell was more relaxed that day than he had been since his arrival at Coniston. There were no reporters to pressure him, Bluebird was running properly for the first time now that the Orpheus was developing full power, and it handled better than it ever had with the Beryl engine. Except for the fact that it was the first time he had run either of the boats or the car without Leo present, it was a throwback to their old times together with the K4. For a brief moment he was the carefree adventurer again. And perhaps he had needed that jolt of sheer exhilaration just to affirm his old skills to himself. When he got back to the jetty, he was elated. For the first time since he had begun the final attempt, the 300mph barrier was in sight. Evans recalled:

He looked completely relaxed, not like a man who'd just driven a boat at 250mph. There was absolutely no stopping him when he got back. He was euphoric. We went back up for dinner, and that was when he opened the present from

David Benson – that bloody monkey with the tin drum. I could have murdered that monkey. Donald'd stick it on the bar and wind it up. Everywhere he went, you could hear this bloody thing. In the end it disappeared, so somebody got their hands on it! Tonia gave him a Mrs Whoppit to go with Mr Whoppit, and Mr Whoppit also got a butcher's apron. And that made me think. Having had a father who was as strict as his, at times like that Donald was reliving his lost youth. He was coming back to the enthusiasm of a small boy that maybe he hadn't been allowed to show when he actually was one.

The day after Boxing Day, Campbell was at it again. He achieved his best speed since returning to Coniston. 'The timekeepers weren't due back until the following day,' Robbie recalled, 'but we worked out the rough speed, which was about 285mph, I think. Obviously that was within reach of the record.' As well as Longines' electronic camera timing, Campbell had access via Norman Buckley to timing gear from the Windermere Motor Boat Racing Club which used a telescope and followed the boat down the course and clicked the watches when it entered the measured kilometre and when it exited it.

Campbell had again launched Bluebird with the delight of a schoolboy sneaking a quick cigarette out by the bicycle sheds. The illicit nature of the enterprise amused him immensely. Common sense said he should not go out with such limited support, but that was the appeal. He could strike back. Evans remembered that the water conditions were nothing like as good this time, but Campbell hit 283mph on his run south, faster than his existing record of 276.33mph. Conditions were deteriorating further as he came back, and by the time he reached the jetty white tops were forming on the lake. Still, he was ecstatic, and he now firmly believed that the record was within reach. His reckless display of bravado and boyish enthusiasm had convinced him not only that the boat could do it, but that he could too. Only the weather was holding him back now.

Villa, who had suspected such a thing might happen, was furious. 'When he came back, virtually in the middle of the run on the 27th, he was absolutely livid!' Robbie remembered. 'And I don't think I was a party to the worst that Leo thought. He had Donald aside on more than one occasion and told him exactly what he thought. And, of course, days later it was brought home to us just how dangerous it all really was.'

23

KISMET

4 January 1967

'I'm getting a lot of bloody row in here . . . I can't see anything . . . I've got the bows up . . . I've gone . . . oh . . .'

DONALD CAMPBELL, CONISTON WATER, 8.51 A.M.

When Keith Harrison, Press Association reporter and secretary of the K7 Club which comprised timers and pressmen, made his habitual trek up to the bungalow early on the morning of 4 January, ready to inform Donald Campbell of the conditions out on the lake, he found him already up and dressed. Campbell had been using field glasses to have a look down the dark water and quite liked what he saw.

'What's the weather like, Keithy?' he asked.

'I've seen it better,' Harrison replied, 'but I've seen it worse. I think we might get a run today.'

Campbell looked out over the balcony at the lake, and replied, 'I think our chances are at best fifty-fifty. I don't like the way the wind is coming from the north-west.' A moment later, he made the decision. The conditions were the best he was going to get. 'All right, Keithy. Get them all out.'

Since 27 December, Bluebird had not run. New Year's Day evening, a Sunday, had been very calm, but the lake had become too ruffled for any runs on the Monday, and Tuesday had brought rain and sleet, then frost. On New Year's Eve, the eighteenth anniversary of his father's death and two years after his own last record, Campbell had thrown a fancy dress party at the Sun. The invitations bore the legend 'Your Hostess – Lady Aitken; Your Host – Old Misery Himself'. Campbell turned up, leading Vi Aitken by the hand, as a French waiter complete with drawn-on pencil moustache. David Benson came as Batman. Dr Darbishire, a big man with a big heart, turned up dressed as a witch doctor. Campbell had a unique ability to make each person feel like the centre of his universe, and he never liked to see anyone with an empty glass in their hand. He appeared relaxed, but subdued. At midnight he shook hands with every man and kissed every woman, and made Connie Robinson cry with a special toast when he thanked her 'for being such a darling mum to us all'. With a smile, he also toasted the assembled journalists, some of them from the now defunct *Daily Sketch* which was supporting the venture, and told them, 'I know that you are all waiting for me to break my neck.' One in particular enjoyed needling him. 'He was always making comments about the runs in Australia, and every time that happened Donald just used to pick his glass up and go round the other side of the bar,' Paul Evans recalled. 'This guy made a comment one night, and Campbell just turned round to him and said, pointblank, "If I have to go, old boy, I hope I'm going ruddy fast at the time." Donald got Leo to wind this guy up by telling him they were putting a second cockpit on the boat, and that the other reporters agreed he was the right guy for it.'

Campbell was always upset by negative stories where the

writer had failed to understand his problems. Like F1 world champion Jim Clark, he would not tolerate inaccurate reporting. On one occasion he had gone down to London to see an osteopath after aggravating his old back injury, and was incensed to read about it in a daily paper after one journalist had eavesdropped on a private telephone conversation. The pressure became greater the longer reporters waited for something to happen. 'I'm sure he felt it,' Tony Robinson believed. 'The media pressure was just one more weight added to everything else. But at the same time he was realistic enough to know that he couldn't have survived at the top in record breaking without being well aware of what he was doing and being on the ball. And he must have been used to handling it.'

Campbell had spent the last night of his life restlessly. Habitually he held a card school at the bungalow, usually accompanied by David Benson and other press buddies. Louis and Julie Goosens looked after everyone. That Tuesday evening he played Russian patience, which he had learned at Lake Mead, while he and Benson awaited the others. In one hand, Campbell had turned up the ace of spades, traditionally the bad luck card, followed immediately by the queen. Campbell called it the death card. He was profoundly disturbed by this omen, and said to Benson, 'That's it. Mary, Queen of Scots drew the same combination the night before she was beheaded.' Benson told him to forget it, and they switched to pontoon. Campbell asked for fresh cards from Goosens, but of all ironies the replacements had green backing and he refused to use them.

Campbell's mood picked up when others joined them, and he played strong hands, frequently consulting for advice Charlie, the small wind-up toy monkey Benson had given him. Though some stories reported that Campbell was

384

drinking heavily during these days at Coniston, Benson was adamant that he had not touched anything for the previous three days. But as usual, Campbell poured generous libations for his friends. Later that evening he became depressed again, as the cards he had turned up continued to prey on his mind. According to Benson, he said at one point, 'I have the most awful premonition that I'm going to get the chop this time. I've had the feeling for days.' Once again Benson told him not to be silly, and argued that the feeling was just the result of hanging around Coniston for so long. 'Well,' Campbell reportedly replied, 'it's somebody in my family that's going to get the chop. I pray to God it's not me.' Gina Campbell, however, disputed this reportage vehemently. 'My father was so worried about everybody else but himself, he would never have wished that on anybody.'

When they finally turned in, Campbell saw Benson to the door and looked up at the dark sky. He managed a wry grin as he told his old friend, 'It looks like tomorrow is the day – I only hope it's not my last.'

Sleep would not come. He called Tonia in Bristol. It was to be their last, poignant conversation. She would later script a reconstruction for the BBC television film *Across the Lake*, claiming it was as verbatim as memory would allow, though she made revisions subsequently for her book *My Speed King*.

The phone rings in Tonia's hotel bedroom.

Tonia: 'Hello'.

Donald: 'Hello, Bobo, how did it go?'

Tonia: 'Oh marvellous. I'm the toast of Bristol, didn't you know?'

Donald: 'Now listen, darling, I'm going for the record tomorrow.'

Tonia: 'Tomorrow?'

Donald: 'Yes. I've told the press and television boys. It's all set. My time's up now . . .'

Tonia: 'You promised them?'

Donald: 'The [Daily Express] Boat Show starts tomorrow, you understand.'

PAUSE

Donald: 'I've been outside. No wind, and the conditions are perfect. I've got it all worked out. We'll go to the Boat Show, celebrate, have a few laughs, then fly off to Courchevel, do some skiing. How about that? I've already cabled Gina, it's all laid on.'

PAUSE

Donald: 'Bobo, are you there?'

Tonia: 'Oh, yes, Donald. I'm sorry. Listen, I'm coming up there, I want to be with you.'

Donald: 'Oh, you will be with me, don't worry. As soon as this is over we'll go away, we'll have a wonderful time. Just you and me.'

Tonia: 'Darling, I should be there. I'm your mascot.'

Donald: 'Don't worry, Mr Whoppit will look after me. He's always here.' (A gentle reproach?)

Tonia: 'Go get some sleep now, yes?'

Donald: 'Yes, I will. Don't worry about me.'

Tonia: 'And you don't take any pills, you old hypochondriac.'

Donald: 'No, I won't. À bientôt.'

Tonia: 'Bientôt.'

PAUSE

Donald (urgently): 'Bobo? Do take care of yourself, won't you? You're awfully important to me, you understand?'

SILENCE

Tonia: 'Donald?'

SILENCE

Campbell also called several old friends that night, particularly those he had not seen for a while. Many noted a hint of desperation in his voice, a need for reassurance, perhaps, to occupy himself with the solace of company. Had they known of these conversations, those who would start to talk of suicide the following day would have had greater ammunition. Louis Stanley remembered, 'He rang very early in the morning, and said he was going to have a go. I said, "Well, are you sure? Why the hurry?" And he said, "The Boat Show is going to be opening in Earls Court, and I've got to get the record broken so that we can announce it and send the boat down there."' Interestingly, Daphne claimed he also spoke with her. 'We were in constant touch,' she said. 'He rang me that night and said, "I am going to have a go at this."' Gina always doubted that claim. 'My father, if he was alive today, would tell you that he came to hate my mother. She deceived him. He could stand anything but deceit and lies. He would give me a routine spanking for lying.' Tonia was also doubtful. 'Donald once said to me, "You know, Tonia, if it wasn't for little Gina I find it hard to believe I ever fucked that woman."'

Were the cards the reason why he phoned so many of his old friends that night? Or was it because this time his father's ghost had not appeared to tell him that it would be all right?

During those final days, Campbell had also spoken to Bill Coley and Peter Barker. 'I didn't go on the last attempt, but we were in contact,' Coley said. 'He wanted me to go up there, of course.' Barker recalled Campbell ringing him 'about three days before, saying please could I go up. I feel I want my old team, as many as I can get, around me. Intimating, I think, that he felt he was being pushed a bit. But I couldn't go.' 'He was lonely, probably,' Dottie said, concern still etched in her voice all those years later. 'And of course Tonia had gone by then. Gina gets very angry about how things are portrayed with Tonia in the film *Across the Lake*, because she knows what went on. But it doesn't do to dwell on these things. Poor Donald, so lonely . . .'

Campbell had also gone to see his friend Hughie Green again at Baker Street while he was visiting the osteopath. 'I remember Donald coming here, and sitting right there on that sofa you are sitting on, just before the end. He was very despondent. I felt like shit because I had to tell him that I had not succeeded in finding him anyone who would put some money up. And he just said, "Oh well, I'll just have to go and do it." I said to him, "Donald, for Christ's sake be careful." And I begged him. I said, "Whatever you do, and I know how anxious you are to get this thing over with, don't you dare be too anxious. Don't make that return before you should."'

Campbell did not call Victor Mishcon, because his old friend had remarried on 1 January and was on honeymoon. But they, too, had spoken just before the ultimate battle. 'I asked him the silly question that I suppose thousands of people would have asked: "How do you feel about this attempt?" And I have never forgotten his answer. He said, "Dead scared."'

The previous Sunday, Campbell had also called Marjorie Staves. 'I think he felt that I was the only one who would understand how he was feeling. We talked, and I said to him, "To be honest with you, I'm not too happy about it." I couldn't let him go without saying that, because I knew I felt there was a disaster. We had to talk very gently. At the end of his life people didn't want to be bothered with him. It made him very nervous and very distressed.'

Whatever his misgivings in those desperate, lonely hours,

Campbell was all action as he strode down to the boathouse just before eight o'clock on Wednesday morning. Much in the way that President John Kennedy's movements in his final hours were accorded greater import than they actually merited, much has been made of Campbell's behaviour at that time. In his book *The Record Breakers*, Villa spoke of feeling dismissed when he tried to give Campbell an update on the water conditions and was told curtly, 'Don't mess about, Unc, let's get her out.' Clive Glynn, however, thought that Campbell was just anxious to get going. 'I said "Good morning, Skipper," in the normal way. He didn't seem any different. The only difference was that he seemed in a hurry.' Several journalists reported that he brushed by them as if preoccupied, rather than giving his usual cheery hello. But these were all indications of a man who just wanted to get the job done, not one who had seen a vision of his own destiny. Anyone who has been around race drivers or record breakers has seen that a hundred times. Evans, forever down to earth, simply remembered, 'The atmosphere was normal until the tragedy.'

These were the major players in that final drama: Campbell was call-signed Skipper; Villa, in one of the Fairline launches with Tony Robinson and photographer Geoff Hallawell, was Alpha; Evans, in Radio Vehicle at Pier Cottage – where Coniston boatman Arthur Wilson had rented space to the team so that they could erect scaffolding to serve as Bluebird's boathouse, and behind which a double garage served as the team's workshop – was Base; Darbishire, on the east shore with Campbell's old friend Andrew Brown in place of the men from Longines who had not returned, was Tango; and Goosens was Charlie, at the southern end with Bill Jordan, close to reporter Keith Harrison in a second Fairline.

At 8.10, Campbell stepped into the cockpit as Bluebird sat by the jetty, but then asked David Benson to fetch the de-mister cloth that he had left in the Land Rover used for launching the boat. As usual, Bluebird's cockpit screen was already misting up. Benson was helping to strap him in when Campbell exclaimed out loud, 'Hell! There's something sticking in my arse!' It was his pipe and tobacco. He handed them to his friend, and they completed the strapping-in process. (Much to Gina's chagrin, the pipe and pouch eventually ended up preserved in Perspex after Benson gave them to Max and Vi Aitken's son, Maxwell. She would frequently be angered to see family possessions, such as Campbell's pilot's licences and some of his guns, included in other people's memorabilia auctions.) There was another minor panic when Mr Whoppit could not be located, and a delay until the bear was found. Though the tension was inevitably heightened by the expectation of a full-blown record attempt, everyone was calm. Campbell, however, had grumbled again about the cards he had turned up the previous evening. Benson once more urged him to forget about them.

At 8.30, Campbell radioed to Harrison for an update on the state of the water. Harrison told him there was a slight ground swell, but that conditions were otherwise moderately good.

But there was another delay. This should have been the first time that Paul Evans had watched a full run. His normal position at Pier Cottage prevented him from seeing any-thing beyond Bluebird leaving to start the southern run, and slowing at the end of its northbound back-up. But this time Campbell had given him permission to take a Land Rover with remote-control radio facilities round to the time-keepers' position on the east shore, so that he could watch everything. But the narrow back road was jammed solid with spectators, and Evans was forced to return to base. His recollection is particularly damaging to those who believed that Campbell was a reckless man on the brink of suicide. 'Donald seemed his normal self,' Evans said. 'There were a few hiccoughs, but nothing major apart from me having to turn round and come back. He was all right on the radio. "Get yourself back here, I'll wait." Time was of the essence and he didn't have time to wait, but he would still rather wait for me even though he knew full well I was in radio contact with everybody. There was no need for that, but he still wanted to wait.'

Several minutes later, with Evans back at base, Campbell called again for a weather update and received the same reply. 'All right then,' he responded, 'we'll have a slow run to see how things are.'

Record runs are rarely given a fanfare. Usually they are dressed up as just another trial run, at least until the halfway point. Nevertheless, everyone dotted around Coniston Water that morning knew perfectly well that this was going to be it. For those in the know, Campbell's deliberately ironic comment was final confirmation.

The lake seemed its usual moody self, even though the early light had filtered sluggishly down from the Grisedale Forest to cast a silvery sheen across the flat, black waters. The wind was gentle still, a ghost's soft kiss on cold cheeks. After all the waiting and all the technical problems, the conditions were finally acceptable. It was now or never.

At 8.41, rockets were fired to frighten wildlife off the water. Campbell went through the starting procedure, and a minute later the familiar whine of the Orpheus broke the morning silence. He gave Benson his usual wave as he set off from Pier Cottage. One of Glynn's jobs kept him ashore at the jetty. 'I would pull the boat round on a piece of rope until it was facing the right way, then it would shoot off,' he said. 'That day, the Skipper hardly gave me a chance to pull the rope off. I only just got it undone. Some days he might take five or ten minutes to get the boat pointing to the south-east. Not that day. He went off in a flaming hurry! I saw him streak off down the lake on the first run, and could hear it all the way down the course. There was a north-east breeze beginning to get up, and the lake wasn't a hundred per cent smooth, but I wouldn't say that was the cause of what happened.'

It was 8.45. Donald Campbell had started his last record attempt.

That first run was the best Campbell ever made in Bluebird K7. Down at the southern end, some of the reporters had gathered just in case Campbell's worst fears were realized and the big blue boat really did run out of lake. But it had roared down the course with perfect stability, entering the kilometre at 8.46, and as usual Campbell made a calm, rational commentary throughout the run. 'I've got a fair amount of water here and, er, without the mask on, just as soon as I'm heading down the lake, er . . . don't know. Here we go, here we go, here we go. Four and five coming up. A lot of water. Nose beginning to lift. Lot of water coming again . . . And the nose is up. Left and right sponsons up. It's up and away. Vision clear. Tramping very hard at 150. Very hard indeed. Trying for full power. I still can't get over the top. Full house, full house, full house. Now that's three.' That last comment meant that the air-speed indicator had flickered to the magic 300mph as Bluebird reached its peak velocity.

The usual strategy was that when Bluebird reached the southern end, Villa would give 'the Skipper' his view of how the boat had looked as it went by his observation point in the measured distance, then Campbell would relate his version of events from the cockpit. Villa would then make the decision on the second run – whether it should go ahead, and when, based on the performance of the boat and the state of the water. If necessary, he would put the brakes on. 'No big foot, Don, boy,' was his frequent caution. On the infrequent occasions when Campbell overrode him, he could be sure of an avuncular bollocking.

Out on the lake, Villa rubbed his hands together to ward off the chill as his Fairline cruiser bobbed gently on the surface, its equilibrium still disturbed by Bluebird's recent passage. The old man scanned the waters and tried to call Campbell. But for reasons that only Campbell himself knew, this time he made only brief contact as twice Villa asked him to communicate. Instead, Campbell was more intent on asking Evans for his speed.

Skipper: 'I'm passing Peel Island, throttling off now, right hand down, brake down, past Peel Island, coming round, dropping to 100. Nose hasn't dropped yet . . . nose down. Leo, do you read me? Over.'

Alpha: 'Read you, Skipper.'

Skipper: 'Base, do you read me?'

Alpha: 'Reading you, Skipper, come in.'

Silence. What was wrong? Why, of all times, should the radio link to the Bluebird suddenly choose not to work? Then Villa was puzzled to hear Campbell's voice again. So the radio was working properly. But Campbell was not talking to him. He was still calling Base.

Skipper: 'Skipper to Base, will you give me my reference on speeds? Over.'

Base: 'Er, roger, er, in actual fact that was Alpha that answered you, Skipper. Over.'

Skipper, (tetchily): 'Roger, never mind about that. I wanted speed progress. Over.'

Base: 'Roger, Skipper. Tango, Tango, do you read? Over.'

Tango: 'Tango to Base. Stand by.'

Soon afterwards Tango came back on again.

Tango: 'Tango to Base, Tango for Base, message for Skipper. Plus 47, plus 47, plus 47. Do you copy that? Repeat, over.'

Base: 'Base to Tango. Roger, roger, roger. Base for Skipper from Tango, plus 47, plus 47. Over.'

So now an impatient Campbell knew his speed. 'Plus 47' meant 47mph over a 250mph baseline. He had achieved an average of 297.6mph on the downward run through the measured kilometre, less than 3mph short of the target. There was now no shred of doubt that he had just become the first man in the world ever to reach a *peak* speed of more than 300mph on water, probably around 315mph.

Campbell was allowed an hour in which to make both runs, under the rules established by the Union Internationale Motonautique (UIM). This was sufficient to allow the wash from the first run to disperse. But habitually he would make his return runs sooner than that. The usual margin was around twenty minutes, but he had done it in four minutes several times, notably at Dumbleyung where he hadn't stopped to refuel. There had been a seven-minute turnaround on 12 December 1966 and only four-minute pauses on the 13th and the 14th. Now, Campbell was on the move again after another four-minute turnaround. During his peremptory requests for his speed he had driven past Goosens, ready with the hose in the refuelling boat, had headed further to the end of the lake, and then turned ready for the return run.

Campbell's refusal to respond to him was what had

prompted Villa to wonder if his own radio was malfunctioning, but Evans tested each radio set every morning. That day all of them had performed, as usual, without any problem. Villa, not knowing this, was still cursing the vagaries of things electronic when, to his complete astonishment, he heard the distinctive whine of the Orpheus spooling up again. With growing alarm, he heard another message crackle over the radio link. Campbell momentarily allowed his strict adherence to radio etiquette to lapse as he came back on to Evans.

Skipper: 'Roger, Paul, I'm starting my return run now.'

The chill Villa now felt in his stomach had nothing to do with the winter temperature. He, of all the men who had camped at Coniston, knew best the pressure Campbell was under after nine frustrating weeks. It was 8.49 a.m., barely four minutes since Campbell had sped from the northern end and through the measured kilometre. The wake from that first pass had not yet dissipated. The factor that Campbell had forgotten to take into account was that he had used the water brake on Bluebird's transom for the first time on the first run, and crucially it had agitated the water even more. That, and the higher speed, would prove critical. The roughened wake had fanned out to the narrow, rocky shores of Peel Island and was even then rippling back onto Bluebird's track. The seeds of disaster had been sown.

What Campbell did in those final moments compounded the mystery of his last day, and perhaps provided the most graphic evidence of the strain he had been under and his determination to win through. It also explained why Villa's radio appeared not to be working.

Evans had carefully lectured everyone not to use the pressel switch on the microphones of the VHF radio system, an override button which, if activated either accidentally or deliberately, meant that everybody else was automatically blocked and could not transmit. Bluebird had had its pressel switch mounted specially by Evans on the floor of the cockpit. Just after Campbell had announced his intention of starting his final run, and just before his final transmission when the run was underway, there was a very long pause. Somebody was activating his pressel button, transmitting but not speaking. Evans had no doubt who it was. 'The strength of that signal was fairly loud. To me, there was only person who had that type of signal strength and control, and that was Donald. The way not to listen to anybody, and to stop anybody contacting you, was to operate the pressel switch. And of course Donald knew that. My personal opinion is this. Plus 47 gave him 297mph. How would you feel? Knowing that you wouldn't get a second chance?'

Campbell had his foot on his pressel switch yet was making no commentary. Villa, like everyone else, had deliberately been kept out of the loop. Evans would forever reproach himself, unnecessarily, for not telling Campbell that he would relay Villa's messages to him.

After the pause, Campbell finally came back on air. In little more than three minutes he had made his first run, had turned around, and was headed back. Villa could not believe his ears. It was against every precept by which Donald Campbell had lived his life. He had never been reckless. He had always consulted him before making his return run. But alone in the cockpit, overriding other transmissions, it would have been easy for Campbell to underestimate the effect of the water brake. He was taking his life into his own hands. It was the one time he had cut Villa out of the communications loop, and it would prove fatal.

Now the old man listened helplessly as Campbell began

transmitting again and entered his last kilometre at 8.50 and 328mph. There is still argument over precisely what he said. This is Paul Evans's transcript, with which many Campbell fans disagree. Other interpretations are in italics.

Skipper: 'The nose is up (*nose up*). Pitching a bit down here as I drive over my own wash (*probably from my own wash*). Stabilizing, up blind track (*straightening up now in my track*) ... rather close to Peel Island, tramping like mad ... er ... full power. And, er, tramping like hell here. Can't see very much, the water's dark and green (*the water's very bad indeed*). I can't get over the top. She's lost a bit of her bloody track (*I'm getting a lot of bloody row in here*). I can't see anything. Hello, the bow's up! I've gone! (*I've got the bows up ... I'm going!*) Oh ...'

In the rough water, Bluebird had begun its characteristic rocking from side to side, which Ken Norris called tramping, and hopped from one sponson to the other. Some 150 yards before the end of the kilometre, seconds later, both sponsons lifted from the water at the same time. Gradually, as if finally seeking its true element after years of obedience to its human master, Bluebird went past its safety angle and climbed gracefully off Coniston Water. It described an eerily elegant arc, thirty or more feet in the air, flipping right over onto its back before plunging back into the water nose-first at an angle of perhaps 45°. Parts flew in all directions as the blue hydroplane shattered. Debris rained down. The impact broke Bluebird in half, sending the sponsons and other components tumbling across the surface, while the rear section of the fuselage aft of the cockpit rolled along the surface before resting there momentarily, like an old lady seeking sanctuary amid an angry welter of spray, too tired to complete her journey. Then it slipped gently from sight, leaving only the disturbed water to mark its savage end.

For moments, there was nothing but terrible silence. Then:

Tango: 'Tango to Base, Tango to Base, over.'

Base: 'Base to Tango, over.'

Tango: 'Tango to Base, Tango to Base. A complete accident, I'm afraid, over.'

Base: 'Roger. Details, over.'

Tango: 'Tango, no details, as yet. Stand by.'

Spellbound, Villa had hunched his shoulders and monitored the boat through his binoculars as it screamed closer, noting the tramping. But then he watched in sheer horror as it increased until Bluebird took off.

'Quick, boy, the Skipper's in trouble!'

The catch of panic grated in Villa's voice as Robinson slashed at the Fairline's mooring ropes. They raced to the accident scene where they circled, waiting frantically for Campbell to bob up. 'I was just transfixed, just sort of stood there,' Robinson recalled.

The first thing I remember is Leo giving me a dig in the ribs and saying, 'Come on, boy, for Christ's sake, get going!' In this sort of total panic we forgot to pull the anchor up, and that was dragging along the surface behind us. Geoff [Hallawell] cut it loose with a knife. We got to the scene, and I'm sure then that it hadn't occurred to Leo that Donald wouldn't survive. We were desperately looking round, and then we saw his lifejacket, and somebody said, 'There he is!' It was all sort of panicky, for me, being the driver of our boat, trying to see his lifejacket and helmet floating there. With a boat it's quite difficult; if something's too close, you've actually got to back off and come back in because you can't go round tight enough. I wasn't getting anywhere, just going round in circles with this thing in the middle and

398

us not getting any nearer to it. Leo was saying, 'Come on, get to it!'

Finally, Hallawell grabbed the object. It was one of the sponsons, and instead of letting go of it he hung onto it and fell out of the boat. 'It was man overboard,' Robinson continued. 'Poor old Geoff was wet through and it was freezing cold, but we had to stay out there. We couldn't leave. We were all still assuming that Donald was going to appear. It was only afterwards when I was talking to Dr Darbishire that he said he simply wouldn't have survived the g forces. He told me that Donald would have been dead before he hit the water.' At the time, Robinson remembered Villa saying, 'Christ, the boat's sunk, it's gone. Where can we get some divers? Get on the radio, get some organized. We've got to get him out.' At that stage the men on the lake still assumed Campbell was strapped into the stricken boat as it had sunk. In retrospect, it is astonishing that there were no real contingencies for any kind of accident.

Piece by piece, items floated to the surface: Campbell's helmet, his socks, one glove, his boots, his lifejacket. Last of all, Mr Whoppit. Together, he and his owner had survived the crash at more than 300mph at Bonneville with the Bluebird car in 1960; now, onlookers prayed silently for another miraculous deliverance.

Back on shore, few observers at the jetty had been in a position to see the accident, but they knew the score because it was broadcast almost immediately as a news bulletin. Word soon began to spread. Everyone knew about the escapade at Bonneville, and many were taking it for granted that Campbell would somehow survive yet again. 'The initial reaction was that nobody believed it had happened,' Evans remembered. 'And then of course people were running around saying that it was OK, he'd got half an hour of oxygen. They sent for divers. But the divers were over in Barrow.' Barrow-in-Furness was some sixteen miles south-west of Coniston; the divers would thus have needed over half an hour to scramble, get to Coniston and spring into action.

While Keith Harrison was out on the lake, David Benson was ashore at Pier Cottage. The pair didn't get on, and Benson held the belief that while he was at home for Christmas Harrison had taken the opportunity to fill his place in the southern boat with someone else. 'I don't think that Keith liked the way that Donald and I were close,' Benson, a difficult man, said. 'I got very upset, but Donald calmed me down. He said it was much better being in the boathouse than way out on the lake. So there I was. I had his field glasses, which were very powerful, and watched the return run. But the bit I saw was not Bluebird taking off, but rolling. I didn't realize until much later that it had somer-saulted, much less that it had broken in half.'

It was Benson who began to circulate the news that Campbell had half an hour of oxygen on board. He even told Tonia that when he telephoned her from the caravan. Some, who had no idea of the severity of the accident, believed it. Frightened men clutched at straws. But those closest to the accident already knew the terrible truth. The oxygen supply had been attached to the helmet, and they already held that in their numb, trembling hands. Bluebird had broken in two just behind the cockpit, so where was Campbell? In the deathly silence that had suddenly settled over the lake, they all watched for the slightest movement.

Waiting, praying. Against all reason, hoping.

As each unrewarded minute stretched those last fragile threads of hope, they snapped one by one, until quietly,

Left: Alfred Owen: industrial knight, lay preacher, non-smoker, teetotaller, abhorrer of cusswords and preternatural do-gooder. A man possessed of a 'streak of self-righteous egotism and a curious inability to accept criticism or even enquiry'. Small wonder that he and Campbell never saw eye to eye.

Below: Typical of the setbacks that Campbell encountered on Lake Eyre in 1963 was the failure of the salt surface to support vehicles such as the 10-ton grader, which broke through with monotonous regularity during costly track preparation. BP

Above: By June 1964 the atmosphere on Lake Eyre had curdled with acrimony as continual weather delays and mechanical problems stretched patience to the limit and made life intolerable for Campbell. BP

Left: On July 17 1964 Campbell finally found his window in the weather and snatched the chance with both hands to set a new wheel-driven land speed record of 403.10 mph, but the courageous success would be an anti-climax. BP

Opposite: During the hour-long turnaround between two almost suicidal runs, Campbell was adamant that he saw the face of his late father reflected in the open cockpit screen, telling him: 'It'll be all right, boy.' BP

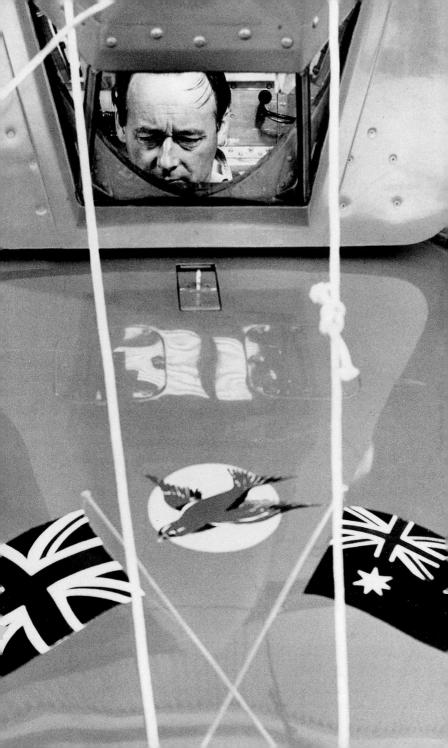

Right: Damning those who believed his demise was suicide, Campbell planned his final record attempt at Coniston Water to raise the funding for a dramatic supersonic Bluebird CN8 that was under design by Norris Brothers. This is the full-scale mock-up.

The people of Adelaide turned out in their hundred thousands to fete Campbell and Bluebird CN7 as he drove the jetcar down King William Street. GINA CAMPBELL

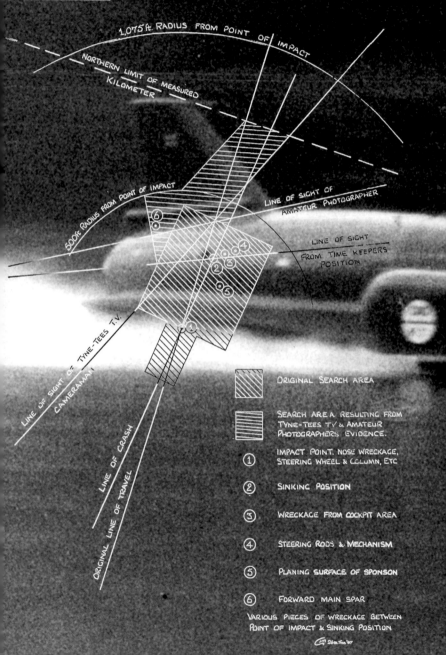

SCALE DIAGRAM OF "BLUEBIRD" CRASH & SEARCH AREAS

SCALE - 1" = 200'

1,075 ft. RADIUS FROM POINT OF IMPACT

NORTHERN LIMIT OF MEASURED KILOMETER

500ft RADIUS FROM POINT OF IMPACT

LINE OF SIGHT OF AMATEUR PHOTOGRAPHER

LINE OF SIGHT FROM TIME KEEPERS POSITION

LINE OF SIGHT OF TYNE-TEES T.V. CAMERAMAN

LINE OF CRASH

LINE OF TRAVEL

ORIGINAL LINE OF TRAVEL

ORIGINAL SEARCH AREA

SEARCH AREA RESULTING FROM TYNE-TEES TV & AMATEUR PHOTOGRAPHERS EVIDENCE.

① IMPACT POINT. NOSE WRECKAGE, STEERING WHEEL & COLUMN, ETC

② SINKING POSITION

③ WRECKAGE FROM COCKPIT AREA

④ STEERING RODS & MECHANISM

⑤ PLANING SURFACE OF SPONSON

⑥ FORWARD MAIN SPAR

VARIOUS PIECES OF WRECKAGE BETWEEN POINT OF IMPACT & SINKING POSITION

Main pic: On his first run on 4 January 1967, Donald Campbell achieved a one-way speed of 297.6 mph, but coming so tantalizingly close to his goal of 300 mph prompted him to take one calculated risk too many on the return. PRESS ASSOCIATION

Below: In the immediate aftermath of the tragedy, Tonia Bern-Campbell lays a small wreath at the side of the lake. WESTMORELAND GAZETTE

Opposite: Lieutenant John Futcher and his team of divers made stupendous efforts to locate Campbell's body, as this scale diagram of the search area attests.

Above: After its final passage through Coniston's measured kilo, Donald Campbell's body is carried ashore on a cold, wet 12 September 2001.

<small>GINA CAMPBELL</small>

Left: Thousands line the streets of Coniston to pay their final respects to the speed king.

<small>GINA CAMPBELL</small>

Right: Campbell's body was finally laid to rest in the cemetery at Coniston, where his spirit still pervades the area in which so many of his life's greatest battles were fought.

You don't often see grown men with tears streaming down their faces. People got very emotional. I was only twenty-six. It was around about that time that I suddenly appreciated how that one guy had affected so many. And there would be a lot of them wishing that they hadn't said things that they had said.

The one thing I will never forget was Leo's face. You know how people describe somebody seeing a ghost – it was just like that. There was no expression whatsoever. His face was just completely bland. I saw Leo go from what I thought was quite an energetic middle-aged man to an old man. He just aged. For him, it was probably a bigger shock than for anybody else.

Out on the water, hope had turned to despair. 'I don't know how long we were out there for,' Robinson said. 'Another boat arrived and we looked round and round. After Geoff's incident we'd collected one of the sponsons, and we got Keith's boat to get the other one. I think by this time Leo had started putting two and two together. He never said so, but he was starting to be affected by shock. Geoff was freezing cold, so they both got in the other boat and they took them and the sponsons back to the boathouse. I was left on my own for the next two hours, just cruising round. In the end it just got too much. If somebody had said I'd got to stay there, I'd have said, "Sod it, that's it." As it was I didn't ask, I just came home.'

Back at the Sun, Connie Robinson put up a large notice. One word: CLOSED. Joan Villa was there with her, as stoic as her husband, and Julie Goosens. 'The place was heaving with people,' Robinson said. 'I always remember walking in, and I saw my mum there, and that was it. Strangely enough, it was David Benson who rescued the situation. He came

over and just took hold of us, took me into the [...] us a drink.'

Evans remembered how there had been a ma[...] hotel after Villa had been brought ashore. 'The [...] were arguing over who had the best shot. Som[...] me what I thought, and I said, "Christ, I never r[...] like that." And then one of the BBC guys said, [...] how the professionals do it now, my son." I [...] clearly fixed in my mind that that was at luncl[...] be totally wrong; it's one of those things tha[...] played a trick on the memory. But I remember[...] back into the bar and there was Fleet Street p[...] Norman Luck and company, and somebody ra[...] and said, "Here's to the Skipper." Everybody just[...] in a trance.'

'Eventually, Stephen Darbishire said there w[...] Robinson said. 'It was just a matter of organizi[...] find him. They'd approached a local sub aq[...] realized that they didn't have the manpower. S[...] touch with the navy, and their divers came do[...] from Rosyth. They started work next mornin[...]

At lunch, and later that evening around [...] place, subdued groups gathered, strained, te[...] easing the atmosphere with fond stories of th[...] brought them all there. Some of them, the ha[...] men of the press, were quite unable to expla[...] selves precisely what it was that had draw[...] Others, his close associates, were left to po[...] and the immediate friendship he had so re[...] them so early in their relationships. And th[...] had created. Villa, who had turned sixty[...] day of November, behaved with heroic dig[...] name. He hid his feelings and did his du[...]

k to the television studios to appear on *Twenty-Four Hours* at evening. Despite his own grief, he pushed on, getting back the Sun at two o'clock the following morning.

Back in London, Hughie Green had been crossing the ad at Baker Street, headed for home, when he saw e lunchtime placards: DONALD CAMPBELL DEAD.

I will never forget that. The tears just flowed. When I got back in the phone was ringing. It was Tonia. Now, a great, great mutual friend of ours, of Tonia's and mine and Donald's, was probably the most loved and the most hated scandal writer in this country, Rex North. He was on the *Daily Mirror*, and he had a power beyond belief. If Rex liked you, then Rex liked you. If he didn't like you ... But Rex adored Donald. I often used to meet Donald at Rex's place. Tonia just said, 'Bluebird has gone down. Will you call Rex? Will you get him to use all his influence to see, if the body is recovered, that it is never shown?' And I think that is the last thing I ever did for Donald. It was Tonia's fervent desire that his body was never seen, by television news people or by photographers. She had made him a promise, you see, which I always thought was a very touch-ing promise between two people, that she would never let he public see him other than standing up.

Donald Campbell was now at one with the shadow of his er. All his life he had lived in it. Now, on that grey morn-in January, it had finally reached out to engulf him. The which had taunted him so cruelly in his early days, and then yielded so much of the subsequent success had made him a national hero, had demanded of him ighest price.

t the day the man died, the real legend was born.

finally, the speedking's stunned friends began to accept the awful reality that they would not see him again. Nobody could possibly have survived an accident of such terrible ferocity. 'When Leo came ashore with the things they had pulled out from the crash scene, like Donald's helmet,' Benson admitted, 'we all knew the truth.'

Gina was in Switzerland. 'My mother called me,' she said. 'I was doing the ironing in the basement dungeon of the Park Hotel in Lausanne. Dad had written suggesting we meet in Courchevel once the wretched record had been broken. I had written back, but he had never got to read it ... Somebody said there was a call for me, and I just knew immediately. Isn't it strange, it never crossed my mind it might be good news.'

Clive Glynn hadn't actually heard Campbell start back. 'The breeze was taking the noise towards the coast. Then we heard that the boat had gone up into the air, and everyone started trying to rush to the scene. The aftermath was awful. It was the first time I'd ever come face to face with that sort of thing. There was just nothing to do. Then gradually they began bringing bits back from the search boats. Louis [Goosens] and I carried the two sponson cowlings back up to the boathouse.'

Everyone automatically congregated outside the radio truck. 'They were all trying to make calls on the one tele-phone in the caravan. It was absolute chaos,' Evans recalled.

Then Clive brought one of the sponson cowlings back, and everybody just went completely quiet. I think it was that moment that brought home to everybody that this was final. As soon as the plus 47 bit had come out a lot of people on shore were getting back to the jetty area to hail the conquer-ing hero.

24

AFTERMATH

January to February 1967

'You will never find another Donald Campbell in this world. He simply does not exist. He was not afraid of what might happen above that 300mph limit.'

LEO VILLA, CONISTON WATER, 4 JANUARY 1967

Only two things mattered now. Where was Donald Campbell's body? And how had the tragedy occurred?

Norris believed that Campbell had been killed on impact and his body ejected from the shattered cockpit. 'As the harness had torn out, I thought it likely that Donald got shot out, forwards, in the first impact. I didn't think it likely that he got shoved back through the engine, even though everything behind him was quite a light structure. That was what David Benson believed. Donald might have been unconscious at the top of the arc, but I'm sure it was the impact that killed him.' It would be thirty-four years before Norris was proved right.

John Futcher, lieutenant commander of the Royal Navy's Scotland and Northern Ireland Command Clearance Diving

Team at HMS Safeguard in Rosyth, Fife, led a ten-man team of divers comprising Petty Officer Shennan, Lieutenant Seamen Kempson, Vernon, Lee and Gallant, and Able Seamen Flynn, Crawford, Porter and Grainger south at 3.15 in the afternoon of Wednesday, 4 January. They made their first dive at 12.30 the following day, working on Futcher's theory that Campbell's body would either be at the point of impact, with the main wreckage, or at a point just ahead. He began to plot the whereabouts of all the parts that had been retrieved and worked back along the line of travel to the point of impact. The fourth dive located the main hull, lying upright 140 feet down, but a detailed search could not be conducted as the diver had only a hand-held torch. Two further dives were made the following day, the 6th, to determine whether Campbell was in or near the remains of the boat. They yielded nothing. Three further dives south of the original datum where the sponsons had come up, working back to the point of impact, all produced wreckage, a fourth did not. Futcher moved the search west and managed to relocate Bluebird's crash path. On Saturday the 7th they found the steering wheel and column, and then the torn bow section of the craft, 280 feet south of the main hull. Futcher believed this marked the impact point. According to Norris, the maximum distance between the point of impact and the sinking position of the main hull could not have been more than 400 feet, based on the maximum speed and the time taken to decelerate to zero miles an hour and sink.

The following Monday, Tuesday and Wednesday, Futcher's team searched areas to the west and east of the travel line, but by the evening of the last day the decision was taken to postpone the attempt. He was then invited to Carlisle to view footage taken by a Tyne-Tees cameraman which showed an object leaving the spray. Futcher and Villa viewed it several times at Border Television studios and formed the view that it could have been Campbell's body.

Dives on Friday the 13th proved fruitless, but then an amateur photographer came forward with still photographs which provided a splash point for the new object, and on the 15th it transpired that it was the forward main spar which connected the sponsons. It was bent, which accounted for it appearing to be the changing shape of a body. Reluctantly, having searched and found the cause of every individual splash shown on film, Futcher abandoned the effort. His team returned to base on the afternoon of Monday the 16th. It would transpire that despite the heroic efforts of his team, they had just missed finding Campbell's body.

Dr Gerry Jackson, a first class diver and a founder fellow of the Institute of Advanced Diving, was part of the team which salvaged the steamship Dolly from Windermere and had previously traversed the bottom of Coniston. He was one of the professional divers first contacted by the police.

When we went out to the accident site, the water conditions were fair. It was cold, of course, but visibility was initially fair, though we couldn't see very much. The bottom of Coniston is muddy and dark and the silt is very easily stirred up. You did everything by touch. There was a press photograph of the boat actually sitting on the bottom with its fin up. After that was published we were provided with underwater cameras, but the visibility became so bad that we couldn't take any further photographs.

I don't think it was a fruitless search, even though we didn't find Donald Campbell. Everyone was efficient at what they had to do. And the wreckage of the boat was located, and several other pieces of the vessel were brought to the surface.

It was dangerous work, and one diver had to go into a decompression chamber because of nitrogen narcosis – the bends. Futcher had his own description of the conditions.

All light from the surface was absorbed by the time seventy feet had been reached, and the bottom consisted of thick mud with a one-foot layer of fine silt on top. Any movement near the bottom caused a disturbance of this silt, which billowed around the diver like a thick fog and rendered the illumination of the hand-held torches completely ineffective.

What happened to the body? One man's theory is as good as the next. My own, now, is that Mr Campbell was catapulted out of the cockpit when the nose of the boat hit the water and broke off. When he himself struck the water he disintegrated, the heavier pieces sinking into the mud of the lake bed and the more buoyant pieces drifting over the silt out of the search area.

Once the divers' search was over, Futcher penned this poignant letter to Villa:

I was terribly disappointed to leave Coniston without having found Mr Campbell's body, but after thoroughly searching the crash area and investigating under and finding the cause of every known splash, the only thing I could have done, even looking at it in retrospect, was to have started a systematic search of the whole lake. This of course was impracticable.

I sincerely hope, Leo, that the shock and personal grief you suffered as a result of the disaster are gradually being dimmed, and that now you are back in your own home you will be able to pick up the threads of your life and continue with the project in which Mr Campbell had placed so much hope.

You can in no way whatsoever blame yourself for the accident. Indeed, if Donald had listened to you he would have been alive today. I know you know this, and I am sure every other thinking person knows it also. However, this gives little relief when the loss is so personal.

There was no shortage of theories as to why Bluebird had crashed. The most obvious was that it had simply reached the speed at which its aerodynamics suited it more for flight. There were suggestions that it had hit a submerged object, such as a log or a tree branch, which had upset the aerodynamic balance; that it had run out of fuel; or that the engine had surged. Suicide theorists believed Campbell had effectively engineered his own death. There was even a ludicrous suggestion that he had not been aboard at all, and that Bluebird was operating under remote control during its last run.

The truth was that a combination of factors created a deadly set of circumstances in which the venerable hydroplane became vulnerable to the aerodynamic forces that had always lain in wait. The late Tom Fink explained why so much effort had gone into making Bluebird K7 aerodynamically stable, and why he felt Campbell had been reckless in the timing of his return run.

From the wind tunnel tests, in which the boat was suspended at various angles, it was very easy to compute a point at which it was bound to take off. It was of the order of five or six degrees, at the speeds he was going to attain. Therefore, it was quite essential that he only run in calm water, so that there would be nothing to throw the nose up.

I think that the maximum speed we told Campbell he should *ever* run the boat in smooth conditions was 240mph. And because of that, it struck me as purely suicidal for him on his last day to have made the return so quickly. On a lake with these steep sides, there would be reflections of his wake which would go on for maybe fifteen or twenty minutes side to side.

Ken Norris instigated an official investigation, helped significantly by the RAF's photographic analysis department. Since Bluebird had sunk, and technology was not sufficiently advanced then to provide a ship-to-shore telemetric link, all they had to go on were Campbell's voice print, still photographs and moving film of the accident. Painstakingly, he, his brother Lew and their aides worked through the evidence, trying to piece together the last moments of a friend whom they had much admired. It was profoundly upsetting work, for both designers felt the burden of responsibility as one question in particular tormented them: could we have done anything to stop this happening? 'You felt these personal recriminations,' Ken Norris admitted.

Maybe I did something wrong. I'm sure I did, looking back. There were things I could have done which might have saved him. I might have stayed there for a start, over that night. And I might have been there to caution him more. But I wasn't. Maybe, technically, we hadn't got enough reserve banked up. Everyone knew that he mustn't get beyond so many degrees at the front. So don't go out if it's rough. If it's smooth, you're not going to pitch up. Those rules weren't to be bent, really. But you still say, 'Christ, why didn't I recognize that? Why didn't I think that?'

When we first considered doing the boat, I knew we had to accept responsibility, and the challenge from the design standpoint. I wrote it up in a little paper and I said that you first had to convince yourself that you are capable because you have this man's life in your hands. You've got to say, 'Can I do it?' And that is always a pretty difficult question.

They had the speed of Bluebird's first run, north to south, as a basis on which to start. The boat had averaged 297.6mph then in calm water, which meant that it had peaked at well over 300mph, but Campbell had kept his foot on the throttle as he exited the measured kilometre and was still accelerating. This proved not only that Bluebird had the power to do the job, but also the stability. Both Norris and Villa observed that it had been running in far more stable trim at very high speed with the revised, forward-biased weight distribution of the Orpheus engine installation than ever it had with the Beryl. 'I was never happy with the way the front water fins were visible at really high speed with the Beryl,' Norris admitted, 'but with the Orpheus she actually rode a lot better. It was lighter, so the weight was further forward, and she ran all the time with the fins immersed. She looked a lot better at speed on her final runs.'

An interesting indication of the forces acting upon Bluebird at very high speeds was given when a technical inspection in 1966 revealed that a fifth of the area of the razor-sharp stabilizing fins – on which Bluebird tended to run, rather than on its planing shoes – had been worn away by interaction with the water, which is 815 times denser than air.

Norris calculated that during the first run Bluebird peaked close to 320mph as it left the kilometre, and the boat remained well within its safe operating envelope. It had a slight nose-down attitude and the trim was perfect.

One significant factor was Campbell's decision not to refuel, which made the boat lighter, but more significant was the use of the water brake. There had always been considerable concern at Norris Brothers that Bluebird might actually run out of water at Coniston. The parachute tried in 1958 had never worked satisfactorily (though the Jim Deist chute used by Lee Taylor on Hustler after his adventure on Lake Havasu in 1964 was rather more successful), so thought had been given to stretching some sort of elastic arrester device across each end of the lake, similar to those used at American drag strips. But then Norris came up with the water brake, a device that increased hydrodynamic drag to slow the boat down. 'It was a simple button on the dashboard that Donald depressed. That would lower a six-inch steel rod hydraulically, relatively slowly. The increased drag would slow the boat quite effectively. To retract it, Donald would press the button again.' Campbell did this for the first time in anger at the end of that first run, and it worked perfectly. But using it badly disturbed the water. 'I think he used the water brake at well over 200mph instead of around that figure, as intended,' Norris theorized, 'so he used it for quite a long period. That meant that on the final run the state of the water was very poor, not from the normal wash or the little bit of swell there, but because the water brake had created bricks on the water, great chunks of wash.'

In the past – at Dumbleyung when time was so crucial; and even during his runs over the Christmas period in 1966 – Campbell had not bothered to refuel and had made his return run between four and seven minutes later. Each time he had got away with it, albeit only just in 1956. But what he didn't take into account in the final calculated gamble of his life was how much the water brake had roughened the water.

He couldn't have known, because the end of that penultimate run marked the first time he had used it at really high speed.

On the first pass, he had run pretty much down the centre of his course. On the return he lined Bluebird up significantly closer to the eastern shore, and he accelerated very quickly, using full power. He had a longer run-up than he had had at the northern end, after pulling back the elastic as far as it would go by deliberately overshooting the refuelling boat, and a lighter boat. But the water on which he was running at higher speed was much less perfect. This he would have known had he consulted as usual with Leo Villa.

Norris likened the effect of hitting a normal swell head-on to a car with stiff suspension settings and damping speeding over a hump-back bridge. The increased water disturbance seriously exacerbated that effect.

From their analysis, Norris and the RAF were able to calculate Bluebird's elapsed time in the kilometre on its return, and to conclude that it had reached a fantastic peak speed of 328.12mph just as it had passed the first marker buoy on the entry to the measured distance. This was a significant increase in performance, even over the first run. But before it reached the point at which it took off, Bluebird had begun to slow. Campbell was travelling at just under 300mph when the bows lifted. 'Donald decelerated,' Norris confirmed, 'and that's another factor as you take the loading off the front planes. If your centre of gravity is slightly below your thrustline, it's like rotating the stick in an aeroplane. You get a couple which says nose up. With the normal screwboat, the thrustline is underneath the centre of gravity, so if you take power off, the boat sticks its snout down. But if you did that on a pure-thrust boat such as Bluebird where the thrustline is above the centre of gravity, you add to the moment which says take off.'

A number of theories were put forward to explain why Campbell had lifted off. One was that he hadn't, but that the engine had surged or the boat had run out of fuel. This went hand in hand with the suggestion that the loss of down-thrust on the bows had caused the flip. When the wreckage was finally recovered from the lake thirty-four years later, however, there was still evidence of fuel in the fuel lines, which finally ruled out that theory.

Another was that mechanical failure had occurred. The wreckage revealed that the mounting rod at the front of the engine had broken. It was the diameter of a ballpoint pen, acted as the third point of support and served to adjust the engine's angle of installation by allowing it to pivot on its two main central mountings. Once adjustment was complete, the rod's position was locked in place, but the pounding it received in a 300mph speedboat might have been sufficient to break it. The medium Marjorie Staves often expressed concern about something having been wrong with the boat during our interview, and when I learned that the rod had broken I inevitably wondered if that could have been what she was alluding to. If it had broken, could that have changed the line of thrust of the Orpheus, with fatal results? Norris didn't think so.

If a thing breaks, then you tend to get some oscillating or a jerky motion. But there's nothing like that before Bluebird hit the water. If you look at the tail fin going through the air during the final run, everything looks in order. It was smooth, and she went up, over the top, and then dived in around 45°. But in any case, the engine only had limited movement, even with the rod disconnected. Once you had it lined up in the boat, Leo would adjust that little extension

414

rod and I would align the axis to get the engine almost horizontal along the thrustline. There was just a little degree of downward angle at the front to help generate download on the front planing points. Then Leo would slide on the other bits of the intake, and this would fix the engine in place at the front while allowing it to slide slightly in its main mountings as it expanded due to heat. At the tail, the jetpipe protruded a little bit through the body cowlings, and there was a stiff rubber seal at the back that went halfway up the side to prevent water ingress. There was a gap at the top to let out the cooling airflow between the engine and the body cowlings, but there was also a turnbuckle tightened around the back of the engine and the seal. That was a pretty tough seal, so realistically it wouldn't have let the engine move very much even if the rod had broken.

Norris also came to dismiss the idea of debris in the lake, despite minor blemishes that were discovered on the sponsons when they were recovered. 'I know there were marks on the steel planing shoe surfaces and that the starboard stabilizing fin showed similar damage,' he said, 'but to me that, like the engine mounting rod, was more consistent with damage sustained when Bluebird broke up on impact. If it was a log or something, again you'd have had a much more violent movement.'

The accident occurred 150 metres short of the end of the measured kilometre, at which point the RAF calculated Bluebird's speed between 285 and 290mph. Had Campbell completed the run, he would certainly have broken his own record, and might just have achieved his mean 300mph goal. Norris added these speeds to the relevant points of Campbell's final commentary:

100mph	'Rather close to Peel Island, tramping like mad.'
	'Full power.'
	'Tramping like hell here.'
200mph	'I can't see very much, the water's very bad indeed.'
	'Wash from water brake on first run getting like concrete with rocks spread on it.'
270mph	'I can't get over the top.'
300mph	'I'm getting a lot of bloody row in here.'
320mph+	'I can't see anything.'
290mph	'I've got the bows up.'
	'I've gone! Oh . . .'
180mph	Impact

Norris explained:

The safety limit on the boat was 6°, but the higher speed and smaller fuel load reduced that perhaps to 5°. If you took the swell into account, the safety limit was reduced maybe another degree and a half, so now it was only 3.5°. But the tramping also had a significant effect. If you accept that one sponson was adjudged by witnesses to be a foot clear of the water, you can calculate one foot over sixteen feet and 3.6° at the sponson, which would mean 1.8° at the centreline of the hull, which would therefore work out at an average of 2.7°. Thus the real safety limit in the conditions that Donald encountered on that final run in 1967 was less than 1°! It was actually around 0.8°. Which on a 26ft boat was a very small operating safety margin.

Norris also calculated that the lower fuel load would have resulted in a reduction of 2,390lbft of download on the bows. Add that to a reduction in download as Campbell reduced engine power, in the order of 1,250lbft, and the potential loss of download on the bows was 3,640lbft. But all of that could have been countered by activation of the water brake. If that had been operated at Bluebird's peak speed of 328mph, it could have generated a download of up to 9,000lbft because of the downward moment it created around the transom of the boat. Even had it been activated at 290mph, when Bluebird was really getting into trouble, it could still have generated nearly 7,000lbft.

The wreckage revealed that the water brake had been activated, but Norris believed that Campbell had used it *after* he had lifted off the throttle. Had he used it *before*, he might have got away with it. The fact that he lifted off first suggested that even at the moment of crisis he was still fighting not only to control Bluebird, but also to maintain his chances of saving his record. When he deployed the water brake, it was the last safety resort available to him, a signal that he had abandoned all hope of 300mph and was now fighting for survival. 'One of the great ironies,' Norris concluded, 'is that despite the fact that it created such havoc with the water after the first run, the water brake could have saved Donald if he had only operated it *before* he backed off the throttle.'

So in the end, the answer was straightforward: Donald Campbell had taken a chance that didn't come off. He had encountered water so rough that it had destabilized Bluebird, and all the pertaining factors had combined to reduce its safe operating margin to the point where it took off, even though he had backed off the throttle in the last seconds of his life.

That left the question why he had put himself in such a position by making his return run so soon. Why, when time was not the critical factor it had been when the Albany Doctor was chasing him down Lake Dumbleyung, had he not stopped to refuel and allow the lake to settle? The answer was that Campbell wanted to beat his wake from the first run, and, rightly as it transpired, knew that he did not need to refuel. Overshadowing both considerations was his elation at his first run speed and his desire simply to get the whole thing over.

There was one other question. Why wasn't Bluebird fitted with a tailplane that might have inhibited its taking off? Fink, who insisted that Ken Warby fit one to his Spirit of Australia hydroplane once Warby had finally been able to persuade him to help on his project, had no doubt that tailplanes were highly beneficial. 'The Bluebird somersault could have been prevented by having a wing. It suffers the same extra upforce when the pitch angle increases for whatever reason. But since it is *behind* the centre of gravity, that upforce acting upon it brings the nose down again.'

'Hah!' Norris exclaimed. 'Tom Fink was always on at me about that! But when the boat was conceived any such aerodynamic aid was illegal, and though the rulemakers looked at several things, they never did look at stability. They always assumed that stability was a magical thing that a boat either had or didn't have.' As he had shown with Bluebird CN7, Norris was always a man to play to the letter of the rules. The closest he had got to any form of wing on K7 was when the hull was reshaped for 1956 to flare out at its base so that the transom formed minor winglets that created some lift. 'It didn't flare out so much with the Orpheus,' Norris admitted, 'but we kept that feature with the different engine. The most important thing with a tail is that it acts like a damper, which could have been beneficial, but the way we interpreted them, the rules said you couldn't use a wing.'

In the aftermath of the accident, inevitably, details leaked out of the dire financial straits Campbell had been in during the last months of his life. Things were so tight that he had not actually paid the premium for the boat's insurance – £500 for £25,000 (£5,500 for £275,000 at today's values) cover. 'We didn't find that out until afterwards,' admitted Bill Coley, for whom 1967 was a doubly tragic year: his son Christopher was also killed, in a motorcycle accident. 'I was his executor . . . The insurance company coughed up. They were very generous. Otherwise there wouldn't have been any estate left.' An ex gratia payment of £24,500 (£269,325) was made. Campbell's estate was finally valued at £38,066 gross (£418,455), but after duty of £917 (£10,080) the net figure was only £10,677 (£117,371).

'I don't know how my father lived the life he lived, financially,' Gina admitted. It was only after his death that she learned that in order to finance construction of Bluebird K7 he had broken into the trust fund set up for her by her grandfather. 'I knew nothing about it. I was advised of it by Victor Mishcon, and dealt with it via my own lawyer. I'd taken a job in Hampshire as a girl groom. My father had left me £500 [£5,500] in his will. Leo and I went off to Reigate Garage and I bought a Triumph Spitfire Mk3, navy blue, soft-top, for £485 [£5,330]. I was absolutely enraptured with it. Later I learned about the trust. Mr Spotnik, my lawyer, told me, "Technically, your father lifted £22,000 [£242,000] of your trust money to finance his life." ' She told him that wasn't a problem. But it also transpired that Daphne had colluded with Campbell in signing the document to get the trust broken. Eventually, Gina accepted a quid pro quo as a result of which she received her father's racing trophies, but Campbell's will was vague about the disposal of them and there was plenty of bad feeling on the subject between her and Tonia over the years. They would argue frequently over the distribution or disposal of her father's silverware and personal possessions.

Allied to the spectacular nature of his death, these factors added up in some minds to one thing: suicide. For many years after the accident, several theories did the rounds. The situation was not helped when his biographer Arthur Knowles, who had never subscribed to the suicide theory, was trapped into suggesting that was what he thought on a radio programme aired on the twentieth anniversary of the accident. In 1987, BBC Radio 4 producer Rod Macrae generated plenty of ink with the suggestion, in a half-hour documentary called *Bluebird, Campbell and Coniston*, that Campbell had been reckless to the point of suicide. 'He reached a point of recklessness where he was as close to suicide as you can get without directly intending it,' Macrae asserted. 'Looking at it objectively, he made a suicidal mistake.'

Many facts militated against the theory, however, not the least of which was Campbell's nature and his determination to scale new mountains. When he climbed into Bluebird on his final day, he did so not as a beleaguered man intent on ending it all, but as a beleaguered man determined to face down his demons and achieve his goal so that finally he could put the prolonged project behind him. He was in a hurry because he wanted to get Bluebird to the Daily Express Boat Show, which opened on the very day of the accident. He planned to go skiing in Courchevel with Tonia and Gina. He was looking towards the future with the supersonic rocket car. He would hardly have bothered waiting for

Paul Evans to get back into position if he had been intent on self-destruction. Nor would he have backed off the throttle, as he so clearly did, once he sensed that the trouble he was in was moving beyond his control. His friends and family have always had one reaction whenever the word suicide is aired. Macrae was roundly condemned for his assertions and heavily criticized for failing to understand Campbell's character.

Daphne Campbell, since remarried and living in Devon, angrily dismissed Macrae's suggestion and referred to the supersonic car project. 'That was not the talk of a man who was going to kill himself.' Jean Wales was livid.

I was staying with friends and picked up the Sunday paper, and it was more or less inferring that my brother had committed suicide. I got on to David Benson and the Press Council. I got nowhere, but no way! No way! No way would Donald do that. This is what upset me, and David was upset about it too. How dare they say that about my brother? It was the most criminal thing to say! Even to infer that he would do it. He would never do that. It was just unfortunate, as Ken Norris said, that he didn't stop to let the wash die down. I think he thought, 'Right, turn and go for it!' But to suggest he committed suicide was just wicked. He just wasn't that sort of man.

The late Stephen Darbishire told reporters, 'I think this is rubbish. He was the last person to be suicidal, because he loved life. He was taking a risk, but it was a calculated one, a fair risk, because he nearly got away with it. I don't think he was reckless.' Norris shared their views wholeheartedly. 'Absolutely, no way! He wanted to get a move on and get down to the Boat Show because of the JetStar, and he was still planning the rocket car. A man like that wasn't going to kill himself. He just wanted to get on with the job. Get it over and finished.' Leo Villa, shattered by the tragedy, refused even to listen to such twaddle in the immediate aftermath, saying instead, 'You will never find another Donald Campbell in this world. He simply does not exist. He was not afraid of what might happen above that 300mph limit.'

Hughie Green recalled a certain morbidity in his friend, but also had no truck with the suicide theory.

I always think that Donald was very ... I won't use the words consumed or interested, I will use the word fascinated ... fascinated by death. In New York one time at the Queen's Tunnel, we twice passed the huge cemetery there. And no matter what we were talking about, Donald changed the subject, 'Look, there's a cemetery . . .' He didn't fear death, but he talked a lot about it.

It must have been a terrible last few seconds. But let's face it, I think it was the way he wanted to go. He was always try-ing to best his father, that's part and parcel of the Donald Campbell story. He was a brilliantly intelligent man, he wasn't a snob, he mixed in any strata of society and he was greatly loved in America. He was the sort of Englishman that could have done a lot for this country. A special person.

Grahame Ferrett summed up the suicide theories in his no-nonsense Aussie manner. 'I was in Perth when that all stuff came out. It was complete shit.'

In Ferrett's homeland, Australia, Campbell's friends and associates shared the grief. The *Advertiser* ran a two-line-deep headline above its lead story on 5 January which said simply: CAMPBELL KILLED IN LAKE CRASH. Above three wire photos of the accident was a lovely shot of Donald and Tonia with Mr Whoppit, taken two years earlier at Adelaide airport as they had prepared to return in triumph to England.

Tributes began to flow in, even from those with whom Campbell had had his differences. Andrew Mustard said, 'Donald would have preferred to die this way than any other. I am certain he was always ready for it. This is the sort of thing one expects if one is the sort of man who goes racing, record breaking or climbing mountains. These occupations need a certain type of mentality, one which is pretty well aware of the risks involved and yet capable of going ahead and doing them despite that.' Stirling Moss said, 'He was a great man who took tremendous risks for his country. He was a very great ambassador, and from the country's point of view he did a very good job. People who do this sort of thing have to have a tremendous strength of will rather than courage. Of course Donald had courage, but he also had the quality of strength and determination over fear. He had a tremendous amount of that.'

On 6 January, Tonia was reported to be under sedation, recovering from a mild but recurrent heart condition. That day, racing driver Innes Ireland made an offer to Leo Villa to carry on Campbell's work if sufficient funds could be obtained. Ireland was a colourful, fun-loving man who undoubtedly possessed in full measure the necessary courage. Years later, he said, 'I had tremendous admiration for Donald and we had met on occasion when our paths crossed. I admired what he was trying to do, and the support he got from Leo Villa and his team. If they had been able to find the money I would have been very keen to have a go, but it was as if Donald's accident had brought down the curtain on an era of record breaking, and nobody could raise the funds to build another boat. I always thought that was a terrible shame.'

Later in 1967, Campbell was posthumously awarded his fourth Segrave Trophy. In a moving speech, Tonia made a gentle attack on those who had believed he had been scared at Coniston. 'Many people today say that Donald Campbell was a big hero,' she said. 'To say it today is one thing, but to have said it yesterday when he was there to hear it is a much more important thing. The Segrave Trophy was given to Donald three times while he was alive. I know how happy he was. This Segrave Trophy honour goes to the Bluebird team and their skipper. Thank you, in his name.'

On Thursday, 23 February 1967, the Church of St Martin-in-the-Fields was packed for Campbell's memorial service. Victor Mishcon delivered the address.

Speed is not the only thing that manages to break through barriers. Amongst nations, amongst various sections of the community within a nation, amongst all creeds and colours, outstanding courage and outstanding character break through barriers too of boundaries, languages, cultures and classes. Donald Malcolm Campbell did not break the sound barrier on land or sea, but he broke those other more important barriers during his all-too-brief life, so that we who are gathered here today are but a few of those who loved and honoured him, and who now mourn him in their many thousands in these islands, in the United States of America, in Australia and throughout the length and breadth of the world, where the spirit of adventure and bravery still thrill the blood of man.

'And thou shalt love the Lord thy God with all thy heart, with all thy soul and with all thy might.' These are sacred words in this House of God, often heard, as they are in the place where I usually worship. If ever a man gave himself with all his heart and soul and might, it was Donald Campbell. So did he love his God. So did he love his Queen and country. So did he love his ever loyal team, with its Leo Villa and the lady whom they called Fred. So did he love the cause of human progress for which in his own field he was prepared to devote and indeed sacrifice his life. So did he love and cherish the memory of his father. So did he love people.

Humbly but proudly, as a friend amongst other friends of his do I pay my tribute to him today in the presence of distinguished personages including representatives of His Royal Highness the Duke of Edinburgh and the Prime Minister, and before members of his family including his wife, his daughter, his mother and his sister. Britain and the world have such need of the indomitable spirit, the sheer determination, the unconquerable determination he had. Our poet Tennyson might have written of Donald Campbell, as he wrote of another:

> Such was he: his work is done.
> But while the races of mankind endure,
> Let his great example stand
> Colossal, seen of every land,
> And keep the soldier firm, the statesman pure;
> Till in all lands and through all human story
> The path of duty be the way to glory.

Dottie missed the service because she was laid up in New Zealand with a head cold, and heavily pregnant with son David. Tonia insisted on sitting with Leo Villa and the team, leaving Jean Wales to look after Gina. Her mother, Daphne, instructed her that under no circumstances was she to cry.

Campbell's will appointed Tonia as Gina's guardian, not Daphne.

By chance, Dory Swann was on one of her annual trips home, and she attended the service. 'I suppose it was meant to be,' she said of the coincidence. Campbell's close friend, the Hon. Greville Howard, acting as an usher, led her to a pew right behind the family, which pleased her. But, poignantly, she left straight afterwards rather than wait to speak with Jean Wales, Norris or Villa. 'I didn't speak to anyone. I was leaving the following day,' is all she will say today. Tonia called her some time later. 'She wanted to have lunch, and I told her no. Later she called again – would I have tea with her? I said no again. Finally I agreed to meet her. It lasted ten minutes. All she wanted me to know was how terrible it had all been for her. I left.'

On 30 June 1967, on Lake Guntersville in Alabama, American Lee Taylor's own brave recovery from injury and disappointment yielded him a new water speed record when he took his Hustler to 285.213mph. Campbell would have saluted his courage and tenacity.

For the next thirty-four years his spirit permeated Coniston Water, guarding it, shedding light like some inspirational guiding beacon. Man and boat lay together at peace beneath the mystic water, but the legend of Donald Campbell and his Bluebird refused to die, and another chapter remained to be written.

25

CLOSURE

March 2001 to October 2002

'I wonder whether Donald himself knew what Donald Campbell really was.'

BARON MISHCON

In June 1967, Leo Villa was awarded the OBE for his services to record breaking. He became the keeper of the flame, the man the followers sought out, until his death from cancer in 1979, at which point his mantle passed to Ken Norris. A clause in Campbell's will had requested Villa to foster fresh attempts to preserve Britain's speed heritage. After Innes Ireland, drag racer Tony Densham wanted to run Bluebird CN7, and Sir Alfred Owen's son David favoured the idea. Craig Breedlove also spoke of Bluebird America in the early 1970s before his wheeldriven record plans matured in another direction. Former Bluebird team member Ken Ritchie also harboured aspirations. 'The Skipper could make me as mad as a hornet, but he was a damned good guy,' he wrote in a letter to Ken Norris, 'and they don't come along all that often.'

In 1973, nineteen-year-old Nigel MacKnight and freefall parachute jump record challenger Peter Dean each tried to revive the Bluebird CN8 project. Neither succeeded, but MacKnight is still working on his Quicksilver water speed record contender, the Norris-designed spiritual successor to Bluebird.

In 1980, thirty-two-year-old Bradford hair transplant centre businessman John Terry, holder of two world parachute endurance records set over Windermere, sought to use the Bluebird name for a water speed record challenge. 'Tonia has been very kind,' he said. 'I am determined to break the record in a boat called Bluebird so that the name of Donald Campbell is never forgotten.' He planned a £600,000 (£1,555,840 at today's values) twin-jet-engined craft designed for 400mph, but like the others the project was stillborn.

In 1988, the BBC documentary drama *Across the Lake*, starring Anthony Hopkins, once again thrust Donald Campbell's name into the headlines, thanks to the actor's fine portrayal of his last days at Coniston. Periodically, national newspapers ran features. Man and machine had become part of the national psyche. Fascination with the legend was limitless. Friends cherished their memories. Despite their argument, David Wynne-Morgan still admired him.

> I couldn't help it. You liked him, warts and all. He was one of the greatest men I've ever met. Because he was absolutely terrified. Everything that he did was in uncharted territory. He was driving at speeds nobody had done before, and nobody could be certain what might happen. He had a sort of death wish in him, in as much as he couldn't stop himself.
>
> I'm afraid it's an awful thing to say, but the man did not

have basic integrity where money was concerned. He had integrity in his efforts to break speed records, but over money he was a nightmare. His lifestyle depended on him raising the next twenty thousand. I don't think his word meant much to him. He felt The Cause took precedence over everything else, and that included Donald's style of living because he saw that as part and parcel of the whole thing. Whatever he had to do to raise the wherewithal to further that, he would do. And if that meant ignoring undertakings he'd made, he never hesitated.

But there was something incredibly likeable about him. He wasn't a phoney. He genuinely worked very hard at something that the world saw as being increasingly marginal, which was sad. He hated that. He was a man of tremendous courage who could be wonderful company, but he had awful bouts of depression.

If I hadn't met Donald Campbell, a terribly exciting part of my life would never have happened. He took me into that *Boy's Own* world, and I am eternally grateful to him. We had some wonderful times tilting at windmills.

If Campbell could be lax when it came to repaying debts, his generosity was limitless, as Grahame Ferrett recalled.

After Lake Eyre, Donald went to see Sir Reginald Ansett [founder and chairman of the airline that bore his name] and arranged to send Leo and Joan, Maurie and his wife Bunny, and my wife Aileen and me to Hayman Island for a fortnight's holiday, all expenses paid.

Then there was Dumbleyung. I had three little kids, and there I was at Christmas, miles from my home in Adelaide. In Perth he bought all these cowboy suits. Spent well over what a person on my income would spend on their kids. I'd introduced him to Wally Grout, the ex-Australian wicket-keeper. He got Wally to help my Aileen set up the Christmas tree and give all this stuff to my kids.

The day he broke the record, Campbell disappeared and left me with all these press people who wanted him, not me. Finally he came back, and I said, 'Where the hell have you been?' He said, 'Oh, I just had something to do.'

New Year's Day was the Perth Cup. Sir Douglas Kendrew, the Governor of Western Australia, had gone to school with Sir Malcolm Campbell. He's arranged for Donald Campbell and his entourage to arrive at the Cup and drive down the straight. So on New Year's Day we've got to Perth airport, and all the air traffic controllers are congratulating him. He's handling it beautifully. It's eleven thirty. I said, 'Come on then, let's get going.' Donald said, 'Let's hang on for a minute or two.' I'm getting impatient. Around noon, in comes the plane from Adelaide. And off gets Aileen. What he'd done in that hour he'd gone missing was to ring Adelaide, get the manager of Ansett to get Aileen to sort out a housekeeper, and arrange for her to get on the plane. Big stuff. A nice touch.

Ferrett never saw any mystery in Campbell. 'I've read some things about him; they might just as well be talking about Hopalong Cassidy. That wasn't the guy I knew at all. We were good mates. We had our fall-outs. After we came back from Dumbleyung, after we were winding everything up, we had a few words at times. But flare-ups were always forgotten. Donald was never a man to bear grudges. He was the straight type, where you knew where you were all the time.'

Ferrett's Dumbleyung stories reflected the man Tony Robinson knew. Robbie agreed that Campbell's generosity

430

owed nothing to how much money he had in the bank. 'Without a doubt he was trying to live up to his father. Donald would not have denied that. But as far as being some little rich kid . . . I don't think he had any money. He was a soft touch for anybody.' In *Across the Lake*, Campbell and Robinson go shopping in Kendal, only for the teenager to discover on Christmas Day that the tape recorder he thought was being bought for somebody else was actually for him. 'I carried this damn thing to the boot of the car, quite unbeknowing. They used the real one in the film.'

After one record attempt here in Coniston they were all invited up to the Windermere Motor Boat Racing Club for an official black tie job. So Donald took them all off to Kendal and bought them dinner suits and ties.

During that last attempt, because people were up here so long, he got Joan to come up and stay for Leo's birthday. As she was getting on the train home at Ulverston, she trapped her finger in the carriage door. Made an awful mess of it. Typical Donald, he had the train stopped at Preston, had a doctor there waiting to dress it for her, and when she got to London she was met and everything was organized to take her to hospital. He did all that on the spur of the moment. And these things weren't one-offs. That's the kind of person he really was.

Paul Evans remembered one time when the bank refused to cash his cheque, so he was unable to buy a round of drinks. When Campbell prised the story from him, he insisted on speaking to the manager to have things put right, and gave Evans some of his own money to tide him over. David Benson told a story of Campbell refuelling his car on the M1. 'It was the place we bought the demister for K7's screen. A young girl was filling up his car, and she said to me, "Is that who I think it is?" looking at Donald. I said, "Yes, that's Donald Campbell." And she rushed off to get her friend to get autographs. The sixties was all about flower power and hippies, and the young tended to make heroes out of the young. But Donald spanned that particular age gap.'

He could relate to anyone. David Richland worked for the Flairavia Flying Club, at Biggin Hill, where Campbell flew in one day.

There was a café there, and Donald landed from Brussels with his wife and daughter. I felt it was odd that there wasn't anybody there to congratulate him, because it wasn't long after he'd broken the land speed record. He headed to the café, and as we had a bar at our place I grabbed a bottle of whisky and headed over. I presented the whisky to him on behalf of Flairavia and offered our most hearty congratulations. He was very charming and asked me if I would like to join him, but I had to get back to the club.

Half an hour later, he just walked in and sat down for a chat. He was extremely pleasant and asked me what we did at the club, what sort of lessons we gave, the leasing we did. We were teaching Honor Blackman to fly after she'd completed that Bond film in which she played Pussy Galore. He was completely charming, approachable and very friendly, and seemed very pleased to have somebody take the trouble to congratulate him. It was only a brief acquaintance, but he didn't appear to have any sort of side. There was no reason why he should have, I suppose, but he was quite a famous person, even more so having just broken the record. He wasn't in the slightest bit condescending, just sat there chatting happily.

Despite the incident with Bluebird CN7, Peter Bolton also remembered Campbell fondly. 'You could not have met a more British man. He was a great promoter of this country. And he was great fun. He once recited "Eskimo Nell" in my house, verbatim. My wife Peggy said, "God, I'd love that in print." And he said, "I'll type it for you, sweetheart." He was only a two-fingered typist, and he sat up all night and typed it. He was a showman. Great to have around.'

'He lived in his father's image, the best way he could,' Marjorie Staves believed. 'He was trying to envisage that glamour and the uplift of his father. That I feel, in part, was rather devastating for him, because he felt that he never made it. He was sincere and he tried hard. By golly, I can tell you that. He deserves full credit for the urge and ambition and impetus that he put into his quest.'

During our interview, Baron Mishcon sat back, steepled his hands. And what he said was perhaps the closest anyone came to the truth. 'I wonder whether I dare say this . . .' he began. 'I wonder whether Donald himself knew what Donald Campbell really was. I say that because at times I think he thought he was a bit worthless, asking people to sponsor this and that, without any real occupation. At other times he felt he was his father all over again and therefore very worthy of esteem. He was a consummate actor, because he was a public figure. People waving and asking for his autograph. And like a film star, I think he was an actor in private life as well.'

Mishcon believed, like Dottie, that the subtitle for this book was absolutely apposite. *Bluebird and the Dead Lake* was one of the greatest books of its genre, but in an irate letter to Villa concerning requested changes that had not been made to the original draft, he said, 'This fellow's managed to make your old pal look like a real mixed-up guy.' Everything had to be scripted, the mask carefully constructed to reflect the image he wanted the world to see. Only those alongside him during the great struggle got to see and appreciate the real Donald Campbell, the man behind the mask, the alternately vulnerable, arrogant, insecure, sensitive, fun-loving, irreverent, moody and abnormally brave fellow who lived his life in the shadow of his father. 'He could command the most complete loyalty,' Mishcon added. 'People like Leo . . . Donald could literally almost make people lie down and die for him.'

And yet, one day in Coniston, when he shopped at the local Co-op and chatted openly with one of the women behind the counter, she was left with the overwhelming image of a very lonely man. But then the cockpit of a race car or a race boat *is* a lonely place. The more so when you are a record breaker rather than a racing driver, when instead of a field of similarly hellbent rivals you coldbloodedly face the enemies of time and nature, and whatever demons have driven you there. Could he have escaped his destiny? Perhaps, but only if he had given up, and that was not a part of his make-up. He lived by a simple code: once you had started something, there could be no turning back.

Jean Wales believed implicitly that her brother was driven by his desire to prove himself worthy of his father. 'He had to, didn't he? For his own satisfaction. It was the Campbell determination. That was it with Dad and with Donald. You set yourself a goal. To begin with, people thought, "Oh, Malcolm Campbell's son, using his father's name." That he was just basking in the glory of it. But he proved to everybody that he'd got the guts to do it himself. I used to stand at the end of the jetty and think, "My God, you're brave! How can you get in that cockpit, shut the canopy and get that frightening jet started up?" It upsets me still, all the problems he was having, all that bad luck. But as he so rightly said, when you start, you've got to finish.' Jean and Gina both believed that, had he lived, he would eventually have gone into politics. 'I could see him doing that,' Gina said. 'He used to make speeches at a few rallies for friends like Greville Howard.'

Dottie's reunion with Gina had helped her to put her life with Campbell, and its aftermath, into better perspective. 'I remember him with affection,' Dottie said. 'With affection and a great deal of respect. And I put that down to Gina, because now I can place it and see it as it was without being hurt, as I felt for many, many years.'

'For me,' Gina said, 'I would best like him to be remembered for his tenacious courage. Like Princess Diana, or Ayrton Senna, he died in a way that immortalized him. I always said that Dad's finest hour was his demise.'

Ultimately, he *had* to do what he did, to live up to his perception of what his father expected of him. But that wasn't enough in itself to drive a man to eight speed records. It wasn't enough to drive him back time and again, especially at the end. He *wanted* to be a record breaker. He liked the fear, living on the edge, though that changed after Bonneville. Then, he wanted to make amends. Brave men often do things without considering the consequences, but the abnormally brave man is the one who has peered over the edge of the pit and weighed them all up, yet still carries on. Courage and patriotism were his driving forces.

Campbell usually kept the lid on his real emotions, but one day prior to the record success on Lake Eyre in 1964 he was walking with Ferrett in Victoria Square in Adelaide when he turned to his friend and said, almost matter-offactly, 'I've either got to do it, or get killed trying to.' When you pared away all the science, all the glamour and romance and mystique, that was so often what record breaking boiled down to.

After the failure to locate Campbell's body, Tonia, Villa and Norris were against trying to raise Bluebird, knowing that Campbell himself had wanted it to stay submerged in the event of an accident. So was Lady Campbell, as diver Gerry Jackson recalled: 'I would have liked to have seen the boat lifted. I mentioned it to Leo and to Lady Campbell. I can't quote her verbatim, but she indicated that she'd like it left there as a memorial to Donald.'

Over the years, bodies have risen from Coniston Water, and each time Campbell's family suffered the inevitable speculation. Gina admitted that she once had a dream in which her father's corpse had been discovered and was being hawked round on public display.

In 2001, a diver from Newcastle called Bill Smith put in train a series of events that would write the final chapter of Donald Campbell's story. They started when Smith, who had dived regularly in Coniston and had in the past explored the wreckage of Bluebird's aft section, applied to the Rawdon-Smith Trust, which owned the national park lake bed, for permission to raise the wreck. In doing so he created a fresh storm of controversy in Campbell circles. Some wanted to see the boat again, others took the view that raising it was tantamount to raiding a war grave. Some believed the real priority was finding Campbell's body.

'People have the misconception that I put Bill onto the trail in the first place,' Gina said, 'but that's absolute nonsense.

He rang me, introduced himself, and said, 'My one goal in the world is to go and find your father's boat.' And I said, 'Oh, good on you,' type of thing. What else do you say? And then he said, 'When I find it, would you like a piece?' I said, 'You what? How dare you!' I really lost my rag with him. After a momentary pause, he said, 'My God, I'm terribly sorry. I really haven't stopped to think. It was just a natural reaction.' He explained himself, and I sort of understood and warmed to him slightly because I sensed a huge amount of humility and embarrassment at the situation he had put himself into.

I never thought about him again until he rang months later. 'Bill Smith here, I've found it, I've found it!' Again, that momentary pause. What are we talking about? Then he told me he'd found the boat. He was excited. End of conversation, until the BBC rang me, Mike Rossiter. 'Obviously you know about the refind of Bluebird. We're making a documentary and we'd very much like your input.' So I went to the Lake District because I wanted to see what was going on. It was pissing with rain. A really dreadful day. And Bill was just walking off the jetty with a group of divers, and supposedly with the first underwater film footage of the boat. We did an interview, Mike and I, and looked at the footage. After you'd seen two minutes, that was all you needed. We had a drink in the Black Bull with all the divers afterwards. And then we went home.

On the way back, she said to her partner, Marshall Capel, 'It's Wednesday today, and they plan to be there until next Monday. What are they going to be doing, Wednesday to Monday? They've already found the boat. So they obviously already had it in their minds – and these are my words – to look for my dad. So I went back up on the

Sunday and spoke to Bill. I said, "Well, you are going to have to bring that boat up a.s.a.p., before the world gets to know about it, and you are going to have to find my father." And Bill said, "Yes, I will do both those things."'

Smith recalled: 'Gina said to me, "I want you to find my dad, I want to put him somewhere warm." She also asked me to recover the wreck and later to bring it back to its original condition.' Gina admitted in 2002, 'I am now faced with huge emotional and financial problems, and the whole kit and caboodle that Bill brought upon us, but I can turn round now and can say very hypocritically that I told Bill to bring the boat up and to find my father. Of course I did. Because he was already sitting there with a BBC film crew. And there was absolutely no choice to be made. I didn't even have to stop to think about it.'

The main wreckage of Bluebird K7 was raised from Coniston Water on 8 March 2001. Bit by bit, in a quite remarkable operation, Smith and his team of divers had relocated it and then recovered most of the other components, including the shattered front end that had been torn away in the impact. After further intensive effort, on 28 May they finally located a headless body just east of the spot where the wreckage of Bluebird had first been discovered by John Futcher and his team in 1967. The remains, which had been remarkably preserved in a waxy form by Coniston's consistent 2° temperature, were placed in a blue box which was draped in the Union Jack flag before they brought it ashore. It meant everything to Gina that they were recovered with care and dignity, as a body. 'It was nice to know he was still a person,' she said. 'He still had his St Christopher on its leather cord, in the chest cavity. His race suit was only thin nylon. It was ripped at the ankles and cuffs but was intact. There was five and fourpence in a pocket, two half crowns and four pennies.'

The recovery of Donald Campbell thirty-four years after his death necessitated an autopsy, a funeral and an inquest. In August, tests conducted by DNA expert Tim Clayton using samples taken from the remains and from Gina and Jean proved that it was 1.9 million times more likely that the samples originated from the father of Gina Campbell than anyone else. Furness coroner Ian Smith told a hearing at Barrow Town Hall that there was absolutely no doubt that the remains, which had sustained massive fractures on the right-hand side, were those of Donald Malcolm Campbell. 'There was always a little bit of doubt,' Gina said. 'Now there is none. There is a sense of closure now. I could have still lived with it, having Dad at rest at the bottom of the lake, but once I knew that Bill had been down there, it changed. Once the mystery of Bluebird and Dad had gone – and Bill violated that – to me it changed everything.'

She wanted a big funeral, with all the people who had so often looked after her father. 'It's not going to be a closed shop,' she told reporters. 'I want it to be a celebration. I don't want it to be a sombre occasion. I want people to come and say, "Wow!" ' It was held in St Andrew's Church in Coniston on 12 September, the day after the Twin Towers atrocity in New York. Campbell's coffin was taken once more through the measured kilometre by launch before pallbearers, who included Smith and Campbell's nephew Don Wales, carried the coffin from the lake to the church in torrential rain. The occasion reunited members of the Campbell family who had grown apart, and brought them, too, a sense of closure decades after the tragedy. Jean Wales, however, was so upset by the turn of events that she did not feel able to attend. Gina and Tonia, who had publicly warred many times in the intervening years and had sat apart at the memorial service in 1967, sat together.

The church was so packed that hundreds of well-wishers congregated outside. The rain did not let up.

Finally, his grave marked by his blue and yellow racing colours, Donald Campbell was laid to rest in Coniston's cemetery.

Now, Gina Campbell ponders the problem of how to finance the restoration of her father's famous old warhorse. 'Donald Wales, his cousins Malcolm and PJ, myself and Jean, we are a pretty poor lot because it's only Donald and I who converse,' she says of the Bluebird Trust. 'Jean just wants us to leave the Campbells in peace. So you've got Donald and me, really. The rebuild has to be a democratic decision, but perhaps we need more trust members, or a subcommittee of people whose opinions we respect. Because once the first hacksaw or acetylene torch goes to Bluebird, you can't go back.' She saw her father's shattered boat several times in Smith's workshop, and admitted that on each occasion she found it more repulsive and distressing.

I came away each time with a different mental attitude. The first time, with the BBC, I felt totally cold. I saw a pile of mangled metal. It didn't mean very much to me. Isn't that strange? It must be the defence mechanism. Then they took me upstairs and showed me the cockpit area, complete save for one side. Bill had managed to decipher which piece of twisted metal went where, and it was held together with tie-wraps. You could see where my father had sat. And there on the side – I've even got the dynatape that he brought back from the States, a great big chrome thing – are the things he printed with it: FUEL PUMP ON, FUEL PUMP OFF. Still stuck there. And to stand there and think, 'My dad sat there, and was killed there . . .' You wouldn't take your kids to see that.

What would people think of us for putting it on display? So what do we do if we don't put her on display? Lock her in the garage and throw away the keys? Dig a big hole and bury her? What do we do with her? She's there, now. Like a huge white elephant.

Tonia admitted that she was ambivalent, and told Gina she would go along with her judgement. The plan is to restore Bluebird K7 to full working order, so that besides becoming a static museum exhibit it may also be demonstrated once a year on the lake. The Orpheus engine will be restricted to 2,500lb of thrust, just beyond what it needs to get up on the plane, and it will probably not exceed 150mph. In the final riposte to the Friends of Brantwood who had opposed Sir Malcolm Campbell in 1939, the work may be carried out in collaboration with Coniston's Ruskin Museum. The Bluebird Trust hopes to secure funding from the National Lottery and commercial sources to complete the rebuild.

On 25 October, an inquest held at the Ruskin School in Coniston sifted through all the known facts gathered by accident investigator Julian Happien Smith, and after a dramatic intervention in which Paul Evans put a more accurate commentary of the final run before coroner Ian Smith, a verdict of accidental death was returned.

And so, nearly thirty-five years after his passing, Donald Campbell made the headlines all over again. He would have loved all the attention. Friends had no doubt that he would be sitting somewhere, exasperating Villa as he chuckled at the arguments raging in his name, digging him in the ribs and demanding to know, 'Who says Campbell's not popular?' Late in 2002, through the efforts of his friends and admirers, he was voted the eighty-ninth Greatest Briton in a

BBC television poll of the top one hundred in history. The vox pop programme's weaknesses were highlighted when 'luminaries' such as radio disc jockey John Peel, actor Michael Crawford, singers Freddie Mercury, Boy George and David Bowie, terrorist Guy Fawkes and Prime Minister Tony Blair polled more votes, and people such as William Wordsworth were ignored altogether. But the remarkable thing was that Campbell was the only motorsporting figure in the poll.

Now, through the efforts of Bill Smith and his team, the speedking sleeps peacefully. But you can still go down to Coniston Water's edge on a cold, black January morning, and above the cries of the wild ducks and the whistle of the wind hear the distant whine of a turbojet engine. And picture the once boyish face of Bluebird's pilot, etched with the worry and tensions of his final months, before the noise rises to a crescendo and once again a spectral blue boat soars across the dark surface until memory catches it in a freeze-frame of suspended motion, leaping for the sky. Man and machine, icons now, forever preserved in the historic amber of their destiny.

Someone – and I hope with all my heart that it will be Gina Campbell because she has the talent, pedigree, guts and, above all, the *right* to do it – will one day demonstrate the rebuilt Bluebird K7 on the lake on which its greatest honours and final tragedy were played out. Where the spirit of her father will continue to walk regardless of what environmentalists may try to do in the name of so-called conservation to a place steeped in the history of speed and all the things he believed made his country great. And somewhere in the crowd that will gather the spark will be ignited again, in young and old alike, and someone else will for the first time be touched and inspired.

And whenever people do remember, the legend of Donald Malcolm Campbell and Bluebird will live on.

NOTES

1 Donald Campbell, in an interview with *Scottish Daily Express* journalist William Allsop, 1964.

2 Donald Campbell, in an interview with *Daily Express* journalist Geoffrey Mather at Coniston, December 1966. As Mather so succinctly summarized, was physical challenge ever so beautifully described?

3 From Lady Dorothy Campbell's *Malcolm Campbell, The Man As I Knew Him*.

4 Ibid.

5 Donald Campbell, in an interview with *Daily Express* journalist Geoffrey Mather at Coniston, December 1966.

6 From *Into the Water Barrier* by Donald Campbell, with Alan W. Mitchell.

7 Ibid.

8 Ibid.

9 Ibid.

10 Ibid.

11 Ibid.

12 Ibid.

13 From Donald Campbell's 'Danger is My Life', *Sunday Express*, November 1964.

14 From *Into the Water Barrier*.

15 From *The Record Breakers* by Leo Villa and Tony Gray.

16 From *Into the Water Barrier*.

17 Donald Campbell, in an interview with John Pett at Coniston for Border Television, 1966.

18 From *The Record Breakers*.

19 Ibid.

20. Donald Campbell, in an interview with John Pett at Coniston for Border Television, 1966.

21 From Donald Campbell's 'To the Water Barrier and Beyond' in *Motorboat & Yachting*, 31 December 1965.

22 Donald Campbell, in written replies to Dennis May, *Car and Driver*, December 1965.

ACKNOWLEDGEMENTS

One of the most hedonistic aspects of researching and writing this book was the support and help I received from so many sources. Like cracks in glass, one contact often radiated into another. Each was seemingly able to furnish the whereabouts of another, hitherto suspected lost, who might be able to chip in with that little bit more insight or that extra anecdote. Thus was the puzzle pieced together, bit by tantalizing bit.

Everyone who helped knows who they are and what they did, and though many usually started an interview fretting about their powers of recall and ended it fearing they had been of little help, they were invariably wrong. This book is testimony to just how valuable their assistance was. Some of it was major, some minor; all of it was willingly given in the name of a great man. Rarely did I find a bad apple in the barrel, and that in its own way is a tribute to the calibre of man Donald Campbell was. He attracted loyal friends. I thank them all.

His daughter Gina and I had known each other on and off over the years – she was an aggressive rival when we both took to the damp streets of Birmingham for a pro-am Renault Five race way back in 1986 – but it wasn't until I spent a thoroughly enjoyable day together with her and her partner Marshall Capel at their home in Leeds that I came fully to appreciate just how proud her father should have been of her. Gina is no slouch when it comes to defending her territory, and truthfulness is her watchword. If her candour offends, well, that's the way it is. Take it or leave it. We were able to dispel a lot of the myths in between scoffing the mountains of food she cooked and trawling through countless evocative photographs. Her crowning gift was to trust me with the only copy of the book Donald Campbell began writing, *The Eternal Challenge*. That, together with Gina's insights, perspectives and yet further contacts, was invaluable. My thanks go to her, too, for writing the foreword. I was deeply moved by it on first reading.

His sister Jean Wales is also an example to all when it comes to loyalty; I owe her a great debt for her kindness and willingness to talk about her illustrious father and brother, and their lives together.

I travelled to New Zealand specifically to visit Dorothy McKegg after the Australian Grand Prix in 2002, courtesy of Gina who 'introduced' us. This demanded a great deal of persistent juggling of my ticketing by Helen Penfold at Travel Places, without whom my regular arrangements would have been about as smooth as the surface of Lake Eyre in 1964. I'd actually been scheduled to visit Dory Swann, only to discover at the eleventh hour that she was *hors de combat*. So New York became New Zealand. Yet again on meeting someone who had loved him, I learned so much about Donald as Dottie shared her sometimes painful memories of the man who led her on such a great adventure for six years before disappearing so suddenly and completely from her life.

Eleven years after I started Desperately Seeking Dory, and after that brief hiatus, I finally got to spend enjoyable hours with her in New York on the way home from the Brazilian Grand Prix. Shrugging off the after-effects of the painfully burned arm that had nixed our original get-together, she took me to Milady's in Manhattan one April lunchtime and taught me the rudiments of survival among the poseurs in SoHo. Hers was perhaps one of the most poignant stories of them all.

Tonia Bern Campbell proved a tough cookie when it came to arranging an interview in November 1992; I told her there had been only one other person in my experience who had been as hard to pin down, and that was Ayrton Senna. Eventually I went to see her up in Big Bear Lake, outside Los Angeles, having told her that I was coming regardless of her apathy and would buy her lunch, pay for it and leave after fifteen minutes if she decided she didn't like the look of my face. As if. She gave a nice laugh, as if she was genuinely amused. In the end we had a few hours of intensive and thoroughly enjoyable conversation at her home. 'I can be difficult,' she conceded when we finally got together, 'but once I agree to do it, I'll do it. And I'll do it well.' Amen to that. Tonia never flinched from even the most probing questions, and volunteered all sorts of details about her private life with Donald Campbell.

Tony Robinson was a similar age to me when he helped Donald on that fateful attempt at Coniston. Besides running the best hotel in the Lake District with his wife Elizabeth, he remains as supportive now to Campbell's followers as he was then to the man himself, and has fine memories that he is always willing to share.

The late Bill Coley was another staunch supporter of Campbell's adventures, and we spent a terrific afternoon together at his home in Walton-on-Thames that was highly illuminating. Until Gina, he was the only person I had ever met who has asked my permission to smoke in their own home.

One of the great pleasures was making the acquaintance of Grahame J. Ferrett, Donald's manager during that bruising yet gratifying 1964 season. He was hospitality with an upper-case H when I paid a visit just before the Australian Grand Prix in Adelaide in 1991. Some of my friends wonder enviously where I got my Bluebird tie. Well, during the course of a lengthy and superbly informative conversation, I mentioned to self-proclaimed 'Fat Ferrett' a comment that Evan Green, his predecessor, had once made about a tie Donald had given him. A while later, Grahame got up from the table and disappeared for a few moments. When he came back he laid such a tie in front of me. It was an act of generosity I still find moving.

Baron Mishcon was a close friend of Campbell's, and he gave me a fabulous interview during which I was touched by his willingness to place trust in me, on first acquaintance, to keep certain subjects off the record. Fellow record breakers Art Asbury and Craig Breedlove were also kind enough to offer illuminating memories. Likewise, entertainer Craig Douglas, sixties radio signalman Paul 'The Corp' Evans and the late Hughie Green were each charming and provided brilliant insights into Campbell's character and his final days.

I was fortunate to bump into my friend Steven Holter on a fairly regular basis when he was working in F1. As ever, he was a mine of information on all things Campbell, and selfless enough to share it openly even though he was writing his own fine book on the same subject. Robin Richardson, founder of the Speed Record Club, is another good mate and oracle on all aspects of record breaking, while fellow Campbell disciples the indefatigable Carolynn Seggie and Neil Sheppard also went out of their way to help on many occasions, and to share their vast knowledge. I also thank Neil for his invaluable and much appreciated help in reading the manuscript. I found much fascinating material on the Speed Record Group website forum (see Bibliography), cleverly managed by Andy Griffin, and this in turn led me to Geoffrey Mather. During the dark days at Coniston, this retired *Daily Express* journalist captured the most meaningful interview with Campbell that I've ever read. He was generosity itself in agreeing to let me quote from it.

Another Speed Record Group member I must thank is Dean Cox, who also runs the excellent acrossthelake website (see Bibliography) dedicated to Campbell. It was Dean who was ultimately responsible for putting me in touch with Dory Swann, via her sister Jennifer Furtney. This was a huge bonus. Like Dottie, I felt Dory's role in the story had never been written fairly and I was determined to redress the imbalance. My abiding fear was that the book would come out without any input from Dory because I'd failed to find her, and that a month later somebody would breeze up and say, 'Hey, why the hell didn't you talk to Dory Swann? How come you didn't know she lives in New York?' Thanks to Dean, that nightmare finally receded.

I also owe Francesca Liversidge at Transworld Publishers a debt for biting the line I shamelessly trailed in the water, and for then selling the idea to her colleagues. It had been in my head for more than a decade, but I'd never got any serious interest from the publishing world. On 10 September 2001 we had lunch to discuss another project. On the way back I mentioned that I was going to Donald Campbell's funeral in two days' time, and slyly suggested that Transworld ought to do a book and that I knew a guy who had ten years' research for it. 'Is he agented?' Francesca asked. I told her that I wasn't. I thus finally found a publisher of the right calibre at precisely the right time.

My friend Nigel Roebuck, the motorsport writer, was instrumental in encouraging me to get started, as a result of lengthy conversations on aeroplanes as we made our way round the world chasing F1 in the early 1990s. My thanks also go to Andrew Wintersgill, who gave me permission to print the words to his wonderful 'Elegy to Campbell'. Man, if I could write like that . . .

And to Bill Smith and his team, whose courage indirectly led to this book's finally finding a publisher.

For posterity, these are the others who also contributed so much, either to Donald Campbell's life and/or to this recollection of it: Peter Allen, of the *Sydney Morning Herald*'s picture library; Ken Archibald; Eloise Asbury; Rosemary Ashbee, archivist at the Savoy; Peter Barker; Graham Beech; Arthur Benjamins, whose paintings of record-breaking boats, and Donald's in particular, are unsurpassed; the late David Benson, of the *Daily Express*; Geoffrey Berry; Peter Bolton; Rod Booth; Sir Jack Brabham; British Petroleum; Michael Burns; Colin Cobb; Peter Collins, formerly managing director of Team Lotus; Kevin Desmond, who supplied encouragement and some addresses early on in the game; Richard Dixon, of the Museum of Speed in Wendover; Novie Dzinora; the late Professor Tom Fink; scrutineer Roly Forss, who went out of his way to help me make contact with his fellow CAMS stewards; Dave Friedman, who gifted me some wonderful photographs; Diana Gaze (formerly Davison); Clive Glynn; A. Harry Griffin MBE; Jack Hutchinson; the late Innes Ireland; Dr Gerry Jackson; Vincent Kearney; the late Arthur Knowles; Barry Lake; Mike Lawrence; Katey Logan, of Castrol's archive department; my mother-in-law Maureen Mitchell; Sir Stirling Moss; the late Reid Railton; Ken Reaks; David Richland; Ian Robinson; Mark Rysiecki; Phil Scott, of *Wheels* magazine; Marjorie Staves; Paul Taylor, of Cummins Diesel; Lord Tebbit CH; Trish Tremayne; the late Leo Villa OBE; Graham Ward; Keith Washington; David Watt; Joan Williamson, at the RAC Library; Nigel Wollheim; David Wynne-Morgan; and Eoin Young.

I have deliberately left one man until last, for Ken Norris deserves to be singled out. I know that he'll be embarrassed by that since he is a most self-effacing individual, but Ken must stand proud, not just for his key role in the Campbell story (including holding things together on treacherous Lake Eyre), nor just for his factual help, personal memories and apparently endless flood of anecdotes, all so willingly, generously and modestly given. For Ken, or 'Mighty Mouse' as he was affectionately known on the Black Rock Desert in 1982 and 1983 during his terms as Project Thrust team manager, also has immense status as the godfather of British record breaking.

All of us captivated by this odd branch of motorsport and its heroes, either as fans or aspirants, owe him a massive debt for his wisdom and guidance, and for his unstinting support, encouragement and genuine friendship. In his time, Ken has worked with the real aces and doers: Donald Campbell, Richard Noble and Andy Green. Yet never has he let any of the rest of us feel he has anything less than 100 per cent belief in our own projects. Truly he is a man who understands the beauty of the dream.

I've known Ken now for more than twenty years, and count that as one of those privileges served up for my occasional good behaviour. He is a prince of a man who reminds us that Donald Campbell was indeed a very good judge of people, and a man who casts his own eternal shadow.

CHRONOLOGY

1885
11 March
Malcolm Donald Campbell
born in Chislehurst, second
child of William and Ada
Campbell.

1913
Marriage of Malcolm
Campbell to Marjorie Trott.

1915
Malcolm and Marjorie
Campbell divorce.

1916
Malcolm Campbell awarded
MBE for services to wartime
aviation.

1920
April
Marriage of Malcolm

Campbell and Dorothy Evelyn
Whitall.

1921
23 March
Donald Malcolm Campbell
born in 'Canbury', Kingston
Hill, the first of two children
of Malcolm and Dorothy
Campbell.

1922
June
Malcolm Campbell
unofficially exceeds land
speed record at 134mph in
350hp Sunbeam on Saltburn
Sands, north-east England.

1923
Jean Campbell, sister to
Donald, born at Povey Cross.

May

Malcolm Campbell breaks land speed record at 136.31mph in 350hp Sunbeam at Fanoe, Denmark, but new mark is not ratified by European authorities.

1924

August

Malcolm Campbell fails in attempt to break land speed record in 350hp Sunbeam at Fanoe, as young boy dies after being struck by a tyre shed by the speeding car.

25 September

Malcolm Campbell breaks land speed record at 146.16mph in 350hp Sunbeam on Pendine Sands, North Wales.

1925

21 July

Malcolm Campbell breaks land speed record at 150.76mph in 350hp Sunbeam on Pendine Sands.

1927

4 February

Malcolm Campbell breaks land speed record at 174.883mph in Blue Bird Napier on Pendine Sands.

3 March

John Godfrey Parry Thomas killed attempting land speed record in Babs on Pendine Sands.

1928

19 February

Malcolm Campbell breaks land speed record at 206.956mph in Blue Bird Napier on Daytona Beach, Florida.

1929

24 April

Malcolm Campbell fails in attempt on land speed record in Blue Bird Napier at Verneuk Pan, South Africa, but sets new marks for the British mile and world five-mile and five-kilometre distances.

1931

5 February

Malcolm Campbell breaks land speed record at 246.09mph in Blue Bird Napier at Daytona Beach, and is subsequently knighted by King George VI.

1932

24 February

Malcolm Campbell breaks land speed record at 253.97mph in Blue Bird Napier at Daytona Beach.

1933

22 February

Malcolm Campbell breaks

land speed record at
272.46mph in Blue Bird
Rolls-Royce at Daytona
Beach.

1935
7 March
Malcolm Campbell breaks
land speed record at
276.82mph in Blue Bird
Rolls-Royce at Daytona
Beach.

3 September
Malcolm Campbell breaks
land speed record at
301.13mph in Blue Bird
Rolls-Royce on Bonneville
Salt Flats, Utah.

1937
1 September
Malcolm Campbell breaks
water speed record at
126.32mph in Blue Bird K3
on Lake Maggiore, Italy.

2 September
Malcolm Campbell breaks
water speed record at
129.5mph in Blue Bird K3 on
Lake Maggiore, Italy.

1938
August
Malcolm Campbell fails in
attempt to break water speed
record in Blue Bird K3 on Lac
Leman, Switzerland.

17 September
Malcolm Campbell breaks

water speed record at
130.86mph in Blue Bird K3
on Lake Hallwil, Switzerland.

1939
19 August
Malcolm Campbell breaks
water speed record at
141.74mph in Blue Bird K4
on Coniston Water, Cumbria.

1940
Malcolm and Dorothy
Campbell divorce.

1945
Marriage of Malcolm
Campbell and Betty
Humphrey, and of Donald
Campbell and Daphne
Margaret Harvey (later Shaw).

1947
June and July
Malcolm Campbell fails in
attempts on water speed
record in jet-engined Blue
Bird K4 on Coniston Water.

1948
28 February
Malcolm and Betty Campbell
divorce.

September
Malcolm Campbell suffers a
stroke.

23 December
Malcolm Campbell suffers a
major stroke and is confined
to his bed.

31 December
Malcolm Campbell dies in bed at home in Little Gatton, Reigate, Surrey.

1949
February
Donald Campbell decides to take up Malcolm Campbell's mantle in defence of his father's water speed record from American attack.

23 August
Donald Campbell 'breaks' his father's record in piston-powered Bluebird K4 on Coniston Water, only to be told the timekeepers made a mistake and that he failed by a few miles an hour.

1950
26 June
American Stanley St Clair Sayres breaks Malcolm Campbell's record with a speed of 160.323mph in Slo-mo-shun IV on Lake Washington, Seattle.

17 August
Donald Campbell fails in new record attempt in Bluebird K4 on Coniston Water.

1951
10 June
Donald Campbell and Leo Villa win the Oltranza Cup for Britain on Lake Garda, Italy, after setting the two consecutive fastest laps during the Oltranza Grand Prix boat race, driving prop-rider Bluebird K4.

25 October
Donald Campbell and Leo Villa escape as Bluebird K4 is severely damaged at 170mph on Coniston Water.

1952
Divorce of Donald and Daphne Campbell.

19 March
Marriage of Donald Campbell and Dorothy McKegg.

7 July
Sayres raises his own water speed record to 178.497mph on Lake Washington.

29 September
John Cobb is killed when his Crusader disintegrates at more than 200mph on Loch Ness during attack on Sayres' record.

1953
Donald Campbell sells shareholding and resigns from partnership in Kine Engineering to concentrate on building new jet-powered Bluebird K7 for attempt on water speed record.

1954
9 October
Racing champion Mario Verga is killed when his Alfa Romeo-powered Laura 3a flips at 190mph during attempt on water speed record on Lake Iseo, Italy.

1955
23 July
Donald Campbell breaks water speed record at 202.32mph in Bluebird K7 on Ullswater, Cumbria.

16 October
Bluebird K7 sinks during test run on Lake Mead, Nevada.

16 November
Donald Campbell breaks water speed record at 216.20mph in Bluebird K7 on Lake Mead.

December
Campbell returns home, receives letter of congratulation from Foreign Office, and is subsequently decorated by Queen Elizabeth II with the insignia of Commander of the British Empire.

1956
5 April
Donald Campbell awarded Segrave Trophy for 1955.

19 September
Donald Campbell breaks water speed record at 225.63mph in Bluebird K7 on Coniston Water.

1957
Divorce of Donald and Dorothy Campbell.

16 August
Donald Campbell fails in attempt to break water speed record in Bluebird K7 on Lake Canandaigua, New York State.

7 November
Donald Campbell sets new water speed record of 239.07mph in Bluebird K7 on Coniston Water.

1958
10 November
Donald Campbell sets new water speed record of 248.62mph in Bluebird K7 on Coniston Water.

8 December
Engagement of Donald Campbell to Antoinette Marie Bern.

24 December
Marriage of Donald Campbell and Antoinette Marie Bern.

1959
Donald Campbell awarded Segrave Trophy for 1958.

14 May
Donald Campbell sets new water speed record of 260.35mph in Bluebird K7 on Coniston Water.

1960
16 September
Donald Campbell suffers fractured skull after crashing Bluebird CN7 at around 300mph on Bonneville Salt Flats.

1963
April–May
Amid acrimony, Donald Campbell's new attempt on land speed record is washed out on Lake Eyre in southern Australia.

5 August
American Craig Breedlove sets unofficial land speed record of 407.45mph on Bonneville Salt Flats.

1964
March–May
Donald Campbell's new attempt on land speed record washed out on Lake Eyre.

17 July
Donald Campbell sets new official land speed record of 403.1mph in Bluebird CN7 on Lake Eyre.

2 October
American Tom Green sets new outright land speed record of 413.20mph in Wingfoot Express on Bonneville Salt Flats.

November
Donald Campbell fails to break water speed record in attempt in Bluebird K7 on Lake Bonney in southern Australia.

31 December
Donald Campbell sets new water speed record of 276.33mph in Bluebird K7 after relocating to Lake Dumbleyung, Western Australia.

1965
September
Donald Campbell announces plans for new supersonic jet-car at press lunch, displaying mock-up and Bluebirds CN7 and K7 at his home, Roundwood, in Surrey.

13 November
American Bob Summers sets new wheeldriven land speed record of 409.277mph in Goldenrod on Bonneville Salt Flats.

16 December
Donald Campbell awarded Segrave Trophy for 1964.

1966
15 June
Bluebird CN7 badly damaged while being driven on test run at RAF Debden by Peter Bolton.

November
Donald Campbell returns to Coniston Water for attempt to break 300mph, with Bluebird K7 now fitted with a more powerful engine.

1967
4 January
Donald Campbell killed as Bluebird K7 lifts from Coniston Water and somersaults.

7 January
Wreckage of Bluebird K7 located on bottom of Coniston Water.

30 June
American Lee Taylor breaks Donald Campbell's water speed record at 285.213mph in Hustler on Lake Guntersville, Alabama.

19 July
Donald Campbell post-humously awarded Segrave Trophy for 1966; Tonia accepts on his behalf.

1979
January
Leo Villa dies.

2001
8 March
Wreckage of Bluebird K7 recovered from Coniston Water.

28 May
Donald Campbell's body recovered from Coniston Water.

12 September
Funeral of Donald Campbell at Coniston.

18 October
American Don Vesco sets new wheeldriven land speed record of 458.440mph, breaking Donald Campbell's 1964 mark for a turbine-powered vehicle. Vesco succumbs to cancer the following year.

THE BLUEBIRD RECORD CARS

Malcolm Campbell

Sunbeam Blue Bird, 1924 to 1925, 146.16mph and 150.766mph

The 350hp Sunbeam with which Kenelm Lee Guinness had set the record at 133.75mph in 1922. Powered by an 18.3-litre 350bhp Sunbeam V12 aero-engine, driving via a four-speed gearbox to shaft final drive. Modified for 1924 with an elongated tail, and for 1925 with a cowled radiator. Currently on display at National Motor Museum, Beaulieu, Hampshire, England.

Napier Campbell Blue Bird 1927, 174.883mph

Campbell's first bespoke record car, designed by Amherst Villiers and Josef Maina. It was powered by a 22.3-litre 450bhp Napier Lion broad arrow twelve-cylinder aero-engine, driving via an FBM three-speed epicyclic gearbox to a shaft final drive.

Napier Campbell Blue Bird 1928, 206.956mph

The 1928 car with the radiators moved to the tail, and sleeker bodywork.

Napier Campbell Blue Bird 1929, unsuccessful

The 1928 car with front-mounted radiator and further revised bodywork by Arrol-Aster. Unsuccessful in attempt on record at Verneuk Pan, South Africa.

Napier Campbell Blue Bird 1931, 246.09mph
The 1929 car fitted with a 1,450bhp 26.9-litre supercharged Napier Lion engine, driving through three-speed gearbox to offset shaft final drive. Elongated wheelbase and dramatically revised bodywork. Campbell knighted after achieving his record in this car on 5 February 1931 at Daytona Beach.

Napier Campbell Blue Bird 1932, 253.97mph
Slightly modified version of the 1931 car, with sleeker bodywork.

Rolls-Royce Campbell Blue Bird 1933, 272.46mph
The 1932 car now fitted with a 2,300bhp V12 Rolls-Royce R aero-engine driving through a three-speed gearbox to offset shaft final drive.

Rolls-Royce Campbell Blue Bird 1935, 276.82mph and 301.13mph
The 1933 car with twin rear wheels and dramatically modified bodywork designed by Reid Railton. Currently on display at the Hall of Fame in Alabama Motor Speedway, Talladega, Alabama, United States.

Donald Campbell
Campbell Norris (CN7) Proteus Bluebird 1960, unsuccessful
Bespoke contender designed by Norris Brothers with honeycomb aluminium sandwich eggbox structure. Powered by 5,000bhp Bristol Siddeley Proteus 705 gas turbine engine driving directly through all four fifty-two-inch wheels. Crashed at 360mph at Bonneville Salt Flats, Utah, in September 1960.

Campbell Norris (CN7) Proteus Bluebird 1962, 403.1mph
Substantially rebuilt version of 1960 car using salvageable components (including much of original chassis), but incorporating modified suspension, locked differentials, revised cockpit canopy and tail fin. Powered by uprated Bristol Siddeley Proteus 755 engine. Currently on display at National Motor Museum, Beaulieu, Hampshire, England.

Campbell Norris (CN8) Bluebird 1965, stillborn project – target speed 840mph
Needle-nosed four-wheeled pure-thrust contender designed by Norris Brothers for supersonic speed, powered by two 4,200lbt Bristol

Siddeley BS 605 rocket-assisted take-off (RATO) engines and running on solid metal wheels. Mock-up constructed in 1965, current whereabouts unknown.

Campbell Norris MacKnight (CNM8) Bluebird Mach 1.1 1973, stillborn project – target speed 840mph
The same car, revived by nineteen-year-old Nigel MacKnight six years after Donald Campbell's death.

THE BLUEBIRD RECORD BOATS

Malcolm Campbell
Blue Bird K3 1937, 126.32mph and 129.5mph
Single-step wood and aluminium hydroplane designed by Fred Cooper and built by Saunders-Roe. Powered by 36.5-litre 2,300bhp Rolls-Royce R V12 aero-engine driving through single two-blade propeller.

Blue Bird K3 1938, 130.86mph
The 1937 boat with revised tail. Currently owned by Paul Ffoulkes-Halberd at Filching Manor Motor Museum, Sussex.

Blue Bird K4 1939, 141.74mph
Three-point wood and aluminium hydroplane designed by Peter du Cane and built by Vosper Thorneycroft.

Powered by 36.5-litre 2,300bhp Rolls-Royce R V12 aero-engine driving through single two-blade propeller.

Blue Bird K4 1947, unsuccessful
The 1939 boat fitted with pure-thrust 5,000lbt de Havilland Goblin centrifugal compressor turbojet and heavily revised upper bodywork. Nicknamed 'The Coniston Slipper'.

Donald Campbell
Bluebird K4 1949, unsuccessful
The 1947 boat returned to 1939 specification with Rolls-Royce R engine boosted to 2,350bhp via revised fuel mix.

Bluebird K4 1950, unsuccessful
The 1949 boat with an additional cockpit on the right-hand side to accommodate engineer Leo Villa.

Bluebird K4 1951, unsuccessful
The 1950 hull significantly revised to operate on prop-riding principles and incorporating a cockpit on either side. Winner of the Oltranza Cup. Destroyed on Coniston Water when boat sank following gearbox mounting failure at high speed. Subsequently stored for years at Coley Metals in Hounslow before ceremonially being burned.

Bluebird K7 1954, 202.32mph and 216.20mph
All-metal three-point pure-thrust hydroplane with outrigged sponsons, designed by Norris Brothers and built by Salmesbury Engineering. Powered by 3,750lbt Metropolitan-Vickers Beryl turbojet engine. Breached 200mph barrier in July 1955.

Bluebird K7 1956, 225.6mph
The 1955 boat, with blown-glass cockpit canopy replacing flat glass screen.

Bluebird K7 1957, 239.07mph
The 1956 boat with minor modifications.

Bluebird K7 1958, 248.62mph
The 1957 boat with modified sponson cowlings and vestigial tail fin to house parachute brake that was not used.

Bluebird K7 1959, 260.35mph
The 1958 boat with minor modifications.

Bluebird K7 1964, 276.33mph
The 1959 boat with minor modifications.

Bluebird K7 1967, unsuccessful
The 1964 boat fitted with a 4,800lbt Bristol Siddeley Orpheus turbojet engine and the tail fin from a Folland Gnat trainer aircraft. Also equipped with foot-operated water brake for first time. Crashed and sank after peaking at 328mph on Coniston Water on 4 January 1967, killing Donald Campbell. Recovered from lake by diver Bill Smith and his team in 2001, currently awaiting rebuild to full working order ready for future display and demonstration runs.

BIBLIOGRAPHY

As befits a character of Donald Campbell's achievements, there has been no shortage of books on his life and records, though few have really probed much beyond the carefully fashioned external veneer, 'the mask'. The following books, magazines and sources either have been consulted or were instrumental in firing the author's interest. I'd particularly like to single out the late Evan Green, Deke Houlgate, the late Arthur Knowles, Geoffrey Mather, Dennis May, Peter Michelmore, Alan W. Mitchell, Wally Parr, John Pearson and Kenneth Rudeen, in recognition of the value of their work. Gentlemen, I raise my metaphorical hat to your skills as wordsmiths. Material from the author's copious collection was also used for research purposes, including personal effects of Leo Villa, Ken Norris and Reid Railton as well as official reports, files and brochures from the Bluebird team.

Books

Blois, Fred, *The Research and Development of Donald Campbell's Bluebird K7 Hydroplane* (self-published, 2003)

Campbell, Donald, with Alan W. Mitchell, *Into the Water Barrier* (Odhams Press, 1955)

Campbell, Lady Dorothy, *Malcolm Campbell, The Man as I Knew Him* (Hutchinson, 1951)

Campbell, Gina, with Michael Meech, *Bluebirds* (Sidgwick & Jackson, 1988)

Campbell, Sir Malcolm, *Speed on Wheels* (Sampson Low, 1949)

Campbell, Tonia, *My Speed King* (Sutton Publishing, 2001)

Clifton, Paul, *The Fastest Men on Earth* (Herbert Jenkins, 1964)

Desmond, Kevin, *The World Water Speed Record* (Batsford, 1977)

Drackett, Phil, *Like Father, Like Son* (Clifton Books, 1969)

Holter, Steve, *Leap into Legend – Donald Campbell and the Complete Story of the World Speed Records* (Sigma, 2002)

Hough, Richard, *The BP Book of the Racing Campbells* (Stanley Paul, 1959)

Houlgate, Deke, and the editors of *Auto Racing* magazine, *The Fastest Men in the World on Wheels* (World Publishing, 1974)

Knowles, Arthur, *Donald Campbell, C.B.E.* (George Allen & Unwin, 1969)

—— *With Campbell at Coniston* (William Kimber, 1969)

Maeterlinck, Maurice, *The Blue Bird* (Methuen, 1909)

Pearson, John, *Bluebird and the Dead Lake* (Collins, 1965; reprinted by Aurum Press in 2002)

Posthumus, Cyril, and David Tremayne, *Land Speed Record* (Osprey, 1984)

Serventy, Vincent, *The Desert Sea – The Miracle of Lake Eyre in Flood* (Macmillan Australia, 1985)

Shapiro, Harvey, *Faster Than Sound* (Barnes, 1974)

Thompson, Mickey, with Griff Borgeson, *Challenger – Mickey Thompson's Own Story of His Life of Speed* (Prentice-Hall, 1962)

Tremayne, David, *The Fastest Man on Earth – The Story of Richard Noble's Land Speed Record* (633 Club, 1986)

—— *The Land Speed Record* (Shire, 1990)

—— *Racers Apart* (Motor Racing Publications, 1991)

Villa, Leo, with Kevin Desmond, *Life with the Speed King* (MHGD, 1979)

—— with Tony Gray, *The Record Breakers* (Paul Hamlyn, 1969)

Young-James, Douglas, *Donald Campbell – An Informal Biography* (Neville & Spearman, 1968)

Magazines

Argosy; Auto; Autocar; Autosprint; CAR; Car and Driver; Classic & Sportscar; Everyman; Hot Rod Handbook; Hot Rod Magazine; Modern Motor; Motorboat & Yachting; Motoring News; Motor Sport; Motor Trend; Popular Mechanics; Psychic News; Radio Times; Road & Track; Sports Car Graphic; Sports Car Illustrated; Sports Illustrated; Sports Review Motorspeed; True, The Man's Magazine; You

Newspapers

The Adelaide Advertiser; The Age (Melbourne); *The Daily Chronicle* (Santa Paula); *Daily Express; Daily Mail; Daily Mirror; Daily Sketch; Daily Star; Daily Telegraph; Evening Mail; Evening Post; Guardian; News* (Adelaide); *The New York Times; Northern Echo; People; Sydney Morning Herald; Sun; Sunday Express; Sunday Telegraph; Sunday Times Magazine; The Times; Today; Westmorland Gazette*

Newsreel and video sources

Across the Lake by Roger Milner and Innes Lloyd, BBC Television

Donald Campbell at Utah (BP)

The Fastest Man on Earth by Tony Maylam

How Long A Mile by Donald Campbell
Muloorina (BP)
Pathé newsreels
The Price of a Record by John Pett, Border Television
Speed King by Nigel Turner, Castle Video
There is No Limit by Melvyn Bragg

Websites

http://groups.yahoo.com/group/speedrecordgroup, run by
Andy Griffin
http://www.acrossthelake.com, run by Dean Cox

INDEX

479

Egypt, 35
Eighty Mile Beach, 277
El Al, 184
Elce, Norman, 132
Eldridge, Ernest: land speed
   record, 51, 52
Endurance, 30
engines
   Alfa Romeo, 134
   Allison, 85, 234
   Bristol-Siddeley: BS 605 RATO,
   346; Orpheus, 29, 364, 370, 379,
   391, 395, 411, 418, 441; Proteus,
   162, 238, 265, 317, 321, 326, 348,
   362
   Britannia, 184
   Chevrolet V8, 219
   De Havilland: Ghost, 120;
   Goblin, 79, 80, 90
   General Electric J47, 235
   Jaguar, 108
   JAP, 40
   Metropolitan-Vickers Beryl, 28,
   29, 31–2, 133, 139, 152, 153–4,
   167, 181, 186, 334, 341, 364, 370,
   379, 411
   Napier, 56, 72
   Pontiac V8, 234, 243
   Railton Mobil, 326
   Rolls-Royce, 56, 72, 91, 92, 116;
   Avon, 131; Griffon, 131, 167;
   R19, 107, 108; R37, 102; R39, 108
   Sunbeam Manitou V12, 47
Enola Gay, 243
Epsom Hospital, 255
Eucla, 277
Eucumbene, Lake, 276, 337
Evans, Corporal Paul, 226–7,
   276–80, 380, 421, 431, 441;
   Coniston (1967), 383, 389,
   390–1, 393–4, 395–6, 401–2, 403
Evans, Robert Beverley, 27
Ewell, 367, 369
Eyre, Lake, 23, 64, 172, 208, 226,
   267–88, 289–308, 306, 307,
   309–27, 329, 333, 335, 339, 340,

342, 344, 347, 348, 350, 372, 429,
435
Eyston, Captain George, 55, 72,
   131, 236

Fageol, Lou, 129
Fairmile, 212
Fangio, Juan Manuel, 134
Fanoe island, 50, 51–2
Farina, Giuseppe, 134
Farnborough Air Show, 119
Fawkes, Guy, 442
Fédération Internationale de
   l'Automobile, 163, 235, 282,
   347–8
Fédération Internationale de
   Motonautique, 282, 348
Ferodo, 164, 166
Ferrett, Aileen, 429–30
Ferrett, Grahame, 226, 268, 290–1,
   292, 297, 299–300, 313–14,
   316–17, 318, 320, 321–2, 330–1,
   429–30, 435; CN8, 346–7;
   Bonney, 335–8; Dumbleyung,
   339–42; Eyre, 429–30; suicide
   theory, 422; tax, 351–3
   film footage, 102, 128, 141, 186,
   246, 254, 288, 406–7, 410, 437
Finger Lakes, 179
Fink, Professor Tom, 122, 125–30,
   136, 137–8, 143, 146, 147, 201,
   409, 418
Flairavia Flying Club, 432
Flapper, see Campbell, Sir Malcolm
Flockhart, Ron, 230
Floyd, Doug, 107
Flying Caduceus, 234, 282
Flynn, Able Seaman, 406–8
Folland Gnat trainer aircraft 28–9,
   364
Ford, 159
Foreign Office, 157, 161
Foresti, Giulio, 54, 102
Forss, Roly, 295, 299, 301, 305–7,
   309–10
Fort Worth, Texas, 174

490

AT THE MERCY OF THE WINDS
by David Hempleman-Adams

Two Remarkable Journeys to the North Pole: a Modern Hero and a
Victorian Romance.

On 28 May 2000, explorer David Hempleman-Adams took off from
Spitzbergen in Norway on what would be a record-breaking flight to
the North Pole. The contents of his balloon's fragile wicker basket
included enough liquid oxygen to allow him to endure the high
altitudes, an inflatable raft plus forty days worth of emergency
rations. He knew that if he survived the week ahead he would be the
first man ever to have reached the North Pole by balloon, but not
the first to have tried.

Indeed, Hempleman-Adams's journey was of great emotional
significance. That he chose to fly in a wicker basket, rather than in
the hi-tech sealed capsule favoured by round-the-world expedition.
In 1897, three Swedes – Salomon Andrée, Nils Strindberg and Knut
Frænkel – tried for the Pole but only days into their attempt, freezing
fog brought them down on the pack ice. Fighting off polar bears,
loneliness, despair and the bitter cold, they managed to survive for
three months. It would be thirty-three years before their bodies were
found . . .

At the Mercy of the Winds tells the extraordinary, compelling stories
of both journeys. Alone in the skies above the frozen and harshly
beautiful landscape, David Hempleman-Adams battled against the
elements to fulfil the dream of those pioneers a century earlier – to
become the first man to balloon to the North Pole.

0 553 81363 3

BANTAM BOOKS

MICHAEL SCHUMACHER: Driven to Extremes
by James Allen

'Fantastic . . . A well-stocked tale, enthusiastically told'
Independent on Sunday

Michael Schumacher is the outstanding formula One driver of the
1990s. Gifted with that blend of superior ability and nerve that
defines a champion, he has earned his place amongst the greats of
the sport. But he is also a highly controversial figure – feared by his
rivals as a ruthless, determined racer who will stop at nothing to
achieve his goals, and criticized on all sides for his unwillingness to
admit mistakes.

Against the backdrop of Schumacher's quest to win the world championship for Ferrari, ITV's James Allen examines the contrasting
sides of the man behind the headlines. With the full co-operation of
Schumacher and the Ferrari team over two Grand Prix seasons, he
tells the inside story of Schumacher's fall from grace following his
cynical foul on Jacques Villeneuve at Jerez in the 1997 title decider,
his doomed pursuit of the 1998 world championship and his
astonishing comeback from a leg-breaking accident at Silverstone
in 1999.

With exclusive insights into Schumacher's methods, both on and off
the track, as well as a close look at the workings of the Ferrari team,
this is the definitive book on Michael Schumacher – in every sense, a
man driven to extremes.

0 553 81214 9

BANTAM BOOKS

MY LIFE ON THE FORMULA ONE ROLLERCOASTER
by JENSON BUTTON
Foreword by Sir Frank Williams

'Who are the three best karters I ever saw? Not three, two. Ayrton Senna and Jenson Button'
Paul Lemmens, owner of the Genk kart track

How does it feel to be a young sportsman on the world stage, weighed down by the burden of others' expectations? What pressures are created when your raw talent excites such dreams that anything other than ultimate achievement will be regarded as failure?

Jenson Button has been winning motor races since he was eight years old, yet even he was surprised to find himself racing in Formula One just weeks after his twentieth birthday. Thrust into the turbulent world of the ambitious BMW-Williams team as the rookie partner of world champion Michael Schumacher's promising brother Ralf, and already tagged by a hungry media as the next Ayrton Senna, he was going to sink without trace, or fight for his corner.

Now a regular in the sports pages and celebrity magazines, here the British star gives his own account of his first season and the career that led him to such a dramatic opportunity. *My Life on the Formula One Rollercoaster* also examines the reasons why his succeeding year demanded a switch to the Benetton-Renault team, and how he fared. It puts the reader right alongside Jenson Button, whether in the cockpit or on the pit wall, a young David taking on the established Goliaths in a razor-sharp sport which takes no prisoners.

0 553 81403 6

BANTAM BOOKS

A SELECTED LIST OF NON-FICTION TITLES
AVAILABLE FROM BANTAM BOOKS

81214 9	MICHAEL SCHUMACHER: DRIVEN TO EXTREMES	*James Allen* £8.99
81403 6	JENSON BUTTON: MY LIFE ON THE FORMULA ONE ROLLERCOASTER	*Jenson Button* £7.99
81556 3	IT'S NOT ABOUT THE TAPAS	*Polly Evans* £6.99
81210 6	A MATTER OF OPINION	*Alan Hansen* £6.99
17521 1	A BRIEF HISTORY OF TIME	*Stephen Hawking* £7.99
81363 3	AT THE MERCY OF THE WINDS	*David Hempleman-Adams* £8.99
81559 8	THE KING	*Denis Law* £6.99
81493 1	FATAL PASSAGE	*Ken McGoogan* £7.99
81385 5	A TIME TO DIE	*Robert Moore* £6.99
81602 0	ALL THE RIGHT PLACES	*Brad Newsham* £6.99
50491 6	JENNY PITMAN AUTOBIOGRAPHY	*Jenny Pitman* £7.99
81417 6	THE GREAT WHITE PALACE	*Tony Porter* £7.99
81554 7	DAD'S WAR	*Howard Reid* £6.99
81269 6	T'RIFIC	*Mike Reid* £6.99
81610 1	THE LAST MISSION	*Jim Smith and Malcolm McConnell* £7.99
81360 9	IN HARM'S WAY	*Doug Stanton* £6.99
81532 6	CUBA DIARIES	*Isadora Tattlin* £6.99
81436 2	RAW: THE AUTOBIOGRAPHY	*Antony Worrall-Thompson* £7.99
81476 1	HALFWAY HOME	*Ronan Tynan* £6.99
81492 3	HUMAN INSTINCT	*Robert Winston* £8.99